LIBRARY

Tel: 01244 375444   Ext: 3301

This book is to be returned on or before the
last date stamped below. Overdue charges
will be incurred by the late return of books.

Chester

A College of the
University of Liverpool

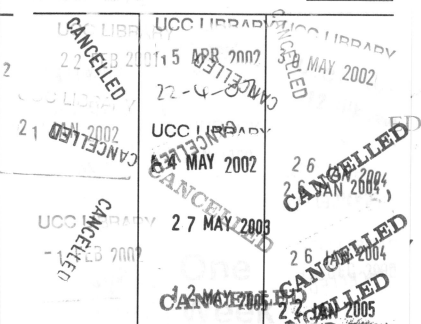

One Week
Loan

One
Week
Loan

J. ALBERTO SOGGIN

JUDGES

A Commentary

Second Edition

SCM PRESS LTD

Translated by John Bowden from the Italian original
Translation © John Bowden 1981, 1987

British Library Cataloguing-in-Publication Data available

334 02108 1
First published in English 1981
by SCM Press Ltd
26–30 Tottenham Road, London N1
Second Edition 1987
Phototypeset by Input Typesetting Ltd
and printed in Great Britain by
Redwood Burn Ltd
Trowbridge

והשופטים איש בשמו
כל אשר לא נשא לבו

ולא נסוג מאחרי אל
יהי זבים לברכה

תהי עצמותם פרחות מתחתם
ושמם תחליף לבניהם

Jesus Sirach, *Ecclesiasticus* 46.11–12

In Judicum libro quot principes populi, tot figurae sunt
Jerome, *Ep.liii,8 ad Paulinum*, PL 22, 540

CONTENTS

Part Three: Appendix on Various Themes (chs. 17–21) 261

PREFACE

As I pointed out about ten years ago in the Preface to my commentary on Joshua, the best preface is useless if a work does not commend itself by its contents. So here too it seems best to do no more than clarify a few points.

1. I think that the hypothesis of a Deuteronomistic redaction of the 'former prophets' has now been established, especially since from 1971 onwards a group from Göttingen, consisting of R. Smend Jr, W. Dietrich and T. Veijola, has developed the theory of a tripartite division resulting in a historical work (DtrH), a stratum influenced by the preaching of the prophets (DtrP) and a legalistic ('nomistic') revision (DtrN). For further details I refer the reader to my *Introduction to the Old Testament*, revised English edition 1980, pp. 164 and xxixf. (third Italian edition, *Introduzione all'Antico Testamento*, 1979).

2. For topographical texts I have continued to make use of the 1:100,000 map produced by the Survey of Palestine, from 1948 the Survey of Israel. All the archaeological sites in the central highlands have been recently surveyed, cf. M. Kochavi (ed.), *Judaea-Samaria and the Golan. Archaeological Survey 1967–1968*, published by The Archaeological Survey of Israel, Jerusalem 1972 (Hebrew). It reproduces some of the 1:100,000 maps just referred to. It goes without saying that I consider this map indispensable for anyone who wants to make a specialist study of the topographical texts. The non-specialist reader will find the 1:250,000 map, in two sheets, quite adequate.

3. The introduction to the commentary has been kept to the minimum. There seems to be no point in repeating what has already appeared in my *Introduction to the Old Testament* or in discussing questions which will be examined in detail in connection with individual passages.

4. This work has been dedicated to St John's College, Cam-

bridge. Two-thirds of it was in fact written during the course of an Overseas Visiting Scholarship in the Michaelmas term of 1978. I doubt whether I would have succeeded in finishing the work without the warm hospitality offered by St John's. I am also indebted to the University of Rome, which readily granted me leave of absence.

5. Rather than attempting to resolve problems, I have tried to point them out and to indicate possible lines of approach. Rather than doing theology and making the texts present a message for our time, I have preferred to show what the texts are concerned to say and the problems with which they tried to cope. I leave it to the reader to judge whether I have succeeded, and if so, whether my approach has been valid and useful.

6. As far as possible, I have updated the bibliographies to the spring of 1978. I would ask the reader to excuse me for any points which may have escaped my notice. F. Crüsemann, *Der Widerstand gegen das Königtum*, WMANT 49, 1978, arrived too late to be used in the original manuscript; it is an important work, and I have tried to incorporate its insights wherever possible.

Rome, February 1979

NOTE TO THE SECOND EDITION

The French edition of this commentary was published by Labor et Fides, Geneva, in March 1987; in it I had updated the bibliographies so that they covered literature up to 1985; I also changed the text in several places, notably that on 5.14, where I have meanwhile opted for a different reading. These alterations and additions have been incorporated in the second English edition, and I have taken the opportunity to correct some misprints. The new bibliographical material is at the back of the book; pages to which it relates have an asterisk against their numbering.

Rome, July 1987

ABBREVIATIONS

A	Aquila, Greek translation of the Old Testament
AASF	Acta Academiae Scientiarum Fennicae, Helsinki
AASOR	*Annual of the American Schools of Oriental Research*, New Haven, Connecticut, later Ann Arbor, Michigan
AB	The Anchor Bible, Garden City, New York
ABLAK	see Noth
ABR	*The Australian Biblical Review*, Melbourne
AHw	*Akkadisches Handwörterbuch*, ed. W. von Soden, 3 vols., Wiesbaden 1965ff.
AION	*Annali dell'Istituto Orientale di Napoli*, Naples
Aistleitner	J. Aistleitner, *Wörterbuch der ugaritischen Sprache*, Berlin 1963 (and reprints)
ALUOS	*Annual of the Leeds University Oriental Society*, Leeds
ANEP	*The Ancient Near East in Pictures*, ed. J. B. Pritchard, Princeton ³1969
ANET	*Ancient Near Eastern Texts Relating to the Old Testament*, ed. J. B. Pritchard, Princeton ³1969
AnBibl	Analecta Biblica, Rome
AnOr	Analecta Orientalia, Rome
ARM	*Archives Royales de Mari*, Paris 1948ff. (cited by vol., no. and line)
ASOR	American Schools of Oriental Research
ATANT	Abhandlungen zur Theologie des Alten und Neuen Testaments, Zurich
AT	Altes Testament, Ancien Testament, Antico Testamento
ATD	Das Alte Testament Deutsch, Göttingen
BA	*The Biblical Archaeologist*, New Haven, Conn., later Ann Arbor, Michigan
BASOR	*Bulletin of the American Schools of Oriental Research*, New Haven, Conn., later Ann Arbor, Michigan
BBB	Bonner Biblische Beiträge, Bonn
BBLAK	*Beiträge zur biblischen Landes- und Altertumskunde* (=*ZDPV* 68), 1951

BDB	F. Brown, S. R. Driver, C. A. Briggs (eds.), *Hebrew and English Lexicon of the Old Testament, based on the Lexicon of William Gesenius*, Oxford 1907 and reprints
BeO	*Bibbia ed Oriente*, Genoa, later Brescia
BG	*La S. Bibbia, edita . . . da Msgr S Garofalo*, Turin
BHH	*Biblisch-historisches Handwörterbuch*, Göttingen
BHK³	*Biblia Hebraica,.* ed. R. Kittel, Stuttgart ³1938
BHS	*Biblia Hebraica Stuttgartensia*, ed. K. Elliger and W. Rudolph, Stuttgart 1978 (= *BHK⁴*)
Bibl	*Biblica*, Rome
BiblOr	*Biblica et Orientalia*, Rome
BJ	*La Bible de Jérusalem*, Paris-Jerusalem
BP	*La Bible de la Pléiade*, Paris 1956
BRL	*Biblisches Reallexikon*, ed. K. Galling (= HAT 1), Tübingen ²1977
BuL	*Bibel und Leben*, Paderborn
BWANT	Beiträge zur Wissenschaft vom Alten und Neuen Testament, Stuttgart
BZAW	Beihefte zur *ZAW*, Giessen, later Berlin
CAH	*Cambridge Ancient History*, Cambridge ³1970ff.
CB	The Cambridge Bible for Schools and Colleges
CBQ	*The Catholic Biblical Quarterly*, Washington DC
coord.	The Survey of Israel (formerly of Palestine): coordinate grid, maps 1:100,000
Dtn	Deuteronomic (writer)
Dtr	Deuteronomistic (writer)
DtrH, DtrN, DtrP	see Preface
EA	*El-Amarma Tafeln*, ed. J. Knudtzon, Leipzig 1915
EB	Echter Bible, Würzburg
EHAT	Exegetisches Handbuch zum AT, Münster im Westfalen
EncBibl	*Encyclopaedia Biblica* (in Hebrew), Jerusalem 1950ff.
EstBibl	*Estudios Bíblicos*, Madrid
ET	English translation
ÉtBibl	Études bibliques, Paris
EThL	*Ephemerides Theologicae Lovanienses*, Louvain
EVV	English versions of the Bible
ExpT	*The Expository Times*, Edinburgh
FRLANT	Forschungen zur Religion und Literatur des Alten und Neuen Testaments, Göttingen
GesB	*Wilhelm Gesenius' hebräisches und aramäisches Handwörterbuch über das Alte Testament*, ed. F. Buhl, Leipzig ¹⁶1915 and reprints
GesK	*Wilhelm Gesenius' Hebrew Grammar*, ed. E. Kautzsch ET ed. A. E. Cowley, Oxford 1910

GesSt	*Gesammelte Studien . . .*
Gordon	C. H. Gordon, *Ugaritic Textbook*, Rome 1965
Greg	*Gregorianum*, Rome
GTT	see Simons
HAT	Handbuch zum Alten Testament, Tübingen
HKAT	Handkommentar zum Alten Testament, Göttingen
HSAT	Die Heilige Schrift des Alten Testament, Cath(olic edition), Bonn; Prot(estant edition), Tübingen
HUCA	*Hebrew Union College Annual*, Cincinnati
IB	*The Interpreter's Bible*, Nashville and New York
ICC	The International Critical Commentary, Edinburgh and New York
IEJ	*Israel Exploration Journal*, Jerusalem
Interp	*Interpretation*, Richmond, Va
IOS	*Israel Oriental Studies,* Tel Aviv
JANESCU	*Journal of the Ancient Near Eastern Society of Columbia University*, New York
JAOS	*Journal of the American Oriental Society*, New Haven, Conn.
JBL	*The Journal of Biblical Literature*, Philadelphia, later Missoula, Montana
JEOL	*Jaarbericht van het genootschap 'Ex Oriente lux'*, Leiden
JJS	*Journal of Jewish Studies*, London
JNES	*Journal of Near Eastern Studies*, Chicago
JPOS	*Journal of the Palestine Oriental Society*, Jerusalem
JQR	*Jewish Quarterly Review*, Philadelphia
JRAS	*Journal of the Royal Asiatic Society*, London
JSS	*Journal of Semitic Studies*, Manchester
JSOT (SS)	*Journal for the Study of the Old Testament* (Supplement Series), Sheffield
JTS	*Journal of Theological Studies*, Oxford
K	Kethib
KAI	*Kanaanäische und Aramäische Inschriften*, ed. H. Donner and W. Röllig, Wiesbaden 1963 (cited by no. and line)
KHCAT	Kurzer Hand-Commentar zum AT, Tübingen
KB	L. Köhler, W. Baumgartner, *Lexicon in Veteris Testamenti Libros*, Leiden 1953, ^{3}1967ff. (only *aleph-nun* published)
KlSchr	*Kleine Schriften . . .*
LXX	Septuagint, Greek translation of the OT (LXX^A = Codex Alexandrinus; LXX^B = Codex Vaticanus; LXX^L = Codices Luciani; LXX^{mss} = manuscripta varia)
MANL	*Memorie dell'Accademia nazionale dei Lincei*, Rome
Meyer	R. Meyer, *Hebräische Grammatik*, 4 vols., Berlin ^{3}1966ff.
MT	Massoretic text

NCB	The New Century Bible, London
Noth,	
ABLAK	M. Noth, *Abhandlungen zur biblischen Landes- und Altertumskunde*, Neukirchen 1971
NTT	*Nederlands Theologisch Tijdschrift*, Wageningen
OBO	*Orbis Biblicus et Orientalis*, Freiburg (CH)
OrAnt	*Oriens Antiquus*, Rome
Orient	*Orientalia*, Rome
OTL	Old Testament Library, London and Philadelphia
OTOS	see Soggin
OTS	*Oudtestamentische Studiën*, Leiden .
PEFQS	*Palestine Exploration Fund Quarterly Statement*, London
PEQ	*Palestine Exploration Quarterly*, London
PJB	*Palästina Jahrbuch des deutschen evangelischen Instituts*, Berlin
PL	Patrologia Latina, ed. J.-P. Migne, Paris 1844ff.
Q	Qere
RANL	*Rendiconti dell'Accademia nazionale dei Lincei*, Rome
RB	*Revue Biblique*, Paris/Jerusalem
RiBibl	*Rivista biblica*, Brescia
RIDA	*Revue internationale des droits de l'antiquité*, Brussels
RSF	*Rivista di storia della filosofia*, Rome
RSO	*Rivista degli studi orientali*, Rome
RSP	*Ras Shamra Parallels*, ed. L. R. Fisher, 2 vols., AnOr 49, 1972 (cited by vol., ch. and no.)
SATA	*Die Schriften des ATs in Auswahl*, Göttingen
SBT	Studies in Biblical Theology, London
Simons,	
GTT	J. Simons, *The Geographical and Topographical Texts in the Old Testament*, Leiden 1959
SMSR	*Studi e materiali di storia della religioni*, Rome
Soggin,	
OTOS	J. A. Soggin, *Old Testament and Oriental Studies*, BiblOr 29, 1975
SS	*Studi semitici*, Rome
SSI	*Textbook of Syrian Semitic Inscriptions*, ed. J. C. L. Gibson, 2 vols., Oxford 1970–75
Syr	Syriac translation of the Old Testament
TDOT	*Theological Dictionary of the Old Testament*, ET of *TWAT*, Grand Rapids, Michigan 1977ff.
Tg	Targum, Aramaic paraphrase of the Old Testament
TGUOS	*Transactions of the Glasgow University Oriental Society*, Glasgow
THAT	*Theologisches Handwörterbuch zum AT*, ed. E. Jenni and C. Westermann, 2 vols., Munich 1971–76

TLZ	*Theologische Literaturzeitung*, Leipzig
TOB	*Traduction Oecuménique de la Bible*, Paris
TR	*Theologische Rundschau*, Tübingen
TWAT	*Theologisches Wörterbuch zum AT*, ed. J. J. Botterweck and H. Ringgren, Stuttgart 1973ff.
TZ	*Theologische Zeitschrift*, Basle
UF	*Ugarit-Forschungen*, Münster in Westfalen
UT	C. H. Gordon, *Ugaritic Textbook*, AnOr 38, 1965
VD	*Verbum Domini*, Rome
VetLat	Vetus Latina, translation of the Old Testament
Vg	Vulgate, translation of the Old Testament
VT	*Vetus Testamentum*, Leiden
VTS	Supplements to *Vetus Testamentum*
WO	*Die Welt des Orients*, Göttingen and Wiesbaden
WMANT	Wissenschaftliche Monographien zum Alten und Neuen Testament, Neukirchen
WZ(H)	*Wissenschaftliche Zeitschrift der Martin-Luther-Universität Halle-Wittenberg*, Halle
ZA	*Zeitschrift für Assyriologie*, Leipzig, later Berlin
ZAW	*Zeitschrift für die alttestamentliche Wissenschaft*, Giessen, later Berlin
ZDPV	*Zeitschrift des deutschen Palästinavereins*, Wiesbaden, later Tübingen
ZTK	*Zeitschrift für Theologie und Kirche*, Tübingen
Θ	Greek translation of the Old Testament by Theodotion
Σ	Greek translation of the Old Testament by Symmachus

GENERAL BIBLIOGRAPHY

1. COMMENTARIES

(Commentaries are cited with the name of the author followed by one asterisk* and the year of publication)

G. F. **Moore**, *Judges*, ICC, 1895; K. **Budde**, *Das Buch der Richter*, KHCAT, 1897; W. **Nowack**, *Richter-Ruth*, HKAT, 1900; M.-J. **Lagrange**, *Le livre de Juges*, ÉtBibl, 1903; G. A. **Cooke**, *Judges*, CB, 1913; C. F. **Burney**, *The Book of Judges*, London ²1919 (reprinted New York 1970 with an introduction by W. F. **Albright**, pp. 1*–38*); H. **Gressmann**, *SATA* I 2, ²1922; R. **Kittel**, HSAT (Prot) I, ⁴1922; W. **Zapletal**, *Das Buch der Richter*, EHAT, 1923; A. **Schulz**, *Das Buch der Richter und das Buch Ruth*, HSAT (Cath), 1926; J. **Garstang**, *Joshua, Judges*, London 1931; F. **Nötscher**, *Das Buch der Richter*, EB, 1950; J. M. **Myers**, IB 2, 1953; É. **Dhorme**, *BP* I, 1956; A. **Vincent**, *Le livre des Juges, le livre de Ruth*, BJ, ²1958; H.-W. **Hertzberg**, *Die Bücher Josua, Richter, Ruth*, ATD 9, ²1959; Y. **Kaufmann**, *Sēfer Šōfᵉṭīm*, Jerusalem 1962 (Hebrew); A. **Penna**, *Giudici e Rut*, BG, 1963; J. **Gray**, *Joshua, Judges and Ruth*, NCB, 1967; R. G. **Boling**, *Judges*, AB, 1975.

2. MONOGRAPHS AND ARTICLES

(These are cited by the name of the author followed by two asterisks** and the year of publication)

O. **Eissfeldt**, *Die Quellen des Richterbuches*, Leipzig 1925; M. **Noth**, *Überlieferungsgeschichtliche Studien* I, Halle 1943 and reprints, 47–61; W. **Rudolph**, 'Textkritische Anmerkungen zum Richterbuch', in *Festschrift O. Eissfeldt zum 60. Geburtstag*, Halle 1947, 199–212; C. A. **Simpson**, *The Composition of the Book of Judges*, Oxford and New York 1957; E. **Täubler**, *Biblische Studien*, Tübingen 1958; G. R. **Driver**, 'Problems in Judges Newly Discussed', *ALUOS* 4, 1962–63 (1964), 6–25; W. **Richter**, *Traditionsgeschichtliche Untersuchungen zum Richterbuch*, BBB 18, 1963; id., *Die Bearbeitung des 'Retterbuches' in der deuteronomistischen Epoche*, BBB 21, 1964 (two basic works on Judges, see the review by W. L. **Moran**, *Bibl* 46, 1965, 223–8, and my review in *AION* 25, 1965, 299–

302); K.-D. **Schunck**, 'Die Richter Israels und ihr Amt', *VTS* 15, 1966, 255–62; D. A. **McKenzie**, 'The Judges of Israel', *VT* 17, 1967, 118–21; **Y. Aharoni**, *The Land of the Bible. A Historical Geography*, London and Philadelphia 1967; T. H. **Gaster**, *Myth, Legend and Custom in the Old Testament*, New York and London 1969; B. **Lindars**, 'Some Septuagintal Readings in Judges', *JTS* NS 22, 1971, 1–14; A. **Malamat**, 'The Period of the Judges', in B. Mazar (ed.), *The World History of the Jewish People* III, London and New Brunswick 1971, 121–63; R. de **Vaux**, *Histoire Ancienne d'Israël* II, Paris 1973; ET, *The Early History of Israel* II: *From the Entry into Canaan to the Period of the Judges*, London and Philadelphia 1978; D. M. **Gunn**, 'Narrative Patterns and Oral Tradition in Judges and Samuel', *VT* 24, 1974, 286–317; A. D. H. **Mayes**, *Israel in the Period of the Judges*, SBT II. 29, 1974; H. **Rösel**, 'Studien zur Topographie der Kriege in den Büchern Josua und Richter', *ZDPV* 91, 1975, 159–90 and 92, 1976, 10–46; O. **Eissfeldt**, 'The Hebrew Kingdom', *CAH* II. 2, ³1975, ch. 34, 553–60.

3. ON THE 'JUDGES' AND ON THE TITLE

(Books in this section are cited with the name of the author followed by three asterisks*** and the year of publication)

O. **Grether**, 'Die Bezeichnung "Richter" für die charismatischen Helden der Vorzeit', *ZAW* 57, 1939, 110–21; M. **Noth**, 'Das Amt des "Richters Israels" ', in *Festschrift A. Bertholet*, Tübingen 1950, 404–17 (= *GesSt* II, Munich 1959, 71–85); G. **von Rad**, *Der heilige Krieg im alten Israel*, ATANT 20, 1951, *passim* (the classic study of the 'holy war' in Israel); W. **Vollborn**, 'Die Richter Israels', in *Sammlung und Sendung. Festschrift H. Rendtorff*, Berlin 1958, 21–31; R. **Smend**, *Jahwekrieg und Stämmebund*, FRLANT 85, 1963, 33–5; W. **Richter**, 'Zu den "Richtern Israels" ', *ZAW* 77, 1965, 40–71 (a fundamental study); G. H. J. de **Geus**, 'De rechteren van Israël', *NTT* 20, 1965–66, 81–100; M. S. **Rozenberg**, 'The *Šōfᵉṭīm* in the Bible', *Eretz Israel* 12, 1975, 77*–86*; T. **Ishida**, 'The Leaders of the Tribal League "Israel" in the Pre-Monarchic Period', *RB* 80, 1973, 514–30.

A bibliographical study, complete up to 1960, has been produced by E. **Jenni**, 'Zwei Jahrzehnte Forschungen an den Büchern Josua bis Könige', *TR* 27, 1961, 1–32, 97–146.

INTRODUCTION

1. THE TITLE

The title of this book, *šōpᵉṭīm* in Hebrew and κριταί in Greek, the second of the 'former prophets', comes from the Hebrew term *šōpēṭ*, plural *šōpᵉṭīm*, and the verb *šāpaṭ*, usually translated 'judge'. The words are used in the book for two types of persons: the so-called 'major' judges and the figures assimilated to them (Judg.3.10; 4.4; 12.7; 15.20; 16.31; cf. also I Sam. 4.18; 7.6, for the noun), and the so-called 'minor' judges (Judg. 10.2, 3; 12.8, 9, 11, 13, 14). However, these are people who are never associated with any function of judgment or arbitration: in fact the 'major' judges have a specifically military role, and sometimes also act as civil rulers. The only exception is 4.4f., where the Israelites 'came up to Deborah . . . for judgment'. However, this is a function which Deborah performs as a prophetess and before being called to be leader of Israel. The two functions combined under the term, to 'judge' in open court or privately, and to command the army, therefore seem to be independent. We have no information about the functions performed by the 'minor' judges. I shall put forward my own conjecture about them in the commentary on 10.1ff. (cf. pp. 196ff. below).[1] Once, in 11.27, the term 'judge' is used in connection with Yahweh.

This evidence has been known for a long time, and many different solutions to the problem have been proposed. They have all been examined and discussed by W. Richter***, 1965,

---

[1]The distinction between 'major' and 'minor' judges has, however, been challenged in recent years, perhaps rightly, though see pp. 197f. below; cf. R. Smend, *Jahwekrieg und Stämmebund*, FRLANT 84, 1963, ch. III; K.-D. Schunck, 'Die Richter Israels', *VTS* 15, 1966, 255–62; W. Richter, 'Zu den "Richtern Israels" ', *ZAW* 77, 1965, 40–72: 68ff.; and, recently, A. J. Hauser, 'The "Minor Judges" – A Re-Evaluation', *JBL* 94, 1975, 190–200.

cf. ** 1963, 319ff.,[2] so there is no need to examine them all over again here. The result of this investigation is that the root *šāpaṭ* and its derivatives can have two basic meanings, distinct yet related (law and order are in fact a fundamental element of good government). The first, better known and more frequent, is 'to exercise the function of judge' (in the context of a court or in private judgment), hence 'judge'; the second, less frequent and less known, is connected with the exercise of some form of government, political or sociological, depending on the context (Ex 2.14; II Kings 15.5; Isa. 40.23; Amos 2.3; Pss. 2.10; 94.2; 96.13; 148.11; cf. perhaps 58.12; 82.2). These two meanings are also attested in Ugarit (Aistleitner no. 2921, *UT* no. 2027, cf. *RSP* I, ii, §§ 156, 275, 365: *ṯpṭ*), while the second appears predominantly in the West Semitic of Mari (*AHw* III, p. 1172: *špṭ*); so far, there is no evidence of the root from Ebla (oral communication by G. Pettinato, on the basis of the vocabularies), but we find the term d i – k u₄ (*dayyānum*, or could it also be read as *šāpiṭum?*) for a high official in the royal palace. The parallels from the Phoenician-Punic world are particularly important, given the similarity between the language and Hebrew, and the constant connections in the political and economic spheres from the earliest stage of the Israelite monarchy. On the sarcophagus of 'Aḥīrām (*KAI* no. 1, line 2) the expression *ḥṭr mšpṭh* can certainly be translated 'the sceptre of his judgment', but it is clear that 'the sceptre of his rule' or 'of his kingdom' is a more obvious rendering and is a better parallel to 'his royal throne'.

---

[2]For the significance of the asterisks see the bibliography at the beginning of this introduction. In addition to the studies by Richter, see more recently C. H. J. de Geus, 'De richteren van Israël', *NTT* 20, 1965–66, 81–100, and M. S. Rozenberg, 'The *Šōfṭīm* in the Bible', *Eretz Israel* 12, 1975, 77*–86*. The work by T. Ishida, 'The Leaders of the Tribal League "Israel" in the Pre-Monarchic Period', *RB* 80, 1973, 514–30, is very useful for the information and the proposals that it contains; see also the annotated bibliography of the most recent studies in H. N. Rösel, 'Die Richter Israels', *BZ* NF 25, 1981, 180–203; H. Reviv, 'Elders and "Saviours"', *OrAnt* 16, 1977, 201–4. The double significance of the root *šāpat* and its derivatives was already noted by H.-W. Hertzberg, 'Die Entwicklung des Begriffes *mišpat* im Alten Testament', *ZAW* 40, 1922, 256–87, an important study not reprinted in his *Beiträge zur Traditionsgeschichte und Theologie des Alten Testaments*, Göttingen 1962. The judicial system as such in ancient Israel has recently been examined by M. Weinfeld, 'Judge and Officer in Ancient Israel and in the Ancient Near East', *IOS* 7, 1977, 65–88.

However, the best known example from Phoenician and Punic history is that of the *Suf(f)ētes*, the supreme magistrates first of Tyre, where there is evidence for them at least after the beginning of the sixth century BC, according to Josephus (*C.Ap.* I.21 = § 157), and then of Carthage and other Punic cities in Graeco-Roman[3] historiography and Punic epigraphy.

However, there is evidence of another title for the judges invested with military leadership: 'saviour' or 'liberator', Hebrew *mōšīᵃ'*. It is therefore probable, as we shall see in § 3 below, that the earliest phase of the book was that of a 'book of saviours', in which heroic or picturesque actions of the people in question were described on the basis of ancient traditions.

The 'major' judges are often presented by the texts as charismatics[4] (cf. Judg. 3.10; 6.34; 8.3; 11.29; 13.25; 14.6, 19; 15.14): the 'spirit of Yahweh' came upon them. This shows that in biblical historiography their power came to be seen as an exceptional measure, reserved for periods of extreme danger and thus justified by the state of emergency. At least in the view of the texts, this led to a centralization of power, albeit purely temporary and provisional, to the detriment of the traditional independence of the tribes of Israel. For these reasons, in the past[5] I have used the institution of dictatorship in the Roman republic as a comparison, and as long as it remains a mere comparison, and is not taken beyond its obvious limits, this parallel is still a valid one. These comments have left the 'minor'

---

[3]Cf. the entry 'Suf(f)eten', in *Lexikon der Alten Welt*, Zurich 1965, col. 2947, and in *Der kleine Pauly* V, Munich 1973, cols. 413f. Cf., also J. Teixidor, 'Les fonctions de *rab* et de suffète en Phénicie', *Semitica* 29, 1979, 9–17. For the 'charisma' of the judges cf. Z. Weisman, 'Charismatic Leaders in the Era of the Judges', *ZAW* 89, 1977, 399–411.

[4]For the judges as charismatic leaders see the now classical work by M. Weber, 'Das antike Judentum', *Gesammelte Aufsätze zur Religionssoziologie* III, Tübingen 1923, 92ff., and A. Alt, 'Die Staatenbildung der Israeliten in Palästina' (1930), *KlSchr* II, Munich 1953, 1–65: 4ff.; ET, 'The Formation of the Israelite State in Palestine', *Essays on Old Testament History and Religion*, Oxford and Garden City, New York 1966, 171–237: 178. The point has again been stressed recently by A. Malamat, 'Charismatic Leadership in the Book of Judges', in *Magnalia Dei – The Mighty Acts of God. Essays in memory of G. Ernest Wright*, Garden City, New York 1976, 152–68.

[5]J. A. Soggin, 'Zur Entwicklung des alttestamentlichen Königtums', *TZ* 15, 1959, 401–18: 407, and *Das Königtum in Israel*, BZAW 104, 1967, 12f. I am now aware that the comparison had already been made by A. B. Ehrlich, *Randglossen zur hebräischen Bibel* III, Leipzig 1919, 75.

judges out of account, but as I have already said, I shall attempt
to present my own hypothesis, which I hope will prove definitive, at the right point.

2. DIVISION AND CHARACTERISTICS

The twenty-one chapters of Judges can be divided into the
following sections (a slightly different division can be found in
J. Gray*, 1967, 204ff.):

(a) 1.1–2.5: narratives connected with the conquest, which
have already been partly examined in my commentary on Joshua.[6] 2.1–5 belong to the latest stratum of Deuteronomy, DtrN,
as we shall see.

(b) 2.6–16.31: the so-called 'main body' of the book. This
describes the exploits of the 'major' judges: Othniel, 3.7–11;
Ehud, 3.12–30; Deborah and Barak, chs. 4–5; Gideon, chs. 6–8;
Samson, chs. 13–16; there are also reports about the 'minor'
judges: Tola and Jair, 10.1–5; Ibzan, Elon and Abdon, 12.8–15.
Another leader, Jephthah (10.6–12.7), not called šōpēṭ, but on
one occasion qāṣīn and on another rō'š (11.8, 11), has characteristics of both categories, as we shall see in due course,
whereas two figures, Shamgar (3.31; cf. 5.6) and Abimelech (ch.
9), do not have anything to do with the judges, but have been
inserted into the text for reasons which we can no longer
establish.

One characteristic feature of the 'main body' of the book is
the insertion of each episode into what has been called a 'framework': this is a kind of preface and a kind of epilogue, which
seek to provide the key for reading the narrative episode and
which we can easily recognize by their schematism: in fact they
remain basically the same for all the episodes, which are as
different as one could imagine. Their characteristics are as follows: the people of God are unfaithful and Yahweh therefore
deprives them of his protection, thus delivering them into the
hands of their enemies; oppressed, the people repent and cry out
to the Lord begging for mercy; the Lord sends help in the form
of a judge who delivers them from their enemies. After a while,
the process repeats itself and continues to do so a number of

[6] *Joshua*, ET, OTL, 1972, 13.

times, giving the impression of a quasi-cyclical conception[7] of time in which *history repeats itself*. The stories of Jephthah and Samson sometimes show a parallelism with earlier episodes and other elements which make it probable that here we have material added at a later stage, in secondary form. We shall see other details in our examination of the texts. Here, too, we find the chronological references which are discussed in the following section.

(c) Chapters 17–18 and 19–21 form an appendix containing two episodes: the conquest by Dan of its own territory in the extreme north of the country, and the tribal war against Benjamin, which is guilty of having refused to extradite some of its members who have committed a barbaric crime. Both these sections have a strong pro-monarchical tone, cf. 17.6; 18.1; 19.1; 21.25, but in the second episode this tone, while retained, is in fact countered by the insertion of the theory of an alternative, tribal authority, responsible for maintaining law and order and capable of mounting, where necessary, police operations pure and simple. Until recently it was thought that the two episodes were free of Dtr revisions; however, recent studies which we shall consider in due course have made it very probable that such revisions are to be found even here, though they have been made in a more subtle way than in the 'main body'. This was probably an earlier phase of the Dtr redaction, DtrH, and perhaps in the case of the second episode, of an anti-monarchical revision of the work by DtrN.

3. REDACTION OF THE 'MAIN BODY'

Bibliography: W. **Richter****, 1963 and 1964, *passim*.

In the following section we shall see that W. Richter distinguishes between judges in the strict sense and judges who in fact are 'saviours'. To have isolated some sections making part of what was originally a 'Book of Saviours' (*Retterbuch*) is another of the merits of the noteworthy labours of this scholar.

An original 'Book of Saviours' was made up of the sections

---

[7]Cf. recently G. Fohrer, *Theologische Grundstrukturen des Alten Testament*, Berlin 1972, 43. I have not been able to go into the problem of whether biblical historiography is to be considered cyclical or linear; for an adequate treatment see A. H. J. Gunneweg, *Vom Verstehen des Alten Testaments. Eine Hermeneutik*, Göttingen 1977, 133ff.; ET, *Understanding the Old Testament*, OTL, 1978, 173ff.

on Ehud (3.15b–26), the only one preserved in its original form; the episode of Jael (4.17a, 18–21 [22]); the following sections of the Gideon traditions: 7.11b, 13–21; 8.5–9, 14–21a; and the conclusion of the work is perhaps to be found in 9.56.

However, the 'Book of Saviours' has been enlarged by a later author, making use of a set of material which transforms the wars fought by the 'saviours' into 'wars of Yahweh', that is, into 'holy wars'. His work can be seen in 3.13, 27–29; 4.4a, 6–9, 11, 17b; 6.2b–5, 11b–17, 25–27a, 31b, 32–34; 7.1, 9–11a, 22–25; 8.3f., 10–13, 22f., 29, 31; 9.1–7, 16a, 19b–21, 23f., 41–45, 56f.

Richter goes on to say that this was followed by two redactions which he calls 'Deuteronomic'. The first inserted the 'frameworks' 3.12, 14, 15a, 30; 4.1a, 2–3a, 23f.; 5.31 (without the number); 6.1 (without the number), 2a; 8.28 (without the number); and perhaps 9.16b–19a, 22, 55. The second presents an 'example' (*Beispielstück*), 3.7–11a (without the number and the formulae in vv. 8, 10f.).

Finally, 2.7, 10–12, 14–16, 18f.; 4.1b and 10.6–16 belong to DtrH in the strict sense.[8]

For a different classification see R. G. Boling*, 1975, 29ff.

For the characteristics of the Dtr history I would refer the reader to what I have said elsewhere.[9]

4. CHRONOLOGY

Bibliography: **M. Noth****, 1943, 18–27; **F. Nötscher***, 1950, 7; **W. Vollborn**, 'Die Chronologie des Richterbuches', in *Festschrift Friedrich Baumgärtel*, Erlangen 1959, 192–6; **W. Richter****, 1964, 132–41; **G. Sauer**, 'Die chronologischen Angaben in den Büchern Deuteronomium bis 2. Könige', *TZ* 24, 1968, 1–14, esp.2ff.; **S. M. Warner**, 'The Period of the Judges within the Structure of Early Israel', *HUCA* 47, 1976, 57–79; id., 'The Dating of the Period of the Judges', *VT* 28, 1978, 455–63.

[8]A computerized study by statistical linguistics has recently been produced by Y. T. Radday, G. Leb, D. Wickmann and S. Talmon, 'The Book of Judges examined by Statistical Linguistics', *Bibl* 58, 1977, 469–99. I must confine myself to the results of this investigation as I am unable, on technical grounds, to check (i.e. to verify or falsify) the validity of the methods followed and the procedures adopted. According to this study there is a very high probability (99%) that the 'main body' of the book is the work of one author, while similar results have also been achieved for other sections, though with lower percentages. If we accept these results, they show us how thoroughly Dtr not only collected, but also reworked his sources.

[9]*Joshua*, 3ff.
Cf. also J. Van Seters, *In Search of History*, New Haven and London 1983, 342–6. For a perspective on one of the subjects of the Deuteronomistic history cf. recently A. Alghisi, 'Il pentimento d'Israele nelle sezioni deuteronomistiche del libro dei Giudici', *RiBibl* 33, 1985, 3–27.

In the traditional scheme of the biblical prehistory,[10] the age of the Judges follows that of the unified conquest under Joshua (Josh. 1–12),[11] and precedes that of Samuel and Saul (I Sam. 1–31). As we have seen, in the present structure of the 'former prophets', the judges arise to liberate Israel every time that Israel repents and cries out to Yahweh. The judges deliver Israel from its enemies. According to the scheme in question, they are to be dated in the last centuries of the second millennium BC, but as we shall soon see, the chronological position is remarkably difficult: as with the conquest under the command of Joshua, though in a very different form, we have here an artificial chronological and historical construction, intent on presenting individual local episodes, in some cases probably traditional and therefore ancient, as representing the liberation of all Israel, united in the sacral tribal alliance, from the oppression of other peoples, an oppression understood, as we have seen, as a deserved punishment for an unfaithful people. And since such a scheme is a typically Dtn or Dtr construction, as has been known for some time, whereas the possibly ancient episodes do not contain any chronological details, it seems evident that the major part of the chronology must be attributed to Dtn and Dtr, i.e. to a school which was not so much interested in historiography for its own sake, but used it to serve the ends of its preaching (because it is essentially a matter of preaching, as H.-W. Hertzberg*, 1959, 162, rightly pointed out), to explain the end first of the kingdom of Israel, the north, in 722–20, and then that of Judah, the south, in 587–86.[12] This end was thought to have been the direct consequence of divine judgment on a process of degeneration in the people of God, the roots of which are to be found in the prehistory of Israel.

[10] I use the term 'prehistory' to denote everything which in Israel precedes the institution of the united monarchy under David; cf. my contribution to J. H. Hayes and J. M. Miller (eds.), *Israelite and Judaean History*, OTL, 1977, 332ff., and 'The History of Ancient Israel', in *Eretz Israel* 14, 1978, 44*–51*. The attempt by S. M. Warner to reverse the traditional chronological order by putting the period of the Judges before the conquest starts from the presupposition that we are dealing with historical sources in the modern sense of the word. As this element can hardly be proved, while there is. much to disprove it, there ought not to be any need to enter into a detailed examination of his theories.

[11] For the historiographical value of this see *Joshua*, 7ff.

[12] As has rightly been noted by W. Richter**, 1964, 133, and L. Perlitt, *Bundestheologie im Alten Testament*, WMANT 36, 1969, 7ff. However, this had already been seen by C. F. Burney*, 1919, liv, who noted 'the hopelessness of any attempt to construct a chronology of our period from the Biblical sources available', while F. Nötscher*, 1950, considered it simply artificial.

On these premises, then, it seems *a priori* impossible to reconstruct a chronology of the period of the Judges on the basis of the biblical material, just as such a task also proved impossible in the case of the book of Joshua. That is true even though some noteworthy attempts have been made in this direction; in fact there is nothing at all which enables us to construct an absolute chronology, and even if a relative chronology were possible, it would not help to establish this general chronology. Thus if, for example, we accept the substantial historicity of the personages mentioned in the book (and this is an admission based on information which is far from being certain), there is nothing to indicate that one 'major' judge could not have been contemporaneous with another: Deborah and Barak could very well have been contemporaries of Samson; Jephthah and Samson could also have been contemporaries, and Ehud could have been contemporary with these two and with Gideon! As for the 'minor' judges, according to the information to which I have already referred, if we leave aside for a moment the theory which would argue for a rotation between various places, they could all have been contemporaries, because they fulfil their office in different areas.

First of all, however, let me try to describe the chronological information given in the text. This can be done in two ways. The first is the easier, which is to note the sequence as it appears: this is the method followed by H. H. Rowley and G. A. Barrois.[13] The other approach tries to distinguish between the chronology of the 'oppressors' and that of the 'saviours', who in part overlap, and was proposed by A. Penna*, 1963, 4. I shall consider them in succession. The two patterns add up to the 410 years of the MT, 420 according to the Septuagint, figures which are evidently too high.

(a) Rowley-Barrois:	MT	LXX
Oppression. Cushan-rishathaim (Judg. 3.8)	8	
Othniel (Judg. 3.11)	40	50
Oppression. Eglon, king of Moab (Judg. 3.14)	18	
Ehud (Judg. 3.30)	80	
Oppression. Jabin, king of Hazor (Judg. 4.3)	20	
Deborah-Barak (Judg. 5.31)	40	

---

[13]H. H. Rowley, *From Joseph to Joshua*, London and New York 1950, 87ff., and G. A. Barrois, 'Chronology, Metrology, etc.', *IB* I, 1952, 142–64: 145. Cf. already G. F. Moore*, 1895, xxxviiff., and J. Garstang*, 1931, 56ff.

Oppression. The Midianites (Judg. 6.1)	7
Gideon (Judg. 8.28)	40
Rule of Abimelech (Judg. 9.22)	3
Tola (Judg. 10.2)	23
Jair (Judg. 10.3)	22
Oppression. The Ammonites (Judg. 10.8)	18
Jephthah (Judg. 12.7)	6
Ibzan (Judg. 12.9)	7
Elon (Judg. 12.11)	10
Abdon (Judg. 12.14)	8
Oppression. The Philistines (Judg. 13.1)	40
Samson (Judg. 15.20; 16.31)	20

(b) Penna*, 1963

Oppressors		Liberators	
Cushan-rishathaim	8 years	Othniel	40 years
Moab	18 years	Ehud	80 years
Philistines	? years	Shamgar	? years
Jabin and the Canaanites	20 years	Barak-Deborah	40 years
Midian	7 years	Gideon	40 years
		Abimelech	3 years
		Tola	23 years
		Jair	22 years
Ammon	18 years	Jephthah	6 years
		Ibzan	7 years
		Elon	10 years
		Abdon	8 years
Philistines	40 years	Samson	20 years

A. Penna*, 1963, rightly takes account of the fact that the 'oppressors' and the 'saviours' to some extent overlap chronologically, but, in view of the silence of the sources, it is not possible to determine to what extent this overlapping affects the general chronology. So, if with his method we succeed in reducing to some extent the figure of 410 (420) years, which we have seen to be excessive, we shall never know to what extent we can in fact reduce it!

There is another feature which catches the eye of the attentive reader: of the eighteen chronological references, seven give stereotyped figures,[14] multiples or fractions of forty, figures which

[14]A.Alt, 'Erwägungen über die Landnahme der Israeliten in Palästina', *PJB* 35, 1939, 8–63; *KlSchr* I, Munich 1953, 126–75: 41/155 n.l.

here are probably reckoned to correspond to a generation; and this makes a total of 280 years out of 410/420. In other words, a little more than two-thirds of the chronology is made up of round numbers! The consequences are obvious, notwithstanding ingenious attempts to reconstruct the chronology of the work and in particular to insert it into the general chronology of 480 (LXX^{BA}:440) years which, according to I Kings 6.1, runs from the date of the exodus to that of the beginning of the work of the construction of the Jerusalem temple. These suggestions have not in the long run produced appreciable results, or at any rate, results proportionate to the labour expended on them. This is also because the nature and the significance of the figure of 480 years has not yet adequately been clarified. It is certainly too high compared with the results of the historical-critical reconstruction of Israelite origins, and in any case has not been handed down in a uniform way (Josephus, *Antt.*VIII. iii.1 = § 61, cf. VII.iii.2 = § 68 and X.viii.5 = §147, speaks of 592 years, whereas in *Contra Apionem* II.2 = §19 and *Antt.*XX.x.1 = §230, he speaks of 612 years).

We have a notable step forward towards the solution of the problem in the studies by W. Richter**, 1964; his theories have been fully accepted by R.G. Boling*, 1975, 23ff. According to Richter, the mistake made by past studies has been not to take account of the literary genre in which the individual chronological details occur. Richter proposes a reconstruction of the figure 480 along the following lines, counting back from the date of the beginning of the building of the temple:

(*a*) Reign of Solomon   4 years (I Kings 6.1)
     Reign of David   40 years (I Kings 2.11)
     Reign of Saul [15]   2 years (I Sam. 13.1)

     Total monarchy   46 years

(*b*) Judges in the strict sense, characterized by the formulae *hū' šāpaṭ 'et yiśrā'ēl* or *wayyišpōṭ 'et yiśrā'ēl*:
Eli   40 years (I Sam.4.18b)
Samson   20 years (Judg. 15.20; 16.31)
Abdon   8 years (Judg. 12.14)

[15]The figure of two years only for the reign of Saul (I Sam.13.1) is often considered to be the product of textual corruption, because it is so low. I am, however, quite persuaded by the arguments in its favour put forward by K.A.D. Smelik, *Saul*, Dissertation, Amsterdam Free University, 1977, 69–71.

Elon	10 years (Judg.12.11)
Ibzan	7 years (Judg.12.9)
Jephthah	6 years (Judg.12.7)
Jair	22 years (Judg.10.3)
Tola	23 years (Judg.10.2)
Total	136 years for judges in the strict sense

(c) 'Saviour' judges characterized by the formula *wattišqōṭ hā'āreṣ*:

After Gideon	40 years (Judg.8.28)
After Barak	40 years (Judg.5.31)
After Ehud	80 years (Judg.3.30)
After Othniel	40 years (Judg.3.11)
Total	200 for the 'saviours'

(d) Periods of oppression

Before Gideon	7 years (Judg.6.1)
Before Deborah	20 years (Judg. 4.3)
Before Ehud	18 years (Judg.3.14)
Before Othniel	8 years (Judg. 3.8)
Total	53 years of oppression

(e) Years in the desert: 40

(f) Joshua and the elders: 5

The sum of all these years amounts to 480.

In this context, there are again some obscurities: first of all, the five years of Joshua and the elders, which are not indicated in the text and are calculated by Richter on the basis of the difference between the sum of the figures and 480 years. Richter has shown that this is probable, given that the author of the chronology in question connects Othniel with Kenaz, brother of Caleb (Judg.3.9). Thus Caleb turns out to be the element which connects the generation of the exodus with that of the conquest, just as later Samuel connects the generation of the judges with that of the monarchy. However, the figure is clearly not certain. Again, we have to exclude from the calculation the three years of Abimelech (Judg.9.22), because he is not a judge; Shamgar, to whom 3.31 does not assign any period of years; and the twenty years given in I Sam. 7.2 for the stay of the ark at Kiriath–jearim, because they belong to another tradition. The eighteen years of 10.8 and the forty years of 13.1 must also be added to the figures not in the reckoning. Richter is well aware that these are objections that can be made to his reconstruction; but there is no doubt that this is the most adequate attempt made so far to reconstruct the official chronology of the book of Judges, an attempt which must form the starting-point for any further examination of the problem.[16] There is, of course, no information relevant to the real chronology.

5. TEXT AND TRANSLATIONS

Select bibliography: **J. Soisalon-Soininen**, *Die Textformen der Septuaginta-Übersetzungen*, Helsinki 1951; J. **Schreiner**, *Septuaginta-Massora des Buches der Richter*, Rome 1957; **S. Jellicoe**, *The Septuagint and Modern Study*, Oxford 1968, 280–3; B. **Lindars**, 'Some Septuagint Readings in Judges', *JTS* NS 22, 1971, 1–14; he also gives a bibliography of other more recent works.

The Massoretic text of Judges is particularly pure; according to some scholars (G.F. Moore*, 1895, xliiiff.) it is the best of the historical books (with the exception, of course, of the song of Deborah, ch. 5, which poses the same problem as all instances of ancient Hebrew poetry, cf. pp. 92ff. below). On the other hand, the Septuagint text presents us with a very complex situation: in fact there is a series of quite remarkable variants between the text of LXX^B and that of LXX^A, which are without parallel in the Old Testament. So great are the discrepancies, that we might speak of two different translations, as we shall see in due course. The text of LXX^A seems to be the older of the two and the quality of the translation is obviously superior; some uncial codices and some minuscules are based on it. By contrast, LXX^B, followed by other uncials and minuscules, presents a different text. So great are the variants between the two codices, and of such a quality, as I have indicated, that in his edition of 1935 A. Rahlfs, on the basis of the work by P. de Lagarde (also accepted with reservations by G.F. Moore*, 1895, loc. cit., and C.F. Burney*, 1919, cxxivff.) prints both on the same page, thus accepting consistently the theory of two different and independent translations. However, this evaluation of

---

[16]Another treatment of the subject can be found in J. J. Bimson, *Redating the Exodus and Conquest*, *JSOT*, SS 5, 1978, 87ff.; however, I am not persuaded by his criticism of W. Richter and R. G. Boling. For this work see my review in *VT* 31, 1981, 98f.

the situation, a problem which we cannot go into in detail in this introduction, is now rejected by most authors (cf. the bibliographies in Jellicoe and Lindars), who think rather of successive revisions of the same text.

Some Hebrew fragments have been discovered at Qumran: 4QJdc[a], which contains part of 6.3–13, and 4QJdc[b], which preserves the whole of 21.12–35 and a fragment of 16.5–7. According to F.M. Cross, the scholar put in charge of the publication of these texts (in a letter to R.G. Boling*, 1975, quoted op.cit., 40), these fragments, so far unpublished (like the other texts entrusted to Cross), except in very fragmentary quotations and extracts, reflect 'the better Septuagint tradition'; however, as Boling rightly observes, such phrases are virtually meaningless if we consider the variants existing between the different recensions of the LXX. So the problem still remains open and we have to await the publication of the fragments in question before coming to a decision.

The translations of the Vulgate, the Peshitto[17] and the Targum are less important: they presuppose the standard Massoretic text.

---

[17]For the Peshitto text cf. P. B. Dirksen, *The Transmission of the Text in the Peshitta Manuscripts of the Book of Judges*, Leiden 1972, and the comments by F. E. Deist, *Towards the Text of the Old Testament*, Pretoria 1978, 145. For the critical edition cf. P. B. Dirksen, *The Old Testament in Syriac according to the Peshitta Version*, Vol. II, 2, *Judges–Samuel*, London 1978.

PART ONE

TRADITIONS ON THE CONQUEST
1.1–2.5

PART ONE

TRADITIONS ON THE CONQUEST

1.1–2.5

Bibliography: (a) *On the whole section*: G. E. **Wright**. 'The Literary and Historical Problem of Joshua 10 and Judges 1', *JNES* 6, 1946, 105–14; H. H. **Rowley**, *From Joseph to Joshua*, London and New York 1950, 100ff.; E. O'**Doherty**, 'The Literary Problem of Judges 1,1–3,6', *CBQ* 18. 1956, 1–7; S. B. **Gurewicz**, 'The Bearing of Judges i–ii 5 on the Authorship of the Book of Judges', *ABR* 7, 1959, 37–40; C. H. J. **de Geus**, 'Richteren 1,1–2,5', *Vox Theologica* 36, Assen 1966, 32–53; A. G. **Auld**, 'Judges 1 and History: A Reconsideration', *VT* 25, 1975, 261–85.

(b) On individual passages: on 1.1–3: G. **von Rad*****, 1951, 16, 24; on 1.1–20: H. **Haag**, 'Von Jahwe geführt. Auslegung von Ri. 1,1–20', *BuL* 4, 1963, 103–5; on 1.3: G. R. **Driver****, 1964, 6; on 1.4: H.-W. **Hertzberg**, 'Adonibeseq', *JPOS* 6, 1926, 213–21 = *Beiträge zur Traditionsgeschichte und Theologie des Alten Testaments*, Göttingen 1962, 28–35; P. **Welten**, 'Bezeq', *ZDPV* 81, 1965, 138–65; on 1.5–8: K.-D. **Schunck**, 'Juda und Jerusalem in vor- und frühisraelitischer Zeit', in *Schalom. Studien . . . A. Jepsen zum 70. Geburtstag dargebracht*, Berlin and Stuttgart 1971, 50–57; M. **Noth**, 'Jerusalem und die israelitische Tradition', *OTS* 8, 1950, 28–46 = *GesSt* I, Munich ³1966, 172–87: 28=172f.; ET, 'Jerusalem and the Israelite Tradition', *The Laws in the Pentateuch and Other Studies*, Edinburgh and Philadelphia 1966, 132–44: 132f.; on 1.14: E. W. **Nicholson**, 'The Problem of *ṣnḥ*', *ZAW* 89, 1977, 259–66; G. R. **Driver**, 'Problems of Interpretation in the Heptateuch', in *Mélanges bibliques . . . A. Robert*, Paris 1957, 66–76; on 1.16: B. **Mazar**, 'The Sanctuary of Arad and the Family of Hobab the Kenite', *JNES* 24, 1965, 297–303; S. **Mittmann**, 'Ri. 1,16f. und das Siedlungsgebiet der Kenitischen Sippe Hobab', *ZDPV* 93, 1977, 212–35; S. **Abramsky**, 'On the Kenite-Midianite Background of Moses' Leadership', *Eretz Israel* 12, 1975, 35–39 (in Hebrew, with English summary); on 1.22–26: O. **Eissfeldt**, 'Der geschichtliche Hintergrund der Erzählung von Gibeas Schandtat' (1935), *KlSchr* II, 1963, 64–80: 73ff.; on 1.22–2.5: H. **Haag**, 'Jahwe, Der Erzieher seines Volkes. Eine Auslegung von Ri. 1,21 – 2,5', *BuL* 4, 1963, 174–84; on 2.1–5: G. **Schmitt**, *Du sollst keinen*

Frieden schliessen mit den Bewohnern des Landes, BWANT V. 11, 1970, 39–41; on Dtr in 2.1–5: R. **Smend**, 'Das Gesetz und die Völker', in *Probleme biblischer Theologie, G. von Rad zum 70. Geburtstag*, Munich 1971, 494–509.

Preamble (1.1–3)

1 [1]After the death of Joshua, the Israelites inquired of Yahweh, 'Which of us shall go up first to fight against the Canaanites?' [2]Yahweh responded, 'Judah shall go up; behold I have given the region into his hand.' [3]And Judah invited Simeon, his brother, 'Come up with me into the territory allotted to me, that we may fight against the Canaanites. Then I will go with you into your territory.' And Simeon accompanied him.

Judah (1.4–9)

4 So Judah went up and Yahweh gave the Canaanites and the Perizzites into their hands; and they smote ten thousand of them at Bezek. [5]Then they discovered at Bezek 'the Lord of Bezek' and fought against him; and defeated the Canaanites and the Perizzites. [6]The Lord of Bezek tried to escape after the battle, but they pursued him, caught him and cut off his thumbs and his big toes. [7]Then the Lord of Bezek exclaimed, 'Seventy kings with their thumbs and big toes cut off used to pick up scraps under my table. As I have done, behold I have been done to!' They took him to Jerusalem, where he died.

8 Then the men of Judah mounted an attack on Jerusalem and took it; they put the inhabitants to the sword, and set the city on fire. [9]They left there to fight against the Canaanites living in the highlands, in the southern desert, and in the lowland.

Judah and Caleb (1.10–15)

10 Then Judah went against the Canaanites who lived in Hebron (the name of Hebron was formerly Kiriath-arba), and they defeated Sheshak, Ahiman and Talmai. [11]From there they went against the inhabitants of Debir, the name of which was formerly Kiriath-sepher. [12]And Caleb said, 'To the one who attacks Kiriath-sepher and takes it, I will give Achsah my daughter as wife.' [13]And Othniel the son of Kenaz, Caleb's younger brother, took it; and he gave him Achsah his daughter as wife. [14]When he came to her, he prompted her to ask her father for a field. { She dismounted from the ass. / She clapped her hands. } and Caleb asked her, 'What do you want?' [15]She replied, 'Do me a favour: since the land that you have given me is dry, you should also give me springs of water.' And Caleb gave her the 'Upper springs' and the 'Lower springs'.

Judah and the Kenites (1.16)

16 The descendants of the Kenite, Hobab, a kinsman of Moses, went up with the people of Judah from the 'City of Palms' to the wilderness of Judah, to the descent of Arad; and they went and settled with the Amalekites.

Judah and Simeon (1.17–20)

17 Then Judah, accompanied by his brother Simeon, went to fight against the Canaanites who lived in Zephath; they utterly destroyed it, so that from then on they called the city Hormah. [18]But Judah did not succeed in conquering Gaza with its territory, or Ashkelon with its territory, or Ekron with its territory. [19]Yahweh was with Judah, so that he succeeded in conquering the highlands, but he did not succeed in prevailing against the inhabitants of the plain, because they had chariots of iron. [20]And they gave Hebron to Caleb, as Moses had said, and Caleb drove out from it the three Anakites.

Benjamin (1.21)

21 The people of Benjamin did not succeed in getting the better of the Jebusites, the inhabitants of Jerusalem, and they have remained in the midst of the people of Benjamin to this day.

Joseph (1.22–26)

22 The house of Joseph also went up against Bethel and Yahweh was with them. [23]Joseph went up to make a reconnaissance in the region of Bethel, the name of which had formerly been Luz. [24]The spies saw a man coming out of the city and made a proposal to him: 'Show us the way into the city and we will spare you. [25]And he showed them the way into the city; and they put the inhabitants of the city to the sword, but they let the man and his family go. [26]And the man went to the land of the Hittites and built a city, and called its name Luz; that is its name to this day.

The tribes of the central northern region (1.27–35)

27 Manasseh did not succeed in subduing Beth-Shean and its territories, nor Taanach and its territories, nor the inhabitants of Dor and its territories, nor the inhabitants of Ibleam and its territories, nor the inhabitants of Megiddo and its territories, so that the Canaanites continued to live in that region. [28]Only when Israel grew stronger could they put the Canaanites under tribute, but they did not succeed in conquering them completely. [29]And Ephraim did not succeed in subjecting the Canaanites who dwelt at Gezer, so that they continued to dwell there; [30]nor did Zebulon succeed in subjecting the inhabitants of Kitron or those of Nahalol, so that the Canaanites continued to dwell there, and became subject to forced labour. [31]Asher did not succeed in subjecting the inhabitants of Acco, of Sidon, of Ahlab, of Achzib, of Helbah, of Aphik and of Rehob. [32]So Asher continued to dwell in the midst of the Canaanites who lived in that region, without

succeeding in subjecting them. [33]Napthali, too, did not succeed in
subjecting the inhabitants of Beth-shemesh and Beth-anath, but dwelt
among the Canaanites, who inhabited the region; however, the inhabitants of Beth-shemesh and Beth-anath were subjected to tribute.
[34]The Amorites drove back the Danites towards the highlands, and
did not allow them to come down to the plain. [35]Thus the Amorites
continued to dwell in Har-heres, in Aijalon and in Shaalbim, but as
soon as Joseph became stronger, they were subjected to tribute.

Edom (1.36)
36 The frontier of the Edomites ran from the 'Ascent of the Scorpions' in the direction of 'The Rock' (Petra?), continuing to ascend.

The angel at Bochim (2.1–5)
2 [1]The 'messenger of Yahweh' went up from Gilgal to Bochim and
said: '. . . I delivered you from Egypt and led you into the land which
I had promised with an oath to give to your forefathers. I said, "I will
never break my covenant with them." [2]Therefore you shall make no
alliance with the inhabitants of this region; you shall break down their
altars. But you have not obeyed my command. What is this that you
have done? [3]So I said to them, "I will not drive them out before you,
and they will turn into a snare, and their gods will become a trap!" '
[4]When the 'messenger of Yahweh' had said all these words to the
Israelites, the people lamented in a loud voice. [5]Therefore they called
the place Bochim ('the weepers') and they sacrificed there to Yahweh.

[1.1] 'After the death . . .' is probably a late addition, serving to
make this passage the sequel to Josh. 24.28–33; however, these last
verses are taken up in Judg. 2.6ff., which thus prove to be the real
continuation of the end of Joshua. So this passage appears to be an
interpolation. 'Joshua': there is no reason at all to amend this to
'Moses', like some less recent commentators (*BHK³* and *BHS* express
their doubts). 'Inquired': root *šā'al*, which in contexts like this always
has the sense of 'inquire by means of the oracle', though the manner
of the inquiry is not stated. We have no mention of a central sanctuary,
nor any implication that there was one, against J. Gray*, 1967, who
thinks of something analogous to 20.18 (cf. the comments on that
passage). 'Shall go': literally, 'ascend', root *'ālāh*, an obvious reference
to the central highlands, to which one 'ascends' from Gilgal; however,
in contexts with a military flavour the verb often has the sense of 'go
on an expedition', with the enemy named after *'al*. This meaning seems
very appropriate here, because the use of the verb does not necessarily
presuppose that the people are at Gilgal (cf. also A. Penna*, 1963),
though the stay at Gilgal is at least possible, at any rate in the mind
of the redactors (cf. 2.1). 'Of us': literally 'for us', 'on our account';
however, the text is not concerned with a group which might go 'in

place of the others; it is concerned only with the order of precedence in the attack, cf. below, 20.18. We must therefore postulate a partitive significance for the prefixed *lamed*, not provided for by traditional grammars. 'The Canaanites': here and in Chronicles always in the singular. In the Pentateuch the term indicates the J tradition, so that we could attribute the earliest elements in the passage to the 'collector' mentioned in Joshua. **[3]** The 'territory allotted to me' is probably a late reference which tries to harmonize this text with Josh. 14.2. **[4]** In the Hebrew there is an alternation between verbs in the singular and verbs in the plural, depending on whether Judah is understood as an individual or a group. It is not possible to imitate this usage in any of the Western languages, which keep exclusively to either singular or plural. 'Smote': in Hebrew military terminology the root *nākāh* indicates the victory of the subject of the verb, leading to heavy human losses on the part of the enemy; the figure given shows this. 'Ten thousand' is a conventional figure and is a generic term for 'innumerable'; cf. I Sam. 18.7 par.: it is not a real figure. 'Bezek': for the place, see the commentary. **[5]** 'The lord of Bezek', Hebrew *'adōnī bezeq*, confirmed by Vg and Targ, is a form with the *yod compaginis*, and therefore not with the pronominal first person suffix.[1] I have translated it literally, without concealing the difficulty presented by a designation of this kind. In fact, in the Old Testament we never find an anonymous sovereign denoted as 'Lord of X'; it cannot be a theophoric name, given that there is as yet no evidence for a deity with this name in the region (Hertzberg*, 1959). Vincent*, 1958, and Penna*, 1963, have proposed an emendation to *'adōnī ṣedeq*, on the basis of the reading in Josh. 10.1–3,[2] but in this text the LXX read *'adōnī bezeq*, a reading which Hertzberg*, 1959, and Noth*, [2]1953, consider the authentic one. The LXX reading in Josh. 10.1ff. simply shows that even in ancient times there was a tendency to confuse the two people, whose names were phonetically similar and who were located in the same region. Of course, those who want to correct the reading to *ṣedeq* seek to connect this text not only with Josh. 10 but also with the biblical traditions associated with Jerusalem, which attribute to one of its kings a name composed of the element *ṣedeq*; these are biblical traditions, because the non-biblical onomastica do not know any king with this name: Gen. 14; Ps. 110. And that is the case even if Adoni-Bezek was not the king of Jerusalem, but of Bezek! According to the story, he was brought to Jerusalem only to die. I have therefore kept MT, with Hertzberg* and Kaufmann*, 1962. The root *bzq* does not appear in the Hebrew Bible, but is attested in Aramaic, where *bizqā*

---

[1]For the form, see the grammar by R. Meyer, §45.3. So it is not necessary to vocalize the word as *'dōnē*, cf. A. B. Ehrlich, *Randglossen zur hebräischen Bibel* III, Leipzig 1910, 58.

[2]Cf. my *Joshua*, 119.

means 'pebble'. It is perhaps a play on words, producing a taunt-name. **[7]** 'They took him': who is the subject? Originally this must have been the king's followers, but the redactors seem to be thinking of the men of Judah. However, the story does not work in either case: in the first because the king had been captured by Judah, and in the second because Judah had not yet occupied Jerusalem (Hertzberg*, 1959)! 'Seventy': this figure is also a legendary synonym for 'many', cf. on 8.30. **[10]** 'Then Judah . . .': Josh. 15.13ff.[3] has 'Caleb'. 'Hebron': LXX has a slightly longer text, cf. *BHK*[3] and *BHS*. 'Kiriath-arba': LXX confuses this with Kiriath-sepher, reading for the latter (v. 12) πόλις (τῶν) γραμμάτων, i.e. *qiriat (has)sōp'rīm*, as in Josh. 15.15. **[14]** 'Prompted': MT has 'she prompted him' (root *swt*), but the reading is obviously wrong, seeing that the 'father' who follows can only be her father, and she is the subject here and in the following verse. Scholars (with the exception of Y. Kaufmann*, 1962) therefore agree on reading *way'sītehā*, 'he (Othniel) prompted her'. But, as I observed in connection with Josh. 15.18, the verb here has a somewhat obscure sense: normally it means 'seduce', 'tempt', always with decidedly pejorative connotations. So while we cannot accept MT because it is manifestly absurd, the emendation does not appear completely free from doubt either. 'A field': with Josh. 15.18 and LXX at this point. The determinative with the noun in MT can only signify the existence of a well-known place, and that is not obviously the case here; I would therefore suppress the article, which is probably the product of a dittography with the preceding *he*. 'Dismounted', or, according to others, 'clapped her hands'. The meaning of the root *ṣānaḥ* is unknown; the LXX has ἐγόγγυζεν καὶ ἔκραζεν, 'murmured and cried out'. Modern authors usually have 'descended', 'dismounted from her ass', a translation recently confirmed by Nicholson; however, Caleb's question presupposes an action out of the ordinary, meant to attract attention, and not simply dismounting from her ass. So here too there is some doubt as to the result. The proposal made by Driver**, 1962–3, 'to break wind', is not to be commended. **[15]** 'Do me a favour . . .': a root *yāhab**, attested in Hebrew only in the imperative, can be found in Aramaic. The text of the verse is slightly different from that in Josh. 15.19, though it is semantically identical. 'A favour': literally, 'a blessing'. 'Dry': Hebrew *negeb*, which is also the name for the steppes south of the central highlands. 'Springs': in this context the term *gullāh*, normally 'bowl', 'basin', or another kind of container for liquids, is obscure; it can only mean 'springs'. It does not seem necessary to read the singular with A, Vg and Syr., given that these are probably proper names. **[16]** 'The descendants . . .', read with LXX[A], cf. 4.11; MT has the phrase 'The sons of a Kenite, father-in-law of Moses', which many scholars consider to be corrupt;

[3]Op. cit., 166.

however, Y. Kaufmann**, 1962, understands: 'The sons of the same Kenite who was the father-in-law of Moses . . .'; similarly Penna*, 1963: 'Those of the Kenite, Moses' father-in-law'. This is grammatically possible, but in that case it is in contradiction with 4.11. LXX[B] has: 'The sons of Jethro the Kenite . . .', but this is an obvious *lectio facilior* which substitutes a well-known name for another which is less known. Apart from the LXX[A] of the present text, 'Hobab' is also attested in Num. 10.29; Judg. 4.11. 'A kinsman . . .': the Hebrew *ḥōtēn* is normally understood as 'father-in-law', but it is difficult to distinguish it from *ḥātān*, 'son-in-law' or 'husband'. Thus the terminology seems somewhat confused: perhaps the terms had different meanings in different periods and different social contexts.[4] 'To the descent of Arad': the LXX has ἥ ἐστιν ἐπὶ καταβάσεως Ἀραδ, i.e. *b'mōrad 'ārād*, a reading which many commentators, and recently Mittmann, prefer. However, it is not clear how we unexpectedly find ourselves in this area (for the location cf. the commentary below), nor is there any geological formation here which can be identified with this description. Mittmann's proposal, that here we have an important reference to the habitat of the Kenites, about which we otherwise know practically nothing, is quite likely. He located the *mōrad* to the south-east of *tell el milḥ*. 'Amalekites': I follow the majority of scholars in reading this for *hā'ām*, 'the people', on the basis of K. Budde*, 1897. The whole verse seems to have connections with I Sam. 15.6. According to Mittmann, it probably goes with the following verse. For the locality, cf. Num. 21.1–3.

[17] 'They called' : I read an impersonal plural with LXX; cf. Vg, *vocatum est*: MT has the singular, with Judah as subject. 'Hormah': a play on words involving the term *ḥerem*, 'ban', 'extermination'. **[18]** 'Not' is missing in MT and Vg, but is to be added with LXX (cf. all contemporary commentators with the exception of J. Gray *, 1967): the point of the statement is that Judah did *not* succeed in occupying the places on the plain, the sites of the cities in question; cf. 3.3, where the Philistine cities are explicitly shown not to have been conquered. **[19]** 'Did not succeed': the verb is presupposed by the phrase, which, however, has only 'did not prevail'; this also appears in the LXX, Vg and Tg. However, it could also be a textual error:

[4]For this information see M. Noth, *Überlieferungsgeschichte des Pentateuch*, Stuttgart 1948, 185f.; ET, *A History of Pentateuchal Traditions*, Englewood Cliffs, NJ 1972, 183f.; W. F. Albright, 'Jethro, Hobab and Reuel in Early Hebrew Tradition', *CBQ* 25, 1963, 1–11; and B. Mazar, art.cit. The lack of precision in words relating to family and social grouping is well known in ancient Hebrew, but not peculiar to that language: it also exists in Arabic, cf. J. W. Rogerson, *Anthropology and the Old Testament*, Oxford 1978, 93ff.: 'Similar difficulties are known to modern anthropologists' because 'social groups are highly complex phenomena which can hardly be adequately explained by modern consciously sophisticated terms, let along by the rough and ready terms to be found in "natural" language.'

dittography of the *lamed* with the preceding *lō'*. In that case we simply read *lō' hōrīš(ū)*, a form used regularly in these passages. The convincing explanation by Kaufmann*, 1962, is similar to this. Here, and in the following verses, we often find the root *yāraš*, 'inherit', 'take possession', 'drive out', 'subject', depending on the context, which is why the reader will find that it has been translated in different ways. 'Chariots of iron': for the war chariot in Syria and Palestine cf. M.G. [Guzzo–] Amadasi, *L'iconografia del carro da guerra in Siria ed in Palestina*, SS 17, 1965; and S.M. Paul and W.G. Dever (eds.), *Biblical Archaeology*, Jerusalem 1973, 237ff. and the illustrations on p. 235. For a more recent period cf. W. Mayer, 'Gedanken zum Einsatz von Streitwagen und Reitern in neuassyrischer Zeit', *UF* 10, 1978, 175–86; these are always two-wheeled chariots. For illustrations cf. Amadasi and *ANEP*, s.v. 'Chariot'. **[20]** '. . .drove out from it. . .': LXX[B] has : 'And took possession there of the three cities of the Anakites', to which LXX[A] adds after 'cities' : ' . . .drove out from there the three Anakites', a phrase which concludes the sentence in the other minor versions. **[21]** 'People of Benjamin': Josh.15.63 has 'Judah'; the confusion is understandable: the place is a frontier point between the two tribes without actually being part of either of them. In Josh. 18.28 Jerusalem belongs to the territory assigned to Benjamin, whereas in our passage it is Judah which attacks the place and destroys it. M. Noth[5] considers the reading 'Benjamin' to be the original reading, which makes improbable the proposal of some authors (*BHK*[3], *BHS*, Kaufmann*, 1962, and perhaps Penna*, 1963) to replace Benjamin by Judah here. **[22]** LXX read 'the sons of Joseph'. **[23]** 'Reconnaissance': the verb *twr* means 'explore', 'spy out', and is the term used in Num. 13–14 (Josh. 2.1ff. has *m'ragg'līm*). **[24]** 'Spies' : Hebrew *haššōm'rīm*; i.e. from the patrol entrusted with the exploration. 'Favour' : *ḥesed* is a technical term connected with the covenant or alliance and indicates the fidelity of the parties involved to what is stipulated or promised; it is often used of the stronger party, as here. **[26]** *'ereṣ*: strange for a noun connected with movement. Should we read *'arṣāh* (haplography of the *he*)? **[27]** We ought to consider the possibility that here the root *yšb* has the technical meaning of 'dominate, rule', as has sometimes been suggested.[6] **[28]** 'Put under tribute': for this rendering cf. E. Täubler**. It is not in fact a question of enslavement, as has often been asserted, but of a form of vassalage. **[30]** 'Nahalol' : the names of the two places are different in the LXX: in Josh. 19.15 and 21.35 we have the phonetic variant Nahalal: the change from *ā* > *ō*, especially in vowels which are long by nature, is typical of West Semitic. **[31]**

[5]M. Noth, *Das Buch Josua*, HAT I 7, [3]1953.
[6]Cf. F. M. Cross, Jr, and D. N. Freedman, 'The Song of Miriam', *JNES* 14, 1955, 237–50; 248f., and recently, W. G. E. Watson, 'David Ousts the City Rulers of Jebus', *VT* 20, 1970, 501f.

maḫᵃlab is attested in VetLat. and in Josh. 19.29 in the metathesis *mēḫebel* ; MT *'aḫlāb* is confirmed by the LXX and Vg. The reading which I suggest is generally accepted, while there are no doubts about *'aḫlāb* being the equivalent of *maḫᵃlēb*, which I have at least corrected in the text. There is the same unanimity over deleting *ḥelbāh* as a duplicate of the two names quoted. *'apēq* is read with Josh. 19.30; here we have the phonetic variant *'apīq*. For *rᵉḫōb* see on Josh. 19.28.

[35] 'Har-heres', probably the Hebrew transcription of 'Mount Horus', i.e. 'of the sun', is identified with the *'ir šemeš* of Josh. 19.41f. It is not clear, in that case, why the place is located in relation to Joseph and not to Dan, but cf. also on chs. 13–16, pp. 231f. below. There remains, however, the problem of the final '*s*', a product of the 'Hellenization' of the name; in Phoenician and otherwise in West Semitic the transcription is always *ḥr*.

[36] 'Edomites': read thus according to the majority of modern scholars,[7] with LXXᴬ and Syr. Hex.; MT has 'Amorites', probably the product of textual corruption (*reš* for *dālet*) and a metathesis. 'In the direction of. . .': Hebrew has *min*, 'from', which is either to be suppressed as dittography with the previous word, or understood in the sense 'in the direction of' or 'as far as', postulating for *min* a polyvalence attested in West Semitic for other prepositions but not for *min*; this last proposal is no more than a hypothesis. [2.1] 'Messenger of Yahweh': or 'angel', 'And said:. . .' the beginning of his speech is missing, and some rabbinic Bibles have a gap, but after *habbōkīm*. 'Bochim': the LXX has 'Bethel', preceded by κλαυθμόνα, 'at the place of weeping'; it probably considered it illogical to mention the new name of the place before it had been given, and tried, probably with reason, to locate Bochim, which it understood as part of the sanctuary of Bethel (perhaps Dtr avoided mentioning Bethel whenever it could). [2] *tittōṣūn*: root *ntṣ*. [3] 'Drive them out': LXX has a longer text, cf. *BHS*: ' . . . I will make them drive out the people, whom I have said that I will destroy'. The phrase presupposes a Hebrew archetype, cf. the Greek τίθημι for *ntn*. 'Noose' goes well in parallelism with the following 'trap', but the *ṣad* of the MT never has this meaning and always means 'flank', a term which is impossible here; perhaps it is a *hapax legomenon* from the Accadian *ṣaddu*, 'noose', cf. *BHS*. Another possibility is the Arabic *ṣaddun*, 'adversary', cf. LXX συνοχάς or Vg *hostes*. An old correction is to read *šārīm* (confusion of *reš* with *dalet*), but this introduces a more generic term which does not fit in parallel with what follows.

1. This section presents a text which, as has been known for a long time and as we have seen,[8] presents a view of the Israelite

---

[7]E. Dhorme*, 1956, thinks not; Y. Kaufmann*, 1962, is non-committal.
[8]*Joshua*, 13.

conquest of Palestine which contrasts with the unitary presentation which appears in Joshua 1–12. By contrast, here we are
shown individual tribes or groups of tribes struggling with the
inhabitants of the country for what is to become their territory.
Verses 1–3, however, presuppose the pan-Israelite vision of the
event and obviously try to mediate between the two conceptions;
the fragmentary account is now presented as a chronological
sequel to the unitary account: after the general assignation of
territory, the individual tribes and the individual groups went
out to conquer their land through a war which has all the
characteristics of the 'holy war'. However, it is clear to any
attentive reader not only that these are two parallel versions of
the same event, but also that the versions are clearly incompatible. Since, then, we have to choose between the two, it is clear
that the fragmentary account is the one closest to the events,
though that does not mean we should fall into a false sense of
security and think that we have here a text which is ancient and
homogeneous in all its parts. It is in fact a fragmentary text, the
individual elements of which will each be examined on its merits.
Thus, as we have seen, the first verses presuppose the pan-
Israelite version of events, and 2.1–5, which is a text which has
evidently been revised by Dtr, is clearly meant to provide the
key for reading all the rest of the text (Smend). However, the
indications of the territory which the tribes did *not* succeed in
conquering bring us to a period before the Davidic monarchy,
though the narrator is writing at a time when these territories
have already been incorporated into Israel (vv.18ff., 27ff.).
Again, v.34 refers to the situation which forced Dan to emigrate
northwards, an element which causes considerable problems;
we shall be concerned with the more important details in discussing ch.13.

On the basis of this information, note should be taken of the
article by S. B. Gurewicz, which has gone almost unnoticed in
the past: according to him, the pericope is to be divided into
three strata: the first original and by an author of the time, the
second the work of a writer from Judah in the monarchical
period, and the third to be attributed to a late author, whose
date can also be put in the post-exilic period: he combined his
own work with the two earlier strata and inserted it into the Dtr
history. C.H.J. de Geus makes a different evaluation: this is a
unitary text, composed *ad hoc* and revised by a Dtr hand, a
result which has been arrived at independently by A.G. Auld.

It seems that the features presented by the text allow of both interpretations, the one certain point remaining the Dtr interpretation and revision of the last section, 2.1–5.

2. On a geographical and topographical level the passage can be divided into two sections: that concerning Judah and the groups connected with it, and that relating to the central and northern tribes. **[4–9]** In the first section we are immediately confronted with the difficulty of locating Bezek. It is true that there is a *ḥirbet ibziq* (coord. 187–197) about ten kilometres north of *tirṣāh* (*tell el far'ah*, coord. 182–188), which corresponds to the Bezek of I Sam. 11.8; but the mention of Judah as the protagonist in the action and the fact that the dying ruler is taken to Jerusalem, make it probable that Bezek must be sought not far from the future capital.[9] It is the name alone, in the region of Jerusalem, which connects the place here with the *tell* of *bezqā'*, in the immediate vicinity of Gezer (coord. 142–140); but the identification is far from certain, as is obvious. Those who continue to maintain an identification with *ḥirbet ibziq* sometimes rely on the evidence for Simeon in the region of Shechem (Gen. 34.1ff. and 49.5–7) along with Levi (though Levi does not in fact have anything to do with it);[10] it is then thought to have been driven out of this area. It would thus have been involved in the episode narrated here while on the journey towards the south. However, our passage speaks only of Judah: Simeon only appears in the preamble (v. 3), in a context provided by the redactors; after that it appears again only in vv. 17ff. Others[11] think that Judah entered Palestine in the course of the last wave, perhaps through the centre, conquering Bezek in the course of its journey southwards; and it is of the conquest of this place that the following verses speak. However, it seems evident that Judah and the groups connected with it made their conquest from the south, and did not come from other regions.

[9] The 'Southern desert' is in the Negeb, the steppe land to the south of the southern highlands, reaching a little beyond Beer-sheba; in its northern part it is partially cultivable after

[9]Against Y. Aharoni**, 197: Vincent*, 1958, and Hertzberg*, 1959.
[10]H. W. Hertzberg*, 1958, and J. Gray*, 1967.
[11]Y. Aharoni, op.cit. However, cf. the recent article by M. Kochavi, 'Khirbet Rabud – Ancient Debir', *Tel Aviv* 1, 1974, 2–33, who confirms the thesis put forward by K. Galling, 'Zur Lokalisierung von Dᵉbir', *ZDPV* 70, 1954, 135ff.: *dᵉbīr* is present-day *ḥirbet rabud* (coord. 152–093).

particularly rainy winters or, in modern times, by means of the use of advanced techniques of agriculture.

[10–15] The 'hill country', Hebrew *š²pēlāh*, is the hilly area situated between the sea and the highlands. For Hebron and Debir cf. on Joshua,[12] so too for the three people, who are also mentioned in Josh. 15.14, cf. 14.12.[13]

[16] Many people[14] identify the 'city of palms' with Jericho, on the basis of Deut. 34.3 and II Chron. 28.15, where this identification is certain. This seems also to have the opinion of the redactors. On the other hand, Jericho is too far from this region and there are no direct lines of communication with it. Consequently two other places have been proposed: *ṣō'ār*, on the south shore of the Dead Sea (coord. 194–049), or *tāmār* ('the palm'), about thirty km. as the crow flies further south (coord. 173–024);[15] the first identification already appears in the Mishnah, *Yeb.* 16.7,[16] and is therefore quite ancient. 'The Negeb of Arad' is the region situated around the city of the same name, mentioned in Num. 21.1 and 33.40; Josh. 12.14; Y. Aharoni[17] locates the Canaanite city on *tell el-milḥ*, Hebrew *tell malḥata* (coord. 152–069), and the Israelite city on *tell 'arad* (coord. 162–076), not to be confused with the modern Israeli city, somewhat further to the east (coord. 170–074).

[17–18] 'Zephath/Hormah' is mentioned with its second name in Num. 14.45 and 21.1–3 (where, however, it appears in connection with Arad in different context, which is difficult to harmonize with this one), and in Josh. 12.14 and 15.30, whereas the first designation is not attested elsewhere. This is probably *ḥirbet masas*, Hebrew *tell maśōś* (coord. 146–069).[18] For three of the five Philistine cities (v. 18) see on *Joshua*.[19]

[21] The mention of Benjamin suddenly after Judah and in relation to Jerusalem seems to reflect the union with Judah in the Davidic monarchy and the Dtr history (Gray*, 1967).

[12] *Joshua*, 125.
[13] Ibid., 170f., 175f.
[14] C. F. Burney*, 1919; E. Dhorme*, 1956, and J. Gray*, 1967; A. Penna*, 1963, and Y. Kaufmann*, 1962, are doubtful.
[15] A. Vincent*, 1958; H. W. Hertzberg*, 1959; Y. Aharoni**, 1967, 198.
[16] Cf. A. Neubauer, *La géographie du Talmud*, Paris 1868, 256, and Y. Aharoni**, 1967, op.cit.
[17] Y. Aharoni, op. cit.
[18] *Joshua*, 152.
[19] For other possibilities cf. A. Penna*, ad loc.

[22–26] For Bethel, see my discussion in *Joshua*,[20] with the reservation that I now accept that it is probably to be identified with the place *beitin* (coord. 172–148), proposed already in the last century by Edward Robinson, and in the present century by W.F. Albright and other archaeologists. The way in which Bethel was betrayed seems to have been as follows: the action presupposes the existence of a postern, normally closed, but capable of being opened from the inside (the kind of emergency exit to be found today in public places); a gate of this kind has been discovered in the excavations at *rāmat rāḥēl*,[21] a place a few kilometres south of Jerusalem (coord. 170–127). It has been observed that the present passage speaks only of Joseph and not (yet?) of Benjamin, to whom Josh. 18.22 assigned Bethel; it is possible that the text refers to a period in which Benjamin had not yet joined the alliance, or had not yet become settled, according to Eissfeldt's theory. 'The land of the Hittites' (v. 26) is the generic term for greater Syria in the neo-Assyrian and neo-Babylonian texts, and then in the Dtr history. However, the usage here is vague and imprecise. If this text is not Dtr, it must go back either to the last years of the Hittite empire (beginning of the twelfth century BC) (J. Gray*, 1967) or rather later, when the region was still studded with Hittite colonies (A. Penna*, 1963); however, the generic character of the note seems more to favour the theory of a Dtr redaction.

[27–35] The places in the centre and north mentioned here, cf. Josh. 17.11ff., are: Beth-shean (coord. 197–212); Taanach (coord. 171–214); Dor (coord. 142–224); Ibleam (coord. 177–205); Megiddo (coord. 167–221); Gezer (coord. 142–140); Kitron and Nahalol are unknown,[22] whereas Acco is the Crusaders' St John of Acre, a few kilometres north of Haifa (coord. 158–258); Ahlab/Mahaleb (coord. 172–303); Achzib (coord. 159–272), scene of the Italian-Israeli excavations of the 1960s (the results of which have yet to be published); Aphik is in the north (coord. 162–249)[23]; whereas Rehob is perhaps *tell bīr el ʿarbi*,

---

[20]*Joshua*, 101ff. Cf., however, the important arguments put forward by J. J. Bimson, *Redating the Exodus and Conquest*, *JSOT*, SS 5, 1978, 215ff., which are quite convincing. He wishes to identify Bethel with *el-bīreh* (coord. 146–171). These arguments ought to be studied carefully before we consider the traditional identification to be beyond reasonable doubt.

[21]Cf. Y. Aharoni, 'Exacavations at Ramat Rahel', *BA* 1961, 98–118: 101, and fig. 4; id., *Excavations at Ramat Raḥel*, Rome 1962, 10ff. and plate 2.

[22]*Joshua*, 192.

[23]Ibid., 193.

Hebrew *tell bīrāh* (coord. 166–256). Beth-shemesh is probably *tell er-ruweisī,* Hebrew *tell rō'š* (coord. 181–271), whereas Beth-anath is perhaps *ṣafed el-baṭṭih* (coord. 190–289). *Har-heres/ 'īr šemeš,* Aijalon and Shaalbim are places examined in *Joshua.*[24]

The picture presented here, in some cases with remarkable precision, is therefore as follows: Israel was not able to occupy the coastal plain either in the south (the Philistines) or the centre (Sharon, south of Carmel), or the plain of Jezreel (which divides the centre from the north); there also remained a kind of corridor between Jerusalem and the sea which the tribes had either to cross with the permission of the city state which controlled access to it or to avoid, making a detour by the rough road which goes to the east of the highlands and to the west of the Dead Sea and the Jordan. Anyone who went from Jerusalem to Bethlehem before the Six-Day War of 1967 will have been able to see the character of the region even today. This is a situation which, according to the sources at our disposal, must have lasted down to the time of David.

[36] The note about Edom (provided that we do not have to read MT), does not have any relationship to its present context and is not very clear. The 'Ascent of the Scorpions', cf. Num. 34.4 and Josh. 15.3, is on a branch of the main road to Eilat, now secondary and almost disused (at coord. 172–035), while 'the Rock' (*hassela'*) is to be identified almost certainly with ancient and modern Petra, II Kings 14.7; II Chron. 25.11f.; Isa. 16.1ff. (coord. 205–020),[25] a place in typically Edomite territory.

[2.1–5] The problem of locating Gilgal has been discussed in *Joshua.*[26] Bochim is mentioned only here in the Old Testament and this passage is its aetiological legend. We do not know where it was; it is possible that we should follow the LXX in locating it in the context of the sanctuary of Bethel. In any case, it must have been a sanctuary with a penitential liturgy, if we accept the substantial historicity of the note – that is, provided that it was not originally a Canaanite sanctuary at which there were celebrations of rites of lament and the struggle over the death of Baal and other fertility gods, as these are attested in

[24]Ibid., 194.

[25]Provided always that this is not a reference to the rock which was the scene of Moses' miracle, Num. 20.8–11, cf. E. Dhorme*, 1956, ad loc., in which case – though it is improbable – the locality remains unknown.

[26]*Joshua,* 9ff.

the Ugaritic texts and in the Old Testament itself (cf. Ezek. 8.14; Zech. 12.11), where there were laments over Tammuz and Baal-Hadad. The character of such rites has been 'historicized', here by associating them with a particular episode in the history of Israel; however, to be on the safe side the narrator prefers to keep quiet about the identity of the sanctuary!

3. Since this whole section is obviously an interpolation between the end of Joshua and 2.6ff., it has been supposed that the interpolation happened after the Dtr redaction of Judges or at least in a final stage of it. It is certain that 2.1–5 is clearly Dtr in phraseology and in its mode of thought:[27] these verses imply that the requirements of Josiah's reform were not carried out and that punishment followed: the exile. So here we find evidence of the last phase of the Dtr redaction, that of so-called DtrN (Smend). This will certainly have worked with earlier material, which it now wants to be understood in accordance with 2.1–5. On the other hand, the redactional preface in 1.1–3 does not seem to be Dtr, though it is familiar with the pan-Israelite account of the conquest, an element which is characteristic of Dtr. Thus the present section will have been inserted in this way into the Dtr history, at a later stage and in an uncertain form. The rest of the passage, especially vv. 22ff., could be attributed to the 'collector' conjectured by M. Noth, the characteristic marks of whom seem fairly similar to those of J.[28] We shall now examine individual details.

[4–9] Judah. The text refers to 'the Canaanites and the Perizzites'; the latter term is one of the conventional names for one element in the pre-Israelite population of Palestine, though we have no criteria for checking the historicity of the detail, much less for identifying it. Most explanations attempted are listed in the study by K.-D. Schunck. No clear historical explanation can be given of the episode of the 'Lord of Bezek'[29] either, and in addition there is no mention of the name of the sovereign or of the exact location of the city. Against the historicity of the statement about the conquest of Jerusalem it has been argued again and again that this was the work of David (cf. also v. 21), so that this would not be a trustworthy reference. Of course it could be noted that the passage does not speak of the occupation of Jerusalem, but only of a successful raid; also, v. 9 seems

[27]Details in J. Gray*, 1967.
[28]*Joshua*, 11.
[29]For a discussion of the name cf. A. Penna*, 1963.

simply to presuppose that once victory had been obtained, Judah had to abandon its future capital.[30] For this reason, the detail need not necessarily be rejected, provided that we do not attribute to it a content which it does not have. It is not possible to say more, even in the most optimistic of circumstances.

[10–15] Judah and Caleb. 'Judah' here seems to be an addition by the redactors. The episode has already been examined in my commentary on Joshua.[31]

[16 (–17?)] Judah and the Kenites. The Kenites are probably the descendants of the Cain whom J places in Gen. 4.1ff. This text, which is often obscure, explains how the Kenites ever came to live in the territory of Judah. Here we have a population whose position *vis à vis* Israel is always presented in a favourable light by the biblical traditions; at worst, it is ambiguous, cf. Num. 10.29–32; 24.20–22; I Sam. 15.6; 27.10; 30.29. Sometimes they appear in a rather obscure combination with the Amalekites, who however are always enemies of Israel, indeed the enemies *par excellence* (Ex. 17.16; I Sam. 15.1ff.). The Kenites also appear in the central plain in 4.17–22 and 5.22ff. (cf. pp. 77f.), a phenomenon which might be explained from their semi-nomadic character; otherwise they seem to have been transferred from the region of Sinai first to the area south of the Dead Sea, and then more to the north-west, in the neighbourhood of the places mentioned.

[17–20] Judah and Simeon. The narrative confirms that to the south, as in the central and northern areas, it was only possible for the invaders to occupy the mountainous regions and the steppe land; not the fertile plains. It is difficult to say whether the text is thinking of a situation before or at least at the time of the arrival of the Philistines in the region; the fact is that they are not mentioned.[32] For the 'chariots of iron' see the studies by Guzzo-Amadasi and by Paul and Dever cited above (p. 24).

[22–26] Joseph. Archaeological excavations have revealed that the last phase of bronze age civilization was destroyed towards the end of the thirteenth century BC; the occupation which followed proves to have been technically much less advanced. It is possible to find here confirmation of the information given in this text, though it is elaborated with legendary ma-

---

[30]Thus H.-W. Hertzberg, art.cit., and *1959.
[31]Cf. *Joshua*, 175f.
[32]A. Penna*, 1963, is in favour of this theory.

terial; and this is the theory put forward by Albright and his disciples. However, even they have realized that it is a matter more of probability than of certainty. European attitudes have been less optimistic: destructions, changes in the standard of living and analogous elements can very well be reflected alongside various factors other than the settlement of a new population: earthquakes, plagues, civil wars, economic crises and other factors must also be taken into account. Furthermore, even if we allow the settlement of new populations, it is by no means certain that these were Israelites.[33] The legendary character of the account and its many imprecisions and generalizations all suggest that we should be very cautious.

[27–35] The tribes of the central and northern areas. The situation envisaged is clearly earlier than the time of David and Solomon: the latter received Gezer (v. 29) as a dowry from the daughter of the Pharaoh (I Kings 9.12–17), whereas the places indicated in vv. 27, 30–33 appear in the list of Solomon's provinces (I Kings 4.7ff.). At the end of the reign of Saul, Beth-shean was still not Israelite, if the Philistines were able to expose the corpses of Saul and those of his sons who had fallen in battle on the walls (I Sam. 31.10–12).[34]

---

[33]For this problem see the fundamental study by M. Weippert, *Die Landnahme der israelitischen Stämme*, FRLANT 92, 1967, passim; ET, *The Settlement of the Israelite Tribes in Palestine*, SBT II.21, 1971.

[34]For this problem see the study by A. Alt, 'Die Staatenbildung der Israeliten in Palästina' (1930), *KlSchr* II, Munich 1953, 1–65; ET, 'The Settlement of the Israelites in Palestine', *Essays on Old Testament History and Religion*, Oxford and New York 1966, 133–69.

PART TWO

THE 'MAIN BODY' OF THE BOOK
2.6–16.31

CHAPTER 2.6–3.6

The Deuteronomistic Introduction

Bibliography: W. **Richter****, 1964, 44ff. (on 2.6–10), 26–40 (on 2.11–3.6), 87ff. (on 2.11–19); A. **Vaccari**, 'Parole rovesciate e critiche errate nella Bibbia ebraica', in *Studi orientalistici . . . G. Levi Della Vida*, Rome 1956, II, 553–66:.554 (on 2.9); H. **Haag**, 'Zwischen Jahwe und Baal', *BuL* 4, 1963, 240–51 (on 3.1–6); R. **Smend**, 'Das Gesetz und die Völker: Richter 2,17.20f.23', in *Probleme biblischer Theologie, G. von Rad zum 70. Geburtstag*, Munich 1971, 504–56; H. **Cancik,** *Grundzüge der hethitischen und alttestamentlichen Geschichtsschreibung*, Wiesbaden 1976, 39–41 (on 2.11–23).

---

2 ⁶After that, Joshua dismissed the people, and the Israelites went each to the territory assigned to them, to take possession of the region. ⁷The people offered worship to Yahweh all the days of Joshua and all the days of the elders who survived him, elders who had seen all the great work which Yahweh had done for Israel. ⁸Joshua, son of Nun, the servant of Yahweh, died at the age of one hundred and ten years, ⁹and they buried him in the territory assigned to him, at Timnath-heres, in the 'Mountain of Ephraim', on the north side of mount Gaash. ¹⁰And all that generation also were gathered to their fathers; and there arose another generation after them which had not known Yahweh or the work that he had done for Israel.

11 And the Israelites did what was evil in the eyes of Yahweh: they worshipped the Baals; ¹²they forsook Yahweh, the God of their fathers, who had led them out of Egypt; they went after strange gods who belonged to the people round about. They bowed down before them and provoked Yahweh. [¹³They forsook Yahweh, to worship Baal and Astarte.] ¹⁴Then the anger of Yahweh was kindled against Israel, and he gave them over into the hands of the enemies who surrounded them, so that they could no longer withstand their enemies. ¹⁵Whatever enterprise they undertook, the hand of Yahweh was against them, as Yahweh had affirmed and sworn to them. Thus he afflicted them greatly. ¹⁶But they cried to Yahweh and he raised up 'judges' who delivered them from the hand of those who plundered them. ¹⁷But no

one wanted to listen to the judges: they prostituted themselves to strange gods and bowed down to them; they soon turned away from the way in which their fathers had walked, to obey the commandments of Yahweh; they did not do the same.

18 Whenever Yahweh raised up judges for them, he was with the judge in question, who saved them from the hand of their enemy all the days he was judge; for Yahweh was moved to pity by their groaning because of those who afflicted and oppressed them. [19]But whenever the judge died, they turned back and behaved worse than their fathers: they followed strange gods, worshipped them and bowed down to them! They did not drop any of their practices or their stubborn attitude.

20 So the anger of Yahweh was kindled against Israel and he said: 'Since this people have transgressed every covenant which I have made, the covenant that I commanded their fathers, and have not obeyed my ordinances, [21]I will not henceforth drive out before them any of the nations that Joshua left when he died, [22]so as to test Israel by them. In this way I shall see whether or not they take care to walk in the way of Yahweh, as their fathers did! [23]And for this reason Yahweh has allowed the people in question to go on existing and has not taken care to drive them out or to give them into the hand of Joshua!'

3 [1]Now these are the nations which Yahweh left, to test Israel by them, that is, all in Israel who had no experience of any war in Canaan; [2]it was only in the interest of the coming generations of Israel, so that they might learn the art of war, at least those who had not learnt it before:

3 The five 'tyrants' of the Philistines, all the Canaanites, and the Sidonians, the Hivites who dwelt in the territory between Mount Baal-hermon and the 'Gateway of Hamath'. [4]They were to put Israel to the test, to know whether or not Israel would obey the commandments of Yahweh, which he gave to their fathers by the hand of Moses. [5]So the people of Israel dwelt among the Canaanites, the Hittites, the Amorites, the Perizzites, the Hivites and the Jebusites; [6]they took their daughters for wives, and their own daughters they gave to the sons of these people, and they served their gods.

2.6–9 is parallel to Josh. 24.18–31; there are a few more details in Judges, cf. v.10; however, these small additions do not essentially change the meaning. The order of the phrases also differs slightly, but this does not affect the content. The order in Joshua seems more obvious; it places the remark about the elders after the death of the leader. The discourse, once begun, is really continued only in Judg. 2.10, whereas the sequence of Judg. 2.6ff. is out of context. We shall consider the problems connected with authenticity in the commentary below. **[9]** 'Territory' is a possible meaning which the Hebrew *gᵉbūl* can have in addition to its more common meaning of 'boundary', 'frontier': i.e., the territory situated between certain boundaries. 'Timnath-heres' is identical with Timnath-serah (Josh. 19.50; 24.30), though there LXX has the same reading as in Judges; cf. there for details. *ḥeres* and *seraḥ* are the same word, the first time read forwards and the second time read backwards; however, it is less difficult to establish the probable reading than it seems: in favour of *ḥeres* is the fact that we also have the same reading in 1.35 (cf. there), i.e. Horus; in that case the metathesis in this text could have taken place deliberately, with the aim of removing a reference to a pagan divinity, which was thought to be inconvenient.[1] Despite what I said in my commentary on Joshua, it now seems more logical to accept the reading *ḥeres*, thus correcting my former proposal. **[11]** 'Worshipped . . .': the root *ʿābad*, 'labour', 'serve', and its derivatives has this meaning in contexts like the present one; cf. also vv. 13, 19, etc. The formula is characteristic of Dtr and the Dtr history.[2] 'The Baals': for the plural, see the commentary, p. 43. **[13]** In the language of Dtn and the Dtr history, 'Baal and Astarte' are the embodiment *par excellence* of the idolatrous Canaanite cult; Astarte is vocalized as *ʿaštārōt*, plural of *ʿaštōret*, reproducing the vowels of *bōšet*, 'shame', 'abomination'; the provision of this vocalization is meant to show that these are the terms that the reader must pronounce instead of the names of the pagan deities. In Dtn and the Dtr history the two names are more symbolic of idolatry in general than a reference to a specific deity. **[15]** 'Afflicted them': I read *wayyāṣar* with LXX: ἐξέθλιψεν, with Yahweh as subject; MT has the paler 'and their affliction was very great'; note the strange vocalization *wayyēṣer*; has the article been incorporated in the conjunction? **[16]** 'But they cried . . .'; I have followed a number of commentators in inserting the phrase; as well as being required by the logic of the text (Yahweh can reply only to a particular request, to a lament) it appears in 3.9,15; 6.6; 10.10 and gives the idea that penitence follows punishment and precedes salvation. **[17]** 'Prostituted themselves': the verb used is a generic term for prostitution (*zānāh*) and not that used for sacral prostitution (*qiddeš*, the verb-form of which is not found either in Ugaritic or in Hebrew). In the context of a relationship between God and the people understood as a marriage bond (cf. the prophet Hosea and Dtn, Dtr), it indicates marital infidelity, adultery, a crime which carried the death penalty. **[18]** 'Those who afflicted and oppressed them': the second

[1]C. F. Burney*, 1919; H. W. Hertzberg*, 1959; E. Dhorme*, 1956; Y. Kaufmann*, 1962; and A. Penna*, 1963. Y. Aharoni**, 1967, 267, is indecisive: he indicates the two readings but does not come down in favour of either of them; Vaccari favours *seraḥ*, cf. also my *Joshua*, 195.
[2]For this formula and the others which are indicated here see the basic study by M. Weinfeld, *Deuteronomy and the Deuteronomistic School*, Oxford 1972, Appendix A, § 1.

term is perhaps a gloss (Vincent*, 1958); in that case, however, it is
hard to see how a rare root has been used to explain another which
is also infrequent; in any case, it does not seem to be an Aramaism,
as Vincent would like to think.[3] **[19]** 'They did not drop . . .': literally, 'They did not let fall any . . .' **[21]** 'When he died . . .': LXX
has ἀφῆκεν, 'when he went away'. **[3.1]** 'Yahweh': LXX[A] and other
versions have 'Joshua', thus linking it with 2.21. This reading is to be
rejected: it is Yahweh, not Joshua, who puts to the test. **[2]** 'In the
interest': MT again inserts 'of the knowledge', da'at; however, yāda'
and its derivatives are transitive, whereas there is no object here; again
the term does not fit well with the following l'lammᵉdām; finally, it is
absent from the ancient translations. I would therefore delete it, despite
the defence made by some scholars.[4] 'Coming' does not appear in the
original, but it is absolutely necessary in any Western translation.
'Had not learnt it . . .': the pronominal suffix refers to the 'wars of
Canaan', v.1; it therefore does not seem necessary to postulate the
presence of a *mem* enclitic, as *BHS* proposes, albeit with reservations.
[3] 'Tyrants': Hebrew sᵉrānīm, construct sarnē (only in the plural and
used solely for the Philistines), has often been associated with the
Greek τύραννος (hence my suggestion between inverted commas) and
can appeal to the Targum, which has ṭūrᵉnē. The question is much
more complex: the term certainly comes from Asia Minor, where the
root ser-* ('above', then a noun and used hierarchically) is amply
attested. It is therefore probable that both the Hebrew and the Greek
terms derive from the same word, originating in Asia Minor.[5] 'Hivites':
this is read by MT, cf. Josh. 13.3, though that reads 'awwīm, and puts
them in the south, in the region of Philistine territory.[6] Here it is often
corrected to 'Hittites', because of Josh. 11.3 and II Sam. 24.6; however,
the first text is inadequate and the second corrupt, whereas II Sam.
24.7 mentions the Hivites in a context similar to this one. If we
remember that LXX tends to confuse the Hittites, the Hurrians and
the Hivites, it is best to leave the text as it is.

1. This text has abundant terms and expressions typical of
the Dtr history. As we have seen, the opening does not refer
back to Judg. 1.1–2.5, but to the end of the book of Joshua. The
sequence of the text in Josh. 24.28–30: dismissal of the people,
death of Joshua and his burial, the religious situation of the

---

[3]It is not listed in the work by M. Wagner, *Die lexikalischen und grammatikalischen
Aramäismen im alttestamentlichen Hebräisch*, BZAW 96, 1966.

[4]E. Dhorme*, 1956; H. W. Hertzberg*, 1959; Y. Kaufmann*, 1962; A. Penna* and
J. Gray*, 1967.

[5]Cf. M. Ellenbogen, *Foreign Words in the Old Testament, Their Origin and Etymology*,
London 1962, 126f., and G. Garbini, 'Ebraico-filisteo sᵉrānīm – "Principi filistei" ',
Ricerche Linguistiche 5, Naples 1962, 178ff.

[6]Cf. *Joshua*, 152.

people during his life and that of the elders who succeeded him, is preferable to that of the parallel text Judg. 2.6–10, which continues the discourse (v.10) indicating that this happened on the death of the elders in question. Furthermore, as Richter has rightly pointed out, the theme of the dismissal should end a book, not begin it; it therefore seems to be in the right place at the end of Joshua, at the conclusion of the assembly of Shechem, and not in Judg. 2.6ff. Again, this last text at least presents an addition, at v.6b: 'The Israelites went each to the territory assigned to them, to take possession of the region. . .', a phrase which presupposes the insertion of 1.1–2.5 and which is therefore subsequent to it; however, this does not seem to be compatible with Josh. 24.18, where the enemies have been driven out. Finally, as we have seen, vv.6,8f. are partly duplicated by Josh. 24.28–30 and are of inferior quality to that passage, because they do not easily fit in with the original Dtr text.[7] It is therefore by no means rash to claim that the repetitions in question necessarily arose after the interpolation of 1.1–2.6, to which they are now subsequent additions.

It is also evident that vv.11–17, 18f., and 20–23 have an almost identical content, though there are a number of variant details: in v.11, worship is offered to Baal and Yahweh is forsaken, cf. v.13, which speaks of Baal and Astarte (probably a repetition of v.11); vv.18f., on the other hand mention 'strange gods'; however, the two themes are absent in vv.20ff.

Of course this argument would collapse if we were to follow M. Noth,[8] E. O'Doherty and others in their theory that 2.6ff. is connected with Josh. 23 rather than Josh. 24, but this theory does not seem easily defensible; as we shall see, Josh. 23 has its proper sequel, if anywhere, in 2.20ff.

Verses 7 and 10 logically follow after Josh 24.28–30 and form the beginning of the Dtr text 2.6–3.6; they require a sequel, which is in fact to be found in vv. 11ff., thus forming the Dtr beginning to the whole of the 'main body' of the book.

Furthermore, as I have noted, this passage is not a unity. The sin of Israel is described in a variety of ways (vv.11,17 and 20); so, too, is the divine punishment (vv.14–22;3.la; 4.1b-2); the functions of the judges also seem different in vv.16 and 17. The topography and geography of the enemies of Israel also seem to

---

[7]Thus from C. F. Burney*, 1919, to A. Vincent*, 1958; for the problem see A. Penna*, 1963, ad loc.

[8]Noth**, 1943, 8 n. 3, 9 n.l.

differ from verse to verse (cf. vv.12, 14 and 21). Furthermore,
v. 13, which does not give any information which is not already
contained in v.11 ('Astarte' is the only addition), and v.17,
which repeats elements contained in vv. 12 and 19 in different
terms (a situation which we probably also find in vv. 17aβ and
19aα, Richter**, 1964), are also later additions. We often find
repetitions of technical terms and typical formulae; in other
instances we have identical concepts expressed in different
forms, producing duplications of style or content. So if the content of vv.11–23 is almost identical, the reader cannot help
noticing remarkable differences of detail. The most obvious is
the description of the people who torment Israel: at one point
these are the 'people round about', v. 12, cf. v. 14 (the expression
is virtually the same as that in Josh. 21.44); elsewhere we have
the Canaanite population which Yahweh did not want to 'drive
out' (v.20); and this presence of the Canaanites has on one
occasion the purpose of passing judgment on the unfaithful
people (v.21a), while on another they are there to 'put Israel to
the test' (vv.22; 3.1), thus serving pedagogical ends; we meet a
third argument in 3.1b-2, where their presence serves to initiate
into the art of war the generation which did not know the
ancient battles. This forms a second pedagogical argument. It
would therefore seem obvious that a number of hands have been
at work in the redaction of this passage, though there is some
degree of agreement among scholars that a new pericope, more
or less parallel to the preceding one, begins with v.20. However,
Richter (**1964) has made it seem probable that vv.20–23 are
simply a series of additions to vv.11–19, given that there is no
original thread which might make one conjecture a parallel
source. Thus we would have to keep in mind the following
phases of redaction: first of all vv.11f., 14–16 and 18f., forming
the central and earliest element; 20–23 would then be supple-
ments to vv.11–19. Verses 6, 8f., 13, 17 and perhaps 15aβ and
18aα (which presuppose the insertion of 1.1–2.5), are late
additions, characteristic because they do not introduce new
elements.

    2. The complex redactional structure of this passage prompts
a search for a unifying criterion, a criterion which in fact can be
the one which inspired the whole of the Dtr work on Judges. It
was described brilliantly by L. Perlitt several years ago:[9] 'The

[9]*Bundestheologie im Alten Testament*, WMANT 36, 1969, 7.

authors of the Dtr history were moved not by a passion for
history writing, but by the necessity of explaining the fall of the
two kingdoms in theological terms.' They therefore provided the
people in exile with a series of ancient texts and authentic pieces
of information with appropriate comments and links, so that
Israel would understand that the exile was the tangible sign of
divine judgment on its sin. Thus the exile is set in the logical
context of the abandonment of the people to the hands of its
enemies and those who exploited it (v. 14, cf. v.16). This is an
explanation which differs considerably from that which sees the
persistence of the Canaanites in the country as a matter of
pedagogy. The explanation of the national catastrophe in terms
of judgment and punishment is carried back in detail to the
time of the judges; even then the people were to blame in the
same way and had been punished; what happened in 587–86
was more definitive: the people's cry of anguish was no longer
capable of warding off, or at least mitigating, the catastrophe.
Here, then, we find ourselves confronted with the extreme,
though logical, consequences of a process which began about
half a millennium earlier and which was realized in the destruction of the state and the deportation of its leading inhabitants. It is interesting to note, as does Cancik, that about a
thousand years earlier the Hittites, too, had developed theories
about history which in many ways were similar to this.

3. (*a*) For the historical, ethnic and geographical elements in
vv.6–10 see on Josh. 24.28–31.[10]

(*b*) The 'Baals' (v.11) is a plural which seems to be typical
of Dtn and the Dtr history. It does not indicate a numerical
plurality of deities bearing this title or name (*ba'al* is originally
'lord', 'husband', a meaning which it continues to have in Hebrew in non-religious texts) so much as the various local mani-
festations of the same deity.[11]

(*c*) The pattern: Israel's sin (idolatry) – divine judgment by
means of the nations – Israel's penitence and cry of distress to
Yahweh – calling of the judge-saviour by Yahweh – appears
throughout the book and already seems to be clearly outlined

[10] *Joshua*, 245.

[11] For the problem, which I cannot go into at any depth here, see the classical study
by O. Eissfeldt, 'Ba'alšamēm und Jahwe', *ZAW* 57, 1939, 1–31 = *KlSchr* II, Tübingen
1963, 171–98; A. S. Kapelrud, *Baal in the Ras Shamra Texts*, Copenhagen 1952; R. de
Vaux, 'El et Baal, le Dieu des pères et Yahweh', in *Ugaritica* VI, *Hommage à C. F. A.
Schaeffer*, Paris 1969, 501–17: 515ff. (with bibliography) and J. Gray*, 1967.

here. One characteristic of the book of Judges is the fact that from 3.7ff. onwards it precedes every narrative episode, the substance of which is usually much earlier. As Richter** (1964, 87ff.) rightly observes, this is a 'historical and theological dissertation', for the purpose of teaching present generations – and perhaps future ones too. It refers to past and present experiences of this kind, and tries to communicate their deeper significance for the present and for the future. Even for these writers it is clear that this significance is not obvious, nor is it the only one possible.

(d) The list of the peoples who lived in Palestine before the 'conquest' (3.5) appears all over the Pentateuch and in Dtr. In Dtn and Dtr it is normally composed of six members, almost always the same (the exceptions are Deut.1.7; Josh.3.10 and 24.11, where it is enlarged); this is a sign that we have here an element which has been fixed from the point of view of tradition, probably handed down by Israel in a very early period. Gen. 10.16 (not Dtr?) and 15.19–21 have more than six members; the latter passage has marked Dtr features. The Canaanites, the Hittites and the Amorites are stereotypes, none of which seems to correspond to any real elements; we know virtually nothing of any of the other peoples.[12]

---

[12]For details see A. Penna*, 1963, 60f., and W. Richter**, 1964, 41f.

The Judge Othniel

Bibliography: E. **Täubler**, "Cushan-Rishataim', *HUCA* 20, 1947, 136–42; R.T.**O'Callaghan**, *Aram Naharaim*, AnOr 26, 1954, 122f.; A. **Malamat**, 'Cushan Rishataim', *JNES* 13, 1954, 321–42; G. **Wallis** et al., 'Die Geschichte der Jakobtradition', in *WZ(H)* 13, 1964, 427–40 (= *Geschichte und Überlieferung*, Berlin and Stuttgart 1968, 13–44), esp. 436–8ff.

3[7] But the people of Israel did what Yahweh thought to be evil: they forgot Yahweh their God and worshipped the Baals and all the Asherim. [8]Then the anger of Yahweh was kindled against Israel and he gave them into the hands of Cushan-rishathaim, king of Aram Naharaim; the Israelites were subject to him for eight years. [9]But they cried out to Yahweh, who raised up a saviour to deliver them: Othniel, son of Kenaz, younger brother of Caleb.

10 The spirit of Yahweh descended on him; he was a judge over Israel and went out to war. Yahweh gave Cushan-rishathaim, king of Aram, into his hands, and he prevailed against him. [11]The land had peace for forty years; afterwards Othniel, son of Kenaz, died.

Verses 7–8a constitute the Dtr 'framework'; in vv. 8b–9 we find a remnant, albeit very brief, of what seems to have been the original narrative. In both passages the text is particularly sound. [7] 'What Yahweh thought to be evil. . . ': literally, here and in the following texts, 'what was evil in the eyes of Yahweh'. 'The *ba'als*' : for the plural see what is said above on 2.6–3.6, § 3b, p. 43. The 'Asherim' were the female counterpart of the *ba'als*, usually vocalized in the plural as though they were masculine, *'ašerīm*; the term *'aštārōt*, 'Astartes', is more common in connection with Baal, cf. above on 2.13, p. 39. As we have seen, it is doubtful whether Dtr had in mind the two deities in question: rather, the terms are indicative of polytheistic paganism in general. [8] 'Gave them': the root *nākar* expresses the passage of property by the free decision of the owner or the legitimate possessor; it is therefore often used for sales or transfers. ' $\,^{>a}$rām nah^{a}r-aim' has traditionally been translated 'Aram of the two rivers', i.e. Mesopotamia; in reality the expression indicates the 'region between the rivers', Egyptian *naharina*, Accadian *(birit) nārim*, a description of the area which lies in the large loop formed by the northern Euphrates;[1] thus the ending of the second word cannot be a dual, which is what the Massoretic vocalization calls for. ' $\,^{>a}$rām': until recently[2] this was usually corrected to $\,^{>e}$dōm (a confusion of *dalet* with *reš*), as has happened in I Kings 11.15: II Kings 16.6; Ezek. 16.57; 27.16; II Chron. 20.2. According to this emendation the 'judge' situated on the southern plateau would have an Edomite adversary, i.e. towards the front, in the East. In that case nah^{a}raim would have to be deleted, cf. also its omission in v. 10. There are also some logical and historical-topographical arguments in favour of this correction: the present form of the name is obviously a parody, a caricature ('the doubly wicked Ethiopian'), whereas *kūšān* by itself would fit in southern Transjordan, where there is evidence of names in – ān (– ōn) (cf. Gen. 36.20–30), whereas in Hab. 3.7 (a notoriously archaic or archaizing text), *kūšān* appears parallel to 'the country of Midian'. Furthermore, the warning issued by Penna, independently accepted by Malamat and implicitly by Wallis, is fully valid here: the correction evidently introduced a *lectio facilior*. It is much more logical to recognize the absence of any further information, cf. also the commentary. **[10]** The 'spirit of Yahweh' often appears as an efficient cause in the calling of a charismatic minister, the terms in which the calling of the 'judges' is presented: 6.34; 11.29; 13.35; 14.6,19; cf. also I Sam. 11.6; 16.13. 'Was judge' or 'exercised his judgeship'. For this meaning of the root *šāpaṭ*, cf. the Introduction above, pp. 1ff.

The episode of Othniel, reduced to the very minimum, begins the Dtr work of revising the earlier traditions. Like the others, the narrative is clearly limited from a territorial point of view: it is set in the area of Debir and its outskirts, not far from Hebron.[3] However, the difficulties connected with the identification of the antagonist, caused by the vagueness of the narrative, make the episode blurred and generalized, and doubt arises as to whether the person of the younger brother of Caleb has not been artificially introduced into a narrative which is itself an artificial construction. A. Malamat's attempt to identify Cushan with an Asiatic usurper in Egypt called Irsu or Arsu

---

[1]Cf. recently R. de Vaux**, 1973, 188ff.; ET, 1978, 186ff.

[2]Cf. also A. Penna*, 1963, though he warns that the new reading 'can be obtained with some ease, but not with any degree of certainty'.

[3]For its location see my *Joshua*, 125f.

(in which case Aram Naharaim would stand for Amurru) does not fare much better. This solution, too, is highly speculative. And this is not the only problem in the present passage; it has no narrative or descriptive element, no form of action. It is therefore not surprising that the episode has been considered a Dtr construction (W. Richter**, 1964), intended to give Judah also a judge of its own (G. Wallis), choosing only the single element of Judah mentioned by name in 1.1–2.6. And in that case we would clearly presuppose the insertion of this passage in the redaction of Judges, the last, latest phase of Dtr. On the other hand, artificial narratives are often distinguished by their exactitude, their historical verisimilitude and the abundance of narrative elements, i.e. precisely the opposite of what we find here. In any case, one firm point is the fact that it is not possible to find any kind of basis in history that we can recognize or that can appear probable.

*

The Judge Ehud

Bibliography: E. G. **Kraeling**, 'Difficulties in the Story of Ehud', *JBL* 54, 1935, 205–10; E. **Täubler****, 1958, 21–42; A. **van Zyl**, *The Moabites*, Leiden 1960, 14; W. **Richter****, 1963, 1–29; G. **Wallis**, art. cit. (cf. the preceding section), 436–9; J. A. **Soggin**, 'Ehûd ed i guadi di Moab, Giud. 3, 28b', *BeO* 15, 1973, 252; ET in *OTOS*, 237; H. **Rösel****, 1975, 184–90; C. **Grottanelli**, 'Un passo del libro dei Giudici alla luce della comparazione storico-religiosa: il giudice Ehud ed il valore della mano sinistra', in *Atti del I convegno italiano di studi del Vicino Oriente antico*, Rome 1978, 35–45; F. **Dexinger**, 'Ein Plädoyer für die Linkshändler im Richterbuch', *ZAW* 89, 1977, 268f.; H. N. **Rösel**, 'Zur Ehud Erzählung', ibid., 270–2.

---

3 [12]But the Israelites returned to doing what Yahweh thought to be evil, and Yahweh gave power to Eglon, king of Moab, over Israel, because it had done what Yahweh thought to be evil. [13]The Ammonites and the Amalekites joined Eglon, so he turned against the Israelites, smote them and occupied the 'city of palms'. [14]And the Israelites remained subject to Eglon for eighteen years. [15]Then they cried out to Yahweh, who raised up for them a saviour in the person of Ehud, son of Gera, a Benjaminite, a man crippled in his right hand. By this man the Israelites sent tribute to Eglon.

16 And Ehud obtained for himself a sword with two edges, about a *gomed* in length, and he girded it on his right thigh, under his clothes. [17]He presented the tribute to Eglon, king of Moab, who was a very fat man; [18]and when he had finished presenting the tribute, he went for a little way with the people who had brought the tribute. [19]However, when he had reached the 'sculpted stones' which are near Gilgal, he turned back and said, 'O king, I have a secret message from God for you.' Then the king said, 'Silence', and dismissed from his presence all the members of his following. [20]Then Ehud came to him, above, in a high room, cool, where he was sitting by himself, and said to him, 'O king, I have an oracle from God for you.' Then Eglon arose from his throne. [21]and at that moment Ehud took the sword from his right

thigh with his left hand and thrust it into his belly. [22]And the hilt went in after the blade and the fat closed over it, so that he could not withdraw the sword from the belly! Then Ehud went out by one of the [courtyards] (?); [23]Ehud went out by one of the [porches] (?), having closed behind him the doors of the upper room and locked them. [24]He succeeded in getting out, whereas the king's courtiers, having seen that the doors of the upper room were locked, remarked: 'He is probably doing business in the cool room.' [25]They waited until they were at a loss, but he did not open the doors of the upper room! Then they took the key, and behold, they found their lord lying on the ground, dead. [26]While they stood there losing time, Ehud succeeded in escaping: he passed the 'sculpted stones' and escaped in the direction of Seir. [27]As soon as he arrived, he sounded the horn on 'Mount Ephraim' until the Israelites came down with him from the 'mountain', with him at their head. [28]Then Ehud exhorted them: 'Go down after me! Yahweh has given your enemies, Moab, into your hands!' And they went down after him and succeeded in seizing the fords over the Jordan against the Moabites, and did not allow anyone to pass over. [29]At that time they succeeded in putting out of action about ten thousand of the Moabites, all able-bodied and strong; not a man escaped. [30]So Moab was humiliated under the hand of Israel, and the land had peace for eighty years.

---

[12] 'Gave power': root $ḥāzaq$, piel. 'Eglon': a name which has every appearance of being a caricature: 'calf' in the diminutive, 'little calf',[1] probably without any cultic connotations. [13] 'He occupied': I read the singular, with LXX and Vg, cf. the other verbs in the sentence and the fact that only one protagonist is mentioned in the story. Here, as opposed to 1.16 (cf. p. 28), the 'city of palms' is Jericho, on the basis of Deut. 34.3 and I Chron. 28.15, though this identification has kept raising substantial doubts. The statement that it was occupied by the enemy of Israel is given on the basis of the defeat of Moab in vv. 29f. by Israel in the course of a holy war, a defeat which could only happen if the warriors who came down from the 'Mountain of Ephraim' were met by an enemy who had crossed the Jordan. This note thus seems to be historically improbable, which puts the first item of topographical information given here in a bad light. [15] 'Ehud' is a composite word formed from the term $hōd$, 'majesty', used essentially of God, especially in relation to his works in nature.[2] Thus the *dramatis personae* are depicted: the fat man with the ridiculous name, the maimed hero, who is no less capable as a result, and who

[1]Taubler**, 1958, 35f.
[2]Cf. M. Noth, *Die israelitischen Personennamen im Rahmen der gemeinsemitischen Namengebung*, BWANT III.10, 1928, reprinted, 146, and Täubler**, 1958, 35.

bears a theophoric name. 'Gera' is a Benjaminite clan, cf. Gen. 46.21 ('P'), where he is the son of Benjamin, and I Chron. 8.3, where however he is his nephew. 'With an impediment': *'iṭṭēr* is a word of the *qaṭṭīl* type, of a kind mostly used to indicate arts and crafts (excluded here) or physical qualities or defects.[3] Some people prefer to understand the term as an equivalent to 'left-handed' (thus recently still Dexinger), while others interpret it as 'ambidextrous' (Rösel**, 1975, 77), which is already the interpretation given in the LXX: ἀμφοτεροδέξιον, and Vg. In fact there are traditions which attribute one quality or another to particular combatants in the Old Testament, especially the Benjaminites, cf. 20.16 below (pp. 291f.) and I Chron. 12.2. In our case, however, everything is in favour of a real physical defect, of a kind that would seriously diminish the capability of a fighting man and make him seem to be harmless. In fact this is the only way in which we can explain how he could ever have been admitted into the presence of the king without any search or any precautionary measures. Another element of the story, which is also implicit, is of course that no one could suspect his skill with his other hand, the left one. Thus if we adopt the translation 'left-handed', we must suppose that Ehud was left-handed of necessity. Note finally the untranslatable play on words between '*(ben-)jaminite*', literally, 'son of the right hand', and 'with an impediment in his right hand'. 'Tribute': Hebrew *minḥāh*, can also be a '(voluntary) gift', and in a cultic context, a 'sacrifice', 'offering'. Following Burney*, 1919, I understand it to mean tribute, on the basis of II Sam. 8.2, 6; I Kings 4.21; II Kings 17.3, etc.: perhaps it is a euphemism (Penna*, 1963). The routine offering of tribute was the ideal way of getting close to a king without being suspected. In the logic of the story, the presentation was made in or near the city of palms. **[16]** 'Obtained for himself': the root *'āśāh*, literally 'made for himself', cf. Josh. 5.2. 'Two edges': *peh*, plural *piyyōt*, referring to a weapon with a cutting edge, indicates the blade. The *'gomed'* is an unknown measure of length, which some people believe to be equivalent to about two-thirds of a cubit, i.e. about 30 cms.[4] For this reason I have translated the weapon as 'sword'. It probably resembled the Roman *gladium*. **[17]** 'Fat' here has a number of connotations: his lack of mobility, his good-natured and therefore unsuspicious character, his ridiculous aspect: all this is pre-supposed for what is about to happen; here, however, the description begins in terms of a caricature. Humour, too, differs from people to people and from age to age. **[18]** 'Finished . . .' indicates some ceremonial connected with handing over the tribute. 'Went with . . .': *šalaḥ* in the piel can mean 'accompany' and also 'dismiss' or 'send away'; the first meaning seems better, given that we see Ehud accom-

[3] R. Meyer, § 38.3.
[4] See A. Strobel, 'Masse und Gewichte', *BHH* II, 1964, cols. 1159ff.

panying his people for some of the way. 'The people': tribute in kind or in precious metal needed people to carry it physically or to guide the beasts of burden. **[19]** 'Near . . .': for *'et* with this meaning cf. *KB*[3]. 'Sculpted stones' or 'images': *p'sīlīm* in biblical Hebrew are usually sculpted images of idols, and therefore the word usually has a pejorative connotation. Here the second meaning seems to be excluded and we must think, rather, of a reference to the Israelite sanctuary of Gilgal, cf. Josh. 4.[5] In any case, such a reference is not explicit here, and there is no negative connotation in the term. Y. Kaufmann*, 1962, has put forward another possibility, that this is a surviving Canaanite sanctuary; in that case, however, we must ask just how many sanctuaries there were at Gilgal. In any case, it seems reasonable to see the place, which was evidently known to the audience, as one of the provisional boundary points between Moab and Benjamin/Ephraim. 'Quiet', or 'Silence', Hebrew *hās*, is equivalent to our 'Hush', and is still used in the same way in Arabic.[6] 'His following': the expression *'āmad 'al* X means 'serve' (cf. the *tiqqūn hassōp'rīm* – scribal correction – in Gen. 18.22); in the context of the court it means the 'followers'. 'Dismiss': with LXX[B], Σ and others: with a slight modification of the vocalization the MT has 'and they went out'. **[20]** 'The cool room': the current translation of *hamm'qērāh* (root *qārar*, 'be cool'). LXX, probably rightly, makes Ehud's speech begin with 'O king . . .', and adds ἐγγὺς αὐτοῦ, 'near' or 'by' or 'alongside him' at the end. **[21]** 'At that moment', lit. 'While he was getting up . . .': added with LXX (ἅμα τοῦ ἀναστῆναι) . . .' The additions of LXX in vv. 20f., while not indispensable, are very useful for reconstructing the dynamics of the action. **[22]** 'Went in': LXX has ἐπεισήνεγκεν, i.e. *wayyābē'*, cf. *BHK*[3] and *BHS*, i.e. 'made it go into . . .' 'With the hilt . . .': *'āḥēr* normally means 'after' something or someone, a meaning which is not excluded here; in fact it is a sequence: first the blade goes in and then the hilt. However, the stress is not so much on the sequence blade-hilt as on the remarkable character of the fact that even the hilt, which would normally remain in the hand of the assailant and outside the wound, penetrates along with the blade. And *'āḥēr* in the sense of 'with', 'together with', is attested in the Ugaritic text Gordon no. 77, 32f.,[7] which is why it is not rash to presuppose it here. 'Courtyard' here and 'porch' in v. 23 are hypothetical translations of two *hapax legomena* indicating two different places in the royal palace; however, their meaning is unknown. Everything suggests that these are two parallel and therefore alternative

[5]See *Joshua*, ad loc., and Rösel.
[6]R. Meyer, § 79.2c.
[7]Cf. among others M. J. Dahood, 'Ugaritic Studies and the Bible', *Greg* 43, 1962, 55–79: 69, and 'Hebrew-Ugaritic Lexicography I', *Bibl* 44, 1963, 289–303: 292f.

descriptions.[8] The LXX does not translate the first term, whereas Vg
and Tg have: 'So that the excrement came out of the body' (as a
consequence of the wound). The 'courtyard' must have been a feature
letting into the 'cool room' the current of air which made it cool. The
translation 'porch' was proposed for the first time by M.-J. Lagrange*,
1903. 'Behind him': this is the only way in which ba‘ădō could be
translated in the present context, cf. *KB*[3] s.v. **[24]** 'Doing business':
here we have the well-known expression 'covering his feet' or better
'opening his feet', root *sākak*, cf. Vg, Tg and Syr: LXX[B] and A have
a synonym ἀποκενοῖ ('empty') τοὺς πόδας (a useless addition): for the
expression cf. I Sam. 24.4 (EVV 3). **[25]** 'Waited': *wayyāḥīlū* here
evidently cannot be the imperfect hiphil of *ḥyl*, 'give birth', and hence
'tremble', 'shake'; it must necessarily be connected with *yāḥal*, 'wait',
following all the ancient translations. It is therefore vocalized as *wayᵉy-
aḥᵃlū* or *wayyōḥīlū* cf. *BHS*; the first reading appears in Gen. 8.10, 12 or
is an anomalous form of *yāḥal*. **[26]** 'To Seir': in the Hebrew Bible the
name is always that of the 'Mountain of Edom', in Transjordan, to
the south of Moab, but here the note appears irreconcilable with the
fact that shortly afterwards Ehud appears on 'Mount Ephraim', i.e.
in central Cisjordan. It also seems improbable that he could have
crossed the territory of a people whose king he had killed. Täubler**
(23) thinks of a region in the Jordan valley, at the foot of 'Mount
Ephraim', on the basis of ancient quotations, whereas J. Simons (*GTT*,
228) has already put this region on 'the Mountain of Ephraim'
(Aharoni does not seem to comment on the problem). However, we
do not have any precise knowledge. Rösel**, 1975, map on p. 189, has
tried to reconstruct the itinerary in question, cf. 1977. **[28]** 'Go down':
with LXX[BA], i.e. *rᵉdū*, root *yārad*; MT has *ridᵉpū*, 'follow me', a prema-
ture exhortation, given that we have not yet reached this stage.
However, Hebrew often anticipates elements which it considers
important, thus putting them chronologically out of context; cf. also
the *wayyērᵉdū* which follows. 'To Moab': the preposition *lᵉ-* does not
seem to indicate direction here, which would be tautologous, nor is it
what has been called a *dativus incommodi*: in Ugaritic the particle is
attested with the sense of 'from', i.e. 'from (the hands of) Moab'.[9]
After what we have seen in connection with v. 13 it is probable that
in the original account the occupation by the Moabites of the fords
over the Jordan had taken place in connection with a raid in Cisjordan,
so that the recapture of the fords by Benjamin (Israel) was aimed not
so much at cutting off the invaders' retreat as at preventing their
crossing the river towards the west.

[8]W. von Soden, 'Zum akkadischen Wörterbuch', *Orient* 24, 1965, 144f., and W.
Richter**, 1963, 15.
[9]Cf. Aistleitner, no. 1422, 4, and Gordon, §§ 10, 11.

1. This narrative is the first in which it is possible to conjecture with good cause the presence of ancient traditions which have been taken up and edited by Dtr as an illustration of its particular argument. Rösel (1977) has also tried to demonstrate that the details of the story are much clearer than they seem, if we examine them organically. Now it is certain that the original introduction seems to have been suppressed, to be replaced by the prologue of the Dtr 'framework'. The transition from this prologue to the original narrative takes place in v. 15. Before being taken over by Dtr, this seems to have been an eminently secular narrative; there are a great many observations of a humorous kind, though this is a humour which now, at least in the West, seems to be somewhat coarse: there is a large number of jokes based on proper names and on physical defects; there is even a scatological theme which contributes to a ridiculous tension (v. 24b). Instead of being proclaimed with prophetic power, or for historical reasons, as is Dtr's wont, the word of God simply serves as a stratagem for Ehud (v. 20), so that he can approach the person of the king for a purpose of which we are well aware.

There are parallels in the history of religion to the theme of the left hand (Týr in Nordic mythology, Yamšid in Persian mythology), and also in ancient epic Roman legends (Mucius Scaevola); these are brought out and commented on in the study by Grottanelli. Given the type of material, it is not surprising to find some topographical details presented in a rather uncertain fashion, so that we do not know whether the action takes place entirely in Cisjordan, near Jericho (as would seem to be the case in the final form of the story), or in part also in Transjordan; for this information cf. Rösel 1975**: for one study of the tradition in general see the same author's work of 1977.

The note about the recapture of the fords (to be understood along the lines mentioned above) probably concluded the original narrative; however, this conclusion has now been mixed up with that of the Dtr framework.

Geographically the story is confined to a clan of Benjamin, that of Gera, and to the area around Gilgal; the mention of the 'Mountain of Ephraim' from which the combatants come is simply an amplification, in that it seeks to include in the action other groups which are at least potentially interested: in I Kings 4.8, 18 the district of the 'Mountain of Ephraim' does not in fact include Benjamin, because the present designation indicates

a wider area. And it is on this element that the pan-Israelite
version of the event has been constructed, certainly present in
the Deuteronomistic framework (vv. 12, 14, 29f.) and perhaps
already in a rather earlier redaction (vv. 27f.), a redaction which
also introduced the theme of the 'holy war'. This is an element
which is not intrinsically necessary for the economy of the ancient narrative,[10] but it is a useful complement in its pan-Israelite
stage.

2. In its present form, the episode is set in Cisjordan. Moab
has crossed the Jordan and has seized Jericho (v. 13, cf. v. 21);
the unusual designation for the city can easily be explained from
the desire of the redactors not to create tensions between the
note and the traditional theory according to which the city was
destroyed by Joshua, only to be rebuilt in I Kings 16.34; however, II Sam. 10.5 already presupposes that the locality was
inhabited in some way. In that case the royal palace will have
been at Jericho, so that the march from and to Gilgal will have
been fairly brief.[11] According to this theory, then, Moab, too,
like Israel, will have tried to enter Cisjordan, succeeding to
begin with, until Israel (or Benjamin and Ephraim) took its
revenge. However, this sequence of events does not seem to be
confirmed by what remains of the earlier version, as we have
seen in the text of v. 13; the earlier version seems to postulate
that the palace of Eglon was in Transjordan, a short distance
from the ford near to Gilgal (Richter**, 1963), otherwise it
would be strange that Ehud came from Gilgal and escaped in
that direction, i.e. from and towards the Jordan; however, this
journey seems probable if the palace was near to the far bank
of the Jordan, and Ehud fled in the direction from which he had
come, i.e. Cisjordan. In any case that the palace must have been
in the depression of the Jordan seems certain from the presence
in it of the 'cool room', a construction that would not be necessary on the uplands, and which plays a crucial role in the
narrative.

In the economy of the more ancient version of the story, the
killing of the king in the circumstances described serves to create

[10]G. von Rad***, 1951, 7; cf. recently M. Weippert, 'Heiliger Krieg in Israel und
Assyrien', *ZAW* 84, 1972, 460–93, who demonstrates the spread throughout the Near
East both of the institution and of the theme of the deity going at the head of his troops.

[11]For this see the important study by K. Galling, 'Bethel und Gilgal', *ZDPV* 66, 1943,
140–55, and 67, 1944–45, 21–34, esp. 144f.

confusion among the invaders or potential invaders, allowing Benjamin to attack and defeat them.

The narrative produces another piece of information which contradicts the traditional theory: according to this, in Transjordan Benjamin was not opposite Moab, but Reuben (cf. Num. 32.37f.; I Chron. 5.8–10); according to the second text, this tribe led a pastoral semi-nomadic existence before it occupied its own territory and settled there. This origin of Reuben is also attested by the ancient song in Judg. 5.15b–16, although its territory is not described. However, the presence of Moab in the region (attested by the mention of the *'arᶜbōt Mō'āb* in Num. 22.1; 33.48)[12], a region which soon afterwards belonged to Ammon, is far from obvious: provided always that we do not deny the ancient story all historicity and regard its contents as being a purely fictitious element, here Moab is probably at its greatest extent towards the north-west, before being forced into its traditional boundaries.[13]

3. Richter's study**, 1963, has shown that if we leave the Dtr redaction out of account, this passage is a unity. The elements which at first were considered to be duplicates (e.g. vv. 19b, 20b) are not so, or at least allow of other more convincing explanations. There are tensions, e.g. between the ancient tradition and its elaborations (Richter). We have found another duplicate in vv. 22f. in the itinerary of the flight from the palace, but its presence seems to be due, rather, to the presence of two terms which are difficult to explain (so that the redactors preferred to give both, rather than suppressing one of them); it is not a true duplicate.

The examination of the text made by Richter (18ff.) leads us to the conclusion that here we have neither a historical narrative nor a purely legendary account: he prefers to talk of a 'committed narrative' (the adjective is meant to be the opposite of 'neutral'). Furthermore, it may well have been familiar to the audience, who would have been captivated by the manner of presentation: interesting details, elements which hold up the action, irony and humour. In the centre of the story is the 'good' protagonist, Ehud, who succeeds in a situation of conflict between his people and a powerful neighbour in carrying out an

[12]Cf. *Joshua*, 27.
[13]Cf. M. Noth, 'Israelitische Stämme zwischen Ammon und Moab', *ZAW* 60, 1944, 11–57 (= *ABLAK* 1971, I, 391–433); 16 = 396ff.; Y. Aharoni**, 1967, 190f., and R. de Vaux**, 576ff., 581ff.

individual enterprise with great astuteness, notwithstanding his personal handicap, indeed putting it to good purpose. There is no real political or theological interest in the ancient narrative: for example, it is significant that Ehud is not presented as a man designated and endowed with the spirit of Yahweh; he appears simply as a representative of his people chosen to bring the tribute to the king. Specifically theological interests only come in with the Dtr redaction: the 'judge' is designated by God, the war which he organizes is a 'holy war'; with the typical formula of v. 28 put on the lips of Ehud, the whole thing becomes an action by means of which the God of Israel once again frees his unfaithful but penitent people.[14]

[14]For this last problem see the details in W. Richter**, 1963, 21ff.

CHAPTER 3.31

Shamgar ben Anath

Bibliography: B. **Maisler (Mazar)**, 'Shamgar ben 'Anat', *PEFQS* 66, 1934, 192–4; A. **Alt**, 'Megiddo im Übergang vom kanaanäischen zum israelitischen Zeitalter', *ZAW* 60, 1944, 67–85 = *KlSchr* I, Munich 1953, 256–73: 72 = 261ff.; E. **Täubler****, 1958, 170ff.; F.C. **Fensham**, 'Shamgar ben 'Anath', *JNES* 20, 1961, 197f.; E. **Danelius**, 'Shamgar ben 'Anath', *JNES* 22, 1963, 191–3; A. **van Selms**, 'Judge Shamgar', *VT* 14, 1964, 294–309; W. **Richter****, 1964, 92ff.; P.C. **Craigie**, 'A Reconsideration of Shamgar ben Anath (Judg. 3.31 and 5.6)', *JBL* 91, 1972; O. **Eissfeldt**, 'Gottesnamen in Personennamen als Symbole menschlicher Qualitäten', *Festschrift Walter Baetke. . .*, Weimar 1966, 110–7 = *KlSchr* IV, Tübingen 1968, 276–84.

3[31] He was succeeded by Shamgar ben Anath, who smote the Philistines with an ox-goad: six hundred men. He too delivered Israel.

[31] 'Goad': the regular translation of the *hapax legomenon malmād*, following Tg and Syr. LXX[B]: ἐν τῷ ἀποτροπόδι, and Vg have 'with a ploughshare', but we know nothing of a particular 'ox's ploughshare': LXX[A] has ἐκτὸς μόσκων, which corresponds to the Hebrew *mill'bad habbāqār*, i.e., 'independent of the herd'; the expression does not make any sense, but presupposes a Hebrew archetype. In any case the emphasis is put on the fact that an agricultural implement, opportunely used, served as an effective weapon of war. 'The Philistines': in LXX always ἀλλόφυλοι, i.e. alien elements to the community, for reasons that we do not know. 'Shamgar', a name which also appears in 5.6 (where it has a chronological function, a sign that this must have been a relatively well known person), cf. also Samgar in Jer. 39.3 for a Babylonian, though the text is corrupt and should probably be read differently, cf. the commentaries. The majority consider the name to be of Hurrian origin; however, it could also be West Semitic, derived from the *šapel* of the root *māgar*, 'submit', in which case it would be

theophoric: 'the deity makes X submit'. The root *mgr* appears in a theophoric name in a seal published recently:[1] *bn-mgr'l.*

The brief narrative of Shamgar ben Anath – 'both the episode and the figure are obscure' (J. Gray*, 1967) – is here inserted into the list of judges, though in a somewhat doubtful form. If it is in fact true that the present context makes him the successor of Ehud as judge ('after him came' or 'he was succeeded by'), it is also true that 4.1 follows after the death of Ehud, jumping over the present passage. From a stylistic point of view, too, it has little in common with the other passages of Judges, whether those concerning the 'major' judges or those concerning the 'minor' judges. As far as the former are concerned, he certainly 'saves' Israel, but only by smiting and killing the Philistines, who are not in fact said to have already been oppressing the Israelites; the only parallel with the latter which is at all clear is that of Samson with the jawbone of an ass, 15.14–17 (see below); in both cases we have the theme of the heroic effort with inadequate weapons. Mention of him here therefore seems justified only because he is used for the purposes of dating in 5.6. Stylistically, this mention has, however, an obvious parallel with the list of David's mighty men (II Sam. 23.8ff.). For that reason it is difficult to say who inserted the hero into the present context: the characteristic Dtr framework is lacking; besides, the insertion was made at a late stage if 4.1ff in fact follows on directly from Ehud. Of course, in itself the note might go back to an ancient tradition.

There are also a large number of foreign names in the list of David's mighty men, but as I have indicated, in this case a West Semitic origin cannot be excluded, especially in the light of the recently discovered seal, even if it does not seem to be Hebrew. According to Craigie's analysis, *ben 'anat* appears in texts from Mari, Ugarit and Egypt, and indicates either the origin of the person in question (in Mari, 'from Hanat' means coming from the sanctuary of Anat, connected with the semi-nomadic Hanaeans), or the person's art or craft: 'son of Anat' can be someone dedicated to the military life, as the deity Anat

---

[1]On the Hurrian origin of the name Shamgar see W. Feiler, 'Hurritische Namen im Alten Testament', *ZA* 45, 1939, 216–29: 219; for the root *mgr*, P. Bordreuil and A. Lemaire, 'Nouveaux sceaux hébreux, araméens et ammonites', *Semitica* 26, Paris 1976, 44–63: no. 33, and F.L. Benz, *Personal Names in the Phoenician and Punic Inscriptions*, Studia Pohl, 8, Rome 1972, 339f., record a name *mgr'l.* I am grateful to my assistant at the University of Rome, Dr Felice Israel, for these references.

was the goddess of war. Both these explanations are possible in the Old Testament, and are not mutually exclusive: in fact we find places which bear the name *bēt 'anat* or *'anātōt*. And in this connection Danelius notes that in Josh. 17.7 we have the reading Δηλαναθ ή ἐστιν κατὰ πρόσωπον υἱῶν ᾿Αναθ in the LXX text;[2] this place would therefore be on the central plateau, near Shechem; however, the name could apply to the person also if we consider his exploit in the military sphere.[3]

Here, then, we would have a Canaanite lordling who fought against the Philistines: in this sense he could have 'saved' Israel, even if Judg.5.6 then presents him as one of the oppressors. This statement therefore has.a certain logic about it, even if it is deduced from some doubtful elements: after all, here were two peoples who were trying to wrest the region from its inhabitants: Israel and the Philistines, and it would not be strange if one allied itself with the other, depending on the situation. So here we would have a Canaanite allied with Israel against the Philistines, while in Judg. 5 a Philistine is at the head of the anti-Israelite coalition.

In this sense, then, the redactors wanted to indicate that Israel is saved by someone who will soon be their enemy *par excellence*, by the work of a person of doubtful historicity, probably not even an Israelite.

[2]Not listed by me in *Joshua*, ad loc.
[3]This explanation is better than the one proposed by J.T. Milik, 'An Unpublished Arrow-Head with Phoenician Inscription of the 11th-10th Century', *BASOR* 143, 1956, 3–6, and taken up by Y. Aharoni**, 1967, 244 n. 180.

Deborah and Barak as Judges

The most salient facts of the judgeship of Deborah and Barak are narrated in chs. 4 and 5, two texts with very different forms: the first is a prose narrative and the second a heroic poem, now considered the oldest Israelite poem that has come down to us. Chapter 4 shows the usual pattern: vv. 1–3, the Dtr 'framework'; vv. 4–10, Deborah and Barak; v. 11, the Kenites; vv. 12–16, the battle; vv. 17–22, the escape and death of Sisera; vv. 23f., the Dtr conclusion. The chronological notes, however, are at the end of ch. 5, a sign that the redactors wanted to take the two compositions together.

(a) Chapter 4

Bibliography: W.F. **Albright**, *Archaeology and the Religion of Israel*, Baltimore ³1953, 117ff., 227; id., *The Archaeology of Palestine*, Harmondsworth ⁴1960, 117; A. **Alt**, 'Megiddo im Übergang vom kanaanäischen zum israelitischen Zeitalter', *ZAW* 60, 1944, 67–85 = *KlSchr* I, 1953, 256–73; S. **Yeivin**, 'The Israelite Settlement in Galilee and the Wars with Yabin of Hazor', in *Mélanges bibliques. . en l'honneur de André Robert*, Paris [1957], 95–104; E. **Täubler****, 1958, 142–69; K.-D. **Schunck**, *Benjamin*, BZAW 86, 1963, 49ff.; W. **Richter ****, 1963, 29ff., 111ff.; G. **Wallis**, 'Die Jakobtradition und Geschichte', *WZ(H)* 13, 1964, 427–40 = *Geschichte und Überlieferung*, Berlin and Stuttgart 1968, 13–44 : 437=39ff.; A.D.H. **Mayes**, 'The Historical Context of the Battle against Sisera', *VT* 19, 1969, 353–60; **Mayes****, 1974, ch. III; P. **Weimar**, 'Die Jahwekriegserzählungen in Exodus 14, Josua 10, Richter 4 and I Samuel 7', *Bibl* 57, 1976, 38–73, esp. 51–62. On v. 2: A. **Malamat**, 'Hazor, "The Head of all those Kingdoms" ', *JBL* 79, 1960, 12–59; V. **Fritz**, 'Das Ende der Spätbronzezeitlichen Stadt Hazor Stratum XIII und die biblische Überlieferung in Josua 11 und Richter 4', *UF* 5, 1973, 123–39. On v. 11: A. **Malamat**, 'Mari and the Bible', *JAOS* 82, 1962, 143–50: 145; W.F. **Albright**, 'Jethro, Hobab and Reuel in Early Hebrew Tradition', *CBQ* 25, 1963, 1–11; G. **Fohrer**, *Überlieferung und Geschichte des Exodus*, BZAW 91, 1964, 25ff.; F.C. **Fensham**, 'Did a Treaty between the Israelites and the Kenites exist?',

BASOR 175, 1964, 51–4; B. **Mazar**, 'The Sanctuary of Arad and the Family of Hobab the Qenite', *JNES* 24, 1965, 297–303; J. A. **Soggin**, 'Heber der Qenit', *VT* 31, 1981, 89–92. On v. 21: B. **Crossfield**, 'A Critical Note on Judges 4,21', *ZAW* 85, 1973, 348–51; E.W. **Nicholson**, 'The Problem of *ṣnḥ*', *ZAW* 89, 1977, 259–66.

(a) Deuteronomistic introduction (vv. 1–3)

4[1] The Israelites began to do what Yahweh thought to be evil, after Ehud died; [2]and Yahweh gave them into the power of Jabin, king of Canaan, who reigned in Hazor; the commander of his army was Sisera, who dwelt in Harosheth, the place of the 'pagans'. [3]The Israelites cried out to Yahweh because he had nine hundred chariots of iron. He oppressed the Israelites for twenty years.

(b) Deborah and Barak (vv. 4–10)

4 At that time Deborah, a prophetess, the wife of Lappidoth, was judge over Israel. [5]She used to sit under 'the palm of Deborah', between Ramah and Bethel, in the 'Mountain of Ephraim', and the people of Israel came up to her for judgment. [6]But one day she sent a message to Barak, son of Abinoam, from Kedesh in Naphtali, and said to him: 'It is certain that Yahweh, God of Israel, has commanded you: Go and take up a position on Mount Tabor, having with you ten thousand men from Naphtali and Zebulon. [7]And I will put in position against you, by the river Kishon, Sisera, leader of the army of Jabin, and all his troops, mounted and on foot, and I will deliver them into your hands.' [8]Barak replied: 'If you will go with me, I will go; but if you will not go with me, I will not go either. I do not in fact know the day when Yahweh will lead me, with his angel at my side.' [9]She replied: 'I will surely go with you; but know that the road on which you are going will not bring you any glory, for Yahweh will sell Sisera into the hand of a woman.' Then Deborah arose and went to Barak at Kedesh, [10]where Barak called to arms all Zebulon and Naphtali; from there he went up on to Mount Tabor, in command of his troops: ten thousand men. Deborah also went up with him.

(c) The Kenites (v. 11)

11 The Kenite group, who had parted from Qayin, one of the descendants of Hobab, a kinsman of Moses, had pitched their tents near to the 'oak of the caravanners' (?), i.e. at Kedesh.

(d) The battle (vv. 12–16)

12 The moment they reported to Sisera that Barak, son of Abinoam, had gone up on Mount Tabor, [13]he called out all his mounted forces: nine hundred chariots of iron, and all the men on foot, his own following, from Harosheth, the place of the 'pagans', to the river Kishon. [14]Then Deborah said to Barak, 'Have courage! This is the day

on which Yahweh has given Sisera into your hands. Indeed, Yahweh himself will go at your head!' And Barak came down from Mount Tabor and the ten thousand men with him. [15]And Yahweh routed Sisera, his chariots and all his army before Barak, and Sisera alighted from his chariot and fled away on foot. [16]And Barak went in pursuit of the chariots and the army as far as Harosheth, the place of the 'pagans'. Thus all the army of Sisera fell to the edge of the sword; not a man of them was left.

(e) *The flight and death of Sisera* (vv. 17–22)

17 Sisera continued his flight as far as the tent of Jael, a woman of the Kenite group, because there were friendly relations between Jabin, king of Hazor, and the Kenite group. [18]And Jael came out to meet Sisera, and said to him, 'Turn aside, my lord, turn aside to me, have no fear!' And he turned aside to her in the tent,

and she { covered him { with a curtain. / with a covering. / wrapped him in a sheet.

[19]Then he said to her; 'Give me, please, a little water, because I am thirsty.' She opened the skin of milk, gave him a drink, and covered him up again. [20]Then he said to her, 'Keep watch at the entrance to the tent, and if anyone comes and asks you, "Is anyone here?", say no.' [21]But Jael, a woman in the group, took a tent peg, and took a hammer in her hand, and went silently to him and drove the peg into his temple, so that it went down to the ground, while he was sleeping deeply from weariness. So he died.

22 Meanwhile, Barak continued the pursuit. Jael came out to receive him and said to him, 'Come and look: the man whom you are seeking is here.' And he went into the tent and saw Sisera lying there dead, with the tent peg in his temple!

(f) *Deuteronomistic conclusion* (vv. 23–24)

23 So on that day God subdued Jabin, king of Canaan, before the people of Israel, [24]and their hand bore increasingly heavily on Jabin king of Canaan, until they succeeded in destroying all the Canaanites.

---

[1] The reference to Ehud is omitted by LXX[A], perhaps in an attempt to make the interpolation of 3.31 less obvious. I have therefore left it as a *lectio difficilior*. [2] The title 'king of Canaan' never existed, cf. also vv. 23f.: the region never enjoyed any political unity, apart from a brief period in the empire of David and Solomon; however, David and Solomon were never given this title. The construct state which governs a proper name prohibits what might seem the most obvious translation, '*A* king of Canaan':[1] thus Burney*, 1919, thinks

[1]Cf. R. Meyer, § 97.3b.

of the city states in the north of the country and Vincent*, 1958, of those in the plain of Jezreel. It is possible that Malamat is on the right lines (1960): the term refers to the fact that the kings of Hazor were the only people to bear this title (Akkadian *šarru*) in the cuneiform texts, cf. also his article of 1962. Another possibility is that the figure of Jabin, associated with Hazor, remained alive in the tradition for a long time after the destruction of the place, Josh.11.1ff., so that the whole passage here is anachronistic, see J. Gray*, 1967. We shall find other traditio–historical details in the commentary. 'Sisera' is the real protagonist in chs. 4–5. The name is not Semitic, but it does not seem to be Indo-European, Illyrian, or Hurrian either.[2] It is increasingly accepted, rather, that this is a Luvian name;[3] in any case, it could be connected with the 'sea peoples' and thus with the Philistines, even though these are not mentioned in the battle. It is certain that the name appears among those who return from Babylon in the sixth century BC, cf. Ezra 2.53//Neh. 7.55, so that it could be a name of foreign origin, which in the course of time had become Canaanized. *ḥarōšet* (= woody?) is shown as an ethnically mixed area, like Galilee in Isa.8.23 (EVV 9.1; a text which is in fact corrupt); and on the basis of what has just been said, it could have been a colony of the 'sea peoples'. Its location is uncertain, and most scholars attempt to identify it as a consequence of v. 7 and the development of the battle. The majority now tend to locate it on *tell el-'ama*, at the foot of the eastern slope of Mount Carmel, in the vicinity of the Kishon and the disused narrow-gauge railway which was once a branch of the *Ḥejaz* route, near the abandoned Arab village (the land of which has been incorporated into the *qibbūṣ ša'ar hā'ᵃᵐmāqîm*, coord. 161–237), which has kept a similar name: *ḥaritīyeh;*[4] this theory is, however, forthrightly challenged by Y. Aharoni,[5] who thinks rather of the forests of Galilee, on the basis of the etymology of the Assyrian *ḥuršānu(m)*, '(wooded?) mountain', cf. *KB*³ and the LXX rendering in v. 16; such an identification would also be reflected in the mention of the 'pagans', perfectly in place in Galilee: the basis of the theory had already been put forward, with slight variants, by Burney, but was rejected by Simons for reasons which I would consider valid: the scene of the battle, the flight and the killing of Sisera (vv. 17ff.) presuppose a series of places situated around the plain of Jezreel. Of course there remains the problem of the different locations of the battle in chs. 4 and 5, which

---

[2]Against: C. F. Burney*, 1919, and J. Gray*, 1967; the latter thinks in terms of a Hittite origin. Cf. M. Noth, *Die israelitischen Personennamen im Rahmen der gemeinsemitischen Namengebung*, BWANT III.10, 1928, 64, and A. Alt, art. cit., 78 = 266 n. 3.

[3]Thus W .F Albright, 'Prolegomenon' to C. F. Burney*, 1919, and recently G. Garbini, 'Il cantico di Debora', *La parola del passato* 178, Naples 1978, 5–31.

[4]Cf. É. Dhorme*, A. Penna*, J. Gray*, A. Vincent*, Y. Kaufmann* and J. Simons, *GTT*, 288f., for whom this identification is problematical.

[5]Y. Aharoni**, 1967, 201ff.

we shall deal with in due course (p. 68 below). **[3]** 'Chariots of iron': the meaning is that they are covered and armed with iron, cf. above on 1.19. The number 'nine hundred', which would carry at least 1800 cavalry, is legendary, not to say extravagant. **[4]** 'Deborah' means 'bee', 'Lappidoth' are 'torches', perhaps 'lamps', while 'Barak' is 'lightning'. There is no kinship between the protagonists on the Israelite side in the neighbourhood, though this has often been conjectured.

[5] 'Used to sit': where she exercised her office as a judge, this time in the forensic sense of the term. The root *yāšab* is primarily 'sit', 'live', but the meaning here is the context of her particular task. 'The palm. . . ', Hebrew *tōmer*, only here and in Jer. 10.5, where it means 'post' or 'scarecrow', instead of the usual *tāmār*: perhaps it is a polemical vocalization with the vowels of *bōšet*, often used for people or elements connected with the Canaanite cult (A. Penna*, 1963). This connection does not seem improbable (as it might appear at first sight), given that the palm tree does not normally grow on the highlands; it could therefore be regarded as a special palm, a sacred tree. The 'oak of Deborah', Rebecca's nurse, Gen. 35.8, is also located in the same area. Despite the homonymy, there does not seem to have been any connection between the two trees, which differ in both species and in function. It should also be noted that the 'judgeship' of Deborah seems to have been used for reckoning time, as we shall see in considering the 'minor judges', cf. below on 10.1–5. 'Ramah' and 'Bethel' are both north of Jerusalem, near the present trunk road between Jerusalem and Nablus: the former is about nine kilometres along the route, probably the present-day *er-rām* (coord. 172–140); for the latter cf. on 1.22ff. Thus the two places are no more than a few hours' journey apart. For the 'Mountain of Ephraim' cf. on 3.27; here, too, the region seems more extended than the Solomonic district of the same name (cf. I Kings 4.8,18), in that it includes parts of Benjamin. 'Justice': Hebrew *lammišpāṭ*; R.G. Boling*, 1975, suggests that this should be understood as replies to specific questions and demands; however, there does not seem to be any reason why it should not be taken as the administration of justice in general and all the problems connected with it. **[6]** 'Kedesh': of Naphtali, to the north of Lake Huleh, reclaimed towards the end of the 1950s (coord. 202–280), attested in Josh. 19.37 and elsewhere. 'It is certain. . .': the particle *hᵃlō'* is usually translated, 'Is it not that. . .?', i.e. as a rhetorical question expecting the answer 'yes'; however, this interpretation seems excluded here, unless we accept that Barak had already received, but rejected, a divine calling, something about which the text says nothing. Otherwise it is obvious that Deborah is announcing a divine vocation to him which Barak could not have known before it was communicated. Thus it would seem better to suppose that here we have an emphatic, asseverative *lamed*. This grammatical form was already known to traditional Hebrew grammar, cf. *GesK* § 150e, and appears frequently in Ugaritic; it is still little known in Hebrew, where there is some uncertainty as to its meaning and functions. 'Commanded ': LXX has σοι ἐνετείλατο, i.e. *lēk-lēkā*. 'Take position' : root *māšak*, literally 'extend (the ranks)', French *deployer*, cf. Vg *duc exercitum*; in Hebrew the word is a military technical term, also 'line up': LXX did not understand: ἀπελεύσῃ, 'leave'. 'Mount Tabor' is the well-known height about five km. east of Nazareth, Arab *ǧebel eṭ-ṭūr* (coord. 137–232), under which ran (and still runs) the main line of communications from southern Galilee to northern Galilee and Damascus. Whereas the reference to Naphtali and Zebulon is historically probable, the figure 10,000 is evidently an exaggeration; nor does it seem possible that here we have mention of 'military units', as G.E. Mendenhall proposed in 1958,[6] of varying kinds. It seems obvious that the epic narrative tends rather to exaggerate figures; for another exaggeration see on v. 3, where it cannot be a matter of 'military units'. **[7]** The subject of the direct speech is always Yahweh. Note how Hebrew makes a different use of direct speech, far superior to ours: for us, it is meant to refer to the *ipsissima verba* of the person speaking, whereas in Hebrew it is more often used for any kind of speech, resulting sometimes in what we find to be the weighty constructions of successive clauses of direct speech, one within the other. 'I will put in position against you. . .': cf. the previous verse for this rendering of *māšak*, except that the subject is now God. Some scholars would prefer to render it 'draw out', but in that case the root would have a basically different meaning from the one that it has in the previous verse, which is at least suspect. The 'Kishon' flows into the Mediterranean north-east of Haifa, having crossed the central plain and skirted the eastern part of Carmel. During the dry summer season, it is completely dried up. Note 'a' in *BHK³* is inaccurate. **[8]** 'I do not know. . . ' is a phrase not very well translated from a Hebrew original which LXX adds at the end of the verse; for the text see *BHS*. It has its real sequel in Deborah's remark in v. 14. **[9]** 'Know': thus LXX γίνωσκε, Hebrew *daʿ*. 'To': *ʿim*, translated εἰς by LXX and *in* plus the accusative by Vg, can mean 'towards' in Ugaritic,[7] which is what I propose here. In fact Barak is already at Kedesh, which is why Deborah cannot go 'together' with him, vv. 6, 11. **[10]** 'Called to arms': *zāʿaq* or *ṣāʿaq* normally mean 'cry out (in pain)', 'lament', and are used in this sense by the Dtr 'framework'; in the niphal they are sometimes used for 'call to arms', 'mobilize', and are therefore technical military terms. 'In command': literally, 'and he went out with ten thousand men at his heels', for the figure see v. 6 above. **[11]** 'The group. . . ': *ḥeber* is generally understood as a proper name (cf. the commentaries); however, the root and the context sug-

---

[6]G. E. Mendenhall, 'The Census Lists of Numbers 1 and 26', *JBL* 77, 1958, 52–66.
[7]Cf. J. Aistleitner, no. 2041.1, and Gordon, § 10.14.

gest, rather, an ethnic unit: 'group', 'clan', etc. (see my recent article). Thus we would have here a Kenite group detached from the rest of the tribe, camping further north, whereas the main body would have remained in the south. 'Kinsman': as in 1.16, here too we have the problem of the exact translation of this title, and therefore of Hobab's kinship or affinity with Moses. *ḥōten* is in fact 'father-in-law', but Num. 10.29 presents Hobab as a kinsman of Moses because he is the son of Reuel/Jethro; LXX has γαμβρός here and Vg *cognatus*. However, an emendation to *ḥātān* does not solve anything because, according to the context, the term means 'husband' or 'son-in-law'. So the problem is insoluble. 'Of the caravanners', root *ṣā'an*, 'pack up' for carriage on a beast of burden, attested once in the Old Testament. In the orthography proposed by the *qerē*, the name is virtually identical with that of the place attested in Josh. 19.33, situated in the territory of the tribe of Naphtali,[8] but there is nothing to indicate that this is the same locality: as is also evident from the text, the name is common and the location remains unknown. According to Simons,[9] the name survives with variants in an Arab translation in present-day *ḥan attuǧǧār*, 'the seraglio of the merchants', situated near the battle area: Simons does not give the coordinates, and I have not been able to find it. 'Kedesh': another name which is very frequent because it becomes attached to a sanctuary of this kind. It can be either that of Naphtali, mentioned in v. 6, or that of Galilee (coord. 199–179); the latter identification is made by those, like Aharoni (see above on v. 2), who would prefer to locate the battle further north. However, it seems only likely that the place was near the scene of the battle, and therefore considerably further south. There is a *tell qedeš* near Megiddo, a little to the south-east (coord. 170–218).[10] The note prepares for what is described in vv. 17ff. **[14]** 'Have courage. . .': literally 'Up!' 'It is certain': for this interpretation of *h'lō'* see on v. 6 above; here it is an oracle of salvation, not a rhetorical question. 'With him': for this rendering of *'aḥ'rayw* see on 3.22. **[15]** 'Routed': root *hāmam*, 'confound'. 'Put to the sword' appears in the text, but is a somewhat inappropriate anticipation of what is to come. I have deleted it, although it is attested in all the ancient translations and should therefore be treated as an ancient textual corruption. Note that the explanation of the Canaanite defeat differs from the one that appears in 5.22ff.; this last is probably a more exact description of what actually happened, whereas here we have a theological explanation of the fact, connected with the 'holy war'. **[17]** 'Friendly relations': *šālōm* indicates more than the absence of conflict pure and simple: it is a positive relationship of friendship or quite simply an alliance. A similar

---

[8]Cf. *Joshua*, ad loc.
[9]Simons, *GTT*, 289.
[10]Ibid.

use is already well-known from the Mari texts, in connection with the Accadian *salīmum*, cf. *ARM*, Vol. I, no. 8, lines 6–8; 71.13; II, 16.16; 44.41; III, 50.15; IV, 20.11f.; see the Lexicon in *ARM* XV, 1954. This is the only explanation of why the general took refuge in the woman's tent. 'The group. . .' for this interpretation of *ḥeber* cf. on v. 11 above, and for Jabin on v. 2. **[18]** We have various readings to indicate what the woman did with the fugitive; LXX^B (and Tg) have: ἐξέκλινεν πρὸς αὐτὴν καὶ περιέβαλεν αὐτὸν ἐπὶ βολαίῳ, 'wrapped him up in a covering. . .'; LXX^A: καὶ ἐξένευσεν πρὸς αὐτὴν . . . καὶ συνεκάλυψεν αὐτὸν ἐν τῇ δέρρει. LXX^A understands the *hapax legomenon* *s*᷊*mīkāh*, probably rightly, as the 'curtain' of skins with which the entrance to the tent was closed, and not as a 'carpet', as J. Gray*, 1967, would prefer; LXX^B ('covering') and Tg (*b*᷊*gūn*᷊*kāh*, 'sheet') have more banal terms, whereas LXX^A has an unusual technical term, probably the exact reading of the MT, but which will have caused some difficulties to the ancient translators. **[19]** 'Skin': note the double vocalization *plene* of the *k*᷊*tib*.[11] 'Milk. . .': probably yoghurt, cf. 5.25; the Hebrew *hem᾽āh* and the present-day Arab/Hebrew *leben*, another form of yoghurt, rather thinner. **[20]** 'Keep watch . . .': the Hebrew has the masculine imperative, preferred by some scholars, with Tg and Syr, to be corrected to *᾽im*᷊*dī*.[12] **[21]** 'Peg': even today among the Bedouin it is the women who put up the tents, so that they are the ones who have the right equipment. 'It went down. . .': the verb *ṣānaḥ* has already been examined in Josh. 15.18//Judg. 1.14; here it seems only to have the meaning 'penetrate', which is how it is usually understood; however, the subject of the action is still Jael and the second verb used is feminine; therefore it is better to consider her as the subject here as well, as Crossfield indicates. Perhaps what we have here is a corruption of *wattiṣrah*, 'and cried out', 'and lamented'? 'Was sleeping': the last part of the verse also presents variants and difficulties: LXX^B has a text which is more or less similar to MT and is followed by Vg; LXX^A has καὶ αὐτὸς ἀπεσκάρισεν ἀνὰ μέσον τῶν γονάτων αὐτῆς καὶ ἐξέψυξεν καὶ ἀπέθανεν, 'jerked between her knees, lost consciousness. . .'; cf. 5.27; the difficulty lies in the use, in Hebrew, of a very concise style, hinging on three key verbs. I prefer the reading of MT, LXX^B and Vg. **[24]** 'Destroying . . .': literally, 'cut away, amputate', root *kārat*.

This text, along with the song in ch.5, is concerned with a pitched battle fought and won by Israel against a much more powerful Canaanite coalition; the event is unusual for the time and was therefore celebrated by Israel as a very important happening, probably a turning point in the troubled relation-

[11]R. Meyer, § 9.3.
[12]The form is explained in *GesK* § 110k and P. Joüon, *Grammaire de l'hébreu biblique*, Rome 1922, § 150a.

ships between the immigrants and the autochthonous population. The heroes on the Israelite side are Deborah and Barak;
the former exercised some kind of judicial and prophetic office;
the latter originally came from upper Galilee, and at least in the
present form of the narrative, does not seem to have had a very
important function. However, the whole narrative, like the song
in ch.5, has a culminating point: the killing of Sisera by a Kenite
woman, in violation of all laws of hospitality; and this climax,
with its individualistic, anecdotal, apolitical character, also suggests the perspective in which the two texts should be read: they
are not history, but epic. On the other side we have a Canaanite
coalition composed of members which the text does not bother
to list; all that is left is their leader's name – he was probably
one of the 'sea peoples'. It is therefore by no means rash to
suppose that if in 3.31 we possibly had a coalition between the
Israelites and the Canaanites against the Philistines, here we
have a coalition between the Philistines and the Canaanites
against the Israelites. In other words, as Mayes has rightly
pointed out in his two studies, we have a break in the earlier
balance of power which is replaced by a new situation; hence a
new form of struggle.

The battle takes place near the river Kishon, which crosses
the plain of Jezreel from south-east to north-west, to flow into
the Mediterranean near Haifa (cf. the comment on the text).
However, as we have seen in examining the text, and as we
shall see in examining the text of ch. 5, the topography of the
battle is far from clear; in this case compare vv. 6–11 and 17b
with 12–16. A comparison with ch. 5 shows that there the battle
takes place more towards the south or south-east side of the
plain, whereas in this chapter it takes place more towards the
north, between Tabor and *ḥariṭiye*; and I have not taken account
of the move even further north proposed by Aharoni! However,
in any case, the two chapters should be taken separately, as
Richter and Mayes have rightly pointed out:[13] in fact the different literary genres should suggest the need for care and an
examination which should begin by being separate (in contrast
to that undertaken by Hertzberg). After ch. 5, I shall examine
synoptically the differences between the two texts; these have
been collected and analysed by Y. Kaufmann*, 1962, in his
commentary. Cf. further pp. 100f.

[13]Richter**, 1963, 29, and A. D. H. Mayes**, 1974.

The division of this chapter is relatively simple. (*a*) Verses 1–3 form the first, opening part of the Dtr framework with its usual pattern: the sin of the people, their punishment, their cry of grief, their liberation achieved by Yahweh through the calling of a 'saviour'. (*b*) In vv. 4–10, Deborah (the one who now becomes the protagonist) and Barak (now a figure on a secondary level) appear and begin negotiations for a common action. It is interesting that in contrast to ch.5, the present text has only two tribes involved in the battle. (*c*) Verse 11 presents a marginal note on the Kenites; this is vital for the conclusion of the episode; the group did not belong to the region, so that it is important to explain why they are here. (*d*) Verses 12–16: a description of the battle under the leadership of Barak, who now assumes the role of protagonist, in categories taken from the theory of the 'holy war'. (*e*) Verses 17–22: the defeat, flight and killing of Sisera: here the protagonist is the Kenite Jael. (*f*) Verses 23f.: the Dtr conclusion, incomplete. Thus the first and last sections form the Dtr additions to the narrative; the other parts belong to the traditional narrative.

At first sight this division seems relatively simple; in reality, as Richter**, 1963, 61, has rightly observed, here we have a complex situation of progressive growth and redactional strata even in the ancient sections (*b*) – (*e*). Because of this, it will be useful to examine individual sections in detail.

[1–3] (*a*) These verses form the Dtr framework (Richter**, 1964, 6ff.); in addition to the usual notes typical of the genre, they present some special features. First of all there are two personal names, Sisera, who reappears in the rest of the narrative and is also a protagonist, especially in section (*e*), and Jabin. The first appears as the commander of the army belonging to the second, and has his home in *ḥarōšet*; he operates from here in a completely independent way, to such a degree that the 'king of Canaan' is mentioned only in v.17 and in vv.23f., and never has any importance for the episode described. Here, as in ch. 5, there is no list of the Canaanite forces nor any indication of their composition. Logic suggests that they must have been the inhabitants of the city-states of the central plain and its immediate environs, cities which according to 1.27ff. Israel was not able to capture (cf. pp. 29f.), and which were only made subject to some degree at a later stage, 'when Israel grew stronger'; probably, as we have seen, at the time of David. However, it is evident that these considerations, logical though they may

be, cannot be more than conjecture, for want of any specific
facts. Jabin appears as 'king of Canaan', a title the absurdity of
which we have already seen (above, p. 62f.). We discussed his
person in connection with Josh.11.1ff.;[14] here he appears as the
immediate superior of Sisera, and is clearly distinguished from
him because he does absolutely nothing. Mention of him therefore seems useless for narrative purposes; at most it adds one
extra fact, that there was another superior authority above the
commander of the coalition; however, this is an authority who
is conspicuous by his absence, apart from the Dtr framework in
vv.2,23. He is completely absent from ch.5. Apart from the
existence of a formal hierarchical relationship, his relationship
with Sisera is also non-existent. Such a precarious presence of
this figure in the present text raises a problem about the relationship between Josh. 11.1ff. and Judg. 4.1ff., the two texts
which mention Jabin in connection with the city of Hazor. The
identity on an onomastic level is obvious, but there is nothing
to suggest that the redactors wanted to identify him and did not
think, for example of a Jabin I and a Jabin II. Nor can we
identify in any way the two battles, the one which led to the fall
of Hazor and the present battle, as some writers have attempted:
the battle of Josh. 11.1ff. takes place much further north,[15]
though we cannot ignore the tendency of some of the data to
place the whole conflict more in that direction (cf. Y. Aharoni,
above, p. 63). Thus as things stand, it is evident, as V. Fritz
has demonstrated, that Jabin appears in this text (and perhaps
also in Josh. 11.1ff.) in a completely secondary form, introduced
by the Dtr redactors for reasons which we cannot now establish.[16] Mayes (88f.) has thought of the possibility of a confusion
between two traditions, one which related to Hazor and Jabin,
confronted by the tribes of Naphtali and Zebulon, and the other
with Deborah and Barak, Sisera and Jabin, but there is no proof
of this.

The second fact which emerges from the Dtr framework is
that of the composition of the Canaanite army. The numbers

[14]Cf. *Joshua*, ad loc., and V. Fritz, art. cit.
[15]O. Eissfeldt, 'Die Eroberung Palästinas durch Altisrael', *WO* II.5–6, 1955, 158–71
= *KlSchr* III, Tübingen 1966, 367–83: 168 = 380ff., and H. W. Hertzberg*, 1959, have
come down authoritatively in favour of this identification. Cf. *Joshua*, 134–7.
[16]So, too, another usually conservative author, Y. Yadin, *Hazor: the Head of all those
Kingdoms*, London 1972, 132: '. . . There was no Jabin, King of Hazor, in the time of
Deborah . . .', cf. 198ff., see also *Hazor*, London 1974, 275; in both works he suggests
that an editor must have been at work here.

both of the Canaanite chariots and horsemen and the Israelite troops are exaggerated. Such notes are completely lacking in ch.5, though this does know of the existence of Canaanite chariots and horses (v.28). The number of 900 'chariots of iron' is evidently very odd, as I have remarked; it is therefore automatically suspect; on the other hand, numbers of this kind are also attested elsewhere for the region, which is rightly considered to have had remarkable economic capacity; after the victorious outcome of the battle of Megiddo during the first campaign of Pharaoh Thutmosis III (*c.* 1490–1436), in about 1468, the annals report the capture, among other things, of 924 war chariots, one of which is gold-plated (*ANET*, 237); however, this information would need at least to be checked on the basis of other documents: in other cases of this sort, the number of chariots captured does not go beyond a few dozen, while the tendency of the royal Egyptian annals to self-glorification is well known. In any case we must exclude the possibility that the Canaanites could have formed some such coalition only against Israel. When the text itself states that the Canaanite concentration only took place when Sisera received information that the men of the two tribes of Naphtali and Zebulon were reunited on Mount Tabor, it admits the local and therefore limited character of the battle (see below); if we accept the substantial historicity of the note and therefore of the figures, it would be likely that the object of the concentration was a more powerful enemy, for example Egypt, which continued to maintain at least two fortresses in this area: Beth-shean and Gezer. And once the army was available, why not also use it in a local policing operation? In that case it would be directed against a group whose presence caused a notable disturbance. An explanation of this kind would fit in perfectly with the economy of the text.

[4–10] (*b*) Here we meet the two protagonists on the Israelite side: Deborah, presented – as we have seen – as a person of paramount importance, and Barak, who clearly seems to be inferior to her (vv.4f.). As we have seen, here we have the only instance in which the forensic function of the judge coincides with the exercise of a prophetic ministry: Deborah is in fact the person who communicates to Barak his designation by Yahweh. It is also worth noting that Deborah is a judge in the forensic sense of the term before being called to be a judge on the political and religious plane, and that during the exercise of this latter office there is no sign of the former. Again, v.4b contains a nominal proposition which belongs to the scheme which appears in the verbal construction introducing the 'minor' judges (Richter**, 1963, 38). Was the forensic judgeship of Deborah similar to that of these figures (cf. further on 10.1ff.)? In any case, it is still remarkable that there is a combination of the prophetic ministry, the judgeship in a forensic sense and the judgeship as announced in this book, a case which could, according to Richter**, 1963, ibid., indicate that at least two hands have been at work on the text. However, notwithstanding this important observation, it does not seem possible to speak of two sources.

The forensic office of judge which Deborah exercised before her calling is outlined better: it is in fact said that people came from afar to present their cases for judgment. We know little about her prophetic ministry, but in connection with Barak she clearly appears as one who brings a divine word for the one who will soon be the leader, an element which across the centuries has been characteristic of prophecy in Israel and also outside it.[17] Of her private life, we are told that she had a husband. Deborah is connected with the 'Mountain of Ephraim'; we do not know whether she had connections with the north before the embassy to Barak (v.6; Naphtali and Zebulon, 5.15; also Issachar, but cf. there), or whether these relations were only established after her prophetic calling, or even – the most radical solution – whether the participation of Deborah was a creation of the earliest redactors at the pre-Dtr stage, to give a pan-Israelite character to the battle, making it a holy war, whereas Barak was the original protagonist on the Hebrew side. In this case the title 'prophetess' (v.4) would have been conferred on Deborah by the redactors in question, on the basis of their own construction.

[6–10] The message from Deborah to Barak is the designation of a leader and the mobilization of the troops for the holy war, by means of a prophet. This follows clearly from other parallels in the book examined by Richter**, 1963, 55; in the formulas attested here there is mention of the groups summoned to muster, and often, also, of the places where they are to concentrate. The message takes the form of an oracle; it begins with the calling of the person to whom it is addressed and ends

---

[17]For the functions of the prophet in the Old Testament see my *Introduction to the Old Testament*, London and Philadelphia [2]1980, 220ff.

with the announcement that victory is certain. Other points to
note are the lack of enthusiasm and the reticence shown by
Barak, elements which here – in contrast to other scenes of
calling – are not connected with a feeling of his own inadequacy
or even unworthiness (in which case they put even more emphasis on the modesty of the hero and the power of God). Such
protestations appear in the accounts of the callings of Moses
and Jeremiah (there are also some noteworthy cases in Judges,
6.15; 13.22; cf. pp. 119, 235), and they are frequent in later
prayers or confessions of faith: here, however, it is a matter of
reticence pure and simple. Barak is ready to go only if he is
offered certain guarantees, even if the guarantee may cost him
his fame. By means of this reasoning, the redactors transfer the
character of protagonist from the person who really had this
role, Barak (cf. vv.12ff.), to the prophetess. The transfer takes
place in a very plausible way: the word of God stands at the
beginning of a process which in a short time will lead to the
victory of the people of God; however, confronted by such an
extraordinary action, Barak, who is a leader and a man of the
world, and therefore accustomed to weigh up the odds, cannot
share the charismatic enthusiasm of Deborah: he cannot endan-
ger himself and others without the necessary guarantees. And
according to the interesting addition of LXX at v.8, he candidly
confesses his own lack of competence in specialized questions
like oracles. Thus the text here contrasts two opposed attitudes:
that of the faith which accepts on trust, sometimes in a way
which humanly speaking can seem almost irresponsible, the call
of the word of God, and which in the face of that authority is
either ignorant of the risks or ignores them; and that of a man
of the world, responsible for himself and others, accustomed to
weighing the pros and cons and only incurring risks on the basis
of certain guarantees. Here, however, we of course have theological notions arising from later reflection, which lead up to the
episode and utilize it as a piece of proof for a particular argument. At any rate, it is clear that in the end it is Barak who
goes out at the head of the troops, and not Deborah.

The content of v.7 also includes a plan of campaign for a
battle: Barak will take up position with his own troops on Mount
Tabor, which dominates the plain towards the east; God himself
will then make Sisera attack from the south-east, from the region
around the Kishon, and will deliver him into the hands of Barak.
The plan presupposed is therefore that the Canaanites will drive

towards the north-east, right under the buttresses of Tabor, where Barak will have laid a trap. The note is in some tension with the locality of Kedesh in Naphtali, situated a good deal further north (cf. on the text), always supposing that this is not Kedesh near Megiddo, in which case, however, this is considerably to the south-west. However, subsequent events (vv. 12ff.) suggest that the defeated general should have fled in the direction of his own base, and not in the opposite direction, as seems to have happened. On the other hand, Tabor is about twenty-five kilometres as the crow flies, i.e., a good day's march from the area of operations, whereas the fact that the enemy knows (vv.12f.) that Barak and his followers are on the mountain contrasts with the obvious secrecy necessary for an ambush. Might it be that originally (or at least in the intention of the authors and the redactors) Tabor was only the operational base for the two tribes?

And speaking of the tribes, it is interesting to note that whereas in 5.14ff. many other tribes are invited to join in the struggle, and some respond to the invitation (cf. further, below, p. 97), including Ephraim, Deborah's tribe, there is no mention of this in the present text. This raises an interesting problem. It is obvious that ch. 5, as we shall see, is the earlier text of the two; on the other hand, it presents a more or less pan-Israelite version of the battle, an interpretation that we know to be later in the context of the 'conquest'. Thus in the earliest text we would have a relatively late outline of the information about all the participants in the battle, and in the later text an earlier tradition which envisages only two tribes being involved in the battle, or at most three, concentrated around Mount Tabor.

[11] (c) In this verse, with which v. 17 should be compared, we have some brief remarks intended to explain the presence in this area of a group which should be located much further south, and which of itself does not belong here. However, its presence is vital for the action of the story, and especially for the conclusion which the two chapters have in common (and which, as we have seen, forms the climax), cf. 4.17ff.; 5.24ff. The style of the note recalls 1.16. The translation which I propose deliberately rejects an individualistic interpretation ('Jael, wife of Heber, the Kenite') in favour of a collective one: the woman is a member of an indeterminate group, of Kenite origin, traditionally akin to Israel through the Midianite father-in-law and relatives of Moses: their habitat is normally the southern desert, towards

the Gulf of Aqaba; and if the group appears in the present sphere of operations, hundreds of miles to the north, it is only because it has separated from the original nucleus. In v. 17 it is said that there was a relationship of *šālōm* between Jabin and the group, i.e., not only an absence of hostility but also harmony, cooperation, alliance, common concerns.[18] In the logic of the narrative, the existence of such relationships explains why Sisera did not escape directly towards his own base, but towards a group which he considered loyal, in order to seek refuge. The group seems to have been of a considerable size: this is the only way in which it could have been capable of providing an effective guarantee of the sanctuary sought. Here, too, the figure of Jabin has no function, and seems to have been introduced later by the redactors.

[12–16] (*d*) Here we have the account of the battle proper; stylistically, however, it seems colourless, especially compared with the conclusion. It has been constructed along the lines of the 'holy war', again a sign of later theological reflection, tending to give all the glory to the God of Israel and to attribute the possession of the promised land to a pattern of promise and fulfilment. This is probably a phase coinciding with the second redaction (Richter**, 1963, 62). One important comment is that the beginning of the operation will have been sparked off by the news of the assembling of Barak and his tribes on Mount Tabor, a note which we have seen to be a contrast with the 'theological' thesis according to which God himself lured the Canaanites into the ambush laid by Israel near to the mountain (v. 7, cf. v. 14). However, this relies on the hypothesis that the Canaanite army will already have been nearby for some operations of greater importance, and while waiting for this could also have been used for a local police operation. Thus Sisera and his troops moved along the Kishon and were confronted by those of Israel, who came down from Tabor. Here we perhaps have two notes combined into one: Tabor was a superb strategical position, provided that the battle took place near it to secure control over the route northwards; the area of the Kishon, where the victory was won and the enemy was routed, is some way away from Tabor. Could it have happened that the battle was first joined by Deborah and a central Palestinian group, who were then

[18]For the alliance, see the classical statements made by J. Pedersen, *Israel: Its Life and Culture*, I–II, Copenhagen 1926, 263ff., and recently, W. Eisenbeis, *Die Wurzel* šlm *im Alten Testament*, BZAW 113, 1969, 107.

reinforced by Barak as a second stage? In any case these are difficulties which the present text simply ignores: by contrast, it seeks to stress the miraculous character of the event: Israel did not have any need to fight, because Yahweh himself inflicted defeat upon his enemies! The note in 5.22ff. seems to be very different. The present text does not say how Yahweh routed the enemy. The text does not say how this happens, but the language recalls Ex. 14.24, cf. Josh. 10.10 and I Sam. 7.10.[19] In a recent paper, which I have been unable to use fully, P. C. Craigie has found some interesting parallels between the Ugaritic myth of 'Anat and the Song of Deborah.[20] And there is a precise analogy with the language of Exodus, where we have three parallel versions of the miracle at the Red Sea (Ex. 24.21bα: the waters which drew back after 'a strong east wind'; Ex. 14.21abβ, 22: the sea divided by Moses, who stretches out his hand above it; and Ex. 14.24: God turns towards the camp and throws it into confusion; these are probably J, P and E respectively). At this point we are probably closest to the last version, Ex. 14.24 (E?). The variant in 5.20 makes the heavens themselves fight against the Canaanites. That here too we have some sort of weather miracle, as we shall see in 5.20, seems proved by the fact that Sisera is forced to flee on foot, abandoning the very vehicle whose speed gave him an advantage when facing the enemy, his chariot now made useless because it was bogged down in the mud. Given the circumstances, and the living record in the tradition that Israel could not win a battle against troops equipped with chariots of iron, the event seems miraculous, a 'sign' of divine intervention into human history: a far superior enemy had been defeated, and moreover without the use of force, by Israel; God had done it all, and all his people had to do was to pursue the consequences.

These consequences of the victory must have been remarkable. First of all in the positive sense: the Canaanites could not keep the plain under their control, and their alliance with the Philistines does not seem to have changed things very much. Israel will have succeeded in maintaining and strengthening contact between the northern and central tribes across the plain. In a negative sense, as Mayes points out, probably rightly, in his writings, the battles mentioned in I Sam. 4 must be con-

[19]For other texts see W. Richter**, 1963, 52.
[20]P. C. Craigie, 'Deborah and Anat: A Study of Poetic Imagery', ZAW 90, 1978, 374–81.

nected with the counter-attack by the Philistines against another group which aspired to possession of the region and which had the means of realizing its aspirations. So if the battle and the victory without doubt had positive consequences, they also led to the greater crisis indicated for the period immediately before the formation of the Israelite monarchy!

[17–22] (e) These verses are the earliest part of the narrative, except for v. 17b, with its mention of Jabin. They describe an episode connected with the battle which, historically speaking, is secondary because of its individualistic and anecdotal character. They are all the more important here from a narrative point of view, because they doubtless constitute the climax of the story. According to Richter, the story was probably handed down among the tribes situated around Tabor, and was then connected with this narrative at a later stage (**1963, 62). The text takes up a phrase from v. 15: 'And Sisera . . . fled on foot.' In the present context, the narrative raises the problem of what seems to be a flagrant violation of the law of hospitality, sacrosanct in the Near Eastern world as it was in the West. The fact that there are notable examples of violations of this kind in the classical world (*Odyssey* XI, 407–13; Sophocles, *Electra* 193–200; Aeschylus, *Agamemnon* 1035ff.), as Penna (*1963, ad loc.) points out, should not make us close our eyes to the enormity of the fact, which is heightened by the existence of a relationship, probably an alliance, with the group in question (cf. the late v. 17b). And a semi-nomadic group like the Kenites must have been particularly dependent on relationships of this kind, if it wanted to be able to obtain pasturage and water along its route, provided that we do not want to regard the Kenites as brigands pure and simple, following the army and living, among other things, on the spoils from the dead and wounded on the battlefield. However, there is no indication of such a characteristic in any of the Old Testament descriptions of the Kenites; furthermore, as here and especially at the end of ch. 5, the texts tend to glorify them; and this eulogy goes far beyond the simple satisfaction provided by the fact that the Israelites had a piece of good luck at the right moment.

At this point, it is worth considering a plausible hypothesis put forward by Fensham: that there was also kinship between Israel and the Kenites, perhaps even an alliance. In other words, the group will have had a twofold loyalty: towards the Canaanites and towards Israel, i.e., towards two groups which up to that point had not been engaged in open conflict. In the new situation, however, in which the Canaanites were allied with the Philistines, the group was forced to make a choice, and chose Israel, to whom it was also bound by common faith and affinity. This seems to be the only possible explanation for the glorification of an action which, while it turned out well for Israel, could in no way be reconciled with existing practice among all civilized peoples from time immemorial. Thus the woman, incapable because of her own weakness of preventing the fugitive general from entering her tent, pretended to accede to his request, only at a later stage to act in accordance with what she considered to be her real duty. The act of the woman should then be seen in the context of a complex conflict of loyalties, a conflict in which the woman had found herself engaged without being responsible for it. However, notwithstanding the explanations we might provide and the clarifications of the situation we might offer, the scene remains sinister; even if one could interpret the glorification of the woman as a glorification not so much of her act as of her choice, it cannot but raise negative reactions in us, in the same way as the classical parallels mentioned above caused their audience to shudder.[21]

This episode concludes the prose part of the narrative. Rich in elements relevant for the historian and the believer, but also in gaps which cannot be filled, it ends with an episode which seems to add to Yahweh's victory in a superfluous, not to say damning way, but which can well be explained as a narrative around which in fact the rest came to be crystallized. Its function within the context of the Dtr history is not very clear: in fact it is obvious that it does more than add something to the theory; it also detracts from it a good deal. Here the affirmation of faith that Yahweh gave the victory to his people is supplemented by an episode which reduces it to a small local feud, to a wretched assassination, against all accepted rules. However, the episode was probably rooted too deeply in the tradition for the Deuteronomists to be able to suppress it; they thus preferred the risk of repeating it to the risk of leaving it out.

[23–24] (f) The conclusion seems incomplete here: it is completed with that of 5.31b, which provides the chronological note now lacking, and which reveals the character of texts cited and

---

[21]For the problem see the study by S. Nyström, *Beduinentum und Jahwismus*, Lund 1946, 109ff.

revised by what was the most notable historiographical school in Israel.

(b) Chapter 5

Select bibliography (in alphabetical order): P. R. **Ackroyd**, 'The Composition of the Song of Deborah', *VT* 2, 1952, 160–2; W. F. **Albright**, 'The Song of Deborah in the Light of Archaeology', *BASOR* 62, 1936, 26–31; A. **Alt**, 'Meros', *ZAW* 58, 1940–41, 244–7 (=*KlSchr* I, 1953, 274–7); J. J. **Bimson**, *Redating the Exodus and Conquest, JSOT*, SS 5, 1978, 194–200; H. **Birkeland**, 'Hebrew *zāē* and Arabic *ḏū*', *Studia Theologica* 2, Lund 1948, 201f.; J. **Blenkinsopp**, 'Ballad Style and Psalm Style in the Song of Deborah – a Discussion', *Bibl* 42, 1961, 61–76; J. **Bowman**, 'Benjamin and Amalek and Paul the Apostle', *Abr Nahrain* 13, Leiden 1972, 88–91; C. H. W. **Brekelmans**, 'Some Translation Patterns in Judges V 29', *OTS* 15, 1970, 170–3; K. J. **Cathcart**, 'The "Demons" in Judges 5.8a', *BZ* NF 21, 1977, 111f.; H. **Cazelles**, 'Débora (Jud. V 14), Amaleq et Mâkîr', *VT* 24, 1974, 235–8; M. D. **Coogan**, 'A Structural Analysis of the Song of Deborah', *CBQ* 40, 1978, 132–66; J. **Coppens**, 'La théophanie de Jud. V, 4–5', *EThL* 43, 1967, 528–31; P. C. **Craigie**, 'A Note on Judges V 2', *VT* 18, 1968, 397–9; id., 'Some Further Notes on the Song of Deborah', *VT* 22, 1972, 349–53; id., 'The Song of Deborah and the Epic of Tukulti-Ninurta', *JBL* 88, 1969, 253–65; id., 'Three Ugaritic Notes on the Song of Deborah', *JSOT* 1, 1977, 33–48; id., 'Deborah and Anat: A Study of Poetic Imagery', *ZAW* 90, 1978, 374–81; F. M. **Cross**, *Canaanite Myth and Hebrew Epic*, Cambridge, Mass. 1973, 100ff.; **Cross** and D. N. **Freedman**, *Studies in Ancient Yahwistic Poetry*, Diss. Phil., Johns Hopkins University, Baltimore 1950, 27–42, reissued Missoula, Montana 1975; A. D. **Crown**, 'Judges V 15b–16', *VT* 17, 1967, 240–2; G. R. **Driver****, 1964, 7–12; O. **Eissfeldt**, 'Gottesnamen in Personennamen als Symbole menschlicher Qualitäten', *Festschrift W. Baetke*, Weimar 1966, 110–17 = *KlSchr* IV, Tübingen 1968, 276–84; D. N. **Freedman**, 'Early Israelite History in the Light of Early Israelite Poetry', *Unity and Diversity*, ed. H. Goedicke and J. J. M. Roberts, Baltimore 1975, 3–34; G. **Garbini**, 'Il cantico di Debora', *La parola del passato* 178, Naples 1978, 5–31; id., 'Parzōn, "Iron" in the Song of Deborah?', *JSS* 23, 1978, 23f.; T. H. **Gaster****, 1969, 418f.; G. **Gerleman**, 'The Song of Deborah in the Light of Stylistics', *VT* 1, 1951, 168–80; A. **Globe**, 'The Text and Literary Structure of Judges 5, 4–5', *Bibl* 55, 1974, 168–78; id., 'Judges V 27', *VT* 25, 1975, 362–7; id., 'The Muster of the Tribes in Judges 5, 11e–18', *ZAW* 87, 1975, 168–84; O. **Grether**, *Das Deboralied*, Gütersloh 1941; P. W. **Lapp**, 'Taanach, by the Waters of Megiddo', *BA* 30, 1967, 9–20; É. **Lipinski**, 'Judges 5, 4–5 et Psaume 68, 1–11', *Bibl* 48, 1967, 185–206; A. D. H. **Mayes**, 'The Historical Content of the Battle against Sisera', *VT* 19, 1969, 353–60; id. **,**

1974, ch. III; P. D. **Miller**, *The Divine Warrior in Early Israel*, Cambridge, Mass. 1973, 87–102; H.-P. **Müller**, 'Aufbau des Deboraliedes', *VT* 16, 1966, 466–59; T. **Piatti**, 'Una nuova interpretazione metrica, testuale, esegetica del canto di Debora', *Bibl* 27, 1946, 65–106, 161–209; C. **Rabin**, 'Judges 5:2 and the "Ideology" of Deborah's War', *JJS* 6, 1955, 129f.; G. **Rietzschel**, 'Zu Jdc 5, 8', *ZAW* 81, 1969, 236f.; id., 'Zu Jdc 5, 14b–15a', *ZAW* 83, 1971, 211–25; W. **Richter****, 1963, 65–112; M. **Rose**, ' "Siebzig Könige aus Ephraim" (Jdc V 14)', *VT* 26, 1976, 447–52; E. **Sellin**, 'Das Deboralied', in *Festschrift O. Procksch zum 60. Geburtstag . . .*, Leipzig 1934, 149–66; C. A. **Simpson****, 1957, 17–24; K.-D. **Schunck**, *Benjamin*, BZAW 96, 1963, 48–57; R. **Smend**, *Jahwekrieg und Stämmebund*, FRLANT 84, 1963, 10–19; J. A. **Soggin**, 'Il canto de Debora, Giudici, cap. V', *RANL* VIII. 32, 1977, 97–112; E. **Täubler****, 1958, ch. v; M. **Weinfeld**, ' "They Fought from Heaven" – Divine Intervention in War in Ancient Israel and in the Ancient Near East', *Eretz Israel* 14, 1978, 23–30 (in Hebrew, English summary); A. **Weiser**, 'Das Deboralied – eine gattungs- und traditionsgeschichtliche Studie', *ZAW* 71, 1959, 67–97; Z. **Weisman**, *'srwth* (Judg. V 29)', *VT* 26, 1976, 116–19; Y. **Yadin**, ' "And Dan, Why Did He Remain in Ships?" (Judges V, 17)', in *Australian Journal of Biblical Archaeology* 1, Sydney 1968, 9–23; H.-J. **Zobel**, *Stammesspruch und Geschichte*, BZAW 95, 1965, 44–52.

The Song of Deborah has been considered by the majority of scholars to be the earliest text in the Hebrew Bible; it is rich in archaic terms and expressions, and does not seem yet to know of the institution of the monarchy in Israel, although the people are already settled in the land of Canaan. The dates which are most frequently given for the battle run from the beginning to the end of the twelfth century BC, usually the latter; recently, however, two British scholars, Mayes and Bimson, have proposed alternative dates. As we saw in the previous chapter, Mayes refers the battle to the period immediately preceding the battles narrated in I Sam. 4 and therefore a little before 1150; by contrast Bimson thinks of a period in the thirteenth century BC. However, to do this is not yet to have dated the text; this can only be done on the basis of objective elements, such as study of the language used and the references in the text itself. This is the starting point for the recent study by G. Garbini, the first which has been concerned with the question starting from objective linguistic data. Garbini comes to the conclusion that here we have a phase of Hebrew earlier than the classical Hebrew of the eighth century but later than that of the agricultural 'calendar' of Gezer, from the end of the tenth century

BC, not to mention Ugaritic and ancient Phoenician (the sarcophagus of Ahiram). The poem in fact already knows the definite article, which does not yet appear in the writings quoted, and it has the normal forms of the plural construct (as opposed to the type *yrḥw* found in Gezer); its poetry, far from falling into the category of 'primitive',[1] shows a great ability in the use of refined techniques like parallelism, which also presupposes a familiarity with the language which can only be the result of long practice. At all events, it seems necessary to reject the theory which associates aesthetic categories (impressions of immediacy, expressive force, barbaric solemnity, etc.) with a possible dating, because this is far too subjective.

Redactional superscription (v. 1)
5 [1]On that day Deborah and Barak, the son of Abinoam, sang the following song:

Invitation to the benediction (v. 2)
2 Because in Israel the people have regained liberty,
because the people offered themselves willingly,
bless the Lord!

Invocation (v. 3)
3 Hear, O kings – give ear, o princes;
to the Lord I will, I will sing,
I will make melody to the Lord, the God of Israel!

Confession of faith (vv. 4f.)
4 O Lord, when you go forth from Seir,
when you advance from the territory of Edom,
the earth trembles – the heaven leaps,
the clouds turn into water.
5 The mountains leap before the Lord,
the Lord of Sinai,
Before the Lord, the God of Israel!

The situation before the battle (vv. 6–8)
6 In the time of Shamgar ben Anath,
in the time of the yoke,
the traders had ceased,
and those who went on journeys

---

[1]I realize that the term 'primitive' is at the least ambiguous in a context like this one. I have used it here to indicate the way in which a not very skilled immigrant makes use of a local language: cf. the text of the *Lex Romana Wisigothorum* or of the *Edictum Rothari*, which use Latin (because the law had to be promulgated in Latin), but a totally inadequate Latin compared with the standard of the language in the Roman empire.

·chose devious routes.
7 The leading class was inactive in Israel,
it was inactive in Israel
until you arose, Deborah,
you arose, O mother in Israel!
8 God chose new men.
In those times there was no defence for five cities,
there were not lances or spears
among the forty groups in Israel!

Invitation to celebration (v. 9)
9 Lift up your hearts, mighty ones of Israel;
those of the people who volunteered, bless the Lord!

Invitation to the song (vv. 10f.)
10 O you who ride on tawny asses,
O you who sit on carpets,
O you who walk by the way,
tell it forth!
11 Louder than the cry of those who distribute water near the
drinking places,
let the glorious achievements of the Lord be sung,
his glorious achievements in directing Israel.
Then the troops of the Lord marched down to the gates.

Invitation to Deborah and Barak (v. 12)
12 Awake, awake, O Deborah,
awake, awake, intone a song.
Arise, O Barak, take prisoner those who have made you captive,
O son of Abinoam!

The roll-call of the tribes (vv. 13–18)
13 Then down marched the remnant with its valiant ones,
the troops of the Lord marched down for him,
together with the mighty ones.
14 From Ephraim the captains arrived from Amalek:
'Following you, Benjamin, with your troops.'
From Machir marched down the captains,
and from Zebulon those who carry the commander's staff.
15 The princes of Issachar are united with Deborah in the revolt,
Issachar was a support for Barak,
entering the Valley behind him.
From the groups of Reuben there were numerous brave hearts!
16 But why did you remain sitting under the pack-saddles,
listening to the shepherds' pipes?
Among the groups of Reuben men were brave only at heart.
17 Gilead continued to camp beyond the Jordan;
Dan, why did he remain among the ships?

Asher remained on the coast of the sea –
and continued to camp near his gates.
18 Zebulon is a people which risked their life to death,
Naphtali, too, on the heights of the field!

The battle (vv. 19–23)
19 The kings joined in combat,
to fight, the kings of Canaan,
at Taanach, near to the waters of Megiddo,
but they did not get any spoils of silver.
20 From heaven the stars also fought,
from their courses they fought against Sisera.
21 The torrent Kishon swept them away,
the torrent attacked them, the torrent Kishon.
May you press down the necks of the powerful!
22 Then the hoofs of the horses clattered,
because of the charges of the charging steeds.
23 'Curse Meroz, says the messenger of the Lord,
curse for ever its inhabitants.
Because they did not come to the aid of the Lord,
to the aid of the Lord with mighty men.'

The flight of Sisera (vv. 24–27)
24 Blessed among all women is Jael,
a woman of the Kenite group,
blessed among all tent-dwelling women!
25 Sisera asked for water
and she gave him milk;
in a cup from a noble banquet
she offered him cream.
26 With her left hand she took up a tent peg,
with her right hand she took the mallet:
she struck Sisera, she split his head,
she shattered his temple.
27 Between her feet he sank, he fell, he lay:
there where he was struck, fallen, dead.

The mother of Sisera (vv. 28–30)
28 From her window she looked, she peered,
the mother of Sisera, through the lattice:
'Why is his chariot so long in coming,
why does the noise of his chariot delay?'
29 The wisest of her women responds to her,
replies with the word that she would like to hear:
30 'Do you not think that they have found spoil,
that they are there dividing it?
One or two maidens each,

a piece of coloured material for Sisera,
a piece of coloured and embroidered material!
Coloured and embroidered material
for the neck of the plunderer.'

Final invocation (v. 31a)
31 So perish all your enemies, O Lord;
but those who love him,
may they be as the sun when it rises,
with all its might.

Redactional conclusion (v. 31b)
And the land had rest for forty years.

---

[1] '. . . and Barak' could be an addition; in fact only Deborah
sings. Hebrew has the feminine singular, which seems to presuppose
a single feminine subject, but a construction of this kind can also
include Barak, cf. *GesK* § 146a. Verse 1, like 31b, is part of the
redaction and not of the song. **[2]** 'Have regained liberty': a contro-
versial phrase because of the double meaning of the root *pāra'*: 'burst
forth', 'liberate' (also in a negative sense, cf. Prov. 29.18), and 'have
long hair' (Lev. 10.16; 13.45). The majority of scholars prefer this
second interpretation,[2] but the first meaning, already suggested by
BDB, seems more relevant both for the parallelism and for the general
drift of the text. Craigie has suggested: 'When in Israel men were
dedicated unconditionally, when the people . . .', probably on the basis
of the study by Rabin.[3] Rabin suggests rendering the second verb 'to
answer the call with alacrity', which would offer a valid alternative to
what I propose here. **[3]** 'I will, I will . . .': literally: 'I to the Lord,
I will sing.' A. Weiser[4] has proposed: 'I belong to the Lord: I will
sing . . .', thus understanding the first two words as nominal propositions: however, this seems improbable. The verbs used here and their
parallelism are already attested in Ugaritic, *RSP*, Vol. I, ch. i, no. 35;
ii, 581. **[4]** With É. Lipiński[5] I have translated everything in the
present: Yahweh has not in fact come from the south solely to join in
the battle; the text is a confession of faith in the God of Israel who
fights alongside his people whenever that seems necessary. The concept, with the same topographical data, also appears in other passages:
Deut. 33.2; Hab. 3.3 and Ps. 68.8, three archaic or archaizing passages.
This conception, which seems to be very old, is in unresolved tension
with the theology which makes the divine name dwell in the temple

---

[2]Cf. T.H. Gaster **, 1969, 418, and R.G. Boling*, 1975, ad loc.
[3]P.C. Craigie, 1968; C. Rabin, 1955, quoting F. Schwally, *Semitische Kriegsaltertümer*
I: *Der heilige Krieg im alten Israel*, Leipzig 1901, 47.
[4]A. Weiser, 1959, 73.
[5]É. Lipiński, 1967.

of Jerusalem, and is probably earlier than that. 'Leaps': LXX^A read ἐξεστάθη, 'remained immobile, astonished': LXX^B read ἔσταξεν, 'stopped'; other LXX readings have ἐταράχθη, 'remained confused', in Hebrew *nāmōgū* and *nāmōtū* respectively: these are attempts which indicate the embarassment already felt by the ancient translators: the first two are hyperbolic, the third is generic. The division of the cosmos into heaven, earth and mountains is also known in Ugarit, *RSP* I, ii, 71, and in Mesopotamia, as well as in the Old Testament, in Isa. 44.23; 49.13, as Lipiński has rightly pointed out. 'The heaven . . .'; *gam* usually means 'also'; for the usage here cf. *GesK* § 154, n. 1(*c*), and *KB*^{3}, s.v., § 8.   **[5]** 'Leap': the Hebrew read the root *nāzal*, 'loosen', 'flatten', but LXX (ἐσαλεύθησαν) and other ancient translations read *nāzōllū*, from *zll*$_{II}$, 'waver'. It is not easy to choose between the two roots, which are very similar phonetically and also semantically (in any case these are figurative expressions). 'The Lord of Sinai', an attribute of Yahweh's, provided that, following an explanation made by Albright and taken up again by Cross,[6] we understand *zeh* = Arab *du* and Ugaritic *d̠-*, i.e. a relative pronoun. However, not all scholars accept this explanation, and it has recently been rejected by Garbini for very strong reasons.[7]   **[6]** 'In the time of the yoke . . .'; the Hebrew has 'In the time of Jael', but the woman plays a role only at the end of the song; the mention of her here does not therefore perform any function. An explanation proposed by W. R. Albright in 1970 (in Burney*, 1919, 'Prolegomenon', p. 13*), '. . . I myself suspect that we should read *Yabîn* instead of *Yaʿēl* in that verse . . .', explains obscurity by even greater obscurity, cf. above, pp. 63, 70. It also seems improbable that we are dealing here with another Jael, as has been suggested by some scholars (cf. Eissfeldt, art. cit., 110 = 277 n. 1). There remains one other explanation, which is now more than forty-five years old, that of E. Sellin. Followed by O. Grether,[8] he has proposed that we should read *bîmē ʿōl*, thus deleting the second *yod* (*bmy ʿl* for *bmy yʿl*) as dittography, a correction which I have adopted. 'Shamgar' is mentioned here only for the purpose of dating the text: our ignorance about his chronology prevents us from making valid use of this information. 'The traders' or 'the caravans'; the term *ʾōraḥ* is rarely used in Hebrew to indicate the actual route: Gen. 49.17; Josh. 2.7; Isa. 33.8; Job 31.32; it therefore seems better to read *ʾorʿhōt*, while its second mention is a repetition which does not make sense and should probably be deleted.[9] 'Had ceased': root *ḥādal*$_I$; but D. N. Freedman has recently argued that it is *ḥādal*$_{II}$, 'grow fat',

---

[6]F.M. Cross, 1973, 20 n.44; this suggestion was put forward for the first time by W.F. Albright, 1936, and has been recently repeated by J. Vlaardingerbroek, *Psalm 68*, Diss., Amsterdam Free University 1973, 36ff.

[7]G. Garbini, 1978, 23 n. 35; but cf. already H. Birkeland, 1948.

[8]E. Sellin, 1934, and O. Grether, 1941.

[9]A. Weiser, 1959, and W. Richter**, 1963.

cf. I Sam. 2.5.[10] In this case we would have 'grew fat at the expense of the caravans'. But who then is the subject? Who grew fat? Freedman suggests that it is the unclear $p^c r\bar{a}z\bar{o}n$ of the next verse who grew fat. Besides, the caravans would not follow devious ways unless they were forced to. It therefore seems markedly better to retain the traditional interpretation of the text. **[7]** 'The leading class', i.e. the leadership of Israel, following E. Sellin and A. Weiser in the translation of the uncertain $p^c r\bar{a}z\bar{o}n$. R. G. Boling*, 1975, has 'warriors', which would also fit the context well; G. R. Driver**, 1964, 'strength', 'prowess'; Garbini, 1978, sees here a reference to 'iron'; Tg and Syr have corrected it to $p^c r\bar{a}z\bar{o}t$, 'villages', to the inhabitants of which the text would make an indirect reference. Thus we would have a description here of the paralysis of the economy before the success. However, the context seems to favour the proposal made by Sellin and Weiser: an ineffective leading class was succeeded by a better one. 'Was inactive', cf. $\d{h}\bar{a}dal_{I}$ in the preceding verse; D. N. Freedman wants to render: 'The rural population grew rich – in Israel there were riches from booty', adding to the verse the first word of the following verse, ^cad, understood as $^cad_{III}$ 'booty'. In that case, in the following verse we would have, 'Because you arose, Deborah . . .', i.e. the enrichment of the rural population is the consequence of the success. Here, too, however, the version which I have proposed is preferable; it describes the misery before the victory, and then the victory itself, a typical element in narratives of this kind. 'You arose', root qwm in the second person singular feminine, with the archaic termination in $-t\bar{\imath}$, which is attested down to the time of Jeremiah (cf. *GesK* § 44h), and preceded by $\check{s}e$ – 'until', which is also archaic. Some years ago I put forward the possibility that this was an ancient causative in $\check{s}$- (the $\check{s}afel$ form), in which case we would have 'Until you, Deborah, launched a counter-attack . . .'[11] However, LXX and Vg both have the third person singular.

[8] This verse is generally recognized as being corrupt, and it can no longer be restored.[12] It is not a very satisfactory solution to delete v. 8 as a gloss which tries to give a theological explanation of the devious routes; in general, explanations, even theological ones, tend to clarify rather than complicate still further. Here I have adopted the interesting proposal made by Craigie (1972), prepared for by the study by Rietzschel (1969), that we should read $^{\prime}az$ $l^c\d{h}\bar{a}m\bar{e}\check{s}$ $^c\bar{a}r\bar{\imath}m$ . . . , dividing the consonants differently, even if this is not definitive: in fact $^{\prime}az$, 'then', appears often in the song, but it is never attested in nominal

[10]D.N. Freedman, 1975. This is on the basis of M.L. Chaney, *HDL-II and the Song of Deborah: Textual, Philological and Sociological Studies in Judges 5*, PhD Diss., Harvard University 1976, and other studies by the same author, to which I have no access.

[11]'Tracce di antichi causativi in $\check{s}$-, realizzati come radici autonome in ebraico biblico', *AION* 25, 1965, 17–30, ET in *OTOS*, 188–202.

[12]D.N. Freedman, 1975; for other proposals cf. J. Gray*, 1967.

propositions (Richter **, 1963). The Hebrew has a rather obscure reference either to bread, *leḥem*, or to the battle, root *lāḥam*; in the latter case it seems unlikely that we should think of the Canaanite god of war, in whose time people laid down or consecrated arms. 'Groups': here the Hebrew *'elep*, thousands, thousand, seems to have the meaning of a unit, probably political and ethnic or military, contrary to what is indicated in 4.6: cf. Mendenhall's article quoted there. D.N. Freedman (1975) thinks in terms of forty units on the basis of the inscription of Mesha, king of Moab, line 20,[13] but the reference is not precise. In any case, it is probable that what we have here is a mention of 'forty groups', and that the note is of the same kind as I Sam. 13.19–22, describing the poor state of weapons in Israel. At the beginning of the verse, many people want to interpret, 'They chose new gods. . .', a solution which K.J. Cathcart (1977) refines to 'They chose new gods – yes, demons – *laḥmu* (attested in Babylonia) at the gate'; the two proposals seem nonsensical in the present context. **[9]** 'Lift up your hearts. . .' with Driver**, 1964, and Craigie, 1972 : this is better than 'my heart is for the mighty ones of Israel'. **[10]** The tawny ass is still much sought after today in the Arab world: for antiquity cf. *RSP* I, iii, 24. 'Carpets' : the Hebrew *middīn* is of uncertain meaning, and Boling*, 1975, thinks of a derivative from the root *dyn*, 'judge', 'sit in judgment', and therefore, 'O you who sit in judgment. . .', cf. Prov. 28.7; however, O. Grether, as early as 1941, followed by W. Richter**, 1963, suggests rather a relationship with *mad*, '(valuable) carpet', similarly KB^3, cf. the Ugaritic *md* (Aistleitner, no. 1517); this proposal seems better, because it brings out the divisions in the invocation: those who ride, those who walk, those who sit, hence 'All you who. . .'. It seems unlikely that we should add the initial *m* of the first word of the following verse to the last word in order to have a *mem* enclitic (Freedman, 1974). **[11]** 'Louder than the cry. . .'; the comparative, usually expressed by the preposition *min*, is suggested here by Weiser, 1959. 'Those who distribute water', with KB^3, on the basis of the scene observed and recorded by Dalman.[14] 'They sing. . .': root *tānāh*, 'repeat, sing (in epic or heroic poetry)', cf. 11.40 and probably Ps.8.2 in my recent suggestion.[15] 'Glorious achievements' is one of the meanings of *ṣᵉdāqōt*, literally 'righteous actions'; R.G. Boling*, 1975, rightly has 'victories'. 'In directing. . .': cf. v. 7a. 'Marched down': probably from the high city, often the site of the temple, to the lower city; however, the text does not place any stress on topography apart from 'the gates'. In ch. 4, on the other hand, we have the descent from Tabor. 'To the gates': in ancient Syria and Palestine the gate of the city performed

---

[13]*KAI* 181; *SSI* I, 71.

[14]G. Dalman, *Arbeit und Sitte in Palästina*, VI, Gütersloh 1939 and reprints, 274ff.

[15]For the verb in this last text see my 'Psalm VIII, vv. 2–3 und 6', *VT* 21, 1971, 565–71. For the Ugaritic, cf. Aistleitner, no. 2898, 2.

the function of the Greek ἀγορά: it was the seat of the assembly of the people and it was here that festivals were celebrated. The text presupposes that Israel is living in fortified villages, if not in cities, another feature which supports Garbini's theory which puts the song at the time of the early monarchy. Verses 11c–18 are corrupt, but Globe, 1975, presents a reconstruction of his own. [12] The song to be sung is not this song of Deborah, but the song which the women, who remained behind in the camp, used to sing during the battle (Gaster**, 1969, 419); the scene is similar to that in Ex. 15.1–21. We should follow Globe, 1975, in noting the untranslatable play on words *d'bōrāh* – *dabb'rī*. 'Who have made you captive': with E. Sellin, 1934, read *šōbēkā* for the Massoretic *šeby'kā* on the basis of a variant reading attested by Syr (*BHS*): here once again we find ourselves in the phase of invocations; it is too soon to have taken prisoners. For a different interpretation cf. H.P. Müller, 1966, 92f. [13] The meaning is doubtful. LXX[B] read: 'Then those who remained came down with the mighty men', a reading which I have adopted with slight changes. 'The remnant': this is not clear. Some authors have proposed an emendation, reading 'Israel' for the compound expression, but this is clearly a *lectio facilior*, as well as being a truism. It could be an unknown military technical term, as the parellelism would suggest. 'The troops of the Lord' is not an allusion to the sacral alliance, which, as we shall see, was not involved, but simply to the participants. [14] Another doubtful verse. Scholars are divided into two camps: those who see the text as a negative comment on Ephraim, which is accused of having put down roots in its own land ('in Amalek': the emended text reads 'in the valley') and therefore of not having joined in the battle despite the summons; and those who, on the contrary, see this as an affirmation that Ephraim did join in the battle in force, following its southern neighbour Benjamin. The choice between these alternative translations depends on which conjecture we make; without one the text is incomprehensible. 'From Ephraim. . .': with E. Sellin, 1934; C.P. Craigie, 1972; and A. Globe, 1975. 'In the valley': the reading of LXX[A] (ἐν κοιλάδι) has usually been proposed by those who consider the Hebrew text, 'in Amalek', absurd. However, quite apart from the methodological problem of extrapolating the meaning of a word or an expression from a translation, the Hebrew text makes sense provided that one accepts that the reference is not necessarily to Israel's ancient enemy, located much further south, but to an Amalek on the high plateau: cf. the commentary and Soggin 1982. This area is identified by 12.12–15 as the region in which the place Pirathon is located, a place now identified almost unanimously with the Arab village of Farata (coord. 166–177); in that case 'Mount Amalek' would be about six miles south-west of present-day Nablūs, near the lorry route towards *qalqīliya*. For a contrary view see the recent study by E. A. Knauf (1983), who suggests the deletion of the phrase *šoršām*

who thinks of the Egyptian term *srs*, or, following the correction proposed by Sellin, 1934, *śārīm*, 'princes', for the Massoretic *śorśām*, cf. v. 14; this reading is attested in LXX manuscripts, but could be a correction to get out of the problem of an incomprehensible reading. 'Following you': literally, 'after you. . .': this is an expression which is also attested in Hos. 5.8f. and is perhaps a war cry: however, in Hosea the text is corrupt and is always emended. Others have proposed a correction to *'aḥīkā*, 'your brother', for reasons which, if they do not resolve the problem, at least show its complexity. 'Commander's staff': *sōpēr* is often connected with the Akkadian *śapāru*, 'have command', or even with the Akkadian *siparru*, 'bronze', and therefore 'sceptre (of bronze)', cf. Boling*, 1975. **[15]** 'The princes of Issachar. . .' with all the ancient versions; MT has 'my princes', which cannot be discarded completely; the subject could be Yahweh, cf. v. 7b; however, it seems improbable, as here we have the older, secular part of the poem. Another more remote possibility is presented by reading the suffix -*ay* as a possessive third person pronoun masculine singular of the kind that we find in Phoenician,[16] following the argument put forward by Globe, 1975 : in that case we would have 'His [the Lord's] princes. . .' G.R. Driver**, 1964, suggests connecting the *b'*- of Issachar with the previous word, producing *w'śārab*, a root attested in Syriac with the meaning 'rebel', cf. Ezek. 2.6 and Ecclus. 41.2, where it appears with *samek*; in that case we would have 'Issachar joined in the rebellion. . .' C. Rietzschel, 1971, on the other hand, thinks that a line has fallen out and suggests the following new reading of v. 15a: *b'yiśśākār 'am d'bōrāh – b''ēmeq śull'hū b'raglayw*, 'With Issachar is the troop of Deborah – on the plain it has followed behind them.' For the second 'Issachar' see C.F. Burney*, 1919; H.–W. Hertzberg*, 1958; A. Vincent*, 1958. A. Penna*, 1963, and S. Mowinckel[17] suggest that we should read 'Naphtali', the tribe in the north which is absent here, but mentioned as a protagonist in 4.6ff.; the correction is accepted by Mayes**, 1974, 86, and considered probable by Gray*, 1967. But Naphtali appears in v. 18b. There are no text-critical reasons for this emendation; the operation confuses the time in chs. 4 and 5; the present text evidently gives the *lectio difficilior* and therefore I have kept it. *kēn* is probably 'support', 'sustenance', 'base', on the basis of the Arabic *kinnu* or *kinānu*, 'covering', 'protection'. 'Behind him', or 'under his command', cf. on 4.10 (Boling*, 1975). 'Brave hearts': here Boling points to the existence of a play on words which can also partly be reproduced in a translation: the 'resolute of heart', and therefore the verbal resolutions, are many, but not everyone gives a specific pledge:

---

[16]Cf. J. Friedrich, *Phönizisch-punische Grammatik*, AnOr 32, ²1970, § 112, 1.I.c, p. 48, an element taken up again by Globe (1975).

[17]S. Mowinckel, ' "Rahelstämme" und "Leastämme" ', in *Von Ugarit nach Qumran, Festschrift O. Eissfeldt*, BZAW 77, 1958, 129–50: 137 n. 15.

points to the existence of a play on words which can also partly be reproduced in a translation: the 'resolute of heart', and therefore the verbal resolutions, are many, but not everyone gives a specific pledge: Reuben remains where he is, cf. also A.D. Crown, 1967. **[16]** 'Pack-saddle': *mišp'taym* is a crux, but it probably signifies the baskets or other items which hang down from the two sides of the saddles of asses and mules, cf. the dual and KB^3; this solution is better than the rendering 'sheepfolds' or 'pens' (Zobel, 1965), or the more recent one of 'embankments' or 'walls' (Craigie, 1977). Here we have an effective and insulting comparison with beasts of burden who, either through laziness, or because their load is too heavy, lie down under their loads; it could also be a sarcastic statement that noble resolutions have not even been taken so far as saddling animals (against Gray*, 1967). 'Only': this has been inserted into the translation to bring out the nobility of the words and intentions, and their ineffectiveness. Thus the last line should not be understood as a duplicate of v. 15b, much less should it be deleted, as some scholars would prefer (cf. *BHS*).

[17] 'Among the ships': W. F. Albright, 1953, 132, followed by KB^3, thinks that the Danites had been recruited as sailors; however, the term, separated as it is from the preposition of usage, should be connected with the Ugaritic *'an*, root *'wn* (Aistleitner, no. 292), 'be strong, secure', here used with disparaging connotations: 'in security, secure': in this case the *lāmmāh* should be deleted, with Vg and Tg (Gray*, 1967, and recently Craigie, 1977), but it seems better to leave it as a rhetorical question. In that case the text would not offer any information about the location of the tribe of Dan. If, on the other hand, we accept Albright's suggestion, we are confronted with the complex problem of the region in which Dan is thought to be located by this text: in the south (cf. also below on ch. 13), or in the north (cf. also on ch. 17). Dan was not by the sea-shore, or near to a lake or river of any substance. Y. Yadin (1968) has suggested that because a part of Dan was still in the south, it would have been thought of as being by the sea-shore. However, the hypothetical nature of these proposals is accentuated further by the difficulty of knowing how to understand the term *'niyōt* properly. **[18]** 'Zebulon' appears here for the second time after v. 14; so would Naphtali, if we were to accept the correction proposed to the same verse; the reasons for this dupli-cation are not clear, but it is certain that according to ch. 4 this is one of the two main tribes in the battle. 'Which pledged', or 'which risked . . .'; cf. KB^3. For the 'heights' which also exist in the flatter plain and have strategic value, cf. II Sam. 1.21 (Boling*, 1975).   **[19]** 'In combat . . . to fight': in this case the Hebrew coordinates, and does not subordinate, as we would do. 'Taanach' is identified with the present-day *tell ta'nek* (coord. 171–214), excavated a short while before the Six-Day War of 1967. It should be noted how the battle takes place further south than in ch. 4.   **[20]** '. . . the stars': the *atnah* goes below *kōkābīm*, thus making a complete phrase; otherwise the proposition remains without the subject. The combination of heaven and stars, rare in the Old Testament, is frequent in Ugaritic, where the latter are one of the sources of rain, cf. J. Gray*, 1967, and *RSP* I, ii, 556. Recently, Blenkinsopp, 69ff.; Mayes, 89ff.; and Sawyer have argued, rather, for a solar eclipse – but in that case why the escape on foot, which would be quite explicable in the case of a downpour? The intervention of the stars in situations of this kind is also known in Babylon. There are other oriental examples in M. Weinfeld, art. cit., who reminds us of a campaign by Thutmosis III in Mitanni, of elements in Greek epic, etc. The connection with a thunderstorm, which would be quite rare during the summer, seems to be an obvious one. **[21]** 'Attacked them': this reading follows the majority of commentators, *BHK*³ and *BHS*: *qiddᵉmām*, for the inexplicable *qᵉdūmīm*, 'primordial'.¹⁸ The functions of the last line in this context are obscure: an augury? The 'neck': note the *yod compaginis*.¹⁹ **[22]** 'Clattered': with W. F. Albright, 1936, and Cross and Freedman, 1950. **[23]** 'The messenger . . .': a term normally used for the angel, a figure which, however, is absent here. T. H. Gaster**, 1969, 419, thinks of some form of prophecy or oracle. The mention of Meroz, a completely unknown locality, presents another difficulty: the logic of the text requires (*a*) that it should be connected in some way with Israel, towards whom it had specific obligations; (*b*) that it was specifically connected with a tribe or group of tribes which came to the battle, cf. O. Grether, 1941, and A. Alt, 1940–41; it would not have any function in the present context as the mention of locality pure and simple, especially if it were Canaanite, in which case its neutrality would have been an advantage to Israel. Alt thinks of a formerly Canaanite locality incorporated into Machir/Manasseh (cf. on v. 14b), in which, suddenly or unexpectedly, there would have been a resurgence of feelings of loyalty towards its own people, or a certain anxiety about the outcome of the battle: because of this it preferred to remain aloof. And this attitude, which Israel would take to be betrayal, would have been caused by its citizens. However, all conjecture is useless, given our ignorance about the location of the village.²⁰ **[24]** 'A woman of the group . . .': cf. on 4.11. For the act cf. on 4.17ff. **[25]** 'Sisera': for the name cf. on 4.2b. 'Milk . . . cream': (not 'butter', given that this is a drink which was offered in a cup); it is a form of curdled milk, *leben* in present-day Arabic and Hebrew, a more liquid form of yoghurt. The parallel 'ask . . . give', absent in Hebrew, is well known in Ugaritic, cf. *RSP* I, ii, 53. **[26]** 'With her left hand'; literally 'with the hand'; however, the parallelism with 'the right hand' implies the left hand.

¹⁸Thus again R. Smend, 1963, 10.
¹⁹R. Meyer, § 45.3.1.
²⁰J. Simons, *GTT*, 559, seems to want to find an identification at any price, whereas Y. Aharoni**, 1967, does not even mention the place.

The parallel is frequent in the Old Testament and in Ugaritic, cf. *RSP* I, ii.218. 'The mallet': the wooden hammer used to knock in the tent pegs. 'Struck. . .split. . .shattered': note the difference from the procedure in 4.22: there she pierces the head of the sleeping fugitive where she has hidden him; here she strikes him on the head, splitting it open, while he is drinking from the cup, on his feet, so that he falls down and lies there (Garbini, 1978) (v. 27). However, I continue to understand *raqqāh* as 'temple'. It is important to see the difference between the two chapters at this point, otherwise the beginning of v. 27 does not make much sense, which is why many scholars delete it (most recently *BHS*). This decision does not comment itself; here we have a dramatic crescendo, in accordance with the technique of climactic parallelism. **[28]** 'Peered': reading *wattabēṭ* with LXX^{BA} (παρέκυψεν and διέκυπτεν), cf. Tg. Incongruously, the Hebrew text anticipates (though sometimes Hebrew style allows this kind of anticipation): 'She lamented'. MT certainly has the *lectio difficilior*. **[29]** 'The wisest. .' reading the singular with Vg; the Hebrew text has the plural, as does Prov. 14.11: for intensification (Brekelmans, 1970)? We might also have an ending in *-at* of a Canaanite type, then misinterpreted by the Massoretes as a plural (Boling, 1975). I have tried to reproduce the sense of what follows in the translation: the literal meaning is 'with her own words'. **[30]** This section could also be the product of a dittography, but cf. v. 27. 'Plunderers', read *šōlēl*, the active qal participle, instead of the Hebrew *šālāl*, 'plunder', with LXX^{BA}.

1. The study of the song of Deborah, one of the earliest pieces of heroic poetry in the Old Testament, is a difficult matter because of a series of objective features: chief among these is the difficulty of the text and the vocabulary. That these are ancient difficulties is clear from recension A of LXX, which in vv. 7, 16, 21, 22 and yet other cases has simply transcribed into Greek letters the Hebrew word which it did not know how to translate, while LXX^B proposes translations which are simply the product of 'the fantastic interpretation of the translator' (Garbini, 1978, 8). In any case, of a total of 30 verses, a full 22 have at least one word, often the key word, which can only be translated in a purely conjectural way; furthermore vv. 2, 10, 11, 13, 14, 21, 22 and 26 are not completely comprehensible. This makes up about a quarter of the whole song (Garbini, 7). Furthermore, the connections with ch. 4 are not always clear. A theory like that put forward by Garbini (25ff.) seems quite probable; according to him the prose version is often simply 'a misunderstanding' of the poetic version and, we might add, was perhaps written precisely because the latter was barely comprehensible even in

antiquity. If this is so, it is also difficult to understand what facts underlie the poem or the prose narrative, even if Mayes (1969, 1974**, cf. on ch. 4) has proposed a theory which seems to make some sense. We will return to it later (p. 97 below).

In part, the only solution to the problems indicated is by way of conjecture. And a good conjecture certainly helps to avoid a dead end and to take us forward, just as medieval maps proved useful to the first navigators.

However, just as the medieval maps could mislead the navigators and make them think, for example, that America was India or that the Caribbean islands were Japan, so faced with conjectures, especially if there are a large number of them as there are here, we need to be very careful.

Again, in the poem there are a number of elements which can be connected with Canaanite poetry of the second millennium BC, especially that of Ugarit. However, difficulties arise as soon as we are called upon to give a critical evaluation of the value of these elements: are they a proof of antiquity or are these simply facts that we have discovered as a result of the new elements with which Ugaritic poetry has provided us? The second of these alternatives seems to be the more probable; these elements which are often called 'West Semitic' in fact appear not only in ancient texts but also in texts which are certainly not old, for example Ecclesiastes and Ecclesiasticus.[21] Thus if we have to recognize the presence of elements known also from Ugaritic poetry, we must remember at the same time that poetry, far more than prose, tends to retain traditional forms, archaic expressions, modes of speech from other times, and does so over a period of centuries. It does not seem, therefore, that the presence of elements which appear in Ugaritic (and which, for example, have been collected and presented in the very useful series *RSP*) can help us to put any kind of date on the text. We must therefore recall the view put forward by Garbini, 1978, and quoted at the beginning of the present chapter: the language of Judg. 5 is older than the classical Hebrew of the eighth century BC but later than that of the so-called Gezer calendar from the end of the tenth century BC, and this fact corresponds with others: the poetry of the song presupposes a poetic tradition of some magnitude and the acquisition of considerable skill;

---

[21]Cf. T. Penar, *Northwest Semitic Philology and the Hebrew Fragments of Ben Sira*, BiblOr 28, 1975, and the bibliography listed there.

there are elements which might suggest a stay of some length in
Canaan. Garbini again notes that here Israel considers itself
quite naturally as master of the land (a fact which is even more
true if v.11c is understood to mean that Israel already lived in
fortified villages or even in cities), and the others as oppressors;
this reflects the point of view of the earlier monarchy, even if
the monarchy is clearly not mentioned. In any case, in studying
the text I have indicated those cases in which the parallelism
with Ugaritic is definite, remembering at the same time, however, that this material is inadequate for dating the poem.

2. An aesthetic and stylistic analysis reveals a series of interesting facts, even if by the nature of things, in many respects
these remain irremediably subjective. In the text I have separated vv. 2, 3, and 4f., but logic would suggest that v. 3 could be
the introduction to vv. 4f.; however, that is not necessarily the
case: the singer's invocation could also refer to v. 6 rather than
to the confession of faith. This latter does not form the object of
the song, and has merely a general cultic value, independently
of the composition in question. The other divisions, however,
are required by the text. A certain break can be noted between
vv. 2–5, 9–11, 13 and 31a, and 6–8, 14–22, with perhaps v. 12
as a connecting link between the two sections, and v. 23 as an
unclear insertion: the blessing, v. 2; the invitation to the song
(addressed to the singer, v. 3; addressed to the 'mighty men of
Israel', v. 9; addressed to the people, vv. 10f.); the confession of
faith, vv. 4f., perhaps meant to correct the mention of the planets
and the stars in v. 20 (Müller). In this, the subject of the action
and the object of the invocation is the God of Israel, described
in terms not unlike those of the orthodox theology of the
eighth- and seventh-century prophets or of Deuteronomy and
Dtr, apart from the mention of his coming from the south. Those
who maintain the theory of the tribal league have plenty of
material in these features to support their theory (but we shall
see in due course that the situation seems more complex); in vv.
9–11, 13 we have other invocations of a Yahwistic type, while
the song concludes with the invocation-curse-blessing of v. 31a.
These are elements which seem to support the theory of A.
Weiser, 1959, that the hymn has its setting in a cultic festival
in honour of Yahweh. In the second part, on the other hand,
we have various descriptions of a heroic type: the situation
before the battle for liberation, vv. 6–8; the invitation to the two
heroes, v. 12, perhaps the 'seam' between the two sections; the

concentration of the tribes summoned to the assembly (vv. 14–18), with exuberant praise for those who take an active part in the battle and with just as heavy reprimands on those who for one reason or another decided to keep away; finally the description of the battle (vv. 19–22). In it, the figure of the God of Israel seems strangely to be absent (as opposed to 4.14ff.), except for a passing mention in vv. 11, 13 and 23; these seem odd, to say the least, after the theological and cultic speech of the other verses; the only elements of a metaphysical character seem to be the planets and the stars in v. 20 (H.-P. Müller, 1966, rightly observes, 449, that they are not in fact taken to be 'in the service of Yahweh'), or 'the messenger' of Yahweh in v. 23, possibly the word of an oracle. Lastly, we have the two anecdotes connected with the person of Sisera: his flight followed by his assassination, in vv. 24–27, parallel to 4.17ff., and the account of his mother, in vv. 28–30, both highly dramatic, but certainly of little value for the historian. It has also been pointed out recently by H.-P. Müller, 1966, that the first of these two last episodes is also the dominant scene here, as in ch. 4. That seems obvious, and is typical of the way in which the stress in stories falls on people and events which are really marginal, but are capable of holding the interest of the audience and arousing its emotions. We find the same sort of thing in all poetry and prose epics. Here too the theological element seems to be missing, whereas in the scene involving Sisera's mother we have a scene like that involving Hector and Andromache in the *Iliad*, Book VI.

Now whereas vv. 2–5 and 9–12 have a dynamic which at first seems independent from that of the rest of the composition, v. 31a makes explicit reference to it, even if it seems applicable to any text which describes the victorious conclusion of a holy war. Furthermore, the two elements presuppose a theological systematization which suggests a later stage of transmission, when the ancient epic was inserted into a theological and cultic context intended to provide an interpretative key: the hymn is no longer about the 'mighty men of Israel' or their commanders, but 'the glorious deeds of the Lord . . .' in leading Israel (v. 11a). The coalition of the tribes of Israel becomes 'the Lord's troops' (v. 11b). We have moved from a war which broke out for political and economic reasons, as the epic clearly affirmed (vv. 6f.), a situation accentuated by the sluggishness of the ruling class in Israel (v. 8), to the 'holy war'; from voluntary participation,

limited to the tribes direcly interested in the enterprise, to com-
pulsory participation (and woe to those who do not come) which
has now become a cultic matter! Thus a different atmosphere
seems to prevail in each of the two sections which make up the
song: furthermore, the one which is rich in cultic elements seems
to have been composed in the train of the second, as it were
'lay', song, which is considerably older; however, the operation
has been performed with skill, so that the two sections reflect a
style and a complex of imagery which is not very different.

Thus 'the actual song of Deborah' (Richter**, 1963, 91) comprises vv. 6–8 and (12)13–30, and is divided into the following
sub-sections: (a) prelude (vv.6–8); (b) the assembling of the
combatants (vv. 13–18); (c) a description of the battle (vv. 19–
22 [23?]); (d) the flight and killing of Sisera' (vv. 24–27); (e) the
waiting mother (vv. 28–30). Richter**, 1963, also includes vv.
9–11, but they seem to belong to another section, the theological
one. Each of the sub-sections in question has its own characteristics, but none of them is likely to have had any independent
existence (Richter**, 102f.).

3. It is apparently quite simple to determine the literary genre
of the song; it is a heroic poem, surrounded with liturgical
elements (vv. 2–5, 9–11, 31a); its aim is to arouse among the
audience a sense of identification with the tribes which responded positively to the call, and condemnation for those who stayed
at home (Richter**, 1963, p. 104: *Werbelied*, that is, a song which
is aimed at arousing dedication in the community in which it is
sung). From this point we can go on to look at its *Sitz im Leben*.
According to the suggestion made by A. Weiser, 1959, to which
I have already referred, the song will have been used in the
context of the worship of the tribal league, a theory which has
also been supported by K.-D. Schunck, 1963; J. Gray, *1967;
and the works of A. Bentzen and W. Beyerlin;[22] the last two
think specifically of the covenant renewal festival. G. Garbini,
1978, also mentions the cultic interpretation with approval, as

---

[22]W. Beyerlin, *Herkunft und Geschichte der ältesten Sinaitraditionen*, Tübingen 1961, 92ff.;
ET, *Origins and History of the Earliest Sinaitic Tradition*, Oxford 1965, 79f.; but cf. already
A. Bentzen, *Introduction to the Old Testament*, Copenhagen ³1957, 138f. Cf. also Schunck,
1963, 52f., and Mayes, 1974, 85. J.J. Bimson, *Relating the Exodus and Conquest*, *JSOT*, SS
5, 1978, 108f., criticizes the argument put forward by A.D.H. Mayes, but goes against
an ever-increasing consensus by assuming that the name Sisera should not be connected
with the Sea Peoples.

1978, also mentions the cultic interpretation with approval, as does J. Blenkinsopp, 1961. However, quite apart from the problems raised by the theory of the amphictyony, if the remarks that I made earlier are valid, there is a difference between the 'main body' of the hymn with its heroic content, from which Yahweh is conspicuously absent, and the liturgical 'framework' in which he seems rather to be the protagonist of the action and the object of adoration. It therefore seems more probable that we should suppose that in the period before Josiah's reform, i.e. in the pre-Dtr period, the heroic song in the strict sense was integrated into the cult. This, however, is an insertion and not its original setting; and as a result of this insertion it is now Yahweh who performs wonders for his people, relegating human factors and agents to a lower plane. It is possible to conjecture that the original song was contained in accounts like the 'Book of the Wars of Yahweh', but we cannot say more than that.

4. Reconstruction of the historical context of the song (as of ch. 4, which precedes it) is a difficult task. We have looked at the theory put forward by Mayes (1969 and 1974**), according to which the battle would be dated a little before the battles described in I Sam. 4: thus the Philistines will have attacked Israel immediately after their defeat on the plain of Esdraelon. It is a theory which makes sense, and is certainly better than those which think of an indeterminate battle in an even more uncertain period. Otherwise, however, the situation seems complex: we are not even in a position to establish which tribes or groups in fact joined in the struggle. Chapter 4 speaks only of Naphtali and Zebulon, but the topography is confused; in ch. 5, according to MT, we have ten tribes, of which Zebulon is mentioned twice, in vv. 14b and 18a. Levi, Simeon, Judah and the southern groups like Caleb and others are not mentioned. Of the tribes mentioned, five or six play an active part in the battle, four stay away although they are invited, and these are groups which as far as we can see did not have a direct interest in the outcome of the battle either because they were in Transjordan (Reuben and Gilead) or because they were situated at the extremities of the country (Asher to the north-west, and Dan, who may already have been in the north, or perhaps still in the south-west of the country). One important piece of information is that the text connects the battle with the control of traffic through the plain of Jezreel, a control which was impossible to apply while the region was still in the hands of the city

states, which according to 1.27ff., Israel had not succeeded in conquering. What is said in 5.6f. is eloquent testimony here. The impossibility of crossing the plain (except by devious routes which will have cost time and money and not been without danger) separated the north central tribes from those of the north.[23]

Against whom did Israel fight? We do not have a list of Canaanite city-states like the list we have of the tribes of Israel. A large number of scholars now accept the possibility that Sisera is a name belonging to the sphere of the 'Sea Peoples', and as we have seen in the previous chapter, this probably allows us to envisage the enemies of Israel as being a coalition between Canaanites and Philistines. That the Philistines had access to the plain appears clearly from the account of the battle of Gilboa in I Sam. 31, and the hypothesis that the name *harošet haggōyīm* should be connected with one of their invasions is at least possible. Whereas in ch. 4 the battle took place in an area some miles to the north, here it is in the region of Taanach towards the upper, south-east reaches of the Kishon. Notwithstanding the learned speculations of W. F. Albright and his followers, it must be said straightaway (with Mayes, 1969 and 1974**) that the mention of this place, as of the 'waters of Megiddo', says absolutely nothing about whether the city in question was inhabited or abandoned: these are purely and simply topographical indications (Smend, 1963; Schunck, 1963). Thus the destruction of Taanach towards the end of the twelfth century BC, mentioned by P. W. Lapp, 1967, 8f., who excavated the place, as a 'very attractive and alluring hypothesis', cannot be accepted. On the basis of what is said in 1.27ff., it also seems improbable that the Israelite victory over the coalition led to the conquest and the destruction of the places in question. So if these were destroyed, we need to attribute their destruction to other agents, and not to the victorious Israelites. Not only does that lie outside the likely scope of the Israelite victory, which will have been to re-establish broken lines of communication; it seems difficult, given the character of these places as fortified cities. And if it is true that these cities came into Israelite hands under David (and therefore appear in the list of districts established under Solomon, I Kings 4.7ff.), we must remember that nothing is said about their being conquered; it therefore seems

---

[23]Thus already K. Budde*, 1897; cf. R. Smend, 1963, 12f.

probable that they were incorporated into the Israelite empire by means of a treaty or through some other peaceful means. Finally, we must remember that heroic poetry is a literary genre which it is difficult to use for history. Maurice Bowra has warned historians about heroic and poetic texts in these words:

> Heroic poetry, then, seems to be on the whole a poor substitute for history. Though it contains real persons and real events, it often connects them in unreal relations and may even add unreal persons and unreal events . . . This means that, except in a few exceptional cases, we have no right to approach heroic poetry as if it were a record of fact . . . It does not record truthfully what happened, but it shows what men believed and felt.[24]

5. At a certain point, then, Israelite faith felt it necessary to provide this originally secular song with a liturgical and theological framework; it may have been for what we might call 'catechetical reasons', or because it was placed in the context of Israelite worship. A song which celebrated the tribes who came to the battle along with their leaders has now become a song which is essentially a celebration of the God of Israel and his glorious achievements: Yahweh who comes from his southern desert sanctuary is the same god who inspires the judges, the saviours of the people, and the prophets who shed light on him through their words; he is the one who fights the peoples' battles, thus fulfilling his ancient promises. The original scope of the song is twisted by this new interpretation, but it is to that conversion that we owe the fact that a considerable part of the song has been preserved.

In this connection we should consider an interesting theory recently put forward by G. Garbini, 1978, which certainly revolutionizes the study of the content of the song. Garbini begins from two features: the names of the participants and the two levels on which the battle develops and is resolved: the earth, but also heaven. As to the names, Barak means 'lightning' and Jael 'she-goat'. Sisera, a name which, as we have seen, is probably connected with the 'sea peoples', seems to be of Cretan origin, where according to a Minoan Linear A text recently published,[25] it is borne by a Cretan deity. Now if it is the case

---

[24]M. Bowra, *Heroic Poetry*, London 1961, 535, quoted by M.D. Coogan, 1978.

[25]G. Pugliese Carratelli, 'ΣΑΙΣΑΡΑ', *La parola del passato* 166, Naples 1976, 123–8: 125, quoted by Garbini, 1978, 20.

that the battle was fought on the ground between Israel and the Canaanites and Philistines, it is also true that the real victor is Yahweh, just as he is the real combatant. In that case the adversary of Yahweh must have been one or more Canaanite-Philistine deities, whom we know essentially to have been gods of the weather. Dagon, one of the Philistine deities, turns out to have been identified later with Zeus Kretogenes, and here seems to have been beaten with his own weapons: the lightning which he held in his hand (so that Barak, the lightning, takes prisoner the one who took him prisoner, v. 12), the stars which fight for Yahweh, while the action of Jael, the she-goat, seems to be diametrically opposed to that of the she-goat Amaltheia performed towards Zeus on Crete: instead of nourishing him and keeping him alive, she kills him, distracting his attention with food. Of course we would have to postulate the identification of Zeus Kretogenes with the deity Sisera. The whole would then have been historicized, leaving little of the ancient myth. This explanation is interesting, but a number of factors tell against it: first of all, it does not take account of the division of our text and mixes up the heroic part with the theological part; if we accept the legitimacy of the interpretation, we should have to accept that it did not go with the ancient heroic poem but with the later theological interpretation. Furthermore, it seems difficult to identify the person of Sisera, a leader of the 'sea peoples', directly with the Cretan divinity of the same name: in the first place, this is probably not a name but a title, and a feminine one at that (Garbini, 1978, 21); and secondly, there is no reason why this should not be a theophoric name pure and simple without any other element. We should also note that this would be the only place in the Old Testament where it was possible to reconstruct the myth which had been historicized with such precision. These features caution prudence, though it is clear that the approach indicated by Garbini could lead to new, interesting discoveries, especially considering the progressive decipherment of Linear A.

6. We can now go on to examine in detail the differences between ch. 4 and ch. 5 (Kaufmann*, 1962; Richter**, 1963, 111ff.). First of all there is a general one: ch. 4 was written in prose and ch. 5 in verse. Secondly, as we have seen, ch. 4 has a Dtr framework, vv. 1–3, (23–)24, and a main body formed of the other verses, whereas ch. 5 has a theological framework, vv. 2–5, 9–11(12) and 31a, in which has been inserted what remains

of the ancient epic song: vv. 6–8, 13–30. In ch. 4, the narrative is now structured in accordance with the scheme of the 'holy war': God gives the enemies of Israel into their hands (14a), and the battle takes place with Yahweh, who 'goes at the head' of Israel and its leaders (v. 14b), and it is he who brings confusion upon their enemies (v. 15a). Chapter 4 again mentions connections with Jabin of Hazor (vv. 1, 17, 23), all to be attributed to the redactors, an element which is absent from ch. 5. The other *dramatis personae*, too, are not always identical: only the tribes of Zebulon and Naphtali appear in ch. 4, and more tribes are mentioned in ch. 5. It is difficult to say which version is closer to the events: Smend, 1963, prefers that of ch. 5, but it is difficult to come down on one side or the other: Barak is a man of Naphtali (4.6), so it seems to be certain that his tribe took part in the battle; Deborah comes from the area called the 'Mountain of Ephraim', but does this mean that she was an Ephraimite? Chapter 4 gives some details about the armaments of Israel's enemies (vv. 2, 13, etc.); ch. 5 puts more stress on the economic and political reasons for the battle, and here hits on an element which seems to be essential. The geographical context also seems to be different: ch. 4 describes the battle as having taken place more in the north, while for ch. 5 it is further south, although the two areas are united by the river Kishon. The way in which Sisera is assassinated also seems to be different: in ch. 4 he is stabbed in the temple with a tent peg while he is sleeping concealed in the tent; in ch. 5 he is struck on the head while drinking the drink offered to him, so that he falls to the ground. Furthermore, ch. 4 does not have the curse on Meroz and the scene with Sisera's mother.

*

Gideon

Bibliography: (a) On the entire section: C.F. **Burney**, 'The Topography of Gideon's Rout of the Midianites', in *Studien zur semitischen Philologie und Religionsgeschichte, Festschrift Julius Wellhausen*, BZAW 27, 1914, 87–99; A. **Malamat**, 'The War of Gideon and Midian, a Military Approach', *PEQ* 84, 1952, 61–5; L. **Alonso-Schökel**, 'Heros Gedeon', *VD* 32, 1954, 1–20; C.A. **Keller**, 'Über einige alttestamentlichen Heiligtumslegenden I', *ZAW* 67, 1955, 154–62; E. **Kutsch**, 'Gideons Berufung und Altarbau', *TLZ* 81, 1956, cols. 75–84; A. **Penna**, 'Gedeone e Abimelek', *BeO* 2, 1960, 86-9 and 136–47; Y. **Kaufmann**, 'The Gideon Stories', *Tarbiz* 30, 1960–61, 139–47 (in Hebrew, with an English summary); W. **Beyerlin**, 'Geschichte und heilsgeschichtliche Traditionsbildung im Alten Testament', *VT* 13, 1963, 1–25; H. **Reventlow**, *Liturgie und prophetisches Ich bei Jeremia*, Gütersloh 1963, 47–51; G.R. **Driver****, 1964, 12–15; W. **Richter** **, 1963, 112–246; 1964**, 97–112; id., *Die sogenannten vorprophetischen Berufungsberichte*, FRLANT 101, 1970, 116, 134ff.; J.A. **Soggin**, *Das Königtum in Israel*, BZAW 104, 1967, 15–20, with bibliography; H. **Haag**, 'Gideon-Jerubbaal-Abimelek', *ZAW* 79, 1967, 305–14; M.-L. **Henry**, *Prophet und Tradition*, BZAW 116, 1969, 19ff.; L. **Schmidt**, *Menschlicher Erfolg und Jahwes Initiative*, WMANT 38, 1970, 5–53, 15–53; A. **Malamat**,** 1971, 141–7; R. **de Vaux**, **,1973, 119–25; ET, 1978, 813–19; H. **Rösel****, 1976, 10–24; J.A. **Emerton**, 'Gideon and Jerubbaal', *JTS* NS 27, 1976, 289–312.

(b) On individual passages: on 6.1–24: A. **de Pury**, *Promesse divine et légende cultuelle dans le cycle de Jacob*, ÉtBibl, 1975, 363f.; on 6.8–24: P. **Kübel**, 'Epiphanie und Altarbau', *ZAW* 83, 1971, 225–31, esp. 227f.; on 6.11–24: G. **del Olmo Lete**, *La vocación del líder en el antiguo Israel*, Bibliotheca Salamanticensis III.2, Salamanca 1973; on 6.25–28: A. **Guillaume**, 'A Note on *happār haššēnī*, Judges VI. 25, 26, 28', *JTS* 50, 1949, 52f.; J.A. **Emerton**, 'The "Second Bull" in Judges 6, 25–28', *Eretz Israel* 14, 1978, 52*–55*; on 6.32: B.O. **Long**, *The Problem of Etiological Narrative in the Old Testament*, BZAW 108, 1968, 27; on 7.1–15: E.L. **Ehrlich**, *Der Traum im Alten Testament*, BZAW 73, 1953, 85–

90; on 7.21: P. **Humbert**, *La 'terou'a', analyse d'un rite biblique*, Neuchâtel 1946, 18; on 8.4–12: S. **Mittmann**, 'Die römische Strasse in der nord-westlichen Belḳa', *ZDPV* 79, 1963, 150–63; on 8.13: id., 'Die Steige des Sonnengottes (Ri.8,13)', *ZDPV* 81, 1965, 80–7; on 8.14; M. **Noth**, 'Überlieferungsgeschichtliches zur zweiten Hälfte des Josuabuches', in *Alttestamentliche Studien F. Nötscher...gewidmet*, BBB 1, 1950, 152–7:154f.; D. **Leveen**, 'The Meaning of *wayikktōb* in Judges viii 14', *JRAS*, 1948, 61f.; D. **Diringer**, 'Early Hebrew Writing', *BA* 13, 1950, 74–95; R. **de Vaux**, *Les Institutions de l'Ancien Testament I*, Paris 1958, 83; ET, *Ancient Israel*, London and New York 1961, 49; O. **Eissfeldt**, *Einleitung in das Alte Testament*, Tübingen ³1964, 916; ET, *The Old Testament. An Introduction*, Oxford and New York 1965, 676; H.-J. **Hermisson**, *Studien zur israelitischen Spruchweisheit*, WMANT 28, 1968, 99–102; H. P. **Rüger**, 'Schreibmaterial, Buch und Schrift', *BRL*, ²1977, 289–92; on 8.18–21: J. **Pedersen**, *Israel: Its Life and Culture*, Copenhagen 1926, I-II, 278ff.; on 8. 22ff.: J. A. **Emerton**, 1976, 298 n.l; G. **Henton Davies**, 'Judges VIII 22–23', *VT* 13, 1963, 151–7; F. **Crüsemann**, *Der Widerstand gegen das Königtum*, WMANT 49, 1978, 42–54; T. **Veijola**, *Das Königtum in der Beurteilung der deuteronomistischen Historiographie*, AASF B-198, 1977, ch. VIII.

1. The complex character of the Gideon tradition is immediately evident even to the non-specialist, as soon as we take note of the following elements. First of all, the double name of the protagonist: *gid'ōn* (eleven times in ch. 6, thirteen times in ch. 7, fifteen times in ch. 8) and *y'rubba'al* (once in ch. 6, once in ch. 7 and twice in ch. 8); moreover the second name also appears outside the Gideon cycle proper: eight times in ch. 9, once in I Sam. 12.11 and once in II Sam. 11.21 (as *y'rubbešet*!). Furthermore, in ch. 9 Abimeleh always appears as son of the second, without the first name ever being mentioned.

Now a double name of this kind would not be impossible in itself; the tradition tells of Jacob-Israel (the second, the eponymous founder of the 'tribal league'), but this designation is also problematical, cf. Gen. 32.28; we also have the case of Solomon/Jedidiah, II Sam. 12.25 (but the second name appears only once); Uzziah/Azariah; Jehoahaz/Shallum, where both the names are well attested, as is clear from the dictionaries and concordances (for other examples see Emerton, 1976, 307ff.), Ezra and Shealtiel, etc. This is leaving aside the instances in which the same person uses two names in succession: Abram-Abraham, Sarai-Sarah, Joseph with an Egyptian name, Jehoiakim, Zedekiah, etc., because in these cases the second name is a *substitute* for the first, which falls into disuse, and does not appear alongside it.[1] In the cases mentioned we often find that a monarch is involved, and we know that in the ancient Near East kings used to have several names, each within the sphere of the functions exercised; or we have a change of linguistic area. Both these cases are quite sufficient to explain the parallelism of two or more names. However, in the case of Gideon the connection between the two names seems somewhat tenuous; *yᵉrubbaʿal* in fact appears to be a surname taken thanks to an affront offered to the Canaanite deity in question, 6.29–32, by means of an etymology of a popular kind, which is in fact erroneous (Emerton, 1976, cf. below). It is therefore difficult to make a decision on the matter: at this point it is enough to say that the Old Testament identifies Gideon with Jerubbaal.

However, there are other elements as well: in ch. 6 various episodes which are related seem originally to have been independent of one another, cf. vv. 11–24, 25–32, 33–35, 36–40; furthermore, they are quite distinct from the Dtr introduction in vv. 1–10. The unifying elements are the person of Gideon and the theme of the Midianite invasion. But there are also tensions in the following chapters: in 7.3–6 and 6.33–35 the members of the 'tribal league' are first called and then sent home for exclusively theological reasons: the presence of divine aid and not human strength is to appear as the decisive factor in the victory; however, hardly have the troops been disbanded than they are summoned back to pursue the Midianites (7.23ff.). Furthermore, in 8.1–3 Ephraim is angry with Gideon for not having been summoned, but this goes directly against what has been explicitly stated in 7.24ff. Nor is it possible to square what is said in 7.1–8.3, where it is the tribal league which fights against Midian, with 8.4–21, where once again the three hundred Abi-ezrites appear. There is also an apparent contrast between the passages in which Gideon is the charismatic leader of his people and appears in continuous dialogue with them, and that where he appears only as vindicator of his brothers killed by the Midianites in circumstances about which we are not told (8.18ff.); in this latter case we evidently have a private or family feud. There is no lack of parallel elements: the building of an altar in 6.11–24 and 6.25–32; the request to God for proof (6.17ff.; 6.31ff., cf. W. Richter **, 1963, 112ff.).

[1]Cf. R. de Vaux, *Les Institutions* . . .I, 74ff.: 78; ET, *Ancient Israel*, 43ff.: 46.

As a result, in the past, the three chapters have seemed to many scholars to be an ideal section for dividing into sources. One authoritative and always interesting attempt is that made by O. Eissfeldt**, 1925,[2] who has been followed more recently by Simpson**, 1947. However, such attempts must be considered mistaken; the only division possible is that between the Deuteronomistic redaction and earlier traditional material. But within this ancient material we have the stratum which refers to the three hundred Abiezrites, and the pan-Israelite material, which extends the action to the 'tribal league'. The seam between these two strata has been produced by the pre-Dtr redaction by means of a narrative device: the tribes appear *en masse* (hence we do not have the problems examined in ch. 5), but the number of the participants, considered too high because the reader could attribute the victory only to the God of Israel, are drastically reduced for theological reasons (7.2b, Beyerlin), by means of two tests: only those who pass them are accepted. Beyerlin rightly observes that here we have an example of the way in which sacred history could be superimposed on secular history. However, the origin of the individual traditions is not uniform either; in 6.11ff., 25ff. we have two aetiological legends on the foundation of two different sanctuaries near to Ophrah (for its location cf. on v. 11), the headquarters of the clan of Abiezer; we also have a reference to two campaigns: one in Cisjordan, 7.1ff., and the other in Transjordan, 8.4ff.

2. Another problem which appears in the text is that of the Midianites. Is it possible to establish whether the text refers to some specific event, and if so to which? Among historians and exegetes there is a tendency not to doubt the substantial historicity of the event, and therefore the difficulties in which Israel found itself,[3] without, however, any success in defining the exact nature of the phenomenon: is it, for example, no more than incursions by semi-nomadic groups, accompanied by plunder and pillaging, or regular transhumance, in which semi-nomadic groups abandoned the desert at the end of the spring to spend some time in the cultivated area now that the harvest was over?

---

[2] See the account in L. Alonso-Schökel, art. cit.

[3] M. Noth, *Geschichte Israels*, Göttingen [2]1954, 148; ET, *History of Israel*, London and New York [2]1960, 161f.; J. Bright, *A History of Israel*, Philadelphia [3]1980, London [3]1981, 180; A. H. Gunneweg, *Geschichte Israels*, Stuttgart 1972, 47ff.; R. de Vaux**, 1978, 813f.; S. Herrmann, *Geschichte Israels*, Munich 1973, 154ff.; ET, *A History of Israel in Old Testament Times*, London and Philadelphia 1975, 115ff.

In such cases clashes and incidents with the local population are always possible, as are reprisals by the latter! This latter theory was put forward by E. Dhorme*, 1956: in 6.2 the phenomenon seems to be repeated at certain intervals, so that when the dangerous season arrives, Israel tries to protect itself by taking measures which seem to be more or less permanent. If this theory is right, then the invasion of the Midianites is not very different from the incursions of the Israelites into the territories near to where they were settled. It is also possible to suppose that the migrating Midianites could be looking for a land, in the same way as the Midianites mentioned in 3.11–30. This would explain the size of the expedition: it was not a matter of just driving back an occasional raid by bandits or semi-nomads, but of providing a remedy for a permanent situation, just as the battle in the previous section could make possible communications among the various Israelite groups. However, such explanations, although they are probable and have the advantage of resolving almost all the problems, are not the only ones possible. Others[4] think rather of an invasion numerically proportionate to the number of the Abiezrites, i.e. a matter of a few hundred. In that case, this would be a single invasion, though spread out over a relatively long period, perhaps by one or more caravans coming towards Midian from the north (Damascus?), which would cross the Jordan at several points and then regroup for the purpose of the raid. That would explain how the groups in Cisjordan were more affected, and not those in Transjordan; they would obviously have been in the front line and would have felt the weight of the invasion to a much greater degree. Furthermore, the route of the flight, first east and then south-east, cf. on 7.22,24b; 8.8,[5] would seem to go against what is said here. In that case, of course, the dimensions of the phenomenon are much reduced, and we simply find a struggle between one clan of Israel and its eastern neighbours. It is certainly a much smaller scale than the first redaction, which speaks of the 'tribal league', would have us believe.[6] Furthermore, the remembrance of these invasions continued to live on in Israelite memory for a long time, cf. I Kings 11.18, and soon took on exemplary value, cf. Ps. 83.10ff. (EVV 9ff.); Isa. 9.3 (EVV 4); 10.26; 60.6; Hab. 3.7, which seems to conflict

[4]Thus, for example, E. Täubler**, 1958, 258ff.
[5]Ibid, 257.
[6]In this sense also R. de Vaux**, 1973/1978.

with the theory that it was a smaller-scale phenomenon. But perhaps not even that: quite independently of the dimensions of the phenomenon, it came to be the symbol of the struggle which Israel had to maintain its own character, especially with people who came from outside (Rösel**, 1976, 10f.).

The problem is not easy to solve, given the difficulties presented by the biblical material. As it stands now, it does not try to give an account of a political and military event, but to proclaim the need for Israel to trust in the God who had also liberated them in the past, rather than in its own might and strength. Given this situation, we must be content with indicating the most probable course of events, even if the texts do not contain elements which the historian would consider fundamental.

3. The very presence of the Midianites in the area is not easy to explain; their habitat is much further south. It is true that v. 3 connects them with 'Amalekites' and with the 'people of the East' generally (this latter term probably describes the inhabitants of Transjordan, cf. 6.33; 7.12: the generic nature of the term prevents it being identified with people known to us, for example the Ammonites, Edomites and Moabites or, later, the Aramaeans), but as we shall see when we look at the text, there are secondary elements here. The Midianites were a semi-nomadic people who inhabited northern Arabia or the Sinai peninsula. They boasted that they were descended from Abram (Gen. 25.2ff.), and one of their caravans took Joseph (Gen. 38.26) and carried him off to Egypt. Moses' father-in-law was a Midianite (Ex. 18.1ff.; Num. 10.29–31). However, already in Num. 22.4–7 we find a coalition of Midian with Moab against Israel, while in Num. 25.6–18, they and Moab lead Israel astray at Baal Peor, cf. ch. 31. These are features which serve to show that groups of Midianites had also reached southern Transjordan. Thus the biblical tradition presents relations between Israel and Midian as variable: sometimes good and at other times bad.

The problem remains open: what are the Midianites doing in central Transjordan, from which they could go over into Cisjordan? Because it is in this particular area that they cross the Jordan and also recross it in their flight. It is less difficult than it might seem to give an answer, which also allows us to resolve the problem of the nature of the incursion. If the mention of Qarqar in 8.10 is really a reference to present-day *qerāqir*, situated in the *wādī sirḥān* (cf. below), we would have a location in the northern *Ḥejaz* and therefore precisely in the region traditionally given as their habitat. They would therefore have left from there for their incursions. And in that case, incursions these would certainly be: the Midianites would then be semi-nomadic raiders, probably not yet in the sedentary stage.

4. One episode to which a great deal of importance has often been attached is the mention of camels in 6.5a; 7.12 and 8.21,26. According to this reconstruction of events, the Midianites will have been a kind of Bedouin[7] who, profiting from the nature of their animals, will have been able to cross deserts quickly and safely, making raids far beyond their own boundaries. However, it is not possible to speak of Bedouin here: the term has a technical significance in ancient Near Eastern studies which is not applicable to the situation of Syro-Palestinian semi-nomad-ism. In any case, according to W. F. Albright[8] and many other scholars in his train, the mention of the camel would be the earliest documentation of a raid carried out with the help of this animal, which had only just been domesticated on a large scale. However it does not seem easy to maintain this theory: we have numerous pieces of evidence that the camel had been domesticated a number of centuries before;[9] moreover, the text speaks of camels only cursorily, and does so in passages coming from the Dtr redaction, whereas protective measures of the kind which appear at the beginning of ch. 6 also can be found in I Sam. 13.6, where there is no mention of camels. This may perhaps explain the remarks made by R. de Vaux**, 1978, 815, 'I am afraid that too much importance has been attached to these camels of the Midianites.' As a result, I shall content myself with pointing to the fact, without attributing more importance to it than it has in the texts.

5. The Gideon cycle can easily be divided into the following units:

(i) The calling and mission of Gideon

   (*a*) The Midianite oppression (6.1–10, Dtr)

   (*b*) Gideon and the altar at Ophrah, under the oak (6.11–24)

[7]See J. Gray*, 1967, and R.G. Boling*, 1975, on the 'Bedouin' character of the Midianites.

[8]*From the Stone Age to Christianity*, Baltimore ²1957, 165ff.; more cautiously in the Introduction to Burney*, ²1919.

[9]Cf. S. Moscati, *Chi furono i Semiti?*, MANL VIII. 8, Rome 1957, 27; cf. R. de Vaux**, 1973, 121; ET, 1978, 815.

(c) Gideon destroys the sanctuary of Baal at Ophrah and builds a second altar (6.25–32)

(d) The call to arms against Midian (6.33–35)

(e) The test of the fleece (6.36–40).

(ii) Campaign in Cisjordan

(a) The army of the sacral alliance and the three hundred Abiezrites (7.1–8)

(b) Favourable omens (7.9–15)

(c) The attack (7.16–22)

(d) The pursuit (7.22–25)

(e) Ephraim's complaint (8.1–3)

(iii) Campaign in Transjordan

(a) Gideon in Transjordan (8.4–12)

(b) Feud and vendetta

(c) Anti-monarchial epilogue (8.22–32)

(d) Dtr conclusion (8.33–35).

(i) The Calling and Mission of Gideon

(a) The Midianite oppression (6.1–10)

6¹ The Israelites did what the Lord thought to be evil; and he delivered them into the hands of Midian for seven years. ²The hand of Midian was heavy upon Israel; for fear of Midian the Israelites made use of hiding places in the mountains, of caves and secluded places. ³Hardly had Israel put in seed than Midian fell upon the countryside, yes, and the Amalekites and the people of the East would fall upon them; ⁴they encamped on their territory, destroying the produce of the land as far as the suburbs of Gaza. They did not leave any sustenance in Israel, no sheep nor ox nor ass. ⁵They used to go on expeditions accompanied by their cattle and their families, coming along as numerous as locusts: they were countless, they and their camels. When they fell upon a region they devastated it completely. ⁶Thus Israel was made very wretched because of Midian, so that the Israelites cried out to Yahweh.

7 When the Israelites cried out to Yahweh because of Midian, ⁸he sent them a man, a prophet, who said to them: 'Thus says Yahweh, God of Israel: "I led you up out of Egypt, and freed you from slavery; ⁹I delivered you from the power of Egypt and from the hands of all your oppressors; I drove them out before you and gave you their country. ¹⁰And I said to you, I Yahweh, your God, that you were not to worship the gods of the Amorites in whose country you lived, but you did not want to listen to my voice." '

[2] 'Hiding places': this is the usual translation of the *hapax legomenon* *hamminhārōt*; from *nāhar* III, it would be 'canals', then hiding places in cracks and fissures in the rocks (the problem here is that the term usually refers to wet hiding places, which would therefore be of little use for hiding perishable objects). It could also come from the Arab *nahāra*, 'excavate (in search of water)', hence hidden deposits of water (Vincent*, 1958: the problem here is that this practice is attested in the desert, where it has a function, but not in cultivated areas, where it does not). LXX^B has τρυμαλία, 'caverns', 'caves', LXX^A μάνδρα 'stables', Vg *antra* (as LXX^B); Tg has the generic term *maṭmōrītā*', 'hiding places': It is best to translate in this latter way: the accent lies on the fact that the harvest had to be hidden; how is only interesting for the philologist and the lexicographer. 'Secluded places', Hebrew *m͑ṣādāh*: the stress lies on the difficulty of reaching them; hence it became a synonym for 'fortress', a meaning which is ruled out by the present context. [3] 'Israel': Dtr also accepts the pan-Israelite version of this happening, given that it is directed towards all the people. The 'Amalekites' and the 'people of the East' are mentioned only in 6.33 and 7.12 and are secondary elements from the point of view of the tradition. The second term is a generic name for the inhabitants of Transjordan. 'Fall upon': *ʿālāh* *ʿal* X often has this sense, even in Ugaritic. 'Yes . . . ': the conjunction should not be deleted; it is an emphatic *waw*, cf. R. G. Boling*, 1975. [4] 'As far as the suburbs. . .': literally 'Up to the point where you arrive at Gaza. . .' The reference to a place which was always in Philistine hands is far from obvious, even if it is only a topographical note. [5] 'Go on expeditions' is missing from Vg and Syr, but it seems to be correct. 'Families', literally 'tents', but *'ōhel* can be one or the other, and the context favours the translation 'family'. In the modern Arab nomadic world, also, 'tent' indicates the family who live in it.[10] 'Coming along': K has *yābō'ū*, Q *ūbā'ū*; the second is preferable because of the conjunction; the tense is less important. 'Locusts', the usual hyperbole in the ancient Near East. [6] The text contrasts the impotence of Israel with the efficacy of the divine action, J. Gray*, 1967. [7] Verse 7a is lacking in LXX^B but not in Vg or Syr, as *BHK*^{3} and *BHS* suggest. 'Because of. . .': LXX^B has ἀπὸ προσώπου i.e. *ʿal p͑nē*. The prophetic invective has the terminology and conceptuality of Dtr, and so it cannot be early, as J. Gray*, 1967, would suppose. [9] 'Drove them out': the normal form with the *waw* consecutive is *wā*^{x}*gāreš*; for the variant *wā*^{x}*gāreš* without the *meteg* cf. GesK § 49c. [10] 'Worship': the literal Hebrew is 'fear'. 'Amoreans' is the generic term for the pre-Israelite population of Canaan in E, Dtn and Dtr.

Once again we have an indication of the cause-and-effect

[10]L. Knopf, 'Arabische Etymologien und Parallele', *VT* 9, 1959, 249.

relationship which is thought to exist between sin and historical catastrophe, the second understood as punishment for the first. Here, too, the audience seems to be the Israelites in exile, 'delivered over into the hands of' Babylon for a final, definitive judgment, just as their ancestors were delivered over into the hands of the surrounding peoples. Thus the present fate of the exiles is given an effective theological explanation, based on the theory that God acts as sovereign in history, even present history, and far from being bound to one people and therefore conquered and disarmed by the Babylonians with the end of his people, he carries on with his own personal plan.[11]

This time, the framework which surrounds the ancient traditions about Gideon seems to provide us with some important historical information: the figure 'seven' in v.1 could be authentic, in which case it would indicate that the Midianite incursions took place at regular intervals. Of course, because this particular figure is used so often as a stereotype, it might also be inauthentic; but for want of any indication that it has this characteristic significance here, we may suppose that it is genuine. Verses 3–6 maintain the theory that even in the past, as in the hearers' own time, Yahweh was accustomed to punish Israel by means of some kind of demonstrable historical phenomenon: invasions, famines and earthquakes.

In the present text the invasion is presented as having been on a vast scale: from central and northern Palestine to the south-west. This information, which is topographically not very appropriate, as we saw in the comments on the text, simply indicates that virtually no one succeeded in escaping the scourge. First of all there is a description of the damage caused by the marauders: they are said to have camped on the fields, presumably laying waste the sown parts and feeding their animals on them (v.3); then we are told how they stole the cattle and beasts of burden. Thus the inhabitants of the regions affected felt forced to hide both themselves (v. 2b) and, as we shall see later (v. 11), their crops; we find a similar situation on the occasion of another invasion, that described in Jer. 6.3; the only natural parallel to this is an invasion of locusts. Among the non-sedentary groups in the Near East in both ancient and modern times the sense of property has always been different

[11]J.A. Soggin, 'Deuteronomistische Geschichtsschreibung während des Exils', in *Oikonomia. Festschrift O. Cullmann*, Hamburg 1967, 11–17; id., *Joshua*, 5f.; id., 'Die Entstehung des deuteronomistischen Geschichtswerkes', *TLZ* 100, 1975, cols. 3–8.

from that prevailing among sedentary peoples; among the former, plundering has never been considered a crime provided
that it happens in connection with groups which are not bound
either by ties of affinity or by alliances (Hebrew *šālōm*, Arab
salām and *sūlḥ*), cf. 4.17.

2. Characteristic of these plunderers is rapid and indiscrimi-
nate pillage, without any thought for the productivity of the
area and hence for its future 'exploitation'; this is an element
not unlike the official version of the Israelite conquest. People
who experience this kind of invasion therefore find themselves
involved in a marked economic crisis caused by the destruction
of their very means of sustenance and not just by the plunder
of their crops, and their yield; that is, if they do not succeed
either in repelling the invasions or neutralizing them by hiding
the crops.

3. In Israel, as Penna*, 1963, 136, rightly observes, the crisis
did not arise simply because of weakness; the lack of unity
among individual groups also prevented Israel from standing
up to the common dangers. The local group was at most connected with the tribe, as clearly appears in the instance described in the Song of Deborah, 5.14ff. (cf. above): any call for
unity tended to fall on deaf ears, because only the groups directly
interested in the battle would tend to respond. The present text,
although the tradition has been revised to refer to all Israel,
clearly retains the fact that it was the Abiezrites who conducted
the campaign. Thus the situation is very like that presented in
chs. 17–21; there was no king and everyone did what seemed
right in his own eyes. This concept seems to underlie what is
said in 8.22–24, which is certainly late, according to which the
people wanted to make Gideon king.

4. A new element appears in vv. 7–10: the message of an
unknown prophet. It is a typically Dtr message, and does not
have any connection with the context. It lacks any logical conclusion, which is a suspect element; if it had been artificial, it
would probably have been constructed in its entirety. It is therefore possible that the notice originally belonged in another context, but that it has been put here to give the Dtr interpretation
greater authority.

The Dtr theory is characteristic of this kind of historiography;
however, it is an element that we find right through the Old
Testament: that the migrations of peoples are not a matter of
chance, nor are they due solely to economic and political factors;

they are elements in the divine plan which is being fulfilled through history. The Old Testament sees the exodus and the conquest in these terms as far as Israel is concerned, but it interprets the movements of other peoples in the same way, cf. Amos 9.7; the return of the exiles in the Persian period was still seen from this perspective: sin is followed by punishment, but conversion will probably be followed by redemption. This is the theory maintained by Ezekiel and by Deutero-Isaiah.

The incomplete character of the episode of the prophet could therefore be an element in favour of its antiquity, even if the text is now hopelessly mutilated and detached from its original context.

(b) Gideon and the altar at Ophrah (6.11–24)

6 [11]One day the messenger of Yahweh arrived and sat under the oak which is in Ophrah, belonging to the Abiezrite; Gideon, his son, was threshing the harvest in the wine-press, to remove it from the Midianites. [12]And the messenger appeared to him and said, 'Yahweh is with you, O mighty warrior.' [13]But Gideon replied: 'With me, my Lord? If Yahweh is with us, how is it that all this has happened? Where are the wonderful deeds recounted by our fathers, according to whom he brought us up out of Egypt? Now Yahweh has surely abandoned us and delivered us up into the hands of Midian!' [14]But Yahweh replied to him with these words: 'Go in this your might and save Israel from the hands of Midian: it is I who send you!' [15]Gideon replied: 'I, my Lord? With what means can I save Israel? My clan is the weakest in Manasseh and I am the youngest in my father's house!' [16]But Yahweh replied to him. 'Surely I will be with you and you shall smite Midian as though it were a solitary man.' [17]Then Gideon said: 'If I really am the object of your grace, then give me a sign that it is really you who are talking with me. [18]Do not go away from here, I beg you, until I return to you, and bring you my offering and put it before you.' He replied, 'Very well, I will stay until you return.' [19]Gideon went and prepared a kid and an *ephah* of flour for unleavened bread; he put the meat in a basket and its sauce in a pot and went out to him under the oak and brought it to him. [20]Then the messenger of God said to him, 'Take the meat and the unleavened cakes. Put them on this stone, here, and pour the sauce on them.' This he did. [21]And the messenger reached out the staff that he had in his hand, and touched the meat and the unleavened cakes with the tip; and fire came out from the stone and consumed them. Then he withdrew from his sight. [22]Then Gideon was persuaded that this was the messenger of Yahweh . . ., and he cried out, 'Alas, O Lord Yahweh, for I have seen the messenger of Yahweh face to face.' [23]But Yahweh replied to him: 'Peace be to

114   JUDGES

you, do not be afraid; you shall not die.' [24]Then Gideon built an altar there to Yahweh and he gave it this name, 'The Lord is security', a name which has lasted down to the present day in Ophrah of Abiezer.

---

[11] 'The messenger of Yahweh': the angel. The expression which I have used here seems better, to keep the distinction from the angelogy of late Judaism, where the angels have an autonomous existence of their own with their own hierarchy. Here, as in other ancient narratives (Gen. 16.7ff.; 21.17; 22.11; Ex. 3.2; Judg. 13.3ff.) and in the present text at vv. 14,16 and 23, the 'messenger' is a being who is interchangeable with Yahweh, identical to him, and does not exist in a separate form, being his visible manifestation. It is thus quite possible, and not a sign of different traditions, that Yahweh and the mal'āk interchange within a short space; there is no particular significance to this.[12] In no way is this an angel with a particular status, nor can the alternation with Yahweh be understood as a sign of different traditions, as is supposed by those who want to divide the text into sources.[13] 'Ophrah': LXX read 'Ephratah', a name which begins with aleph and which therefore seems excluded here; perhaps the error comes from the reading 'oprāt in v.24. The geographical location of the place is disputed: F.-M. Abel,[14] followed by Vincent*, 1958, thought of et-tayībe (coord. 192–223), about 10 km east of the hill of Moreh (see on 7.1); Y. Aharoni**, 1967, 240ff.,[15] puts it near 'affūlāh (coord. 177–223); others would prefer it to be nearer to bēt š'ē'ān, a little to the north of the area. In any case, the area in which the events narrated take place is south-south-east of the plain. 'Was threshing': the first task in producing grain by hand, that of beating it;[16] the difference here is that it is not being done in the open air but in the vat used for pressing the grapes.[17] This will be a construction excavated from the rock, made up of two or more vats connecting at different levels, so that the grape juice flows from the upper one to the lower.[18] By means of this operation it seems to have been possible to keep the harvest from the

[12]Cf. W. Baumgartner, 'Zum Problem des "Jahwe-Engels" ', Schweizerische Theologische Umschau 14, Berne 1944, 97–102: Zum Alten Testament und seine Umwelt, Leiden 1959, 240–6.
[13]Cf. the studies by E. Kutsch, 1955; W. Richter, 1970; and L. Schmidt, 1970; already cited.
[14]F.-M. Abel, Géographie de la Palestine, II, Paris 1938, 402.
[15]Z. Kallai-Kleinmann, The Tribes of Israel, Jerusalem 1967, 356 (in Hebrew).
[16]A.S. Kapelrud, 'Dreschen', BHH I, 1962, cols. 355–7.
[17]Thus J. Gray*, 1967: better than the 'mill' for the olives, even if the Hebrew uses gat for both.
[18]Cf. G. Fohrer, 'Kelter', BHH II, 1964, col. 939, with plans and sections; at col. 1356 we have the mill, also with illustrations; cf. Ahlström, 'Wine Presses and Cup-Marks of the Jenin-Megiddo Survey', BASOR 231, 1978, 19–49, with many illustrations of wine-presses; however, the operation evidently refers to the first artifact. In Sardinia today, vats scooped in the rock are still in use for pressing valuable grapes.

plunderers, though it is not clear how: perhaps by covering the vat with branches and thus hiding it from view? The text does not say that the rock mentioned in vv. 20ff. was identical with the vat, nor is it even certain that the two elements belong to a single complex, even if we might (cf. Keller, 156) suppose that the rock was in some way an extension of the vat; and from the combination of the two elements it could be possible to explain the union of the two traditions, a problem that we shall be concerned with later. 'To remove it' is better than 'hide': *nws* is literally 'escape' (Driver**, and Boling*, 1975). It is sometimes argued that vv.11a, 18f. and 21–24 are a first tradition and vv.11b–17 a second;[19] in any case, the question, which we shall consider further below, cannot be decided on the basis of the alternation between the 'messenger' and Yahweh. **[12]** 'Appeared to him': the verb *rā'āh* in the niphal is a technical term for the divine manifestation: it is not enough that the person is present; he needs to reveal himself, to 'appear' to man in the sense of being perceived by him. For the translation 'salvation' cf. further on § 4. 'Mighty warrior': the free man, well-off and able-bodied (Richter **, 1963, 147; Gray*, 1967); hence it became synonymous with 'warrior' and in this sense is an expression for a sociological category. Boling wants to render it 'you aristocrat', but this goes beyond the sense of the expression, all the more since it is not clear what such a term would mean in a structure that was still tribal. 'With you': with the preposition *'im*. This alternates with the expression *bī* on Gideon's lips; it is much less strong and therefore has undertones of scepticism and irony; it is a polite way of expressing doubt. That seems better than 'Pray, sir' (Gray) or 'Pardon me, sir' (Boling); this also emerges from the following verse. **[13]** The formula *bī' ᵃdōni* is a courteous but firm way (from an inferior to a superior) of showing disagreement.[20] Verse 13b is an addition to the text in Dtr style, so I have translated the direct speech in Hebrew with indirect speech. Here, too, I have translated the term *hᵃlō'* as though there was an emphatic *lamed*, cf. on 4.6. 'Recounted': lit.: 'Which our fathers have narrated'. R. G. Boling*, 1975, recalls that 4Q Judgᵃ has the expression *śsprw*, with the prefix *śĕ-*, which he considers an archaism (cf. 5.7b); however, this could be a late form of the kind that appears in biblical writings of the late post-exilic period, here (wrongly?) introduced by the Qumran copyist. **[14]** 'Yahweh': LXX, to harmonize, has 'the angel': in its time the distinction between Yahweh and the angel was clear; MT has the more difficult reading. The verse follows the formula of the investiture of the 'saviour'. 'It is I. . .' once again a translation of the emphatic *lamed*: the rhetorical question does not make any sense here, given that

---

[19]Thus E. Kutsch, W. Richter and L. Schmidt.
[20]Cf. I. Lande, *Formelhafte Wendungen der Umgangssprache im Alten Testament*, Leiden 1949, 16ff., and W. Richter, 1970, 136ff.

Gideon could not know who was commanding him. 'In this your might. . .'; there is no need to understand the second person pronominal suffix as an emphatic *kaph*: 'With the force of him who . . .', i.e. Yahweh (D.N. Freedman, in Boling*, 1975): the text clearly implies that Gideon's might is of divine origin. **[15]** 'My Lord' is *'ᵃdōnī*, not the *'ᵃdōnay* of MT: Gideon has not yet recognized the person who is speaking to him, cf. v.22. I have thus followed LXX in reading κύριε μου; the *Domine* of Vg allows of both meanings. In any case, the messenger's speech is full of allusions and implications, suitable elements for arousing suspicions in Gideon about the real identity of the person talking to him; that is why in v. 17b he asks for 'a sign' which will help him to overcome all his doubts. 'Clan': this is a rendering of 'thousand', cf. 4.6. **[16]** 'Yahweh': once again, LXX has 'the angel'. 'I will be . . . ' LXX has Κύριος ἔσται. . ., i.e., 'If the Lord is with you . . . ', a good variant compared with the Hebrew text. In Hebrew we have a play on words similar to that in Ex. 3.12–14 (Boling*, 1975).

[17] Gideon's affirmation, 'That it is really you who are talking with me' might seem to be a tautology: who else could be talking with him? It is not. More than once we have accepted that Gideon would already have some suspicions about the true identity of the person talking to him. According to Rudolph**, 1947, 201f., we should insert Yahweh, and *mᵉdabbēr* should have the article, thus reading: *šā'attāh Yhwh hammᵉdabbēr* . . .; this 'Yahweh' is supposed to have fallen out as a result of haplography of the repeated *he*. In any case, this seems to be the sense of the text. Here too the prefix *ša-* instead of *ˣšer* should be noted; it is either archaic or late, cf. on v.13. **[19]** An *ephah*: an unknown measure of capacity for solids (cereals, etc.), but certainly amounting to tens of litres. In any case it is a quantity disproportionate to a meal for two people. Of course it could be a reference to the ritual of the sanctuary, in which case it is an obvious anachronism, given that the sanctuary does not yet exist; however, eating the sacred food could be derived from this episode. 'The. . .sauce': the Hebrew *mārāq* is used either for sauce or for meat stock; Syr has *maṣlōl*, 'wine (filtered)': the offering of food and wine is more regular than that of meat with its sauce or stock. 'Brought it to him': the verb *nāgaš*, literally 'bring near' (to offer); however, here we have a combination of *wayyaggēš*, 'and offered it' (thus Vg, Syr and Tg) and *wayyiggaš*, 'and brought' (thus LXX^A); LXX^B has 'and worshipped'. In any case, it is not a matter of 'divining', as Boling*, 1975, would suppose; despite the presence of the tree, there is no question of oracles here. **[20]** 'Of God': LXX^A, Vg, Targ and Syr read 'of Yahweh'. 'On this stone here. . .': *hallāz* is a demonstrative with a local sense: 'this here'. **[23]** 'Peace be to you. . .': *šālōm*, offered by God to man, signifies security, the security which is offered by the fact that he is in communion with him. The danger to human life in the case of irregular relationships with the deity is a real one (Boling*, 1975), hence the formula 'Do not be afraid', with which God reassures the man. **[24]** The termination *'ophrāt* is remarkable: perhaps it is archaic or perhaps a construct, but in that case it goes with *pataḥ*. 'To the present day' is usually the sign of an aetiological legend.

It is a widespread view, as I pointed out in my comments on the text, that here we have what were originally two more or less parallel narratives: the first, comprising vv.11a, 18f. and 21–24 (the division can vary from author to author),[21] would relate the founding of a sanctuary with an altar under an oak; in it, Gideon has the function of mediator between the divinity who appeared there and the worshippers. This note could originally have described the history of the transfer of a Canaanite sanctuary to Israel. The second narrative would comprise vv.11b-17 and would describe the calling of Gideon to be a military leader with charismatic elements. Both would then have been combined with considerable skill, so that they can only be separated by very acute analysis; and those authors who accept the existence of two narratives through our text are agreed in recognizing that the separation in question is not that of two complete texts capable of an autonomous existence. In turn, Dtr collected the now unitary narrative comprising the cultic legend of the sanctuary at Ophrah; here, at the place where the sanctuary was to be founded, the angel appeared to Gideon and was his guest; it was here that he communicated to Gideon his calling to be the leader of his own people, the Abiezrites, with a view to liberating them.

A later phase then extended to 'all Israel', the tribal league, this narrative which originally was limited and on a local scale.

[11] The nucleus of the sanctuary in question seems to have been the sacred oak and the altar called *Yhwh šālōm* (v. 24), still existing at the time of the first tradition and situated in the territory of the clan of Abiezer, near to the winepress hollowed out in the rock which traditionally belonged to Gideon. In the present narrative the accent has now been totally shifted to the precariousness of the situation in which the people now find themselves; on the one hand the grain harvest is threshed in conditions of semi-secrecy, while on the other, the group does not seem to have had any chance of success in fighting against the invader.

---

[21]L. Schmidt, 53, is the most subtle.

[12–13] As a result, the messenger's announcement to Gideon falls on barren soil. Leaving aside the typically Dtr insertion of v. 13b, with its stereotyped reference to the exodus, the speech seems clear: the Lord cannot possibly be with him if he allows this sort of thing to happen to his own people. The typically Dtr insertion takes up the theme of the exodus in terms which recall Ps. 78.3–8 and that of the conquest in terms similar to Ps.44.2ff.[22] It is much better fitted to the situation of the exile than to that of the end of the second millenium BC.

The greeting of the messenger to Gideon can be understood in two ways, and is therefore somewhat ambiguous in character; however, this is a frequent feature where we have divine speech addressed to men. It is either a common salutation, 'The Lord *be* with you . . .', or a statement, 'The Lord *is* with you', i.e. an oracle of salvation (thus H. Reventlow). The latter seems to be the meaning which Gideon himself attaches to the greeting, otherwise the somewhat polemical reply would not make any sense: thus it challenges the validity of the oracle, because its message does not correspond with the present situation. Granted, it could also be intended as a play on words, rather as if someone said 'Good day,' and received the reply, 'What good day? I'd call it terrible.' That notwithstanding, given the character of the text, it seems probable that here we have a formula which is at the same time an oracle of salvation. Richter**, 1963, 147, underlines the semantic and syntactical ambiguity of the nominal proposition in the formula. In any case, the meaning is made more specific in v. 16 with the use of the verb in the imperfect, which, if nothing else, shows how a later generation understood the content of the oracle.

It is interesting to see how Gideon's reply, with or without the Dtr addition, reveals his ignorance of any prophetic message capable of explaining the situation, and therefore the independence of the text from vv. 7ff. On the other hand, in all ancient literature, both Eastern and Western, it is regular to introduce into speeches references to events later than the situation of the protagonists and sometimes even of the audience: cf. the discussions in Ezek. 11.22–25, dating from the sixth century BC, in which the 'glory of Yahweh' abandons the temple and the people a little while before the events of 587–6.

[14] However, Gideon is gifted in a special way, charismati-

---

[22]I. Lande, *Formelhafte Wendungen*, 11ff.

cally, for his task. This element is expressed by means of his calling in vv. 12ff., in the expression 'this is your strength', cf. 3.28, where the element appears in connection with the Holy War. It is not clear from the text if this strength was there before his calling, so that it is already latent in Gideon (cf. v. 12b, where the messenger calls Gideon a 'mighty warrior') and that therefore the calling simply brings it to light; or whether Gideon receives a particular gift in the course of his calling. In the Old Testament, concepts like election and vocation never have a theoretical value, as though they were a privilege; they always exist in connection with a mission. That is already the case with the election *par excellence*, that of the people of God. It is also a characteristic feature of the Dtn and Dtr doctrine that this election of the people does not come about for any merits; it is always in the light of the mission which the people is given. And here it is a matter of 'saving', root *yāša'* (v. 14a), Israel from Midian. Gideon thus appears as a 'saviour', according to the ancient traditions whose existence has been made probable by Richter (cf. the introduction above, pp. 103ff.), and it is with a view to this mission that Gideon receives his particular gifts (v. 16b). This being the case, the discussion whether Gideon already had certain gifts or whether he received them in the act of his calling, becomes unnecessary. Even Gideon himself does not seem to be much preoccupied with this; however, he stresses his own inadequacy for the mission to which he has been called, either because he is a member of a small group with scanty resources or because he is the youngest member of his family. On the other hand, the theme of his unworthiness is part of the stereotyped response made by the person called on the occasion of his calling, so that it is not clear whether what we have is intended as a realistic appraisal of the situation (and if so, to what extent), or whether the statements are purely and simply a matter of courtesy.

[15] It is often asserted (Schmidt, 43) that Gideon here is not yet an independent man, whereas in 8.20ff. he already had a firstborn son capable of bearing arms – so much so that he invites him to kill the two Midianite prisoners: therefore 'the historical Gideon does not correspond with the picture given of him in 6.15': furthermore, the family of Gideon was far from being insignificant, seeing that in 8.18 it is said that two of his brothers resembled princes. The first point is based on a phrase in v. 15, which stresses the unworthiness and weakness of Gid-

eon, connected with the lowly character of his own clan. However, as I have said, the contradiction is more superficial and formal than real and substantial: any man called directly to serve the God of Israel is by the nature of things unworthy, so that the theme appears on many occasions. In I Sam. 9.21 Saul, too, is defined in these terms, though he belonged to a powerful family and had an imposing bearing, I Sam. 9.1f.; David is certainly the youngest member of a family which is not very well known (I Sam. 16.6ff.), whereas even Jeremiah (cf. 1.6–8) tries to put forward reasons of this kind, although he belonged to a priestly family. In Isa. 6.1ff., the prophet stresses his own sinfulness, which derives from that of his people. Thus we have a series of instances in which these declarations are simply more or less rhetorical confessions, 'well-mannered', as we would say today, without any sociological or theological content; in other cases, it is true, the divine choice is presented as a choice of the lowliest, the individuals whom man would not choose (cf. I Sam. 2.1ff.).[23] In the first instance the formula serves to bring into relief the honour of which the person elected is the object, an honour which is all the greater in proportion to the worth of the person who makes the choice and the unworthiness of the person who is chosen. In theological contexts it serves to give God absolute glory.

[16] Thus we have here an element which could be paraphrased with the formula *soli Deo gloriae*, which is present in all the accounts of calling, whether the person called underlines his own unworthiness or whether this unworthiness is real and the person called really comes from the ranks of the poor and insignificant. This is not necessarily a late feature: we already find it in the second phase, the 'theological' phase, of the Song of Deborah (cf. above); however, it is not a very early element either, given that it presupposes some reflection on the theme. But once it has entered the Bible it can be found right through both Old and New Testaments, cf. I Cor. 1.29ff. Thus Yahweh will be with Gideon, who will be able to defeat his enemy almost as a matter of course, as if Gideon had a large following. Furthermore, the theme of its own vocation and election follows Israel from its beginning right down to the present day, and

---

[23]For the problem see I. Lande, *Formelhafte Wendungen*, 68ff., esp. 74ff.: 'self-injury' (*Selbstbeschimpfung*). On the motive of the divine call see N. Habel, 'The Form and Significance of the Call Narratives', *ZAW* 77, 1965, 297–323, esp. 279ff.; W. Richter, 1970; and G. del Olmo, op. cit.

often involves it in polemic with people of greater military strength, technically more advanced, and artistically and legally further developed; it has also entered into Christian doctrine. It was easy for the Dtr school to associate itself with this doctrine and to make it an important element in its preaching.

[17–22] Gideon calls on the mysterious personage for a proof: he perceives the person with whom he is dealing, but given the importance of his own mission, he feels that he needs to know quite definitely who has sent him and therefore in whose authority he is acting. Such proofs, which the New Testament writers do not like at all (cf. John 20.29, among other passages), are by no means thought to be illegitimate or even strange in the Old Testament. Indeed, they often form part of a narrative in which a person is blamed for not having asked a sign from God, as the prophet told him: in Isa. 7.10–25 King Ahaz is reproached for refusing to ask the Lord for a sign (vv. 11–13); in the New Testament, by contrast, faith has to do without signs.

Here the sign belongs in the sphere of the cult and, one might say, to an earlier phase: the deity has to consume, root *'ākal*, literally 'eat', the offering in a particular manner (v. 21b). It is consumed by means of a fire which devours it from the rock, cf. also I Kings 18.38 (where, however, the fire seems to come from heaven). The offering (*minḥāh*, which in 3.15ff. we have seen to mean 'tribute') of v. 18 is normally one of food and is therefore bloodless: here, in fact, the 'meat' is already cooked and therefore, seeing that it has been made into food, is no longer a bloody sacrifice; it is accompanied by unleavened bread, cf. Lev. 2.11, and the sauce or stock of the meat (but cf. the interesting variant in Syr, which read 'wine': this is the liquid which in the history of religion normally goes with sacrifice, whereas the 'stock' or 'sauce' is an unusual element). It would not be surprising if the remarkable quantity of flour or the combination of meat with its sauce or broth made up the original elements of the sacred food in the sanctuary of Ophrah, in which at a later stage the 'messenger' was again the guest, this time an invisible one. The food would be traditionally derived from the institution of the sanctuary by Gideon. This is one of the many rituals which probably came to an end when Josiah reconquered part of the north (II Kings 23.16–20//II Chron. 34.6f.), with explicit mention of Manasseh, the tribe to which the clan of Abiezer belonged.

[21] Of course, once the messenger has revealed his true identity, he has to disappear, given that his action now transcends the human form which he has assumed; we shall also see a similar case in 13.19ff., probably composed on the model of this. However, Gideon, who has seen the 'messenger' face to face, feels lost (v. 22). His reaction is no different from that of Isaiah in 6.5; besides, even a person like Moses could only see God from the back (Ex. 33.18–23), a passage which is certainly late and of uncertain derivation, situated in an extremely fragmentary context. The theme of fear is usually to be found at the beginning of a vision, but here, for obvious reasons, it only appears at the end: at the beginning Gideon did not know that this was a vision.[24]

[23–24] Here we have the oracle of salvation which has already been considered (cf. note 24): perhaps its origin is to be sought in the doctrine of the holy war, an element which seems relevant even if it is somewhat late and evidently belongs to the redaction which, at latest, immediately preceded that of Dtr. God responds in a reassuring way to the lament of the man who feels that he is lost because he has gone beyond the limits which it is permissible for a man to reach: this is not a case of impiety on man's part; it is the divine will. Thus Gideon is 'secure', a concept effectively expressed by the term *šālōm*. *Šālōm* with its various meanings is a complex word, but it expresses virtually everything that can be included in a positive relationship between two parties: alliance, agreement, peace, co-operation. Thus a new relationship is established between the God of Israel and the one whom he has newly elected by means of the divine initiative, and the sanctuary founded by Gideon remains a perpetual memorial of the event.

(c) Gideon destroys the sanctuary of Baal at Ophrah
(6.25–32)

6 [25]That same night Yahweh said to him: 'Take your father's best bullock, the one which has been fattened; pull down the altar of Baal which belongs to your father and cut down the Asherah which stands

[24]For the formula cf. J. Begrich, 'Das priesterliche Heilsorakel', *ZAW* 52, 1934, 81–92 = *Gesemmelte Studien*, Munich 1964, 217–31, and recently P. E. (H.M.) Dion, 'The "Fear Not" Formula and Holy War', *CBQ* 32, 1970, 565–70; however cf. already id., 'The Patriarchal Traditions and the Literary Form of the "Oracle of Salvation" ', *CBQ* 29, 1967, 198–206. See also A. de Pury, *Promesse divine et légende cultuelle dans le cycle de Jacob*, Paris 1975, 222–40 and 363f.

beside it. [26]Then build a proper altar on the top of the fortress; then take the best bullock and offer a holocaust with the wood of the Asherah which you have cut down.' [27]Then Gideon chose ten men from among his servants and did as Yahweh had commanded; however, he was afraid to act by day because of his family and the inhabitants of the neighbourhood, so he acted by night. [28]The next morning, when the people arose, they saw that the altar of Baal had been destroyed and that the Asherah beside it had been cut down. The young bullock which had been fattened had been offered as a holocaust on the altar which had just been built. [29]Everyone said to his neighbour, 'Who has done such a thing?' They made inquiries and collected information and came to the conclusion, 'It was Gideon, son of Joash, who did all this.'

30 Then the inhabitants of the place said to Joash: 'Bring out Gideon, that he may be put to death: he has destroyed the altar of Baal and has cut down the Asherah beside it!'

31 But Joash said to those who stood around him: 'Do you want to defend Baal? Do you want to come to his help? [If anyone wants to defend Baal, let him be put to death before morning!] If he is god, let him defend himself, since someone has demolished his altar.' [32]On that day they called Gideon *Jerubbaal*, since he had said: 'Let Baal fight with him, since he has pulled down his altar!'

---

[25] Note the redactional shift from the preceding episode to this one by means of the formula 'that same night'. Thus the redactors envisaged a rapid succession of events: the calling of Gideon, the beginning of the fight against Baal, the foundation or the appropriation of local sanctuaries. This appears more probable than the statement of Gray*, 1967, that we can no longer determine if these elements belong to the original or to the redaction. 'The bullock': *pār* often appears in contexts in which it is a sacrificial animal. In the present state of MT we find two, one the property of Gideon's father, which no longer appears, called *pār haššōr*; this is an unusual expression, the regular one being *pār ben bāqār*. There is also a second, always called that even when the first one is no longer mentioned, and which later is sacrificed as a holocaust, vv. 26, 28. MT, confirmed by LXX[B], Vg, Tg and Syr, therefore reads: '. . . Which belongs to your father, and a second bullock, seven years old . . .' However, here and in v. 28 LXX[AL] reads: τὸν μόσχον τὸν σιτευτὸν . . . τὸν ἑπταετῆ . . ., a reading which presupposes a Hebrew *'et happār haššānī ben šeba' šānīm* . . .; and this reading is proposed by Guillaume and partly accepted by Driver**, 1964 (the rest of his proposals are not, however, convincing), and followed by many scholars today. However, they substitute the corresponding Hebrew 'grown' (*šānī*) for the Greek 'fattened': in fact, *siteuton* never renders *šāmēn*. Thus we have a shorter

and better text, even if it is not the *lectio difficilior*. So much so that L. Schmidt (6f.) prefers to read *pār haššōr* throughout; however, his proposals seem to complicate the problems of the text rather than to simplify them, and he too arrives at the conclusion that there ought to be only one animal. A better solution is perhaps that proposed by Emerton, 1978: for *šēnī* read *šānī*, root *šn'*;[25] on the basis of its meaning in Syriac and Arabic, this root probably means 'sparkle', 'catch the eye', and therefore indicates the best; perhaps in that case we should read *šeba'*, 'fattened', for the Massoretic *šeba' šānīm*, 'seven years old'. However, yet another possibility ought to be explored: that the ritual described here is parallel to that indicated in I Kings 18.23ff., where two bulls are also mentioned, one to be offered by Elijah and the other by the prophets of Baal. In our case this would mean that one bull was intended to be offered by Gideon, the other by the priests of the shrine of Baal. However, little more can be said, as the sources convey virtually nothing. The text remains a typical crux and at present its reconstruction is impossible: an attempt made by Rudolph**, 1947, is not at all convincing in any respect.

One explanation of the corruption of the text could be that this is another fragment of the ritual of the sanctuary which at that time was no longer understood; in that case we should certainly not rule out the possibility of two or even more animals: some were offered and others not. Or we could leave the reading 'seven years': the age of the animal could indicate its adult character or the duration of Midianite supremacy, two explanations which are not mutually exclusive.

The Asherah is a symbol of the Canaanite deity of the same name; for its form cf. K. Elliger, 'Aschera', *BHH* I, 1962, cols. 136f. It should not be confused with Astarte. It is 'cut down' for the reasons indicated in connection with the next verse.

[26] The 'fortress', Hebrew *mā'ōz*, is architecturally connected with the sanctuary; it is probably a version of the fortified Canaanite temple:[26] a temple which was consecrated to Baal is now consecrated to Yahweh. The reference to the 'fortress' also caused difficulties for the ancient translators, all of whom tried to get rid of it, cf. LXX[BA] and Vg, as later did Kimchi and the Hebrew exegetes. 'Proper': literally 'in a row'. The Asherah serves as firewood, a deliberate piece of sacrilege. **[27]** LXX[A] has 'thirty men'. **[28]** For the text see on v. 25.

[31f.] The difficulty of the texts consists in the word-play contained in the new name. In the various schemes the root *ryb* signifies: I, 'Litigate', 'put on trial', and II, 'Defend' or 'assume the defence of

---

[25]J. A. Emerton, 'The Meaning of ŠĒNĀ' in Psalm CXXVII', *VT* 24, 1974, 15–31, esp. 25ff.

[26]Cf. B. Mazar, 'Migdāl', *EncBibl* IV, 1962, cols. 633–5 (in Hebrew); in the bibliographies there is a number of references to 'an unpublished paper by Professor Mazar' on the argument; its content should be substantially identical with this article. Also G. E. Wright, *Shechem*, New York 1965, ch. VI.

someone', in each case in a legal context. We have the play on the popular etymology of the name on the basis of these two meanings. There are two ways of resolving the difficulty: either we have here the above-mentioned root *ryb*, in which case we ought to have *yārīb*, or we have the root *rābab*, 'be great', so that the name would mean 'let Baal prove himself to be great':[27] the word-play thus hinges on the assonance of these two roots. Thus the name seems to be theophoric in the positive sense of the term: either 'Baal is great' or 'Baal make (you) great', and only the Israelite anti-Canaanite polemic could detect a sarcastic undertone: notwithstanding the play on words this appears forced, and we are prompted to ask whether, starting from the existing name, popular etymology did not simply want to give it a meaning in connection with the story, so that investigations of etymologies and meanings would prove useless. Finally, we have something that may have been a more or less pious marginal gloss which has now entered the text: it threatens the death penalty for those who worship the Canaanite gods and is a manifest contrast with the invitation directed to Baal to defend himself (Schmidt). The context recalls that of I Kings 18.21ff., even if the outcome of the narrative is much less bloody. 'Called him': the Hebrew *wayyiqrā'* suggests an impersonal subject, 'they called him', 'he was called' (Gray*, 1967), but it is probable and also logical that the subject here is Joash: Gideon is as it were reborn, and his father gives him the name; the exclamation in v. 31 is in fact based on the new name.

1. As L. Schmidt (5ff.) has rightly indicated, the present text poses two problems which appear afresh in any discussion. (i) Was the account in the beginning concerned with the events by which what was originally a Canaanite sanctuary became Israelite (of the type, as I have said, which is to be found in I Kings 18), or was it constructed to illustrate an aetiological interest of that kind? A variant of this was once suggested by H. Gressmann*, 1921, 205: perhaps we have the recollection of a later reform. J. Gray*, 1967, 224, adopts the first solution. (ii) Is the popular explanation of the name in v. 32 part of the original narrative, or is it too a later aetiology which seeks to identify two different people? A third theory has been proposed by W. Richter**, 1963, 157–68: vv. 25–27a and 32 belong to a pre-Dtr redactor of the 'Book of Saviours', whereas vv. 27b–31bα belong to an ancient narrative, which no longer has its

---

[27]M. Noth, *Die israelitischen Personennamen . . .*, BWANT III.10, 1928, 206, and *Geschichte Israels*, Göttingen ²1954, 141; ET, *History of Israel*, London and New York ²1960, 152f.; cf. also W. F. Albright, *Archaeology and the Religion of Israel*, Baltimore ³1953, 112, 206: 'May Baal increase'.

original conclusion. For that the aetiology of the name Jerubbaal
has been substituted, whereas the beginning of the narrative has
been revised to emphasize the work of Yahweh (p. 164). The
scope of the original narrative would only have been that of
describing the small clashes, the petty incidents (*Plänkeleien*,
skirmishes) which took place between the adherents of the two
cults, living together in the same territory. For Schmidt (8) there
is still a tension between vv. 25f. and v. 30, so much so that the
two units cannot be attributed to the same author: the first text
in fact speaks of the desecration and the destruction of the
symbols of the Canaanite cult (v. 25) and of the order to build
an altar to Yahweh on the fortress (v. 26a), where the bullock
has to be offered as a holocaust (v. 26b); v. 30, on the other
hand, only knows the destruction and desecration of the Canaanite cult and uses the verb *nātaṣ* instead of *hāras* for the
destruction, cf. also vv. 28–32. For Schmidt it is impossible that
the accusation of the people of Ophrah could concern only the
destruction and desecration of the symbols of the Canaanite cult
and not also the building of the altar on the fortress and the
subsequent sacrifice there. He points to further discrepancies:
for example that in v. 31aβ the accent falls on the impiety of
the people of Ophrah, whereas vv. 25ff. stress rather the courage
of Gideon. Again, as Richter (161f.) and Rogerson indicate,
v. 31 presupposes that Baal has reacted in some way to the
challenge directed to him by Joash, which does not in fact
happen; therefore v. 32 cannot be the narrative continuation of
v. 31; this is, however, very understandable, but simply as a
pointer towards the aetiology of the name.

2. It in fact seems most improbable that the original conclusion of the narrative has fallen out, to be replaced by the aetiology of the name.[28] Such a conclusion could in fact only have
told how Baal made an effective response to the challenge, in
the end remaining defeated and put to shame: certainly this
would be a conclusion that was very favourable to the present
theory which the text puts forward. In fact it is the root *ryb/rbb*
which is the key to v. 31, in that the whole speech revolves
around it; it is also the key to v. 32, which now forms its conclusion. Only in this way, as Schmidt rightly points out, can the
figure of Joash assume the importance that it has in the present
narrative. This seems all the more remarkable if, with Schmidt,

[28]L. Schmidt, 10ff., and J. Gray*, 1967, 224.

we take Joash to be the subject of *wayyiqrā'* in v. 32, quite a reasonable probability.

To ask a deity to show his power by punishing the impious is an unusual procedure, to say the least; it is normally the community which punishes the impious one, and steps in this direction are in fact taken by the people of Ophrah. If, then, we have this kind of challenge here, notwithstanding the people's request that the impious person should be put to death, it is a clear sign that Joash did not believe in the power of the god; or if in fact he was wrong, Baal would have vindicated his honour not just on the one who had committed sacrilege but on the whole of the community, which, by not punishing him, would in fact have declared its approval of him.

Schmidt seems less convincing, however, when he sets vv. 25–27a over against v. 30; the first verses would belong to the re-elaboration. According to Schmidt, the destruction and desecration of the symbols of the Canaanite cult did not result in the building of an altar to Yahweh (contrary to the narrative of I Kings 18). Therefore, along with Richter he denies that the text was intended originally to tell how the Canaanite cult was replaced with that of Yahweh, and wants, rather, simply to narrate the etymology of the name; in reality there is no aetiological and cultic interest at all: the interest is in the success of the hero, not in that of Yahweh. The argument is based on the relevance or otherwise of the mention of Baal in v. 30; however, is this really a relevant fact? It does not seem to be: the Ophrathites do not censure Gideon's family for having honoured and sacrificed to their own deity, but for having demolished and desecrated the symbols of their god. Thus, confronted with a relatively tolerant paganism (all the Mediterranean and Eastern religions have been generally tolerant, except perhaps towards those who attacked the very foundations of the system, as did, for example, the primitive Christians), Yahwism proves to be intolerant, a phenomenon clearly attested by the prophet Elijah at an early stage and which would reach its culmination with the great prophets of the eighth and seventh centuries BC and then with Josiah's reform. On the other hand, that is not to say that the phenomenon began with the great prophets; it could have been much older.

Whereas the symbols of the Canaanite cult ought to be found in the place reserved for them in the temple, so that in the morning, everyone would suddenly realize what had happened, the altar to Yahweh was built 'on the summit', v. 26a, and that too, especially in a syncretistic context, could not cause major disturbances. It was the destruction of the symbols of the pagan cult which created the tension.

If there is a tension in the present text, it is to be found in the order addressed by Yahweh himself to Gideon; however, it is possible that originally the story simply gave the account of a minor local conflict, ending with the elimination of the cult of Baal. But now this narrative has been inserted into the account of the calling of Gideon, thus taking on a certain degree of symmetry with the previous narrative: in this former account Gideon is called on to fight against an external enemy; here the fight is with those within. However, this is a symmetry which presupposes the religious situation of the eighth and seventh centuries.

3. In the view of almost all scholars, the request made by the Ophrathites for the death penalty on the author of the act of sacrilege seems to be the most ancient part of the account. Joash dissents from this request with an intervention which H. W. Hertzberg*, 1959, calls 'courageous and skilful' at the same time, and which he compares with that of Gamaliel in Acts 5.38ff. In the present version of the passage, the intervention points on the one hand to Baal's impotence and on the other to the Ophrathites' feeble commitment towards their faith: instead of insisting on the imposition of the penalty for sacrilege, they allow themselves to be convinced by an argument which clearly left them out of the procedure. The Old Testament knows of other instances in which the zeal of the interested party is considerably greater: 11.29ff.; I Sam. 14.36ff. In these episodes a vow has to be fulfilled, even when it seems to be inhuman. The situation again recalls Elijah's reproach to the people assembled at the sanctuary on Carmel, I Kings 18.21, where the keyword is uncertain, but the generally accepted translation runs: 'How long will you keep on limping with both feet?', i.e. not taking either one or the other faith seriously.

4. The narrative does not say whether or not Baal reacts; it seems that he does not, otherwise Gideon's surname would not make much sense. This surname appears rarely in chs. 6–8, but frequently in ch. 9.

In the economy of the narrative as we now have it. Gideon is ready for the fight against the outside enemy, an enemy which at the same time is the punishment for the inward sin of Israel.

(*d*) The call to arms against Midian (6.33–35)

6 [33]One day all the Midianites and the Amalekites and the people of the East came together, crossed the Jordan and camped in the plain of Jezreel. [34]Then the spirit of the Lord came over Gideon; he sounded the horn and the Abiezrites mustered behind him. [35]He immediately sent messengers throughout Manasseh who also mustered behind him; then he also sent them to Asher, Zebulon and Naphtali. These, too, left on the expedition to confront the enemy.

This short section shows analogies to elements in both 6.1ff. and ch. 7; it therefore does not seem to constitute an original tradition, but simply takes up other themes (Rösel **, 1976, 11). From a textual point of view the section is marked by considerable variant readings in the ancient traditions at almost every point. This is a sign of a troublesome tradition.

[33] The people concerned are again those of 6.3, cf there. The 'plain of Esdraelon' is that which runs from the beginning of the depression of the Jordan, towards Beth-shean, in a north-westerly direction; it divides the central plateau from Galilee.

[34] 'Came over', root *lābaš*, 'clothe'; the expression seems to be a late one, cf. I Chron. 12.19; II Chron. 24.20; Job 29.14 with other elements (e.g. 'curses', Ps. 109.18); it is attested through the exile. In LXX it is confirmed only by the Lagarde edition; LXX^{BA} have ἐνε-δυνάμωσεν, probably *way'ammēṣ* or, perhaps better, *wayḥazzēq*. 'Mustered': root *zā'aq* (also *ṣā'aq*); for this meaning cf. on 4.10 (where besides we have the unusual hiphil); 12.1; 18.22f. and I Sam. 14.20. In the qal the root has the meaning of 'lament', 'call for help' and is typical of the Dtr framework. LXX^A ἐβόησεν, Vg *convocavit*, and Syr *waqo'l* read Gideon as the subject and the verb in the qal: *wayyiz'aq*, whereas LXX^B has ἐφοβήθη, subject Abiezer, which does not make much sense. MT therefore seems to be in order.   [35] Note the emphatic position (first in the phrase) of 'messengers', and the same phenomenon a little later. As a result I have translated it 'immediately'. 'Mustered': cf. on the previous verse, also for LXX^A. LXX^B has a single list of those to whom messengers were sent, whereas Vg suppresses the second verb. However, this seems to be more a stylistic adjustment than a real variant. 'To confront the enemy'; the Hebrew has literally 'to encounter' or 'to come to grips with them', respectively with the Abiezrites or with the enemy: in Hebrew the third person plural pronominal suffix is ambiguous. LXX^A and Vg read the third person singular pronoun, i.e. 'with Gideon'; for LXX, on the other hand, it is Gideon who goes against the allies. This is improbable. However, the presence of *'ālāh* seems to indicate the military expedition against the enemy, not the journey to reach his people. There

is a relationship between this verse and 7.23, but we cannot call them duplicates. Cf. there.

1. As I have indicated, the section has analogies with elements contained in 6.1ff. and with 7.12; the list of peoples hostile to Israel, elements which we have seen to be secondary (cf. on 6.3), and which belong to the pan-Israelite version of 7.2ff., 23ff. Thus the text does not belong to the earliest phase of the traditions which sees only a confrontation between the Abiezrites and the Midianites, the only invaders who came from Transjordan (cf. 7.13–15, 25; 8.1, 3, 5, 12, 22, 26, 28).

2. In its present state, as in 6.1ff. the text sets out to show that the invasion from the East is not an occasional, contingent affair limited in time, in space or in the participants, but an integral part of a coherent plan in which a coalition of peoples from the East invades the land of Israel. Therefore the time is ripe for a general call to arms of all the northern tribes. Thus Manasseh, the tribe of the Abiezrites, Zebulon and Naphtali suddenly appear from the north of the plain, along with Asher, a little remote because it is situated at the north-west extremity, along the Mediterranean. There is no mention of dangers for the other tribes situated further south, as 7.1, 4 would suggest.

In its present position and context, the thesis of the narrative is that Gideon, designated by God, can now be endowed with the spirit of God, fortified as he is by the fight against Canaanite syncretism (see my comments on 3.27). The author moves within the categories of the sacred war, waged by members of the tribal alliance, even if not by all of them.

However, the logic of the account would require a different order of events: first, a local victory with local forces, that is, with the three hundred Abiezrites, and then a campaign of larger dimensions and of greater extent, with the participation of surrounding tribes (cf. 7.1, 8, 23ff.). However, here we have attitudes typical of Hebrew style: elements considered relevant in the economy of a narrative are often brought out at a prior chronological stage; here it is thought relevant that it is the tribal alliance, or a qualified part of it, which is at work, and that therefore the operation goes beyond all local limitations. However, what we have here is evidently a historical speculation which is probably a theological speculation as well: not only the tribal alliance but also its God. W. Richter**, 1963, gives a useful list of stylistic analogies between the present passage and the others mentioned.

3. It is also worth noting that the present passage seems originally not to have known the preceding episodes: the possession by the spirit obviously does not presuppose either the calling or the fight against the Canaanite cult. We have a parallel case in Saul, though with different terminology: in I Sam. 11.6ff., 'The spirit of God began to work (*wattiṣlāḥ*) in Saul . . .' Thus, like Saul, Gideon becomes a 'charismatic'. However, the reunion of different elements in a single context seems to be the work of the final redaction, at most that of the immediately pre-Dtr redaction; thus here we are confronted with something like the third calling of Gideon, a phenomenon very similar to that which we have in the case of Saul in I Sam. 11; 8.1ff. + 10.17–27; 9.1–10.16.

(e) The test of the fleece (6.36–40)

6 [36]Then Gideon said to God, 'If you really think that you will save Israel through me, as you have said, [37]behold I am laying a fleece of wool which has just been sheared on the threshing floor: if there is dew on the·fleece while the rest of the ground stays dry, I shall know that you want to save Israel through me, as you have said.' [38]And so it happened. As soon as Gideon arose the next morning he squeezed the fleece and wrung water out of it, enough to fill a bowl. [39]Then Gideon said to God: 'Do not be angry with me if I dare to address you a second time: let me put the fleece to the test a second time; let the fleece only be dry, and let dew cover the ground.' [40]And that is what God did during the night: only the fleece stayed dry and there was dew on the ground.

---

[37] 'Laying': the root *yāṣag* indicates 'laying' something out without pulling it. 'The fleece': Hebrew *gizzāh*, a *hapax legomenon* attested only here: the root is *gāzaz*, 'shear', hence '*gēz*', 'shearing'. The root signifies shorn wool, whereas *ṣemer* signifies a fleece that has not been shorn, the pelt, cf. *GesB*, *KB*[3] and H.-W. Hertzberg*, 1959. However, the translation of the term seems far from clear, and *BDB*, *KB*[2], Gray*, 1967, and Boling*, 1975, would prefer the opposite meaning: *gizzāh*, 'pelt'. Thus there are two notable differences over the meaning of the technical term; however, the nature of the operation seems clear enough. [39f]. Twice we have *'el* for *'al*, a common change in two prepositions which are phonetically and semantically similar.

1. There cannot be any doubt that this passage is not in its

proper place: the proof which Gideon asks of Yahweh is connected with his calling, cf. vv. 17ff., to which this text seems to be a parallel; in any case it seems out of the question that it could stand after the conferring of the spirit and after the call of the people to arms. Thus this text is completely isolated from what has gone before, nor do the connections with what follows in 7.1ff. seem any better: there Gideon leaves with the people who are with him. Furthermore, in this last passage he bears the name Jerubbaal (this is one of the rare occasions in chs. 6–8 on which he does so), an element which connects this passage with 6.32. However, the presence of the people associates it with vv. 33–36. What we have here, then, is an isolated passage, to some degree parallel to that in which Gideon asks for a proof from the one who calls him (6.17). It is also possible that vv. 33–35 should be transposed, in which case the present text could have been inserted, though not without some difficulty, after v. 32.

For Y. Kaufmann*, 1962 (cf. the pointer in this direction which was already made by E. Dhorme*, 1956), the passage follows 6.11–24; yet other authors, all from the first half of this century, regard vv. 11–24 and 36–40 as parallels, in that both sections describe the proof requested by Gideon from God. However, this argument does not seem convincing: in 11–24 the request for a proof is not the primary element, whereas here it is; there the proof is meant to reassure Gideon of the identity of the person who is talking to him, while here it is concerned with the outcome of his mission, and therefore takes on the role of a prediction. It therefore seems possible to follow Kaufmann in reading 11–24 and 36–40 as a sequence: first the proof of identity and then the proof and forecast of the success of the mission. On the other hand, the literary genre of the two texts seems to be different: the first is the cultic legend of a sanctuary, and therefore a well-defined genre, whereas the present text is an anecdotal legend in its pure state, with the same kind of moralizing and edificatory tendencies as those that we find in rabbinic Judaism, where people from ancient history (David, Solomon, etc.) put a 'strange' request to God or receive an equally strange one from God. The response to this is often a miracle or, on man's side, a particularly acute observation.

2. As I have indicated, here we might have a reminiscence of an instance of divination: before the battle, the combatants used to collect favourable and unfavourable omens by means of trad-

itional techniques, and the proof of the fleece with the dew has all the signs of being one of these. The interpretation and the later redaction then eliminated all the elements that might be considered scandalous because they were connected with techniques of divination, substituting the present narrative for them even in the pre-Dtr period. In the biblical world, from time immemorial dew was considered to be a gift from heaven (Gen. 27.28; Deut. 33.13), a miracle of divine grace, in the same way as rain, which partook of these characteristics to an even greater degree. In the summer, Syria and Palestine are completely dry regions, so that the dew is the only element which guarantees a minimum of humidity; for this reason dew is particularly prized. In a universe conceived of as being on three levels, heaven, earth and underworld, the dew and the rain are a gift from heaven. Thus Gideon asks for a sign from heaven, a request which, as we already saw in v. 17, is not in fact a sign of doubt, unsure faith or impiety in the person who makes it. The theme of the rain and the dew which moisten some places and leave others dry is also well known, cf. Amos 4.7 and, for the theme, also T. H. Gaster**, 1969, 419f., 530f., and R. G. Boling*, 1975. B. Margalith 1982, however, supposes this is an ancient technique for collecting dew or nocturnal humidity, a possibility which does not exclude divination.

3. As we have seen, not all the details connected with the giving of the proof are clear; for example, the object which is either moistened or left dry. Although it is connected with a fleece, we do not know precisely what it was. The action of spreading out the material which is moistened (cf. v. 38) suggests wool that has already been shorn, which could have been put on the threshing floor for ventilation. Part of the logic of the action is that the wool absorbs water in a more evident way than the beaten earth of the threshing floor. Thus this is not a miraculous sign so much as one which is unusual from a statistical point of view.

4. The reverse of the test (vv. 38–40) seems less obvious; here, however, we have the character of proof which is absent in the preceding element. The style of the discourse recalls that of Abraham in Gen. 18.32f. and seems to bear witness to Gideon's awareness that he is asking for an absurdity; this remains despite the use of those elaborate forms of courtesy which are typical of the Near East right down to the present day when an inferior addresses a superior, and which serve to maintain, if not to

and then Dtr, had in mind when they added this brief passage. This degree of obscurity explains why the fathers of the church sometimes resorted to allegory in their attempts to explain the episode. In that case the dew becomes grace, the wool the people of God; however, these are explanations which, quite apart from the illegitimacy of allegorical exegesis, could hold for the first part of the test, but not for the second. The only possible explanation is that the sign motif was always part of the Gideon cycle and therefore could not be suppressed, but only transformed. At the same time, from a stylistic point of view, the story has the important function of building up suspense.

(ii) Campaign in Cisjordan

(a) The troops of the tribal league and the three hundred Abiezrites (7.1–8)

7 [1]Jerubbaal, that is Gideon, and all his people arose early and encamped near the spring of Harod; the camp of Midian was to the north, under the hill of Moreh, in the plain.

2 Then Yahweh said to Gideon, 'The people with you are too many for me to give Midian into your hands, lest Israel vaunt themselves and say that their own power has liberated them. [3]So make an announcement to the people in these terms, "Let anyone who is fearful and trembling go home!" In this way Gideon put them to the test, and of the people twenty-two thousand went home and ten thousand remained.

4 But Yahweh said to Gideon, The people are still too many. Make them go down to the water where I will put them to the test, and he of whom I shall say to you, "This man will go with you", he shall go; and all those of whom I say to you, "This man shall not go with you", shall not go.' [5]Then Gideon made the people go down to the water. And Yahweh said to Gideon: 'Everyone who laps the water with his tongue, like a dog does, you shall put aside; and everyone who kneels down to drink, conveying the water to their mouth with his hands, you shall also set him aside.' [6]And the number of those who lapped the water with their tongues was three hundred men, whereas the rest of the people knelt down to drink, and conveyed the water to their mouths with their hands. [7]Then Yahweh said to Gideon, 'With the three hundred men who lapped I will deliver you, and will give Midian into your hands! Let the others go back home.'

8 $\left\{\begin{array}{l}\text{Then the three hundred took provisions}\\\text{Then Gideon took the jars}\end{array}\right\}$ from the hands of the people, and also their horns, and he sent the rest of Israel every

man to his tent, keeping instead the three hundred men. And the camp
of Midian was below him, in the valley.

It is not easy to translate the present passage, one of the best known
in the Old Testament, because the text is often corrupt and its details
are sometimes obscure. However, most of the time we can reconstruct
it with a reasonable degree of certainty. The fact that vv. 1b and 8b
are virtually identical shows that we are almost certainly dealing with
an interpolation (Richter**, 1963, 120; Rösel**, 1976, 11).

[1] This continues on from 6.34 and 36–40; the reading *y'rubba'al*,
which does not appear in the sequel, seems to be secondary (Richter**,
1963, 186, and the bibliography there). The topographical details,
which are not always clear, serve to connect the verse on the one hand
with the account of the battle, 7.9–22, and with the request for a sign,
6.36–40, and on the other hand with 6.33f., cf. 7.23f. and 7.25–8.1
(Richter**, 1963, 187). 'Arose': the traditional version, which I accept,
is better than that proposed by R. G. Boling*, 1975: 'They busied
themselves'. 'Near': the preposition *'al* here does not mean 'at the
waters', as H. W. Hertzberg supposes, but 'near the waters', a sense
which the preposition has in Ugaritic (Aistleitner no. 2030. 4), but
often also in Hebrew, cf. 5.19; Pss. 1.3; 23.2; 42.5f.; 81.8; 137.1f.[29] 'The
spring of Harod' or *'ēn ḥ'rōd*, in Arabic *'ēn ğālūd*, is characterized
by a strong jet of water, probably spasmodic: the verb *ḥārad* in fact
means 'tremble', so that there is a play on words with v. 3a; today the
area is fed by an artificial reservoir and an irrigation system. It is half
way up the trunk road from *'affulāh* to *bet šeʾān*, a few hundred metres
north of it, under the range of *gilbōᵃʿ* (coord. 184–217).

As I have said, the topographical indications are not very clear, cf.
the comments by A. Penna*, 1963, and Rösel**, though I do not
follow these entirely. Penna points out the parallel with I Sam. 28.4,
where Saul is encamped near Gilboa, probably at the same place as
Gideon (even if, against Penna, the place is not specified); by contrast
the Philistines are at *šūnēm*, Arabic *śūlam* (coord. 181–223). However, if we insert *mittaḥat l'gib'at* and delete *miggib''at* (cf. v. 8b, and the
discussion in Burney*, 1919, but not more recent commentators), we
obtain the text which I suggest. In any case, Gideon's camp is thought
to be on a hill, cf. the descent to the spring in v. 4, and the contrast
with the camp of Midian, which is in the plain (v. 8b). H. Rösel**,
1976, 11ff., however, points to the note given in Ps. 83.10ff., which
runs: 'Do to them as you did to Midian . . . who were destroyed at *'ēn
dōʾr* . . .' (note the unusual spelling, instead of *dōr*); and this is the
place where Saul had his encounter with the witch (I Sam. 28, coord.
187–228). This represents an obvious *lectio difficilior*. However, a great

many commentators on the Psalms think that there is a corruption of
ʿēn ḥᵃrōd, the original reading, deleting Midian in v. 10, as Rösel
recognizes. So after having examined four possible readings (including
that of Burney, which I have just proposed), he decides on the following: *ūmaḥᵃnē midyān hāyāh miṣṣāpōn lᵉgibʿat hammōreh*, 'the camp of
Midian was to the north of the hill of Moreh', so that Gideon and his
followers would be on the height in question. He affirms this on the
basis of Ps. 83.10ff., which I have just examined, cf. also A. Malamat**, 1971, 143f. However, quite apart from the problems connected
with the psalm (which I have also just examined), it is difficult to see
why the insertion, the topography of which seems to be connected
with I Sam. 28.4, did not make the Israelites drink in a less remote
place. 'Moreh': a proper name, or 'heights of the master', or, 'of
instruction, of the oracle', cf. C. F. Burney*, 1919: 'hill of the oracle
giver', or R. G. Boling*, 1975, 'teacher's hill'. This is usually identified
with *ğebel nebī dāḥi* (coord. 184–225).

[2] I have rendered the original direct speech after 'and say' as
indirect speech. 'Power': literally 'hand'.

[3] 'Make an announcement . . .': literally, 'Cry in the ears of the
people'. 'And Gideon put them . . .': the text is damaged: the Hebrew
has 'And Gideon . . . [verb *ṣāpar*ᵢᵢ, of unknown meaning] . . . from
the mount of Gilead', a phrase which does not make sense, though it
is explicitly defended by E. Dhorme*, 1956, who thinks of something
like the return by devious ways, via the mount of Gilead. For the
discussion cf. Burney 1914 and *1919, who thinks, among other things,
of an original *wᵉyaʿᵃbōr*, 'and went beyond', hence 'withdrew'; cf. LXX
καὶ ἐκχωρεῖτο; Vg *et recesserunt*; however, this seems to be the *lectior
facilior*, and even actually more convenient. G. F. Moore*, 1895, and
M.-J. Lagrange*, 1903, followed today by A. Penna*, 1963, and J.
Gray**, cf. *BHK*³ and *BHS*, proposed that we should read *wayyiṣrᵉpēm
gidʿōn*, a reading which I adopt. 'Twenty-two thousand . . . ten thousand': here we cannot read 'twenty-two units' and 'ten units' respectively, following the proposal made by Mendenhall and mentioned in
connection with 4.6; it is clear that the biblical tradition understood
these to be real figures, evidently much inflated, to make the miracle
of Gideon's three hundred seem all the greater. Another difficulty in
the text is the mention of 'Gilead' to which I have referred; C. F.
Burney*, 1919, and R. G. Boling*, 1975, would prefer to connect it
with the Arabic name *ğālūd*, rather than with the Transjordanian
region of the same name, whereas *ḥᵃrōd* would arise from the play of
words mentioned in v. 1. The correction of *gilʿad* to *gidʿōn* proposed
by Gray*, 1967, seems simpler, and I accept it.

[4] The brook *ḥᵃrōd/ğālūd* runs eastwards and flows into the
Jordan.

[5f]. Verses 5b–6a are also in obvious disorder and there are marked

variants, especially between MT and LXX^A. However, it is only possible to reconstruct the text because of all these variants. Boling* gives a useful synoptic table of all the variants (p. 145); cf. also the discussion in A. Penna*, 1963.

In v. 5b LXX^A, cf. Vg and Syr, adds at the end μεταστήσεις αὐτὸν καθ᾽ αὐτόν, i.e. *taṣṣīg ʾōtō lᵉbād*, a reading which I have adopted. However, it seems obvious that in v. 6a the reference to the person who conveys the water to his mouth with his hands is to the person who drinks kneeling and not to the one who 'laps like a dog'; therefore I have inserted this element, taking it from its present position, even though that is attested by LXX^{BA}. LXX^A has a further peculiarity: after 'anyone who laps' it adds the expression 'with the tongue' (Rudolph**, 1947); the present displacement of 5b to 6a may perhaps be explained as an instance of homoioteleuton: six words in v. 6b end in *mem*, a situation which, according to Boling*, 1975, explains the phenomenon.

There is considerable confusion about the character of the test. It is not in fact easy to establish why the one who 'laps with his tongue, like a dog' should be better suited for the holy war than the one who drinks kneeling, conveying the water to his mouth with his hands. T. H. Gaster**, 1969, 420ff., 531, followed by Boling*, indicates numerous parallels from the history of religions and from ethnology, from which it emerges that those who tend to drink (or to eat) like an animal show that they have no preoccupations, whereas those who drink kneeling stay on the alert, ready to respond to an attack from the rear. However, the more ancient interpretation differs from this: Josephus, *Antt.* V. vi. 3 =§§216f., and later, the church father Theodoret, see here rather a sign of fear, and comment how God chooses inadequate men so that all may redound to his glory: in that case Gideon's three hundred men would be not only few but also neither wary nor able-bodied. Inadequate though these explanations may be, they are in any case better than the more common one, that the speed with which the three hundred throw themselves down beside the water indicates 'courage and fighting *élan*' (Penna*, 1963); the opposite could also be the case; it could be an indication of irresponsibility and lack of control, and therefore of small aptitude for fighting. It is probably more reasonable not to think in terms of any particular meaning; we are dealing here with a test, a kind of ordeal by which God selects his own men.

[8] Another difficult text: what is the subject, which must be plural, of the initial verb? The three hundred or 'the people'? This latter possibility seems remote: syntactically, in fact, the subject usually follows the verb, except when it is emphatic, in which case it precedes it.[30] However, the second verb *šillaḥ* and successive verbs have Gideon

[30]R. Meyer, III, §91.1.

as subject, so that we may conjecture that he is also the subject of the first; in that case it should have read *wayyiqqaḥ*: thus K. Budde, 1897, and C. F. Burney, 1919, and more recently, J. Gray*, 1967. This is a practical way of getting out of the difficulty: in that case it is the commander who does the assigning. Another possibility is to read ἐπισιτισμὸν τοῦ λαοῦ with LXX^BA, i.e. *'et ṣēdat hāʿām*: the people go, but leave with the combatants the provisions they have brought; in that case the three hundred are the subject. The objections made by G.F. Moore*, 1895, and by Burney *, 1919, that the provisions for so many people would have been too many for only three hundred suggests, however, that we should read *kaddē hāʿām*, 'the jars of the people', which would anticipate a theme which proves vital in vv. 16–22 and perhaps was no longer understood later. One apparent difficulty, however, is the fact that while the presence of provisions is obvious, that of the jars is not mentioned explicitly, and in vv. 16ff. it appears as a completely new development, but in a context in which it has its natural position. However, while accepting this difficulty, we need to ask whether the mention of the horns, too, which here is made in an obviously secondary way, relating somewhat obscurely to what has gone before (why ever would the people going home have had so many horns with them?) and very much at odds with what the text says, is not also itself an anticipatory mention of vv. 16ff. (Rudolph **,1947); these verses speak (cf. the comments there) of horns, jars and torches in an indeterminate form (without the article), implying that they are items which appear only at that point, and are previously unknown. 'From their/his hands': there is no need to read *miyādām* for *bᵉyādām*: in Hebrew, as in Ugaritic, *bᵉ* can have the meaning of 'from', as indeed in Phoenician (cf. Aistleitner, no. 486.3d and *KB³*, s.v., §13, against J. Gray*, 1967, and R. G. Boling*, 1975; the latter has 'into their [i.e. the three hundred's] own hands'. Others (Rudolph**, 1947, Penna*, 1963, and *BHS*, but not *BHK³*) suggest a correction to avoid the awkwardness indicated by Burney*, 1919: read *bᵉdayyām* (metathesis) 'in accordance with their need', 'as they required', but this does not seem necessary. 'To his tent. . .': one might think of the semi-nomadic origins of the tribes of Israel; however, the expression soon became synonymous with 'going home', as is clear from II Sam.20.1b and I Kings 12.16: ((Each one) to $\begin{Bmatrix} \text{his} \\ \text{your} \end{Bmatrix}$ tent, O Israel . . .!'

The redactors of this text, probably pre-Dtr, but late, were interested in showing that the tribal league, albeit in reduced numbers (only Manasseh, Asher, Zebulon and Naphtali joined in, first in the assembly, 6.34f., and then in the pursuit, 7.23f.), was the protagonist in the campaign under the leadership of

Gideon, but that the real protagonist of the operation was the God of Israel. However, it was difficult to reconcile an argument like this with the earlier tradition which had only the three hundred Abiezrites of Gideon as the architects of victory. The difficulty is resolved here on a narrative theological plane: the number of three hundred heroes remains, but it is shown that this number was arrived at by means of two successive reductions in the number of the partipants. The first was voluntary, in the sense that anyone who had any kind of doubt about his capacities and his courage was allowed to go home. This is a procedure in Deut. 20.8, at the end of a series of instances of exemption from military service, though for different reasons from those given here: concern that the fearfulness of the cowards may infect the brave (Hertzberg*). The second reduction is achieved by means of a test to which the participants are subjected without being aware of it, a kind of ordeal in which God chooses his own. This produces just three hundred men, all Abiezrites. That the victory, and hence all the merit, must belong only to the God of Israel is one of the fundamental themes of the institution of the holy war,[31] cf. among other passages Judg.5 in the second phase, with its theologizing approach (above, pp. 99f.), and also I Sam. 14.6; Isa. 10.12; 59.16; I Macc. 3.19. R. G. Boling*, 1975, 148, also observes that we should note that all ch. 7 serves to provide a theological perspective on ch. 8, on the events and especially the victory described here, seeking to reduce all human merit to a minimum. So much so, that there are plenty of texts in which the human initiative is even considered to be a negative factor, cf. I Sam. 25.26,33 (Penna*, 1963). In 6.27ff., the text simply takes note of Gideon's initiative, without either praising or condemning him. It is also interesting to note that whereas the earlier text attributes divinatory practices to Gideon, the present one attributes them directly to God himself, in that an ordeal is used to recognize the people whom he wants to choose as his troops.

[31]G. von Rad***, 1951, *passim*; P. D. Miller, *The Divine Warrior in Early Israel*, Harvard Semitic Monographs 3, Cambridge, Mass. 1973, *passim*.

(b) Favourable omens (7.9–15)

7 ⁹That same night, Yahweh said to him, 'Arise, go down against the camp, because I have given it into your hands, ¹⁰and if you are afraid to go down by yourself, go down to the camp with your shield-bearer Purah. ¹¹You will hear what they say and be encouraged to attack the camp.' Then he went down together with his shield-bearer Purah in the direction of the outposts of the armed men that were in the camp. ¹²The Midianites, the Amalekites and all the people of the East had invaded the plain, as numerous as locusts; they had countless camels, as many in number as the sand on the sea shore.

13 When Gideon arrived, there was a man there who was telling his companion about a dream. He said, 'Behold, I had a dream: a loaf of barley bread rolled into the camp of Midian; when it came to the tent, it struck it and made it fall and turned it upside down. Then it lay there, flattened!' ¹⁴His companion replied: 'That can only mean the sword of Gideon, son of Joash, the Israelite: God has given Midian and all the camp into his hands!'

15 When Gideon heard the telling of the dream and its interpretation, he knelt before Yahweh in prayer and then returned to the Israelite camp. Then he said, 'Up, for Yahweh has given the camp of Midian into our hands!'

The text of this section seems to be in good condition. The formula 'Yahweh said (to him) . . .' (v. 9), which serves to interpret the tradition (Richter**, 1963, 206f.), is also typical of J and the 'collector'. Thus we have a tradition which, with the exception of vv. 12 and 14, has all the marks of authenticity and which is probably part of the earliest stratum of the story. 'That same night. . .': we do not know whether this is the same night as that mentioned in 6.25ff., or whether the narrator meant another one. **[10]** 'Shield-bearer' is one of the meanings which the term *na'ar*, normally 'young man', can take on in contexts of this kind. The person in question does not have any function in the narrative other than that of accompanying Gideon and bearing silent testimony to what he sees and hears. **[11]** 'Be encouraged': literally 'strengthen your hand'. 'Outposts of the armed men': the expression seems pertinent, even though it is difficult, perhaps made up of technical terms. 'The outposts' are denoted by the same term as 'extremities': *ḥᵃmūšīm* are 'the armed (men)'. LXX πεντήκοντα has misinterpreted it as *ḥᵃmiššīm*, 'fifty'. **[12]** This verse again belongs to the tradition of the three peoples. It has nothing to do with the present passage; indeed, it contradicts it because it does not presuppose a camp under guard but an open and scattered encampment. *šeʿal* : note here, as in 5.7b and 6.17, the prefix *še-* which appears in archaic and late texts. **[13]** 'I had a dream. . .', an expression attested for

Joseph, Gen. 37.5–10; 40.5–9; 41.11–15 and 42.9; for the (false) prophets, Deut. 13.2–6 (EVV 1–5); cf. Jer. 29.8 and 23.28 (without a verb); the people in Joel 3.1 (EVV 2.28); cf. also Dan. 2.1ff. Thus the usage seems to be concentrated in passages which refer to Joseph and in Dtn and Dtr. The last part, 13bβ is somewhat harsh, and perhaps some of its elements have been deleted, cf. *BHS*. However, this is not a necessary conclusion. The variants, K: *ṣᵉlûl*, Q:*ṣᵉlîl*, should be noted; the term is not clear. For some scholars it is 'slice' or 'shape', but the former cannot roll, so it must be a 'loaf' (Rösel **, 1976, 14). For its condition and ingredients (fresh or stale, leavened or unleavened), cf. G. R. Driver**, 1964, 13. 'The (one) tent' is a symbol for all the camp.

[14] The explanation of the dream given by the man talking to the person who dreamed it is evidently meant not for the dreamer, but for Israel; furthermore, v. 15 refers only to the account of the dream and not to its explanation. A Midianite would have difficulty in recognizing the name and the patronym of his adversary, whereas the reference to the 'sword of Gideon' recalls his future war-cry (7.20). The mention of 'God', stressed in LXX^A (*Kyrios*), is another element in this direction.   [15] 'In prayer': LXX has 'Yahweh', a reading adopted by many commentators, but not by Hertzberg, 1959, or by Gray*, 1967; others (Hertzberg and Penna) render it 'knelt in prayer', a translation which I have adopted: this is the sense of *ḥāwāh* in a cultic context like ours; it is lacking in the Greek, so that LXX had to be specific.

This text introduces another element connected with divination: a prediction given by means of a dream. This time the protagonist is the enemy himself, overheard by Gideon and his shield-bearer during a nocturnal reconnaissance. The circumstances make the best of both worlds: on the one hand the author of the prediction is Yahweh, and Gideon is strengthened in his intentions by hearing it; on the other hand, it is the enemy who has the dream, which excludes practices of this kind in Israel and at the same time heightens the tension, the suspense, in the text.

As an element of divination, the dream is well attested elsewhere in the Old Testament, as we have seen in connection with the text. It can be found both in the Joseph story and in the Dtn and Dtr preaching on false prophecy; then, much later, in Daniel. However, the theme is also widespread throughout the ancient Near East.[32] Here, as Pedersen rightly indicates

[32] J. Pedersen, *Israel: its Life and Culture* I-II, Copenhagen and London 1926, 133–40; A. L. Oppenheim, *The Interpretation of Dreams in the Ancient Near East*, Philadelphia 1956; and of course the basic study by E. L. Ehrlich, *Der Traum im Alten Testament*, BZAW 73, 1953.

(p. 137), it is the psychology of imminent defeat which produces this kind of dream: the enemy is beaten before the battle proper has been lost. Thus as far as the Midianites are concerned, we have a nightmare.

The 'loaf of barley bread' is clearly the symbol of Israel. The text does not say whether this is enormously large (H.W. Hertzberg*, 1959, *ungeheuer*); rather, it seems that here too the stress is laid on its smallness, its inadequacy in producing such weighty results. Furthermore, the identity of the loaf with Israel is indicated by the exact but pedantic explanation in v. 14. However, barley, like any form of cereal crop, presupposes agriculture and therefore a sedentary state, or its equivalent for Israel, whereas 'the tent', one which represents the whole camp, is the typical sign of the nomad. Thus once again (cf. Cain and Abel, Gen. 4; Jacob and Esau, Gen. 27) a biblical account contrasts the nomad with the settler; and here, as in the other cases, the settler wins.

Gideon goes down with his shield-bearer, a feature also attested in I Sam. 14.1ff. and 26.6ff., for Jonathan and David respectively. The reason why the two go together here is Gideon's fear of being left alone, which is expressed only in the presence of Yahweh; however, the fact that Gideon then does in fact go with the shield-bearer shows that this fear really continues. This is probably meant to underline the fact that even the leader whom Yahweh has foreordained for a mission of this kind cannot do anything without divine aid, although this is in contradiction to the greeting of the angel in 6.11ff. However, whereas in the other passages mentioned the presence of the shield-bearer has a purpose, and he is involved in the action, even being engaged in continuous dialogue with the protagonist, here we have someone who does not do that, says nothing, and is completely unnecessary for the purpose of the narrative.

For the redactors of the cycle, the stage is now set for the battle.

(c) The attack (7.16–22)

7 [16] Then Gideon divided up the three hundred men into three columns and put a horn in the hand of each of them and an empty jar, with a torch inside the jar. [17]Then he said to them: 'Look at me, and do likewise: when I come to the outposts of the camp, do as I do. [18]When I blow the horn, I and all who are with me, then blow your horns too, around the camp, and say, "For Yahweh and Gideon!" '

19 So Gideon and the hundred men who were with him arrived at

the outposts at the beginning of the second watch, when the sentries had just been set; they blew the horns and broke the jars which they had in their hand. ²⁰Then the three columns blew their horns, broke their jars, holding the torches in their left hands and the horns to blow in their right, and cried, 'A sword, for Yahweh and for Gideon!' ²¹Every man had taken up position in his proper place, surrounding the camp. And the whole camp leapt to its feet and fled. ²²When the three hundred sounded their horns and let out their war cry, Yahweh directed each man's sword within the camp against his companion, and the camp fled to Beth-shittah, towards Zererah, as far as the boundaries of Abel-meholah, near Tabbath.

The text is probably early, and has been transmitted with care, even if there are a number of tensions: between Gideon and the three independent columns (vv. 16f., 20) on the one hand, and Gideon as commander of one of them (vv. 18f.) on the other; between the general flight of the enemy in vv. 21, 22b and the theme of the reciprocal killing in v. 22a. However, these are inconsistencies which can be explained in the context of the transmission of the text and therefore do not suggest the presence of two sources (thus perhaps A. Penna*, 1963, but against W. Richter**, 1963, 199). For the other features see the commentary. **[16]** The division into 'three columns' (Hebrew ra'šîm, literally 'heads') goes well with the figure of three hundred men, even if it is somewhat mechanical; it is also attested in I Sam. 11.11, where, however, it is intrinsically logical. **[19]** An LXX tradition, based on the Lucianic recension, reads the singular, thus having only Gideon himself as the subject. In that case we would have a text which read (cf. BHK³ and BHS): wayyitgaʿ baššôpār wᵉnāpîṣ hakkād ᵃšer bᵉyādô, a reading which we must in any case adopt in a translation into a Western language: in Hebrew MT's reading is hard, but not impossible, given that Hebrew often tends to anticipate events or facts which it considers particularly important, thus giving rise to dyschronological narratives, as they have been called. In a translation into a Western language, a stylistic figure of this kind is impossible. 'The beginning of the second watch': in Israel the night was divided into three watches, each of four hours, a principle similar to that of the Roman vigiliae, except that in Rome each watch lasted for a period of three hours. The 'third watch' appears in Ex. 14.24 and in I Sam. 11.11, and is also called 'the morning watch'; watches are also attested in Jub. 49.10–12. In late Judaism there could also have been four watches, probably following the example of Rome, cf. Mark 13.35 in the New Testament and Ber. 3ab in the Talmud. 'Broke': infinite absolute with a finite meaning. **[20]** Some authors (cf. BHK³ and BHS) would like to read haḥereb instead of MT haššôpārôt litqōᵃ', which would make better sense; however, such a reading is not supported by any authority. Furthermore, it seems to be an attempt to straighten out the confused state of the text. I do not accept it, as it is a *lectio facilior*. **[21]** 'Leapt to its feet . . . ': from Moore*, 1895, onwards, many authors tend to read *wayyīqaṣ*, root *qyṣ*, 'woke up', though it is never attested in this form; those who keep it with MT translate it as 'escape', 'run away', root *rwṣ*, which is also never used in this sense besides being a duplicate with what follows. G. R. Driver**, 1964, has shown that *rwṣ* can have, on rare occasions, the meaning of 'leap', 'jump (to one's feet)', cf. Gen. 25.22; Joel 2.9; Nahum 2.5 (EVV 4); Ps. 18.30, a meaning which it has here. 'And fled': K read a hiphil of *nws* not attested elsewhere: *wayyānīsū*: 'And (the Israelites) shouted out and put them to flight.' The Q, *wayyānūsū*, with the camp as subject, seems better. However, in that case we have another problem: the use of *wayyārī'ū*, root *rw'*, almost always in the hiphil, indicates the war cry or the acclamation in the religious or political sense of the term, so that it does not seem applicable to the Midianites, who if anything are uttering cries of terror: KB^2 and other dictionaries also indicate that this meaning is extremely rare. Instead, P. Humbert suggests that the verb should be transposed to v. 22, after 'sounded the horns', a proposal which I accept. **[22]** 'Let out their war cry. . .'; cf. the comments on the preceding verse. None of the places mentioned here has been identified with any degree of certainty, though it seems obvious that they must all be located to the east and the south-east. *bēt šiṭṭāh* could correspond either to the Arab village of *šaṭṭah* (coord. 191–217), to the west of *bet š'an* (thus E. Robinson, who was opposed by Moore* and Burney*, and now by Boling* and Rösel**, 1976), or to a locality immediately beyond the Jordan, *ṣ'rērāt*, a word which should not be changed and is probably a phonetic variant of *ṣar'tān*, the present-day *tell es-sa'idīya* (coord. 186–205, Pritchard), or the *tell umm hāmad* (coord. 172–205, Aharoni**, 1967): here at any rate it is to the south-east of *'abel m'ḥōlāh*, probably beyond the Jordan. *'abel m'ḥōlāh* can be either *tell abu sifri* (coord. 197–197), or *tell el maqlūb* on the *wādī yabiš*, coord. 214–201 (improbable, cf. on 21.1–14, where I identify this *tell* with *yābeš*), or again *ḥirbet el ḥilū*, coord. 192–197 (Aharoni**, 1967), or also *abū ṣūṣ* or *abū 'aṣūṣ*, coord. 203–197 (Rösel**, 1976); this *tell* has two fords in the vicinity. The location of *ṭabbat* is also uncertain: perhaps *rāš abū ṭabat*, near *'aǧlūn* in Transjordan (coord. 223–192, against Rösel). Notwithstanding the uncertainty of all these locations, it is possible to note two directions of flight: one more or less in the area in which the battle took place, and the other much further away, towards the south and south-east, perhaps this was a divergence of different groups (A. Penna*, 1963).

The reader will immediately notice that at first sight everything happens with virtually no human contribution, at least of a military kind: in v. 22 it is God who 'directs the sword' of each Midianite 'against his companion' instead of against the attackers. So it is not as if the Midianites lacked the will to fight, but rather that they lacked the capacity to discern their real enemy. This theme can also be found elsewhere in the Old Testament: in II Chron. 20.1–30, esp. vv. 22f., the Amorites and the Edomites, allied against Judah, destroy one another after the liturgical action performed by Judah under the direction of the pious King Jehoshaphat; and it is in fact God himself who 'laid ambush (to them)'! The similarity between the two situations is remarkable, even if authors are agreed in attributing the present passage to an ancient tradition.

Furthermore, it seems that there is no liturgical action here. However, it is not completely absent, although it is not as evident as in the Chronicles passage already mentioned. The sounding of the horns cannot in fact be understood as a secular act, seeing that here we have the *šōpār*, the ram's horn, which is still sounded in acts of solemn worship even today. The human involvement in the operation, which at first sight seems important in the stratagem, is in fact reduced to a very small element, seeing that the stratagem is followed by panic and rout in the enemy camp; however, it is also evident that the stratagem in itself does not have a definitive function: an adversary in good order, disciplined and ready for battle, could easily have recovered.

Still, it should also be noted that v. 22 seeks in some degree to correct v. 21: the victory of Israel or better, of the three hundred, is not caused by the stratagem, but by divine intervention. That the verse is in fact an interpolation intended to provide a theological explanation is also evident at a stylistic level: v. 21 ends with *wayyanūsū*, and v. 22b begins again with *wayyānos hammahᵃneh* . . . with the only difference the third person plural of v. 21 and the third person singular of v. 22.

However, there are other features which it is important to note. As H.-W. Hertzberg*, 1959, pointed out, there is a certain tension between the sound of the horn and the war-cry. It is not that the presence of both of these is technically impossible, but it makes the narrative all the more improbable, seeing that v. 20 felt the necessity of giving a detailed explanation of how this could happen. Furthermore, to break the jars with the torches alight inside them and to hold horns in the other hand is quite a difficult operation; to sound the trumpet holding a torch in the other hand, and alternating between blowing the horns and uttering the war-cry is a complex operation at the best of times. Perhaps we can recognize the following phases in the narrative:

(*a*) The story of the stratagem: kindled torches are hidden in the jars and are suddenly shown when the jars are broken; this unexpected sight, which will certainly have been sinister at night, accompanied by the war-cry, threw the enemies of Israel into confusion and they fled.

(*b*) The immediately pre-Dtr redaction found that the narrative did not have any theological elements and sought to remedy this. It introduced the horns, obtaining an effect like that produced in the siege of Jericho, Josh. 6.1ff.: the three columns of the attackers became a procession, and it is God who gives the final victory in an operation similar to that mentioned in II Chron. 20.1–30, without any help from human agents: the decisive element continues to be the divine intervention in v. 22a. Here, then, we have a slight cultic coloration which at the same time provides the key for a theological reading of the whole passage.

(*d*) The capture of two princes of Midian (7.23–8.3)

7 [23]Then the men of Israel mobilized themselves, from Naphtali, from Asher and from all Manasseh, and pursued Midian. [24]Gideon again sent messengers throughout the 'Mountain of Ephraim' with the following message: 'Come down against the Midianites and cut off the fords of the Jordan against them!' So all the men of Ephraim mobilized and seized the fords of the Jordan. [25]They also captured the two princes of Midian, Oreb and Zeeb; the first they killed at the 'rock of Oreb' and the second at the 'wine press of Zeeb'. They continued to pursue Midian, but they brought the heads of Oreb and Zeeb to Gideon beyond the Jordan.

8 [1]But the men of Ephraim said to him: 'What is this that you have done? You went to fight against Midian without calling us!' And they upbraided him violently. [2]He replied to them: 'What have I done in comparison with what you have done? The gleaning of the grapes of Ephraim is certainly better than the vintage of Abiezer! [3]God has delivered the princes of Midian, Oreb and Zeeb, into your hands, and what have I been able to do in comparison with you?' Then their anger against him was abated, when he had said this.

[**23**] For ṣā'aq/zā'aq, 'mobilize', cf. 6.34 and the note there. Here too LXX reads ἐβόησεν/-αν, the active, with Gideon as subject. The

tribes called with the same technique as in 6.35 are the same tribes, except for Zebulon; in 7.11ff. they had been sent home because the troops were too numerous. **[24]** 'Cut off. . . .': for this use of *lᵉ* in *lāhem* cf. on 3.28. Here and in v. 24b MT continues, 'the waters as far as Beth-barah and the Jordan', but this does not make any sense. C. F. Burney* proposes *'et ma'bᵉrōt hayyardēn*, a reading which I accept; the situation is identical to that described in 3.28 and 12.5f.: the present text seems to be the product of the dittography of *ma'bᵉrōt* and the confusion of *reš* and *dālet* (Burney). The 'Mountain of Ephraim' is the name of a region which also includes Manasseh, cf. Josh. 17.15; 20.7; Judg. 4.5 (cf. there); in I Kings 4.8 it is one of the northern districts, created under Solomon. It is probable (and is generally accepted), though it cannot be demonstrated, that the tribe of the same name took its name from the region, and not vice versa. The note given here does not fit very well with that of 8.1–3, where the Ephraimites complain that they were not called; however, the text seems rather to want to convey that they complained about the subordinate position assigned to them first in the campaign and then in the battle, a position which Gideon then redefines. **[25]** The names of the two princes who are captured and put to death are 'crow' and 'wolf' respectively, and they are then given an aetiological relationship (thus, rightly, W. Richter**, 1963, 208, against R. G. Boling*, 1975) with two places which have not been identified. Purely and simply for reasons of assonance scholars have thought of the *'ušš eǧ ǧurāb* ('crow's nest') and the *tuwāl eḍ-ḍihāb* ('wolf's cave'), both a little to the north of Jericho – the respective coordinates are 193–145 and 191–147 – but these places are evidently too far south (Burney): however, it could be an Ephraimite tradition (Rösel**, 1976). The text puts these places in Cisjordan, cf. v. 25b, whereas Gideon would already be in Transjordan. Aetiological as it is, the mention of the two princes must be secondary compared with what follows in 8.5ff., 10ff., 24f., even if it is reported by Isa. 10.26a and Ps. 83.12. 'Pursued': read *'et* for *'el* ('towards the Midianites') with the ancient translations. **[8.2]** The quarrel is settled by Gideon with a *bon mot* or a proverb, which Gideon brings up to date, applying it to the situation (Richter**, 1963, 208): whatever Abiezer can have achieved is less than the least of the achievements of Ephraim. 'Certainly . . .': here too I prefer to render *hᵃlō'* as an emphatic affirmation rather than as a rhetorical question (cf. 4.6).

As we have seen, the episode which we have just examined contains a number of contradictions, appearing as it does between the decisive victory over Midian and the final pursuit; on a logistical level it seems absurd that Gideon first sent home a large part of his confederate troops and then recalled them the next moment; such a procedure will certainly have taken time and is hardly compatible with the speed of the pursuit; however, this is a pan-Israelite version of events which is harmonized with the tradition of the three hundred Abiezrites, which is undoubtedly original; there is another seam in 8.2, where only Abiezer (and not the other groups) is contrasted with Ephraim.

The purpose of the information introduced here is by no means clear, except as an explanation of the two names connected with the region of 'Mount Ephraim' and the affirmation that Ephraim is the most important of all the tribes. Furthermore, this statement reflects its later position, whereas here, as we have seen, it is a purely verbal declaration, meant to 'save face' and not create difficulties for Gideon with other groups. The whole thing would therefore suggest a relatively late composition, perhaps written on the basis of the traditions of Ehud, the actual foundation of which is the reminiscence of a quarrel between Ephraim and Manasseh about the division of the spoil, a quarrel which was resolved when the former accepted the explanation given by the latter. Now the narrative has been completely, albeit precariously, inserted into the traditions of the Gideon cycle.

(iii) Campaign in Transjordan (8.4–35)

(a) Gideon in Transjordan (8.4–12)

8 ⁴And Gideon came to the Jordan. He crossed it with his three hundred men, tired and hungry. ⁵He said to the inhabitants of Succoth, 'Please give loaves of bread to the people who follow me, because they are exhausted; I am pursuing Zebah and Zalmunna, kings of Midian!' ⁶But the officials of Succoth replied: 'Is the power of Zebah and Zalmunna already in your hands that we should give you bread for your army?' ⁷Gideon replied to them: 'Because of this, when Yahweh has delivered Zebah and Zalmunna into my hands I will flail your flesh with the thorns of the wilderness and with briars!'

8 And he went up to Penuel and spoke to them in the same way; but the men of Penuel replied to him like those of Succoth. ⁹Then he replied to them: 'When I return safe and sound, I shall break down this tower!'

10 Now Zebah and Zalmunna were at Karkor with all their troops, about fifteen thousand men, all who were left of the people of the East: one hundred and twenty thousand of them had fallen, all able-bodied men. ¹¹Gideon attacked by the caravan route which runs east of Nobah and Jogbehah and fell on the army when it thought that it was safe.

[12]Zebah and Zalmunna fled, but he pursued them. He captured the two kings of Midian, Zebah and Zalmunna, and routed all their troops.

---

[4] 'Crossed it . . .': the Hebrew has the active participle qal, but the readings *wayya'ªbōr* or *wayya'ªbᵉrēhū* (imperfect qal with *waw* consecutive) or even (Hertzberg*, 1959) *we'ābar* (perfect qal with *waw* copulative) are usually preferred, cf. LXX, Vg and Syr. 'Hungry': the Hebrew has 'exhausted and pursuing', not impossible but rather strange. I suggest that we should follow LXX[A] and Syr in reading *ūrᵉ'ēbīm*, which would explain better the request for food rather than a place to rest. [5] 'Succoth' has always been identified with *tell dēir 'alla*, coord. 209–178 (cf. S. Mittmann, 1965), but this identification has recently been questioned by the director of the excavations on the *tell*, J. H. Franken,[33] followed by R. de Vaux: it has been proposed recently, though only tentatively, by H. Rösel**, 1976, 24, and R. G. Boling*, 1975.

The verse unexpectedly names two Midianite 'kings', an obvious parallel to the two 'princes' of the previous section. The first name means 'sacrifice' or 'sacrificial victim', the second is a composite word (a very rare occurrence in Semitic languages): *ṣel*, 'shade' (here in the sense of 'resting place', 'refuge', cf. *KB* s.v.), and *munnā'*, pual participle without prefix[34] of *māna'*, 'withhold, refuse'; thus the name would mean 'protection withheld' or 'shelter refused'. These are obviously (sur)names which allude to the fate the bearers were to suffer at Israel's hands. For similar instances cf. 1.5 and 3.8. The inhabitants of Succoth, and, shortly after, those of Penuel, evidently thought that Gideon's enterprise had by no means come to a favourable end, and indeed that it might be doomed to failure; furthermore, they do not seem to have seen the Midianite invasion as a danger *per se*, or they saw it as an inevitable evil for which there was no remedy. Their ironical reply might suggest that in the description implied by the narrative they perhaps profited directly from the invasions, acquiring booty or exchanging it with the raiders. [6] 'Replied': the Hebrew has the singular, corrected into the obvious plural by the Massoretic *šᵉbīrīn*, cf. *BHK*[3] and *BHS*, cf. also the ancient translations. 'The power . . .': literally, 'the hand of . . .' some would prefer to correct it into the interrogative *ha'ap* . . ? 'Are not already . . .?' (Gray*, 1967). [7] 'Because of this . . .': *lākēn* gives a reason for the announcement of punishment. 'I will flail . . .': the root *dwš* denotes the threshing of grain, done by means of a special sledge or a cart with a large number of wheels, provided with metal spikes or splinters of rock and drawn

---

[33]H. J. Franken, *Excavations at Tell Deir 'Alla*, Leiden 1969, 4ff., 19ff., followed by R. de Vaux**, 1973, 122; ET, 1978, 816.
[34]*GesK* § 52s, where however the examples used are for the most part passive qal participles.

by animals.[35] The verb is also used in Amos 1.3, where Damascus is condemned 'because it threshed Gilead with flails of iron'. It is difficult to say whether the expression in both cases is intended only in a merely figurative sense or whether it is meant to express a particularly cruel form of reprisal in which the sledge or cart in question is hauled over the bodies of the vanquished, here stretched out on thorns and briars; the present passage and Amos 1 do not exclude the second possibility. 'Along with . . .': some authors object to the use of *'et*, 'with', and instead propose *b^e-* or *'al*, cf. LXX ἐν. However, this could be an idiomatic expression. 'Briars': *barqān* is a thorn bush to which we cannot give a precise botanical identification, which even LXX[A] was content to transcribe.   [8] Penuel, also the scene of the struggle between Jacob and the angel, Gen. 32.24ff.; Hos. 12.4, is now usually identified with *tulul eḏ-ḏahāb* (coord. 215–174), in a great bend of the Jabbok, the present *wādī ez-zarqā'*, flowing into the Jordan from the left. Mahanaim, mentioned in the story of Jacob referred to above, is in its immediate vicinity; it is probably the present-day *tell ḥaǧǧāǧ* (coord. 214–177). Thus it is one of the areas which the fugitives tried to cross in order to reach the desert whence they came. The route is probably like the path made of beaten earth which even now connects the area with the region of *es-salṭ*, passing through *ṣubeḥi* (coord. 216–173), the *wādī ez-zarqā'* and the *wādī ḥaǧǧāǧ*, and which in part follows the trace of the ancient Roman road which in turn was built on traces of the ancient path (S. Mittmann, 1965; H. Rösel**, 1976, 23, with the bibliography there). Today it has fallen into disuse, and has been replaced by the modern trunk road through *es-salṭ*, which was given an asphalt surface a few years ago.   [9] 'This tower', Hebrew *migdāl*, is unknown. The term can refer either to a particular feature of the fortifications of the place or to its temple, cf. 6.26; 9.46ff. The two theories are not incompatible. 'Safe and sound': Hebrew *b^e šālōm*, 'in peace', i.e. synonymous with 'victorious'. Note the difference in the treatment of the two places, a feature which the text does not explain. [10] 'Karkor', here called the place where the people of the East are encamped, is a place which has not yet been identified with any certainty. Eusebius, *Onomasticon* 272, knows a Karkaria, one day's journey from Petra (coord. 205–020), i.e. considerably to the south: today we also know a *qubbān qarāqir* in the *wādī sirḥān* in the northern *ḥeǧaz*, about 160 km. east of the Dead Sea as the crow flies. This is a place which the explorations of Alois Musil[36] have shown to be rich in springs and well protected by natural barriers. If this identification could be maintained (only the distance tells against it, and as we shall see that is not an essential feature), here we would have a reference to

---

[35]There is a reproduction in *BHH* I, 1962, col. 356.
[36]A. Musil, *The Northern Heǧaz*, New York 1926, 184, and J. Garstang*, 1931, 321ff. and map 17; R. de Vaux**, 1973, 120; ET, 1978, 817; Rösel**, 1976, 18 n. 58.

the great caravan route which crosses the Transjordan from north to south. This is the so-called 'royal road', Hebrew *derek hammelek*, Arabic *tarīḫ es-sulṭān*, Num. 20.17, which even now connects Damascus with northern Arabia, running parallel to the Mediterranean and to the Dead Sea. The route going from west to east intersects the route at this point (cf. map 17 in J. Garstang*, 1931, though he makes it run a little further north), theoretically making a right angle with the royal road, which today is a north-south trunk road. It is also used by pilgrims to Mecca as an alternative route to that parallel with the coast (Simons, *GTT*, 295). *qarāqir* was also the scene of important events in the earlier history of Islam: Ḥalīd ibn al Walīd passed through it on the expedition which in 634 took him from Iraq to Syria across the desert; he turned northwards from it in his march on Damascus.[37] Another *qarqār* is that situated to the north of Hamath, where the battle between the Assyrians and the western coalition took place in 853; however, this seems automatically to be excluded because it is too far north. Given that this is the place to the south-east, at the end of the caravan route (v. 11a), the problem of distance no longer seems unsurmountable: the narrative has Gideon attacking the very base of the enemy, so far away and well protected that it is virtually unguarded (v. 11b). **[11]** 'Attacked': one of the senses of the verb *'ālāh*, as we have seen on a number of occasions. In effect Gideon does not 'go up', but follows the route and 'attacks'. 'The caravan route': literally 'the route of the inhabitants of tents', the expression is made up of a construct preceded by the article to show that this is a unique combination, *GesK* § 130a, n. 2. For the translation cf. H.-W. Hertzberg*, 1959, '*Beduinenstrasse*', so also Gray*, 1967, and Rösel**, 1976, 17f. 'Which runs . . .': implied, cf. Rösel, loc. cit. The first place has not been identified, the second seems to be *ḫirbet el ǧubēha*, the orthography of which is not always constant, coord. 231–159 (Rösel, 18 n. 54). Instead, LXX[A] has inserted ἐξ ἐναντίας Ζεβεε, 'pursuing Zebah', which Boling*, 1975, wants to insert into the text. **[12]** 'Routed': Hebrew *heḥ'rīd* (*ḥārād*, 'frighten', and hence 'rout'). The expression is rather weak and some scholars have wanted to put forward corrections: C. F. Burney*, 1919: *heḥ'rīm*, 'put them to the ban', 'exterminated them'; others *hikḥīd* in the hiphil, 'exterminated them'; *heḥ'rīb*, 'he put them to the sword', or *hikrīt*, 'he cut them in pieces', cf. LXX[A], ἐξέτριψεν, and Josephus, *Antt.* V. vi. 5 = § 228, διέφθειρε (*BHK*[3], *BHS*). However, the original Hebrew does not necessarily need to be changed (Garstang*, 1931; Penna, 1973; and Gray*, 1967); if it does, Burney's proposal is the one to be preferred.

In 1927, J. C. Duncan excavated the remains of the ancient Roman road which led from the Jordan valley to the plateau of

---

[37]P. K. Hitti, *History of the Arabs*, London [9]1967, 147–50, esp. 149.

Transjordan, where it ended near to *es-salṭ*; in 1962, members of the *Deutsches Evangelisches Institut für das Heilige Land* made an expedition along that part of it which could still be identified (S. Mittmann, 1963 and 1965). Thus it has finally been possible to put the information contained in this passage on an objective topographical basis. At first it was often thought to be part of an inauthentic tradition because of the conventional terminology which is used: 'Gideon attacked . . . and smote' (v. 11): the two kings 'fled and he pursued them. . .', 'captured . . . and routed . . .' (v. 12), cf. also H. Rösel **, 1976, 18f., who in n. 58 makes concessions to the theory put forward by Musil, op. cit., and admits that the mention of Karkor could be authentic.

One can never be too careful in instances of this kind, especially in view of the fact that to a certain degree 7.22 – 8.3 and 8.4–12 are parallels: they have in common the element of the pursuit, capture and killing of two Midianite princes, but differ over the location, the first being situated in Cisjordan and the second in Transjordan. There remains the problem whether we have the same episode transmitted twice with different details, or whether we have four distinct people, killed in different historical and topographical circumstances. The second alternative has a good deal in its favour: for example, that the names in the first episode are connected with particular topographical features in Cisjordan, 7.22ff., and in particular with the territory of Ephraim, whereas in 8.4ff. the names are clearly surnames and do not serve as aetiologies. On the other hand, the mention of Karkor seems historically important, notwithstanding the obvious problem of its distance from the scene of the battle. In this tradition there would be nothing strange in seeing it in fact as the base, the site of the principal Midianite camp, from which the group would make raids on the surrounding country and also, as in this case, much further. The locality would have served well for this purpose, being rich in water and natural defences (rocks which allow virtually only one route of approach).

So in the present version of events, Gideon arrives in the camp, which he destroys, thus exterminating the root of all evil. In the present text much is left to the initiative of Gideon, and there are no traces of a substantial theological revision. This is one more feature which supports the probable authenticity and antiquity of this section.

(b) Gideon's feud and vendetta (8.13–21)

8 [13]Then Gideon, son of Joash, returned from the battle by the 'Ascent of Horus'. [14]He captured a young man belonging to the men of Succoth and questioned him; and he wrote down for him the names of the princes of Succoth and its elders: seventy-seven men in all. [15]Then he came to the men of Succoth and said, 'Behold, Zebah and Zalmunna, about whom you taunted me with the words, "Are Zebah and Zalmunna already in your hands that we should give bread to your men who are faint?" ' [16]Then he took the elders of the city, and he took thorns of the desert and briars, and threshed the men of Succoth with them; [17]and he broke down the tower of Penuel and killed the men of the city.

18 Then he said to Zebah and to Zalmunna, 'What can you tell me about the men whom you killed on Tabor?' They replied. 'They were like you, every one of them; they resembled the sons of kings!' [19]He replied, 'They were my brothers, the sons of my mother. As Yahweh lives, had you left them alive, I would not kill you!' [20]Then he said to Jether his firstborn, 'Rise and slay them!' But the young man could not draw his sword from the scabbard for fear: he was still a boy. [21]Then Zebah and Zalmunna said, 'Strike us yourself, for as a man is, so is his strength!' Then Gideon arose and killed Zebah and Zalmunna, and took the crescents that were on the necks of their camels.

---

[13] The 'Ascent of Horus' is an ancient crux, which can now be said to be resolved after the studies made by Mittmann (1965). In fact, it was already a crux for a fragment with Palestinian vocalization which read *hehārīm*, 'by the mountains'.[38] However, this reading must almost certainly be rejected, as it replaces the *lectio difficilior* with an easier, vaguer and trite one, notwithstanding Σ and Θ (see below). It is a mountain pass, as MT shows, with the expression *mil‘ma‘ᵃlēh hehāres*, translated by LXX as ἀπὸ ἀναβάσεως Αρες τοῦ δρομοῦ (Σ: τῶν ὁρῶν), whereas LXX[B] has ἀπὸ ἐπάνωθεν τῆς παρατάξεως Αρες, Vg *ante solis ortum*, and Tg *mē‘al šimšā'*. Thus the expression does not seem to have been understood by some of the ancient translations, either LXX[A], A, Σ, Θ (for Σ and Θ we have the readings τῶν ὅρων and ὅρους respectively; the problem here is whether they either simply transliterated Hebrew which they did not understand, or presuppose the variant Palestinian reading). Furthermore, the expression seems to presuppose the present MT. As a result of this we can understand how many commentators have wanted to correct the expression or even to delete it. However, the term *ma‘ᵃleh*, as well as meaning 'tribune' or 'podium', always signifies 'the ascent' of some kind, whereas

[38]Cf. B. Chiesa, *L'Antico Testamento ebraico, secondo la tradizione palestinese*, Turin 1978, 163, 294f.

we have seen that *ḥēres* is Horus, cf. 1.35 (*har ḥēres*) and 2.9 (*timnat ḥēres*). (However, for one still unsolved problem of this identification, see below.)

Mittmann supposes that the descent was made by the pass which, though steep, is easy and quick, especially on the way down; it was also used later by the Roman road; it has the advantage of leading directly to *tell dēir 'alla*, which is in all probability Succoth (see the square 210–215/175–180 on the map) instead of Penuel, which Gideon and his followers would have reached first had they returned by the same route.

[14] It does not seem necessary to transpose the *atnaḥ*, as *BHK*³ and *BHS* would like. The difficulty presented by the verse is that we do not know the exact meaning here of the term *na'ar*. Usually it means 'young man', but it often has other meanings: 'companion', 'shield-bearer' (cf. 7.10), 'servant', 'champion' (cf. II Sam. 2.14ff.), etc. The problem, then, is whether we have an ordinary young man, in which case the fact that he knew how to write would indicate a high general level of literacy, or whether he is a 'servant', someone employed in the area and therefore a scribe who by the very nature of his work was able to read and write. The majority of scholars decide for the first alternative: there was evidently widespread literacy in Israel in pre-monarchical times, if it is the case that any young man, picked up on the road, was able to write.[39] However, there are very few substantial pieces of evidence to support this first theory: first of all, it is not in fact certain that Succoth was an Israelite city at this time, and Y. Aharoni**, 1967, 241ff., says that we do not know what kind of inhabitants would have lived in the cities in this area. He goes on to say that the context strongly suggests that this was a Canaanite enclave in the region of Gad-Gilead; in any case it would be unwise to use this evidence to draw any conclusions about the situation in Israel; besides, we would need to know whether the man wrote himself or whether what he said was written down by a scribe (which is the conclusion of the important, but little noted study by Leveen), not to mention the possibility, in general, of inferring information of this importance from a casual remark such as this. Even in the eighth century, Isa. 29.12 is aware of the existence of illiterates who seem to be as numerous as those who know how to read and write (and even that would indicate a high literacy rate for this period), so that it would seem absurd to suppose that literacy was on a very high level as early as this. These reasons seem sufficient for us to accept the second suggestion for

---

[39]See the books and articles by M. Noth, D. Diringer and R. de Vaux cited above; for the second alternative see already K. Galling, 'Ein Stück judäischen Bodenrechtes in Jesaja 8', *ZDPV* 56, 1933, 209–18, esp. 215 n.1; J. Leveen and H.-J. Hermisson; O. Eissfeldt and A. Penna give the two positions without taking sides. See recently K. A. D. Smelik, *Saul. De voorstellingen van Israëls erste koning in de Masoretische text van het Oude Testament*, Amsterdam 1977, 34f.

interpreting the episode. Note finally the distinction made in the text between 'princes' (perhaps chiefs in the military sense) and 'elders' (probably those responsible for the government of the city'.[40] But it also seems rash to seek to derive exact information about the government of the city from the information given here. **[15]** This is an almost verbal repetition of v. 6, probably to stress the retributory character of the cruel measure.   **[16]** 'Threshed': read *wayyādoš*, with all the commentaries, instead of the incomprehensible *wayyōda'*, 'and taught them . . .', with LXX^B ἠλόησεν ἐν αὐτοῖς (sc. the thorns), whereas LXX^A has a notably longer text which could be the original version and which I adopt in the text: for the Greek see the apparatus of *BHS*; the Hebrew would then be *wayyiqqah 'et ziqnē hā'îr, waydūšēm 'et qōšē hammidbār w°'et habbarq°nim*.   **[17]** Note the different order of the two places. We do not know why, but perhaps the route by the 'Ascent of Horus' led Gideon first, as we have seen, to Succoth; however, this could also be a literary construction.   **[18]** The interrogation of the two kings introduces a new theme: that of the blood-brothers ('sons of my mother', i.e. not just sons of his father, in which case they could also have been his half-brothers) of Gideon, whom they had killed. 'What can you tell me . . .?' with G. R. Driver**, 1964, 15, who rightly points out that the translation of *'ēpōh* with the usual 'where . . .?' does not make any sense here; he therefore takes up a suggestion made by Ehrlich. The action of Gideon is thus a personal vendetta in the context of a family feud. The presence of Mount Tabor (cf. on 4.6) here is nothing short of amazing, but it could be a feature in favour of the authenticity of the tradition; it should not therefore be emended. **[20]** Up to now we have heard nothing of the firstborn son. It presupposes that Gideon was of mature years, though the boy seems very young, frightened and inexperienced.   **[21]** What seems to be a popular proverb is quoted here (Richter**, 1963, 227), so that we should not emend. The 'crescents' are ornaments, or, better, amulets worn as ornaments.

This text is composed of two episodes: the first, vv. 13–17, which describes the reprisals taken by Gideon on the places of Succoth and Penuel, following his threats in vv. 5ff.; the second, vv. 18–21, speaks of a personal vendetta for a wrong done by the Midianities to Gideon's closest kinsmen.

[13–17] In the first case we have an episode typical of the two rules with which war was waged at that time, not mitigated by any international conventions; on the other hand we have seen that in Amos 1.3ff. Damascus is condemned for having

[40]J. L. McKenzie, 'The Elders in the Old Testament', *Bibl* 40, 1959, 522–40 = *Studia Biblica et Orientalia* I, AnBibl 10, 1959, 388–406, esp. 527/393f.

adopted similar measures against the men of Gilead, a sign that even at that time, notwithstanding the obvious harshness, the victor's right to dispose of the vanquished could not be limitless. The text insists that this is a reprisal and not a gratuitous act of cruelty; it thus seems to accept the criterion in question: that even if we have reason to doubt the validity of the reprisal itself, there is no proportional relationship either between the offence suffered and the punishment inflicted or between the different manners in which the two places are treated, seeing that they are both guilty of the same crime. After all, neither of them was allied to Israel and therefore did not have any legal or moral obligation to victual the troops; still less did such an obligation exist where the cities will have been allies of Midian, in which case they would only have undergone the treatment reserved for the vanquished enemy, harsh though it could have been in those days. The story evidently wants to affirm that Gideon, as well as inflicting a very hard blow on the enemy, also means to discourage the places situated along its route and to deny the enemy their aid. Of course this is a speech in which it is impossible to discern any theological or ethical dimension: the criterion adopted here is that of military reprisals and reasons of state.

[18–21] The second episode, however, is different. We now know the two kings, who appear unexpectedly in v. 5, even if it is perhaps an interpolation. The text reveals here the real reasons which had prompted Gideon to the war and the pursuit: the blood vendetta is an episode of family feud. However, this is an episode of which nothing else is known; we know nothing of the killing of Gideon's two brothers, whose family is presented here not as lowly and on the lowest social level, but with at least physical characteristics like those of kings (cf. 6.15 with 8.18). The mention of Tabor, which might perhaps suggest an intervening episode in the course of a shared ceremony, here reveals the existence of a perhaps greater cultural exchange between Israel and Midian than the present redaction of the text would like to admit.

The blood vendetta is an institution which is still accepted today in the Bedouin world and also in certain Mediterranean regions, where it sometimes leads to interminable feuds. In the Old Testament it is codified in Deut. 19.21 and Lev. 24.17; cf. Ex. 21.23. The text of this last passage is not easy. The vendetta is regulated in accordance with the *lex talionis*, which works with clear limiting functions: the vendetta may not go beyond the wrong received. The Old Testament does not say who must pursue it; it is therefore probable that it was to be pursued by the closest relatives of the victim. Gideon expressly says that he would have spared the life of his enemies had they not been guilty of the killing of his relatives. This vendetta as the original motivation for the campaign recalls that of Abraham in Gen. 14.14ff., a text which, moreover, is certainly later. At a much later stage it has been combined with the theme of the divine calling to lead all Israel to victory and liberation; here it seems inextricably connected with the theme of the killing of the two kings.

The dialogue between Gideon and the two kings follows canons which we might call those of epic chivalry; in this context it seems to have been the rule to spare the conquered and captured enemy; there is no sentimentality, but everything takes place as in a rite 'in which question, answer and action follow one upon the other' in an established order (Pedersen, 1926, 379). Only the institution of the vendetta prompts Gideon to the killing (v. 19b). Furthermore, the killing is motivated, and this is a feature which need not necessarily have been known to the interested parties: they remember the episode (v. 18b), but can connect it with the person of Gideon only after he has given his explanations (v. 19). The choice of Gideon's small son also enters into this logic (v. 20): the two have killed the brothers of Gideon, and now a son of his will kill them. This logic, too, seems to be fully accepted by those who are about to die, who exhort Gideon to proceed only when they see that the boy is not going to be successful (v. 21). For the rest, the event returns to the ethical, juridical and logical categories which they also accept (Pedersen: 'Both parties agree that whatever happens must happen and no one tries to shirk'); they only ask that the act should be performed by a qualified and experienced person. Here, too, the account has no theological and ethical elements, but remains interesting for the details of customs which it contains.

(c) Anti-monarchical epilogue (8.22–32)

8 [22]Then the men of Israel said to Gideon, 'Rule over us, you and your son and your grandson; you have delivered us from the hands of Midian.' [23]But Gideon replied to them: 'I will not reign over you, nor will my sons reign over you; it is Yahweh who will reign over you!'

24 Then Gideon added, 'Allow me to make a request; let every man give me the earrings from his spoil.' Being Ishmaelites, the enemy wore golden earrings. [25] They replied, 'We will certainly give them to you.' They spread out a cloak and each one threw the earrings from his spoil on to it. [26] The weight of the golden earrings which he asked for was one thousand seven hundred shekels of gold, besides all the crescents and pendants and purple garments worn by the kings of Midian, and the collars which were round the necks of their camels. [27]And Gideon made them into an ephod, which he put in his own city, at Ophrah. And all Israel prostituted themselves to it there, and it became a snare to Gideon and his house. [28]Thus Midian was humbled before the Israelites and could not lift up its head again; and the land had peace for forty years in the days of Gideon.

29 And Jerubbaal, son of Joash, went and lived in his own house. [30]Gideon had seventy sons, all his own offspring: he had many wives.. [31] His concubine who lived at Shechem also bore him a son, to whom he had given the name Abimelech. [32]Then Gideon, son of Joash, died in peaceful old age and was buried in the tomb of his father Joash, at Ophrah of Abiezer.

[**22f.**] Again the pan-Israelite version; at least, the tribes which were summoned and took part in the enterprise. 'Reign': note the use of the root *māšal* instead of the more usual *mālak*. This choice of word seems to be deliberate here and in 9.22 which follows, even if, as is likely, the verb is neither Dtn or Dtr, although it is probable that in the theocratic ideal which Dtr attributes to the pre-monarchical period, *melek* can only be Yahweh. That God in fact had this title appears from passages which are often considered old, like Ex. 15.18; Num. 23.21; Deut. 33.5; however, the Dtr theory is that the title in question was exclusively theological.[41] For this reason, the verb, and therefore the phrase in which it appears, seems suspect. Implicit in Abimelech's demand in 9.2 is the thought that Gideon should have accepted the kingship, handing it on to his seventy legitimate sons, cf. ad loc. in all the commentaries. Thus the present passage clearly proves to be an interpolation of a later date, with an ideology similar to that of I Sam. 8.1ff. and 10.17–27.[42] That makes it possible that this passage, too, belongs to the last phase of Dtr, DtrN, even if this does not seem to have been sufficiently proved (against Veijola); or should we think of the last,

[41]See my articles 'Mālak' and 'Māšal', *THAT* I, 1971, cols. 908–20, 930–3. F. Crüsemann, op. cit., 50ff., differs. He maintains that the title 'king' for Yahweh is late. The problem seems to me to be more complex, cf. my 'Gott als König in der biblischen Dichtung', in *Proceedings of the Fifth World Congress of Jewish Studies, Jerusalem, 1969*, I, Jerusalem 1971, 126–33. However, we really need a completely new study of the problem of 'ancient Yahwistic poetry' in Hebrew.

[42]Thus J. A. Emerton, 1976, rightly, against the position which I put forward in *Das Königtum in Israel*, 15ff.; cf. also T. Veijola, *Das Königtum in der Beurteilung der deuteronomistischen Historiographie*, AASF B–198, 1977, 100–3.

pre-Dtr phase of the redaction of the story (so Richter**, 1963)? This would explain why earlier authors attributed the text to E. Where would we put the Dtr mention of the ephod? However, it is probable that vv. 24–27 form another, different, tradition. **[24]** 'The earrings' could also be 'nose rings', but in the Old Testament these are worn only by women, cf. Gen. 24.47; Isa. 3.21; Ezek. 16.12. The Eastern custom (which can also be found throughout the Mediterranean) for men to wear earrings is already attested by Pliny, *Hist. Nat.* XI.50 = §136 (Burney). 'Ishmaelites': the term is interchangeable with Midianites; in the genealogy of Gen. 25.1–6, Midian appears as a half-brother (the same father but a different mother) of Ishmael and we find an alternation between Midian and Ishmael in Gen. 37.25ff.; 39.1ff., where such an alternation is a classic starting point for teaching source criticism to beginners. **[25]** 'They spread': LXX has the singular, with Gideon as subject. **[26]** The 'shekel' weighs about 11.424 grams,[43] so that the weight of the objects collected by Gideon is a little less than 20 kg. It is possible that v. 26b is an addition; it interrupts the narrative with a list of materials which have nothing to do with the making of the ephod. **[27]** For the nature of the object see the dictionaries and encyclopaedias. Here is seems to be something capable of becoming an object of idolatrous worship. **[28]** The end of the verse has chronological information typical of Dtr : a multiple or fraction of forty. Verses 29–32 introduce ch. 9. **[29]** 'Went and lived. . .': for *wayyēšēb* some would prefer to read *wayyāšob*, root *šwb*: 'And Gideon. . .returned to his own home.' **[30]** The number 'seventy' is a round figure for 'many', cf. 1.7 (seventy kings taken prisoner); II Kings 10.1 (Ahab has seventy sons); and the inscription of Panammuwa II, *KAI* 215, *SSI* II, p. 14, line 3 (the father has seventy relatives and they are all killed), etc. (Burney).[44] 'All his own offspring', literally 'came forth from his loins'; for the expression cf. Gen. 24.2,9, and 47.29: it seems to be a euphemism for the *membrum virile*. **[31]** 'Concubine': *pīlegeš* is in fact a legitimate wife, but of second rank.[44] We meet here with a figure typical of sovereigns, but rare in the private sphere: another element which points to the regal character of Gideon. It is difficult to say whether this is at least a *ṣadīqa* marriage (cf. on 14.15). 'Had given the name': the expression with *śym* is rare; the verb *qārā'* is normally used. 'Abimelech' is a good West Semitic name, also attested in Ugarit for a scribe. **[32]** 'In Ophrah': to be read in the construct, or 'of Abiezer' is to be taken as a gloss.

The present passage is made up of various elements, all of

---

[43]See A. Strobel, 'Masse und Gewichte', *BHH* II, 1964, cols. 1159–69, esp. col. 1167.
[44]M.–J. Lagrange*, 1903; cf. H.-W. Jüngling, Diss. (see p. 279 below), 147 and note; cf. F. C. Fensham, 'The Numeral Seventy in the Old Testament and the Family of Jerubbaal, Ahab, Panamuwa and Athirat', *PEQ* 109, 1977, 113–15.

which can be separated from one another: vv. 22f., the offering
of the kingship to Gideon; vv. 24–27, the making of the ephod;
v. 28, the conclusion of the cycle; vv. 29–31, the descendants of
Gideon (introduction to ch. 9); and v. 32, the death of Gideon.
I shall take them all together.

[22–23] The episode of the offering of the kingship, which is
refused for theological reasons, has all the characteristics of
relative lateness; here we have the pan-Israelite version instead
of the list of tribes which took part in the action, or even of the
Abiezrites; the theocratic version of the text does not correspond
to the description in 9.2, where the sons of Gideon exercise
power based on heredity on their father's side and which seemed
burdensome to some Shechemites (always with the use of the
root *mšl*). Thus even if we consider the theme of theocracy to
be early (however, it should be noted that it is always inserted
into contexts with the literary genre of a hymn, so that we
should use such material with caution), it is used here in a
similar way to that in I Sam. 8.7b: 'They (Israel) have not
rejected you, but me (Yahweh) from being king over them' (here
with the root *mlk*). The opinion of G. Henton Davies, followed
by many (there is a list in F. Crüsemann), according to whom
Gideon's refusal is not a real refusal, but simply a polite form
which entails final acceptance (something like what we found in
6.13), is therefore hardly pertinent. The proposal made by F.
Crüsemann, op. cit., 47ff., 82ff., seems very interesting: this text
must be considered together with Num. 23.21; Deut. 33.5; I
Sam. 8.7; 12.12 and dated during the first half of the first
millennium BC between King Solomon and the end of the northern kingdom. According to Crüsemann, these texts express the
opposition of certain groups to the royal ideology centred on
Jerusalem, especially the temple and the royal palace.

[24–27] The episode of the ephod made with the gold taken
from the spoils of war ends with a typically Dtr phrase, even if
this has not been a feature of the preceding material: perhaps
what we have here is originally a cult object existing in the
sanctuary of Ophrah, which later fell under the Dtn prohibition.
The use of gold would suggest, rather, some form of statue.

[28] The conclusion has the Dtr chronology, v. 28b, but otherwise, v. 28a, could well have been the conclusion of the original
cycle.

[29–32] Finally, the details of Gideon's descendants and the note of his death are additions which serve well to introduce ch. 9 and which therefore cannot be dated.

(d) Conclusion (8.33–35)

8 [33] But when Gideon was dead, the Israelites continued to prostitute themselves to Baal, and made Baal Berith a god. [34]They did not remember their God, Yahweh, who had delivered them from the power of their surrounding enemies, [35]and they did not show any loyalty to the house of Jerubbaal, that is Gideon, for all the good that he had done to Israel.

---

[33] 'Baal Berith' is the deity to whom the temple of Shechem is dedicated in 9.4ff., cf. there. [35] 'Loyalty', or 'fidelity', Hebrew *ḥesed*. It is not easy to say whether Dtr here wants to condemn the Israelites for their rebellion against the sons of Gideon in favour of Abimelech, ch. 9, or not (Hertzberg*, 1958; Gray*, 1967).

Thus ends the Dtr framework of the Gideon cycle: the people, saved and free, return to their old faults, as in other episodes. Here the idolatry is made specific: it is connected with the patron deity of Shechem, in which it is most likely that only the inhabitants of the place and the surrounding districts will have been involved.

CHAPTER 9

The Reign of Abimelech

Select bibliography: R. J. **Williams**, 'The Fable in the Old Testament', in *A Stubborn Faith, Papers . . . presented . . . to W. A. Irwin*, Dallas, Texas 1956, 3–26; W. **Harrelson**, 'Shechem in Extra-Biblical References', *BA* 20, 1957, 2–10; B. W. **Anderson**, 'The Place of Shechem in the Bible', ibid., 10–19; E. **Nielsen**, *Shechem*, Copenhagen 1959, 147–53; M. **Adinolfi**, 'Originalità dell'apologo di Jotam (Giud. 9, 8–15)', *RiBibl* 7, 1959, 338–42; E. **Maly**, 'The Jotham Fable—Anti-Monarchical?', *CBQ* 22, 1960, 299–302; A. D. **Crown**, 'A Re-Interpretation of Judges IX in the Light of its Humour', *'Abr Nahrain* 3, 1961–62, 90–98; V. **Vilar**, 'El templo de Baal Berit en Siquem', *EstBíbl* 24, 1962, 65–7; G. **Wallis**, 'Die Anfänge des Konigtums in Israel', *WZ(H)* 12, 1962–63, 239–47 = *Geschichte und Überlieferung*, Berlin and Stuttgart 1968, 45–65; R. G. **Boling**, 'And who is Š-K-M? (Judges IX 28)', *VT* 13, 1963, 479–82; R. J. **Bull** and J. F. **Ross**, 'The Biblical Traditions of Shechem's Sacred Area', *BASOR* 169, 1963, 27–32, esp. 28ff.; W. **Richter****, 1963, 246–318; H.-J. **Stoebe**, 'Das deutsche evangelische Institut für Altertumswissenschaft des Heiligen Landes, Lehrkurs 1964', *ZDPV* 82, 1966, 1–45, esp. 11ff.; S. H. **Horn**, 'Shechem – History and Excavations of a Palestinian City', *JEOL* VI, 18, 1964, 284–306; G. E. **Wright**, *Shechem. The Biography of a Biblical City*, New York 1965, 123–8 and passim; M. **Reviv**, 'The Government of Sichem in the Amarna Period and in the Days of Abimelek', *IEJ* 16, 1966, 252–7; J. A. **Soggin**, 'Bemerkungen zur alttestamentlichen Topographie Sichems, mit besonderem Bezug auf Jdc.9', *ZDPV* 83, 1967, 183–98; H. **Haag**, 'Gideon – Jerubbaal – Abimelek', *ZAW* 79, 1967, 305–14; G. R. H. **Wright**, 'Temples at Shechem', *ZAW* 80, 1968, 1–35; R. E. **Clements**, 'Baal Berit of Shechem', *JSS* 13, 1968, 21–32; V. **Eppstein**, 'Was Saul also among the Prophets?', *ZAW* 81, 1969, 287–304, esp. 291ff.; H. H. **Schmid**, 'Die Herrschaft Abimeleks (Jdc 9)', *Judaica* 26, Zürich 1970, 1–11; G. R. H. **Wright**, 'The Mythology of Pre-Israelite Shechem', *VT* 20, 1970, 75–82; J. A. **Soggin**, 'Il regno de 'Abî-mélek in Sichem ("Giudici" 9) e le istituzioni della città-stato siro-palestinese nei secoli XV–XVI avanti Cristo', in *Studi in onore di*

Edoardo Volterra, Milan 1972, VI, 161–89; B. **Lindars**, 'Jotham's Fable – A New Form-Critical Analysis', *JTS* NS 24, 1973, 355–66; G. R. H. **Wright**, 'Temples at Shechem – A Detail', *ZAW* 87, 1975, 56–65; H. **Rösel****, 1976, 24–31; S. **Talmon**, 'Har', *TWAT* II, 1977, cols. 459–83, esp. 471–83; ET, *TDOT* III, 1978, 436–47, esp. 427–47; T. **Veijola**, *Das Königtum in der Beurteilung der deuteronomistischen Historiographie*, AASF B–198, 1977, 103–14; F. **Crüsemann**, *Der Widerstand gegen das Königtum*, WMANT 49, 1978, 19–42. For archaeological excavations, which are only of peripheral interest here, cf. (until the definitive reports have been published) the provisional reports in *BASOR* 144, 1956; 148, 1957; 161, 1961; 169, 1963; 180, 1965; 190, 1968; 204, 1971; 216, 1974; and 223, 1976.

1. Chapter 9 has been placed by the redactors directly after the Gideon cycle, chs. 6–8, and is joined to them by means of the statement that their protagonist, Abimelech, is a son of Jerubbaal/Gideon. By eliminating his half-brothers, he succeeds in assuming royal power with the consent and support of the assembly of the city state; however, this consensus is very soon shattered and a military conflict between the king and the assembly follows. Technically speaking, the king emerges victor in the conflict, but at the price of the destruction of the city and some neighbouring localities, the extermination of their populations and even his own death; a real Pyrrhic victory, which produces nothing: the restitution of the monarchy at Shechem does not seem to have had any impact on growing Israel or on the city-state itself.

2. The facts listed in this way immediately show that at this point, in contrast to the earlier stories in Judges and Joshua, we do not so much have material of a heroic and religious type as a narrative with a political background. There is no Dtr framework, even though we may perhaps detect it in the Dtr conclusion to ch. 8, and the Dtn chronology is also absent. The text speaks of the civic assembly and its functions, the monarchy in a city state, the difficulties which soon arose between the new king and his subjects, the former trying to concentrate as much power as possible in his own hands and the latter, as an assembly, not prepared to yield on this point, which they considered to be fundamental. Thus this is a typical case of conflicts over power and competence between what today we would call the legislative power (the assembly) and the executive power (the sovereign).

3. The present text has little interest in theological themes, in particular in the basic themes of the history of salvation; it does not even seem to be particularly interested in problems connected with divine intervention: in vv. 23f. it is God who, by means of an evil spirit, sows dissension between the king and the assembly, with the aim of punishing the mass murder committed by Abimelech at the beginning of his career; it is thus a variant of the Dtn and Dtr concept of retribution, which is also to be found in wisdom literature. In vv. 56f. God brings down their sins on the heads of the king and his Shechemites, as in the preceding instance. However, it is clear that this is not a theme which is typical of the religion of Israel: other deities outside Israel could act in the same way; what was done would therefore have been normal. Still, it is now these scanty elements which offer the key for reading the present text.

4. Thus it is probable that in Judg. 9 we have a narrative composed on the basis of material which is like a chronicle or a set of annals, and is therefore important as a historical source. However, it is impossible to check it in the light of parallel material; we have no text, in Israel or outside, which speaks of the events discussed here: still, in every case it seems that we should presuppose the basic historicity of what is narrated here. If for the moment we leave aside the apologue made by Jotham, moreover, the narrative has a strongly unitary character. On the other hand, if a superficial reading suggests that this is the case, a closer look will reveal the existence of a number of tensions. The fact that there is no agreement among scholars about their extent and their nature does not detract in any way from this fact. Here I follow the analysis made by Richter**, 1963, 246ff., in whose work we can also find a thorough examination of the theories put forward earlier.

First of all, as I have already indicated, we have the problem of the apologue in its present context (vv. 7–21: vv. 8–15 contain the apologue proper, and the rest serves as a framework); then in v. 45 Abimelech destroys all the city, but in v. 46 he also destroys the 'tower of Shechem'; in v. 40 Abimelech gives chase to Gaal and wins a victory, whereas in v. 42 the people go out into the fields the day afterwards, as if nothing had happened; in v. 23 we have the mention of the 'evil spirit' which causes the dissension between Abimelech and the assembly (cf. above, § 3), but in vv. 26ff. we have a kind of conspiracy, devised by Gaal, mentioned above, a newcomer to the area, and by his

family; in vv. 34ff. we have tensions between a pitched battle
and an ambush, with a somewhat obscure relationship between
this episode in vv. 34–40 and the following vv. 42–44: in the first
text we have four groups and in the second three; again in vv.
6–20 there is mention of a *millō'*, a term which is still obscure,
whereas in vv. 46–49 we find a *migdāl* ('tower', but also used
for a particular form of temple); again, vv. 16ff. talk of the
gratitude which the Shechemites (– or is the text really thinking
of Israel?) should have towards Jerubbaal and therefore his
sons, a theme which appears in 8.35. This last, as we have seen,
is a Dtr text, except that instead of *ḥesed* we find *ṭōbāh*; the
mention of 'Israel' in vv. 22 and 55 also seems strange when the
narrative is always only concerned with the Shechemites: perhaps this text, too, was soon subjected to a revision along pan-
Israelite lines? All these are elements which show that the narrative was not composed straight off; it is the product of a
number of quite complicated factors. Notwithstanding that, we
have to say that as a complex the narrative gives the impression
of being a unity; the tensions indicated all seem necessary: for
example, the contrast between Shechem and the 'Tower of
Shechem' could be due to the fact that these are two different
places, even if they are connected, as the name seems to suggest.
We shall consider this problem in due course. One could produce a similar argument in connection with *millō'*. The dualism
between the 'evil spirit' from Yahweh which provokes discord
and Gaal's conspiracy is probably better explained by the concept of 'dual causality',[1] frequent in the Old Testament, and
which for some time has been the object of some important
studies. Thus the differences indicated can be considerably reduced; there remains only the contrast between the pitched
battle and the ambush, where two elements of different origin
may have been combined, whereas vv. 16–20 could be a Dtr-
type insertion which sets out to explain the events in Shechem
in terms of retribution for the ingratitude of Israel towards
Gideon and for the sins of Abimelech and the assembly at
Shechem. In any case, it seems difficult to support the argument

[1]I. L. Seeligmann, 'Menschliches Heldentum und göttliche Hilfe', *TZ* 19, 1963, 385–
411; cf. again C. Schmidt, *Menschlicher Erfolg und Jahwes Initiative*, WMANT 31, 1970.
In a recent paper, G. Garbini, ' "Narrativa della successione" o "storia dei Re"?',
Henoch 1, Turin 1979, 19-41, esp. 31ff., has considered the story of Abimelech to be part
of a major 'history of the kings', which includes the 'succession narrative', Abimelech,
Saul and David before his enthronement, and afterwards, Ahab, Jehu and perhaps
Zimri.

put forward by Richter**, 1963, 322, that vv. 1–7, 16a, 19b–21, 23f., 41–45, 56f. are to be attributed to a single author, that of the 'book of saviours'. More probable is the suggestion made by F. Crüsemann, according to whom an 'ancient nucleus' is probably to be found in vv. 23, 25, 42, 43–54.

5. As things stand, we can divide the chapter into the following sections:

(a) Abimelech becomes king (vv. 1–6)
(b) Jotham's apologue (vv. 8–15)
(c) Jotham's speech (vv. 7, 16–21)
(d) First difficulties between Abimelech and the people of Shechem (vv. 22–25)
(e) Gaal's conspiracy (vv. 26–29)
(f) Abimelech's first campaign (vv. 30–41)
(g) Abimelech's second campaign (vv. 42–45)
(h) The destruction of the 'Tower of Shechem' (vv. 46–49)
(i) The death of Abimelech (vv. 50–55)
(j) Theological conclusion (vv. 56–57).

(a) Abimelech becomes king (9.1–6)

9 [1]Abimelech, son of Jerubbaal, went to Shechem, to his mother's kinsfolk, and said to them and to their father's kinsfolk: [2]'Say to all the "notables" of Shechem: "Which is better for you, that seventy people (all the sons of Jerubbaal) should reign over you or that one should rule over you? Remember that I am bone of your bone and flesh of your flesh!" [3]And his mother's kinsmen reported these things to the 'notables' in Shechem, who made the decision to follow Abimelech. For they said, 'He is our kinsman'. [4]And they gave him a large sum of money from the temple of Baal Berith, and with this Abimelech hired adventurers who followed him. [5]He went to his father's house at Ophrah where he killed his half-brothers (the sons of Jerubbaal, seventy of them) upon one stone; only one of them, Jotham, Jerubbaal's youngest son, survived because he managed to hide.

6 Then all the 'notables' from Shechem and all Beth-millo met in assembly to crown Abimelech by the 'oak of the pillar' which is in Shechem.

The text of this section is particularly sound. [1] 'Abimelech' is a good West Semitic name, often attested already in Ugarit (Aistleitner no. 25, 'abmlk) and in the archives of el-'Amarna (abimilki), and also in Phoenician. Composite names in 'abi-X are frequent in Mari, though this one has yet to be found; on the other hand, it already appears in the West Semitic of Ebla in the form *a-bu₃-ma-lik* (oral communication by G. Pettinato). The name declares the kingship of the *theos patrōos*, or the divine sonship of the person who bears it: '(My divine) father is king', or 'My father is (the god) *malik*'. 'Shechem': present-day *tell balāṭa* (coord. 177–180), near the eastern suburb of *nablūs* which has the same name, and about eight kilometres away. It was discovered and identified by H. Thiersch in 1903 on the basis of the outer edges of a 'cyclopean' wall; it became the object of a first exploratory archaeological campaign in 1911, which was followed by two others in 1913 and 1914, all carried out by E. Sellin and C. Watzinger; a last archaeological campaign took place in 1926 under the direction of the same E. Sellin, assisted by F. M. T. de Liagre-Böhl and the architect G. Welter; another campaign was led in 1927. The polemics which followed Sellin's comments on the results of the excavations led to his dismissal by the *Deutsches Verein für die Erforschung Palästinas*, the patron of the excavations, and his replacement by G. Welter. Sellin again participated in the very brief campaign of 1928, while between 1928 and 1932 an uncertain number of campaigns were directed by Welter. In 1933 Welter, too, was dismissed and replaced by Sellin, assisted by the architect H. Steckeweh. Meanwhile contributions to the expedition by German agencies had decreased, and this, together with the disorders which broke out in Palestine in 1936, prevented the work from being taken further. As a result of the Second World War it was then postponed indefinitely. Sellin's notes and a large amount of the material which he had collected were destroyed in 1943 during the course of an air raid. The work was taken up again in 1954 under the patronage of Drew University, Madison, New Jersey; McCormick Theological Seminary, Chicago; and the American Schools of Oriental Research, and excavations were resumed again in 1956 by an American expedition. From then on there have been various campaigns, concluding with the ninth, of 1969; after that year there were only controls and checks *in situ*.

'Kinsfolk': it does not seem probable that the term *'aḥ* here has the meaning of 'physical brother'; evidently, as in v. 3, this is the larger family group within which there were precise rules about solidarity. Their kinsmen's kinsmen, *mišpaḥat bēt 'ābī*, were also involved (note the first person suffix: perhaps this is one of the instances in which *-y* can have the meaning of the third person singular masculine, as in Phoenician? Cf. on 5.15). I have dealt with the problem posed by the imprecision of ethnic and kinship terms above, in connection with 1.16. The significance of the last note is obscure. **[2]** 'The "notables" ': the expression *ba'ᵃlē-X* with the name of the place has been interpreted by scholars in different ways; for a survey see Soggin, 1972, 180–3. In this context it appears again for *migdal šᵉkem* in vv. 46f. and for *tebeṣ* (v. 51); it appears again for Jericho in Josh. 24.11 and for *qᵉ'īlāh* in I Sam. 23.11f., for *yābēš* in II Sam. 21.12 and, outside the Old Testament, in the inscriptions of Sefire, *KAI* 222 A, line 4, and B, lines 4f.; 224, lines 23, 26 for *b'ly ktk* and *b'ly 'rpd*; finally, on stele III we have *b'lyh* (their *ba'al*), the contractual party in the alliance and therefore belonging to the nobility; all the stelai use *'m* (*'am*) for the 'people' proper. Thus in the case of Shechem and the other places it means 'notables' as landowners (one of the meanings of the term *ba'al* in West Semitic); these formed the civic assembly. Hence to translate 'citizens', as is often done, is not incorrect, but it is insufficient. 'Say . . .': lit. 'Speak into the ears of . . .', cf. v. 3. 'Seventy': not necessarily to be taken literally, cf. on 8.30. Cases of the extermination of all possible heirs to the throne by a usurper are not uncommon, see II Kings 10.1ff. and the inscription of Panamuwwa II (second half of the eighth century BC, *KAI* 215, line 3); in both texts they number seventy! Is this perhaps a rhetorical figure of speech only? **[4]** 'The temple . . .': literally 'the house' (*bēt*). This is the first temple mentioned; the other, the temple of *'el b'rīt*, is connected with *migdal š'kēm*. *b'rīt* is a technical term for 'covenant', 'alliance', and sometimes means 'pledge'.[2] At present we only have one instance of the expression outside the Old Testament, in the Hurrian text of Ugarit, RS no. 24278, where it appears in lines 14f.[3] 'A large sum': literally 'seventy (shekels) of silver': the figure seventy stands here (as in v. 2 and in 8.30) for a large, indeterminate quantity. 'Adventurers': literally, 'worthless and reckless men', i.e. characters who could be hired for somewhat dubious enterprises. **[5]** The theme of the 'one stone', cf. v. 18, is interesting if only for the stress on a detail which seems to us to be secondary. Saul, too, sacrifices on one stone in I Sam. 14.33f., and it is possible that this was the abattoir where animals were killed in the requisite ritual form. The stone made certain that the blood would flow out, G. F. Moore*, 1895 and C. F. Burney*, 1919. The mention of the escape of Jotham, along with everything else which follows, is an interpolation: after the massacre the text continues in vv. 22ff. Thus we have the theme of the sole survivor, which serves to introduce both the apologue inserted into Jotham's speech and the comment of a Dtr type. **[6]** '*bēt millō*': we do not know exactly what this was, but from the root *mālē*' which underlies it, it seems that this was an acropolis constructed artificially by filling in; it would therefore be the acropolis of the area, whose inhabitants, soldiers and priests, would take part in an assembly functioning as an independent entity. The term *millō*' also appears for Jerusalem, II Sam. 5.9; I Kings 9.15–24; 11.27; II Kings 12.21 (EVV 20); I Chron. 11.8; and II Chron.

---

[2]E. Kutsch, '*B'rīt*, "Verpflichtung" ', *THAT* 1, 1971, cols. 339–52 and M. Weinfeld, '*B'rīt*', *TDOT* 2, 1977, 253–79.

[3]Cf. É. Lipiński, 'El-Berit', *Syria* 50, Paris 1973, 50ff.

32.5. Here, too, the allusion is obscure: the excavations carried on in Jerusalem in 1961 and 1967[4] revealed an artificial filling which the excavator, K. M. Kenyon, identified with *millō*'. In this case the interpretation of it as the acropolis formed in the manner just described would fit in well with the excavations at Shechem, which have revealed the ruins of a temple situated on an artificial mound of earth. It is therefore probable that this was the *millō*', even if there clearly can be no definite proof. 'The oak of the pillar' is probably a sacred tree growing in the area of the sanctuary. Sellin discovered some pillars in the course of excavations. It is unconvincing to emend the text, which probably refers to a proper name.

1. It is possible to extract some important historical information from this episode: (*a*) That in traditional folk lore, quite independently of whether Gideon did or did not accept the kingship, his sons exercised in the region a *de facto* power which amounted to royal power, and which provoked discontent in a non-Israelite city-state of the kind that Shechem was; (*b*) that the city state of Shechem was governed by an assembly of 'notables', probably land-owners, and that this assembly had important functions: the designation of a king, and, as appears from vv. 23ff., also the censuring of him and possibly his removal, fell under its authority, as did the disposition of the temple treasure and yet other prerogatives; (*c*) that notwithstanding everything, Abimelech did not have any right to the crown, so that he could not present himself directly to the assembly. He had to use intermediaries, his kinsmen on his mother's side. On the other hand the theme of maternal kinsmen, though justified here by the narrative, also appears elsewhere in the ancient Near East, cf. the text on the statue of Idrimi, king of Alalaḫ (*ANET*[3], 557ff.), where the protagonist, a fugitive from 'the house of my father', as the residence is called (line 3), takes refuge at Emar with his maternal kinsfolk (line 25). From there, and after a number of vicissitudes, he succeeds in regaining the throne which he had lost as the result of a plot which had obliged him to flee. The theme of the legitimacy of Idrimi on the throne of Alalaḫ underlies the narrative: the king wants to indicate that he is not an usurper but the legitimate claimant to the throne, a throne of which he had once been deprived; therefore it is difficult to say whether his claim is real or whether it was simply a pretext so that he could appear to

[4]K. M. Kenyon, *Digging up Jerusalem*, London 1974, 100–3.

have a legitimacy which he did not in fact possess;[5] in the case
of Abimelech, on the other hand, the legitimacy does not derive
from his parentage, but only from the decision of the assembly.

2. By then Shechem had already had a long history: there is
evidence of the place in neolithic times and, as the archives of
el-'Amarna reveal (cf. letter no. 289 and all those that mention
its sovereign Lab'ayu without directly mentioning the locality),
in the second half of the second millennium it was one of the
largest city states in the region. No text indicates how it had
been inserted into the territory of the tribes of Israel; we only
know that this must have happened towards the end of the
thirteenth or the beginning of the twelfth century, and in an
essentially peaceful way: the excavations in fact show no trace
of any kind of destruction of the strata which relate to this
period. However, the explanation put forward by Reviv seems
probable, even though it is not demonstrable and must remain
a hypothesis: as in the fourteenth century Shechem had chosen
to collaborate with the invaders, and even chose a sovereign
from their number, the same thing had happened when it was
faced with the Israelite tribes of the region, and especially
Manasseh.

If we can trust our text, the position of the city will not have
been without tensions, and Abimelech will have made skilful
use of these. By making himself the spokesmen of certain elements in the assembly who were concerned for restoration, he
could present himself as the leader of the revolt against a negative development in the political and economic sphere which
incorporation into Israel had created, and against the greed of
the dominant parties which appears from the criticism of the
régime led by Gideon's sons. Thus it is in this context of
discontent that Abimelech could hire adventurers and proceed
to eliminate his adversaries, then having himself crowned king.

3. In connection with the topography of the area, it has been
widely held[6] that *ba'al b'rīt* and *'el b'rīt* are the same deity, and
that therefore we have different but similar designations for the
same temple. Now, however, as long as the identity or at least
the equivalence of the two terms *ba'al* and *'ēl* in this context
has not been demonstrated, we have here two different deities,

---

[5]For this argument and for the whole theme connected with it see the important study
by M. Liverani, 'Partire col carro, per il deserto', *AION* 32, 1972, 403–15.

[6]Most recently H. Rösel**, 1976, 29; in n. 105 he also wrongly attributes this
identification to me, but cf. Soggin, 1967, 196f.

and therefore two sanctuaries. The places Shechem and *migdal*
š^ekem, mentioned in vv. 46ff., are therefore different; for further
details see there.

(*b*) Jotham's apologue (9.7, 8–15)

9 ⁷The matter was reported to Jotham. He went and stood on
the summit of Mount Gerizim, and there cried out to them:

Listen to me, you notables of Shechem,
and may God give a hearing to you.
⁸One day the trees decided to crown a king over them.
The said to the olive tree,
'You reign over us.'
⁹But the olive replied,
'Shall I give up my fatness
which gods and men prize in me,
to sway over the trees?'
¹⁰Then the trees said to the fig tree,
'You become king over us.'
¹¹But the fig tree replied,
'Shall I leave my sweetness and my good fruit,
to sway over the trees?'
¹²Then the trees proposed to the vine,
'Arise and reign over us.'
¹³But the vine replied,
'Shall I give up my wine
which refreshes gods and men,
to sway over the trees?'
¹⁴Then all the trees proposed to the bramble,
'Arise and reign over us.'
¹⁵And the bramble said to the trees,
'If in truth you intend
to crown me king over you,
come and take refuge in my shade!
Otherwise may fire come out of the bramble
capable of devouring the cedars of Lebanon.'

(*c*) Jotham's speech (9.[7]16–21)

9 ¹⁶Now therefore, if you acted in good faith and with honour when
you proclaimed Abimelech king, and if you dealt rightly with Jerubbaal
and his house, and finally if you acted towards him as his deeds

deserved ([17]for my father fought for you and risked his life to save you from the hands of the Midianites, [18]but you are rebellious today against the family of my father and have slaughtered his sons, seventy persons, on a single stone, and have made Abimelech, the son of a slave girl, king over the notables of Shechem, simply because he is your kinsman), [19]if then, as I said, you have acted today in good faith and honourably with Jerubbaal and his house, then rejoice in Abimelech and let him rejoice in you. [20]But if not, let fire come out of Abimelech and devour the notables of Shechem and all Beth-millo, and let a fire come out of the notables of Shechem and out of Beth-millo and devour Abimelech.

21 Then Jotham ran away and fled for fear of Abimelech, his brother, and went to Beer, and lived there.

---

[8] 'Crown': literally, 'to anoint a king over them'.[7] The expression evidently refers to the sacred oil used during the coronation ceremony, but by this time it had become a technical term for the ceremony. 'Reign': the variant between K and Q is not relevant for our understanding of the text. [9] 'Gods': I follow the majority of commentators (Burney is doubtful) in taking ''elōhīm as a plural: the expression is strange where it is applied to Yahweh, but normal when applied to pagan gods, known for their banquets. 'Which they prize in me' with MT and LXX$^{A;}$ LXX^{B,} however, has 'with which ($\dot{\epsilon}\nu$ $\hat{\dot{\eta}}$, i.e., $b\bar{o}$) men honour God . . .', while Syr omits 'men', leaving an impersonal text: 'with which God is honoured'; Vg has a variant from MT and LXX^{A}, 'Qua utuntur dii et homines.' Tg proposes what seems to be a compromise: 'with which God is honoured and in which men delight'. These are all readings which presuppose $b\bar{o}$ in the Hebrew instead of $b\bar{\imath}$ and, with the exception of LXX^{B}, also an impersonal verb, the niphal yikkabdū. However, with Hertzberg*, 1959, and against almost all the commentaries, I prefer the reading of MT and LXX^{A}: LXX^{B} and Syr show their intention of eliminating an originally polytheistic text, whereas Vg inserts a new element, that of the use of oil by gods and men, while leaving the polytheistic interpretation. The formula reappears, but with notable syntactical variants, in v. 13. [14] 'The bramble': generally identified with Lycium Europaeum, the 'thorns' often mentioned in the New Testament. Beautiful for its flowers in spring, it was in ancient times regarded as a nuisance to flocks. We now know that it is very useful in preventing mountain slopes from eroding. [15] 'Out of the bramble': LXX has $\dot{\alpha}\pi$' $\dot{\epsilon}\mu o\hat{v}$, i.e. mimmenī, 'from me'. The sense is the same. [16] 'In good faith and with honour', cf. v. 19, are terms indicating the right attitude in the context of an alliance ($^{\prime e}$met – tāmīm). 'Rightly', ṭōbāh, is an analogous concept in a similar con-

---

[7]For the theme and the problem of anointing, cf. E. Kutsch, Salbung als Rechtsakt im Alten Testament und im Alten Orient, BZAW 87, 1963, and THAT I, cols. 913f.

text.[8] The text elegantly suggests that, given the incompatibility of the two attitudes, they cannot both be held in good faith, honourably and rightly. Verses 17f. are an obvious gloss, probably Dtr, the aim of which is to explain the statements which have preceded it. This kind of gloss can be recognized not only because it interrupts the speech by making it more precise than is necessary, but also by its form, which is often, as in this case, somewhat crude: not only does it leave nothing to the hearer's imagination, but it attributes to the Shechemites here the need for feelings (of gratitude) towards Gideon-Jerubbaal which they cannot possibly have had. There is a parallel to I Sam. 10.18b–19a (Veijola, 111). **[17]** 'Risked his life' or 'put his life in jeopardy', literally 'threw his own life forward'. It does not seem necessary to read *minneg'dō*, which is preferred by the majority of commentators, *BHK*[3] and *BHS*. **[18]** 'The son of a slave girl', is not quite correct, cf. 8.31. Is this an unintentional mistake due to insufficient information, or a deliberate insult? In any case it seems to be proof of the chronological distance between the gloss and the original text.   **[19]** This takes up the speech interrupted by the interpolation and develops the themes sketched out earlier; I have indicated the resumption with 'as I said'. The argument is: it is not possible to be faithful to the family of Gideon-Jerubbaal and to its exterminators. **[21]** In the translation I have modified the order of the text, following H. W. Hertzberg*, 1959; in Hebrew this is correct and need not be changed. '*b'ēr*' is an unknown place, perhaps imaginary, given that it is a generic term for 'well', J. Gray, 1967, proposed that we should read *b'ēdōm*, 'in Edom' (*reš* for the original *dalet*, and omitting the *mem*), but this modification seems improbable. It is better to continue to suppose that this is a narrative element, originally independent of the present narrative and inserted later.

1. There are two problems in these sections, which are so closely interconnected, at least in their logic, that I prefer to treat them together: the first is the relationship between Jotham's speech as a whole and its present context; the second is that of the relationship between Jotham's apologue and his speech, and therefore with the rest of the context. I shall begin with the apologue or fable – whatever it should be called (according to some scholars it is a parable, but this term does not seem precise: the parable presents human beings).

2. The problem of the relationship between the apologue and its two present contexts is complex and old; it has been discussed now for more than a century.[9] First of all, is it a piece which has

[8]J. C. Croatto, '*Ṭōbā* como "amistad (da alianza)" ', *AION* 28, 1968, 285–9.
[9]For an examination of the solutions proposed, cf. W. Richter**, 1963, 248ff.

been composed for the present text, so that it appears incomprehensible apart from it, or is it a text which could have an autonomous existence, and which has been inserted here only to heighten the tension? Without claiming to give a solution to this old and complex problem, I would at least point out:

(*a*) The apologue is poetry and the rest of the text is prose. Thus the apologue stands out directly on a formal level both from Jotham's speech and from the more general context.

(*b*) As to its content, the trees look for a king to whom they may offer the crown, and in fact offer it to various species, all of which, apart from the last, refuse it. On the other hand, the men of Shechem are approached by Abimelech and are convinced by him that they should make him king, after he has shown them his capability and his strength. As Richter rightly observes, this presupposes a different setting of the speech.

(*c*) The meaning of the apologue is clearly that only the worst, the least qualified, is disposed to accept responsibility on the political level ('Shall I sway over the trees?', vv. 9b, 10b, 13b, is a phrase which seems to want to bring out both the general arbitrariness and the futility of the power when it is confronted with real problems; the verb *nw'* also appears in Isa. 7.2, which is a markedly ironical text). However, this situation is hardly applicable to Abimelech, who has always been the sole candidate, so that there is no question here that the worst person accepts: it is simply that there is no choice. Furthermore, when Jotham is speaking, Abimelech has already been crowned: in v. 6 we have the verb *mālak* in the hiphil, and not *māšaḥ*, as in v. 8, a lexicographical detail of some importance; the apologue is evidently talking of royalty in general and the context is concerned only with the specific case of Abimelech. At this point in the narrative the coronation of Abimelech is irrevocable, but Jotham speaks as though it were not, as if there were still some sort of choice left.

(*d*) The apologue has no evident connection with either the previous or the subsequent passages (cf. Richter and Veijola): it is restricted to a general critique of the institution of the monarchy (we shall consider this in greater detail in due course) from the point of view of wisdom, but through the eyes of those who are subject to it and not those who exercise power.

(*e*) The question is made even more complex by the fact that authors are not agreed on the character of the conclusion in v. 15: is this the original conclusion (thus Richter and Veijola), or is this a conclusion added at a later stage, and replacing an original conclusion (thus Maly, Lindars, Boling*, 1975, and Crüsemann)? The latter seems the more probable, as the cedars of Lebanon do not otherwise appear in the story and introduce a new concept into it. One thing seems certain: since the rest of Jotham's speech explicitly refers to v. 15 (cf. vv. 16, 19), it is clear that this is at least the point of juncture, though redactional, between the apologue and Jotham's speech. More than that, however, it is difficult to say.

(f) Another feature which stands out is the political character of the apologue, vv. 9b, 13b, as opposed to the general theological neutrality of the text, if we omit the Dtr or Dtr-type passages, which are of course pro-Yahwistic, in ch. 9 (against Adinolfi).

(g) The fable has been interpreted by v. 57 as a 'curse'. Quite clearly this is not original, but a later development.

(h) These are features which make it very probable that the apologue was originally independent of its two present contexts, even though the matter cannot be considered to be settled decisively. Moore*, 1895, and Burney*, 1919, rightly observed that the apologue fits 'somewhat precariously' into its present context, though they find this fact easy to explain in the light of the oriental way of reasoning, which differs from Western logic.

3. The olive, the fig and the vine are three very typical trees, much prized in Syria and Palestine even today; the fourth valuable tree is the almond, which is not mentioned here. Thus as I have indicated, the 'moral' of the apologue is very negative and polemical: not only does someone who successfully pursues an autonomous and recognized productive activity refrain from seeking political power, but he even refuses it when it is offered to him. This concept does not seem very different from the modern dictum 'power corrupts': not only does it offer to those who exercise it occasions for licence and illicit actions which are not to be found elsewhere, but it also detracts from productive and honest work. The symbol of those who are very ready to accept power is the bramble: it produces nothing but rather beautiful blossom in spring, but this is difficult to pick because of the thorns and does not seem to serve any purpose. It is only recently that we have learnt that brambles are in fact the best antidote to erosion on mountains which have been robbed of their natural vegetation; however, for antiquity the bramble was the most obvious antithesis to the trees mentioned above. It

therefore seems obvious that v. 15a is the point of the story: the bramble offers a protection which it is unable to give, and we should remember the protective function of the 'shade of the king' in the ideology of ancient Near Eastern kingship: it is a widespread theme (Crüsemann), especially in Egypt and Mesopotamia. In the Old Testament it appears for the 'shade of God', but at least once (Lam. 4.20) also for the king.

4. We have seen that quite apart from the question whether or not it is original, v. 15 is an element which allows the transition from Jotham's apologue to his speech, and therefore allows the apologue to be applied to the case of Abimelech. Here we must stop to consider a number of features:

(a) The first of these is the manifestly absurd claim made by the bramble that the other trees can come and take refuge in its shade. Absurd though it may be, it is not the only instance in the Old Testament: in a similar apologue, which is much briefer (II Kings 14.9), 'the bramble of Lebanon' asks the 'cedar of Lebanon' for its daughter as a bride for the bramble's son. Thus the two apologues, and especially the present one, are directed against the aberrant and sometimes absurd pretensions of power.

(b) When it comes to power, the bramble again promises something which it evidently cannot perform. Just as it cannot give shade, so too it cannot give the security which is often expressed by the term 'shade' ($ṣēl$, cf. Ps. 91.1).

(c) A third feature is the threat against those who will not accede to the requests of the bramble, which are both arbitrary and absurd, and do not want to accept its promises, which clearly it cannot keep.

5. Animal and plant fables are a feature of wisdom, both in Israel and throughout the ancient Near East.[10] It is here, therefore, that we must look for the origin of Jotham's. However, there is a considerable difference: while in the ancient Near East kingship seems both obvious and necessary, and is coveted by all, here it appears to be fundamentally negative, and only desired by the wicked.[11] In no way is the fable a 'curse', as indicated in v. 57. This time the wisdom seems to be popular wisdom rather than the wisdom of the court. In fact it is the product of the experience which centuries of subjection have

[10]Cf. W. G. Lambert, *Babylonian Wisdom Literature*, Oxford 1960, 150ff.
[11]Cf. recently F. Crüsemann, op.cit., 28ff.

created in those who experience power, in those who are governed: the irrationality and arbitrariness of the claims, the emptiness of the promises (remember the expression 'sway over the trees', Isa. 7.2, considered above, §2(c)), and finally the threats of repression against those who do not accept the rules of the game as they are imposed by the other party. This explanation is better than the one proposed by Maly and Lindars, according to which the fable does not criticize kingship as such, but only the attitude of those who refuse to assume certain civic responsibilities, thus leaving them to wicked persons. Such a trend can already be found in LXX^A (πεποίθατε, 'obey') and in Josephus, *Antt.* V. vii. 2 = §236ff.·

Thus here we have a deliberate rejection of the institution of the monarchy as such, and not just of some of its worse aspects. There is a very different attitude here from that which we find, for example, in chs. 17–21, where the origin of all the ills which the people have to suffer is seen in the absence of the monarchy (17.6; 18.1; 19.1; 21.25). M. Buber[12] has spoken of 'the most powerful anti-monarchical composition in the literature of the world', while T. Veijola sees its insertion into the present context as the work of a later, exilic stage of Dtr: DtrN. The way in which the problems caused by the monarchy are presented here strongly suggests that the fable in its present form originates in Israel (Crüsemann).

6. Thus the literary genre that we find here is a wisdom-type apologue, a genre well attested in the literature of the ancient Near East and also in the West: one might recall the apologue of Menenius Agrippa on the occasion of the secession of the Roman *plebs* on the Mons Sacer, at the gates of Rome; this last instance, however, offers a defence of the usefulness of power given by a representative of it.

The Old Testament refers to 'three thousand proverbs', dealing with 'the trees, from the cedar of Lebanon to the hyssop . . .', and which I Kings 5.9 attributes to Solomon. This is a genre which is rarely attested in the Old Testament, seeing that it appears only here and in II Kings 14.9, already referred to, where we have the antithesis between the bramble and the cedar.

7. Jotham's speech, in which the apologue has now been inserted, forms a contrast to this: it is addressed to a conven-

---

[12]M. Buber, *Königtum Gottes*, Heidelberg ³1956, 24.

tional situation. A group of people have been exterminated and only one has survived, in circumstances which are not narrated but which we may imagine to have been dramatic. And it is this very person who, instead of keeping clear, content to have escaped the danger, takes a role of prime importance in subsequent events; only in these verses, however, because he is completely absent from the rest of ch. 9. If there was still any need for proof that this passage did not originate in its present context, here it is. We have a similar case in II Kings 11–12, when the boy Joash escapes the massacre ordered in the name of Athaliah and regains his throne, albeit many years later.[13] These are themes which belong to fable and folklore, not to history. It is therefore useless to ask (like G. F. Moore*, 1895, or even J. Gray*, 1967, and R. G. Boling*, 1975) on the basis of the topography of the area how and where it was possible for Jotham to speak to the notables of Shechem 'from the summit of Mount Gerizim', or to ask whether by summit is meant the highest point of the massif or a platform half-way up, noted by travellers (Moore), or a ruin about 400 metres up, above present-day *nablūs*. We shall consider the problems of the topography of Shechem in due course (pp. 188ff. below) and shall not anticipate them here. It is enough to recall the theory put forward by K. Budde*, who in 1897 indicated the probability that the speech along with the apologue had been inserted into this context with a view to heightening the suspense, though the two are irrelevant from the point of view of the information which they offer: their presence adds nothing and their suppression does not detract in any way from this point of view. We accept them as elements of a literary kind. From this point of view they are important, especially the apologue, but otherwise they are conventional, inserted into the present context only for narrative reasons and perhaps to offer, in the Dtr redaction, the key to the way in which this episode is meant to be understood.

From a redactional point of view, then, these are late elements, even if there is no intrinsic element which helps us to date them. The wisdom-type apologue could be traditional, derived from Near Eastern wisdom and therefore more certainly ancient in itself than in its present context. It is probable that it has a literary history all of its own.

---

[13]A noteworthy article by M. Liverani, 'L'histoire de Joas', *VT* 24, 1974, 438–53, which is a sequel to the one quoted in n. 5 above, connects together the themes in question, from Joash to Idrimi.

Verses 56f., the conclusion of the chapter, make specific reference to Jotham's speech. This is a Dtr piece which Veijola (n. 9 above) also believes to be part of DtrN. It is therefore probable that the present passage belongs there too, even if, as I have said, the apologue is a wisdom text of considerable antiquity and importance.

(d) First difficulties between Abimelech and the men of Shechem (9.22–25)

9 [22]Abimelech ruled over Israel for three years.
23 God sent an evil spirit which came between Abimelech and the notables of Shechem; and they rebelled against him. [24]This happened to avenge the violence done towards the seventy sons of Jerubbaal and to make rebound on Abimelech, their brother, the blood of the brothers whom he had killed, and on the notables of Shechem, who had encouraged him in this direction.
25 The notables of Shechem organized ambushes on the mountain tops and robbed all the travellers who passed along that way. This happened against the wishes of Abimelech, to whom the matter was soon reported.

---

[22] 'Ruled': wayyāśar, root śārar, but vocalized as though it was the root śwr. For the date cf. the commentary.

[23] 'Which came between . . .': literally, 'an evil spirit between Abimelech and the notables of Shechem'.

[24] 'To avenge . . .': I read the hiphil lᵉhābī' with some commentaries, BHK³ and BHS, and with LXX ἐπαγαγεῖν. Another possibility is to read lābī'; in this way we avoid MT with its clumsy syntax, 'So that the violence rebounded . . .' 'Encouraged', literally 'had strengthened his hands'. The Hebrew repeats the note about the killing of the brothers, which I have omitted here. I have also restructured the syntax of the sentence; however, it remains equally clumsy.

[25] 'This happened . . .' the Hebrew has only 'against him', an ambiguous expression. The commentators agree (against Crüsemann, 94) in understanding the lō of the text to mean 'to his detriment', which means that this is a dativus incommodi (cf. GesK §119s, which does not, however, quote this instance). This is therefore different from what we find in 3.38; 7.24 and 12.4; cf. the commentary there. Nor can we render it 'against him', as though he had been the object of the ambushes: the objects of the ambushes are the travellers, even if the affair was damaging to Abimelech (against G. A. Cooke*, 1913, and now TOB; cf. the criticism made by Burney*, 1919).
Verses 23f. are from the Deuteronomistic redaction and try to ex-

plain in terms of retribution the difficulties which Abimelech had with
the government of the city-state.

1. The chronological note given here is of particular importance, even if originally it had nothing to do with the present
context. Various elements tell against its originality; in the first
place Abimelech was never a 'ruler over Israel' (so too v. 55);
he only ruled over the city-state of Shechem and its territory
(as, moreover, is explicitly affirmed in v. 6), and this territory
included placés like *'arūmāh* (cf. on v. 41 and on v. 31 for the
problems) and *tebeṣ* (vv. 50ff.). In the second place, again
according to v. 6, he really bore the title 'king' and not just that
of 'ruler', which prevents us from seeing this as a continuation
of v. 6 (Veijola). Now we also find the monarchy described with
another verb in 8.22f. (cf. there): *māšal*, instead of *mālak*, along
with the pan-Israelite theory; we must therefore also attribute
9.22 to this stage of the tradition, which we have seen to be late,
or to something similar. T. Veijola thinks of DtrN, a possibility
which must be considered seriously, even if it does not yet seem
to have been sufficiently proved.

Thus the note certainly seems to be an interpolation, even if
we do not know for certain who put it here. However, its purpose
is to give some chronological information.

2. Some scholars do not think that this date has any value,
but there is no reason to take such a negative attitude towards
it: rather, it resembles other notes of this kind scattered through
the 'former prophets': the dates of the 'minor' judges, which we
shall consider in due course; I Sam. 13.1: the 'two years' of the
reign of Saul;[14] the two years of the reign of Ishbaal,
II Sam. 2.10;[15] the seven and a half years of the reign of David
at Hebron, II Sam. 2.11. Thus if we strip the present text of
later elaborations, what we have left is a chronological note of
undoubted value; there is no valid reason for doubting that the
reign of Abimelech lasted for only three years.

3. In v. 23 we have one of the few passages in our text with
a clear theological colouring: God (note that the passage does
not use Yahweh; and the note could be found in any kind of

---

[14]For the precision of this figure (not of the former one, on the age of Saul), which is
unanimously challenged by critics, see recently K. A. D. Smelik, *Saul*, Dissertation,
Amsterdam 1977, 69ff.

[15]For the figure, see my 'Il regno di 'Ešbaʿal, figlio di Saul', *RSO* 40, 1965, 89–106,
now in English in *OTOS*, 31–49.

religious text) sent an 'evil spirit' which disturbed the harmony between the monarch and the assembly which had elected him. We also find spirits of this kind elsewhere in the Old Testament; in I Sam. 16.14 and 18.10 one takes possession of Saul, producing in him signs of neurosis and mental instability; in I Kings 22.21 'a spirit' makes the prophets pronounce lying oracles, deceiving King Ahab. It is characteristic of the present text that this spirit here acts independently, interposing itself between the two parties.

4. Apart from the mention of the 'spirit', the text says nothing about the reasons which led to the break between Abimelech and the assembly. Is it possible to discover other elements in our text, for example of an economic or political kind, which could help us to find the reasons for this break?

First of all, it should be said that in any case the break cannot have been caused by the foreign origin (or partly foreign origin) of Abimelech. As Reviv demonstrates (a point to which I have already referred, p. 170), it emerges with a considerable degree of probability from texts in the el-'Amarna archive (middle of the fourteenth century BC) that the Shechemites tended to choose a ruler from among the foreigners who represented a major threat to the area. On the other hand, Abimelech was only half a foreigner; in other respects, as we have seen, he was a true Shechemite who must have had particularly good qualifications. However, the same archives from el-'Amarna also show us that rebellions among the assemblies of all the city-states in the region were frequent;[16] many sovereigns complain to the Pharaoh that they have been driven out and are forced to live the lives of refugees and exiles. The case of Abimelech does not seem to have been very different: the assembly which nominated or confirmed the sovereign (if he was the hereditary ruler) seems also to have taken over the right to censure him, and in more serious cases, to deport him or drive him out. This right was clearly challenged by various kings. That Abimelech was king in the sense of the monarchy of the Canaanite city-states seems to be quite clear from the study by Wallis, which shows how Abimelech had made use of these very political structures to attain the monarchy. But just as he made use of these structures, so it seems probable that the notables of Shechem had also wanted to make use of them to gain the ends which they had in

[16]Cf. G. E. Wright, 1965, Appendix 2, 191ff.

mind with the restoration of the monarchy. It is here that we might insert the conjecture put forward in his 1972 study, on the causes of the conflict.

In the Old Testament sources, Shechem never seems to be invested with any kind of political function, except in the last quarter of the tenth century BC, when for some decades it became the capital of the kingdom of Israel, born out of the break-up of the personal union between Israel and Judah, which regrouped the tribes of the centre and north, with the exception of Benjamin, cf. I Kings 12 (c. 926 or 922 BC). In other instances, however, the place only appears as a religious centre, the location of important sanctuaries. It is only in this respect that its name has been handed down in the Dtr history.

However, it emerges clearly from the el-'Amarna letters that Shechem was in fact the largest city-state in the whole of the highlands, if not the largest city-state in Palestine – the only one, at any rate, to have a substantial amount of territory. Even if the biblical sources do not give us any details of the extent of its territory during the last centuries of the second millennium BC, we may conclude from the essentially peaceful way in which Israel succeeded in settling in the area that the political and economic importance of Shechem was now much reduced.

Thus it is in no way strange that the notables of the city should have thought that they would find in the person of the new king of their choice someone who belonged both to the invaders and to the city, and who had already shown a remarkable capacity for making decisions combined with a complete lack of scruples, a man who could restore to their city its ancient splendour, if necessary with the agreement of Israel, and otherwise independently of it.

Thus it is hypothetically possible to find the origins of the conflict between Abimelech and the city-state in the delusions of its notables in the face of the hope which they placed in the new king; in fact, as far as we can see, he did not even reside in his capital (vv. 31, 41).[17] One specific instance which could have led to the break could have been the Shechemite practice of imposing a tax on passing travellers, a practice which Abimelech wanted to bring to an end, or at least to profit from, so that the proceeds came into the royal treasury.

The region was very suitable for brigandage, and is still so

---

[17]E. Täubler**, 1958, 270ff.

even today: travellers have to go through the valley in which present-day *nāblus* is situated, and from the top of the mountains, particularly from Garizim, it was possible, as it is today, to see them coming from a long way off. This is the meaning of the text in v. 25, where it speaks of 'ambushes on the mountain tops', as Gray*, 1967, rightly indicates. Gray also recalls that such practices have continued until quite recently: during the Arab revolt in Palestine against the British in 1936–37, the localities of *nāblus, tul-karem* and *ǧenin* formed the so-called 'triangle of terror'.

5. In any case, the situation of conflict outlined here was only in its initial stages; it had not yet reached crisis point. However, it could change if an occasion presented itself, and the enemies of Abimelech will have had the men and the means to take advantage of it in an effective way. Such an occasion arises in the next section, which must therefore not be considered as a mere duplicate of this one, as often happens.

(e) Gaal's conspiracy (9.26–29)

9 ²⁶ One day Gaal the son of Obed moved into Shechem with his kinsmen; the notables had confidence in him. ²⁷One day they went out into the country, gathered their grapes, trod them and held a festival; they went into the temple of their god to eat and to drink. And there they spoke disparagingly of Abimelech.

28 Gaal the son of Obed said, 'Who is this Abimelech, and who are we, Shechem, that we should submit to him? Is not this the son of Jerubbaal and his lieutenant Zebul? Be subject to the men of Hamor, who bear the name of Shechem! Why should we be subject to Abimelech? ²⁹If only I were allowed to command this people, then I would think of removing Abimelech. I would say, "Strengthen your forces and go out to fight!" '

---

[26] 'Gaal, son of Obed': the names have been handed down with remarkable variants between the different versions. MT has the phrase *ben ʿebed*; LXX^B has Γαλααδ υἱὸς Ἰώβηλ, LXX^A Γαλααδ υἱὸς Ἄβεδ; Josephus, *Antt.* V.vii. 35f. = § 240ff. has Γυάλης. This last name seems to presuppose an original Hebrew reading *gōʿel/gōʿāl*. Vg and Vet Lat have *Gaal filius Obed*. We do not have to examine the problems presented by the first name: LXX^B is probably the result of a confusion; in Josephus we have merely a phonetic variant, which is understandable in an unvocalized text. The position over the patronym is more complex and more interesting. Ιωβηλ is almost certainly Ιωβηδ

(a confusion between Λ and Δ, which is frequent in uncial texts), i.e. *ʿōbēd*, always provided that this is not the Greek rendering of *yōbaʿal* or *yōbēʾl*, a theophoric name which combines Yahweh and Baal. In both cases we can explain the substitution of *ʿebed*, 'servant', made by MT, which evidently has a contemptuous sound: *ʿōbēd* is a name which frequently appears in theophoric combinations like *ʿōbēd-X*, while in the second case the onomastic combination of a syncretistic type is sufficient explanation for its suppression and substitution. However, whereas the first name is often attested in Israel, the second is not, so that notwithstanding its interest in this context we must prefer the first.   **[27]** 'Festival': *hillūlīm* is the festival of praise and thanksgiving connected with agriculture and the consecration of the first fruits, here the grapes which have just been picked (cf. Lev. 19.24); we probably have a similar instance, but without the specific term, in Judg. 21.19ff. (cf. there) in the region of Shiloh, again connected with the harvesting of the grapes. 'Spoke disparagingly': *qālal* in the piel is normally 'curse', which is the way in which most scholars translate it. Here, however, it has a rather different meaning; the term seems to be used in a broader and less specialized sense from a cultic point of view (J. Gray*, 1967, and R. G. Boling*, 1975). The context here seems to rule out the possibility that this was some rite of cursing.

[28] The text is not easy; for an account of the explanations put forward, cf. W. Richter**, 1963, 267 n. 58. 'Who are we, Shechem. . .?' forms a natural contrast with the 'Who is Abimelech. . .?' which has preceded it, but the former is literally, 'Who is Shechem. . .?' 'Be subject': I have kept the imperative of MT; the speaker first insinuates doubt about the possibility of continuing the course they have undertaken into the mind of his audience and then puts forward an alternative course, which is simply to return to their traditional ways. With the emendation we would have to read, 'Abimelech and Zebul. . .have been subject to the men of Hamor . . .' (for the expression, see the commentary), but in that case we would have to shift the *ʾatnaḥ*. The name Zebul is attested in the Old Testament, but it already appears in Ugaritic as an attribute of deities like Baal and Yam: it means 'lord'.   **[29]** 'If only I were allowed. . .': literally, 'If only you would give this people into my hands!' 'I would say': MT read 'he said', which Boling wants to keep. However, it seems better to accept the reading of LXX, ἐρῶ, i.e. *wāʾōmār*. The phrase is absent from Vg. R. G. Boling*, 1975, as we have seen, leaves *wayyōmer*, but explains the preceding *lamed* as a *lamed* vocative, 'Hey there, Abimelech'; however, quite apart from the problem of this form, the existence of which is postulated in Hebrew, against traditional grammar, on the basis of Ugaritic (and most of the time its connotations are rather doubtful), this interpretation is improbable: Abimelech was not in the city (cf. v. 41), and had to be warned by means of messengers (v. 31).

'Strengthen. . . .': literally, 'increase your army. . . .' is the language of defiance; it contrasts with that of military strategy, which is meant to affirm one's own superiority, not that of the enemy. Note the anomalous form *rabbeh*, for *rabbēh*, piel of *rābāh*.

1. This passage and the one which follows are remarkably effective pieces of narrative. The occasion which was to make hostilities break out between Abimelech and the notables seems to emerge following the arrival of Gaal and his brothers in Shechem: it is around them that the discontent crystallizes which, when spread, is transformed into specific hostility. We do not know who the people in question were. Gaal seems to have had some relationship with Shechem, and perhaps he was even a Shechemite: speaking to the notables he in fact uses the first person plural (v. 28), and to accept that he was one of them gives the whole speech an internal logic. Reviv has suggested that they were a group of mercenaries, a proposal which has been accepted by Gray and Boling; if this proposal is acceptable, it provides a good explanation for his presence in the locality and his familiarity with the notables: the official version was that they were travellers; the reality, on the other hand, was that they were a group of armed men, hired by the notables to organize resistance. The message of the lieutenant to Abimelech reinforces this theory: Gaal and his followers must have been a well-known group; so much so that in v. 40 he is actually invited to fight, a somewhat unusual invitation if it is addressed to a simple traveller in transit.

The occasion for the conspiracy is provided by the grape harvest and the festival which followed it. This could easily give cover for a seditious gathering: even the cry against Abimelech could be made to seem like an inconsequential drunken uproar.

2. Gaal's speech gives rise to arguments of a nationalistic kind. The foreigner Abimelech (notwithstanding his Shechemite mother) and his lieutenants (who are also of unknown origin) are not worthy to reign over a group of ancient nobility like the 'men of Hamor'. The Hebrew word which means 'ass', and analogous expressions (for example, 'sons of Hamor', semantically equivalent in a text like this one) always appear in relation to Shechem (Gen. 33.19; 34.1–26; Josh. 24.32 in addition to this text), and seem to be the name or the title of the dominant group.

Its origins are unknown. However, it has often been connected with the usage, attested among semi-nomadic groups in circulation around the Western Mesopotamian city-state of Mari in the eighteenth and seventeenth centuries BC, of killing an ass in the course of the ceremonies for celebrating an alliance; and the connection with Shechem happens through its temples, which are dedicated to Baal Berith and El Berith respectively (vv. 4, 46).[18] The comparison, which has been made often during the past twenty-five years, is remarkably suggestive (cf. some other information in W. Richter**, 1963, 266 n. 57), but is rash, not to say arbitrary. Besides, it does not make any contribution to the history of Shechem or towards understanding the texts which speak of it.

Thus in the present state of research we can only affirm the existence of this title, without being able to say more about it.

(f) Abimelech's first campaign (9.30–41)

9 [30] When Zebul, the governor of the city, heard the words of Gaal son of Obed, his anger was kindled. [31]He sent messengers secretly to Abimelech with the following message: 'Gaal, son of Obed, and his brothers have come to Shechem and are stirring up the city against you. [32]Now march this same night, you and the troops behind you, and take up position in the fields. [33]In the morning, when the sun rises, get up early and move against the city. When Gaal and his troops come out, you can do with them whatever circumstances call for.'

34 Abimelech and his troops made haste, and that same night hid near Shechem, in four companies. [35]Gaal, son of Obed, went out and stood in the gate of the city, while Abimelech and his troops came out from their hiding place. [36]Then Gaal said to Zebul, 'I see troops coming down from the mountain tops.' Zebul replied to him, 'What you see are the shadows of the mountains which look like men.' [37]But Gaal said again, 'Look at the troops which are coming down from the "navel of the world", and one company is coming from the direction of the "diviner's oak"! [38]Then Zebul replied, 'Where is your big mouth, with which you said, "Who is Abimelech that we should serve him?" These are the people whom you despised. Go out now and confront them!'

[18]Cf. V. Willesen, 'Die Eselssöhne von Sichem als Bundesgenossen', *VT* 4, 1954, 216f.; M. Noth, 'Das alttestamentliche Bundesschliessen im Lichte eines Maritextes' (1955), *GesSt* I, Munich [3]1966, 143–6; ET, 'Old Testament Covenant-making in the light of a Text from Mari', *The Laws in the Pentateuch and Other Studies*, Edinburgh and Philadelphia 1966, 108-17; H.-W. Wolff, 'Jahwe als Bundesvermittler', *VT* 6, 1956, 316–20; B. W. Anderson, 1957, 13–15; G. E. Wright, 1965, 130ff.; R. G. Boling*, 1975, ad loc., etc.

39 Then Gaal went out at the head of the notables of Shechem and fought with Abimelech. [40]But Abimelech put him to flight and he had to flee. And many of his men fell dead before they reached the gate of the city.

41 Abimelech continued to live at Arumah, whereas Zebul drove out Gaal and his brothers, so that they could not live on at Shechem.

---

[30] 'Governor': Hebrew *śār*, instead of the previous *pāqīd*. The two terms are not contradictory, despite what is often claimed (Richter*, 1963, 267). *śar hā'īr* appears on two recently published seals from late pre-exilic times, probably Hebrew.[19] [31] 'In secret': thus in the MT, LXX[B], Vg and Syr. But LXX[A] has μετὰ δώρων, i.e. *bit'rūmāh* (a technical term for the offering in the cult), a word which does not make sense unless we understand it as a corruption of *'arūmāh*, the place mentioned in v. 41. On the other hand, MT has the *hapax legomenon tormāh*, which Kimchi already considered to be a deviant and for which he substituted a combination of *mirmāh* and *tarmīt*. As a result, a large majority of scholars, followed by *BHK*[3] and *BHS*, prefer to read *bā'rūmāh*, on the basis of LXX[A], cf. the discussion which can already be found in G. F. Moore*, and Soggin, 1967, 190.[20] However, despite all this, the Hebrew here seems preferable, provided that the meaning of the phrase is 'secretly', or 'by a ruse' directed to Abimelech, cf. G. R. Driver**, 1964, 15, and R. G. Boling*, 1975: the secret character of the delegation and the nature of the dialogue at the gate the following morning, vv. 36ff. 'Are stirring up...': *ṣwr* in the transitive is rare, but it has precisely the meaning, as Boling* rightly indicates, cf. Deut. 2.2,19 and Esther 8.11. With *'al*, on the other hand, it means, 'lay siege to', 'besiege'. Thus the textual emendation which is generally put forward is neither necessary nor legitimate. [33] 'Troops': this is my translation, here and in the following verses, for the Hebrew *'am*, generically 'people', with Moore* and others. [34] 'Near...' for this meaning which *'al* sometimes has, see on 7.1. [35] 'The gate' is the outer gate, always open except in cases of siege; only the inner gate was shut at night, and then it was opened again in the morning. I shall consider its topography in due course, in connection with § 2; for a plan of Shechem see Wright, 1965, figs. 9,13,20 for the north-west gate and 24,26,27,29 for the south gate. [38] 'These are...': once again, cf. on 4.6. I have translated the Hebrew *h*^*lō'* in this way. [40] 'Of the city...': added with 1Q 6, LXX[A] and Vg. 'Him': 1Q 6 has the plural 'them'. [41] 'Continued to live': root *yāšab* in MT and in Vg (*sedit*): LXX[B], however, has εἰσῆλθεν, which

---

[19]Cf. F. Vattioni, 'Sigilli ebraici III', *AION* 38, 1978, nos. 394 and 402, with bibliography. I am grateful to my assistant Dr Felice Israel for this reference.
[20]Y. Aharoni**, 1967, 242, however, thinks in terms of two names for the same locality.

seems to presuppose *wayyāšob*, root *šwb*, 'turned', a reading which some scholars (Hertzberg*, 1958, and Vincent*, 1958) prefer. However, in that case we have the unaccustomed use of b^e- to express movement from place to place. R. G. Boling*, 1975, is right to observe that *yšb* here has the meaning of 'exercise power' ('presided'). The 'residence' is therefore an official one, i.e. a palace. 'Arumah' is usually identified with *el-'orme*, about 8 km. south-south-east of Shechem (coord. 180–172), but there remains a difficulty which is hard to get over, the transition from the initial *'aleph* to *'ayin*.

1. The first of Abimelech's campaigns against a rebellious Shechem is described in a text which is basically sound and which creates a remarkable literary effect (Richter**, 1963, 266–71). One of its chief characteristics is the essential character of the elements which make it up: there are no glosses, insertions or elements which are in any way superfluous and which can be deleted without the text having to suffer as a result. A second characteristic is the narrative technique: action and dialogue alternate, giving place to a narrative which, while simple, is effective. A number of brief scenes follow one after the other, each one with its protagonists and with its climax. Finally – and this is the proof of a superlative narrative technique – there is the fact that the royal protagonist never speaks: Abimelech is always silent; he only acts. Instead, the dialogue is carried on by the secondary figures, Gaal and Zebul, though the reader is never in any doubt as to who is the real protagonist.

Once again, the narrative is not interested in matters of worship or faith, nor does it contain any reflections of a political kind. It is only interested in human figures, specific people, with their aspirations and their anxieties.

The campaign described here ends with the defeat of the rebels and the killing of a number of them in battle. However, it does not seem as if the place is subjected to punitive measures of any kind. It is probable that Abimelech thought that a military defeat and the pursuit of the agitators would be enough to restore peace. It might also be that he did not want to attack the massive fortifications of the city, preferring to wait for a more propitious time, cf. the following episode. It is difficult to decide.

2. The present text is also important because it gives some details of the topography of Shechem and the complex of sanctuaries for which Shechem is famous in the Old Testament and

is also mentioned in a number of Near Eastern texts. I shall summarize here the results of my study on the question (Soggin, 1967), taking advantage of the opportunity to correct some points and add others.

[37] The 'navel of the world' and the 'diviner's oak' seem to be two elements in the complex of sanctuaries situated at Shechem and in its neighbourhood, cf. Soggin, 1967, 190. Gaal and Zebul stand at the gate of the city, v. 35; as I pointed out in connection with the text, we know of two gates: the first is the north-west gate, discovered and excavated in 1914 and again in 1926, which looks out towards Mount Gerizim. The other is the south gate, discovered in 1926 and definitively excavated in 1956 and 1957; this looks out towards the plain. It is almost certain here that the gate is the one facing north-west: the sanctuaries were around Gerizim, the sacred mountain, and could only be seen from there. Furthermore, the LXX has an addition, κατὰ θάλασσαν, Hebrew *miyyām*, 'from the sea', but also 'from the west'. Thus the two stand looking westwards, and that is possible only if the gate is the one to the north-west.

The 'navel of the world'[21] is a name which is confirmed by LXX and Vg and is taken up by the Mishnah and also by the Talmud. By contrast, the Targum translates the passage 'the fortress of the country', an element taken up again by Rashi and Kimchi. This last translation of the Hebrew *ṭabbūr*, 'fortress', is taken up by S. Talmon in his recent studies, but his arguments have not convinced me: the term 'navel' is also well known in other places with sanctuaries, whereas 'fortress' or even 'height' seems rather generic, especially on the lips of someone who wants to indicate the origin of a group of people. In any case, come what may, it is clear that it is connected in some way with Mount Gerizim, towards the west for anyone who is keeping watch at the gate, and is also in full sight. The 'oak' is confirmed by LXX[B], whereas LXX[A], A and Vg presuppose a term connected with 'vision' (but this could have happened under the influence of the augurs). It is in the same direction, but does not seem to be visible to anyone looking from the gate; in any

---

[21]For the expression, cf. again Ezek. 38.12 and Jub. 8.19, and S. Terrien, 'The Omphalos Myth and Hebrew Religion', *VT* 20, 1970, 315–38; S. Talmon, 'Ṭabūr Ha'arez and the Comparative Method', *Tarbiz* 45, 1975–6, 163–77 (in Hebrew: English summary); id., 'The "Navel of the Earth" and the Comparative Method', in *Scripture in History and Theology. Essays in honor of J. C. Rylaarsdam*, Pittsburgh 1977, 243–68; cf. *TDOT* III, 438, and recently 'The "Comparative Method" in Biblical Interpretation – Principles and Problems', *VTS* 29, 1978, 320–56: 348–51.

case it is independent of the 'navel' (against Soggin, 1967, 190f.).
We have various mentions in the Old Testament of trees connected with the cult of Shechem: in some instances the translators are not fully agreed as to the exact species: Gen. 35.4:
hā'ēlāh; Josh. 24.26: *hā'allāh*; Gen. 12.6 and Deut. 11.30: *'ēlōn
hammōreh*; Judg. 9.6: *'ēlōn muṣṣāb*, and v. 37 here. The fact that
this tree is always mentioned in the singular perhaps means that
it is always the same one in the same sanctuary, even if the trees
may have been different down the centuries. It is probable that
this is a sanctuary which was first pagan (hence the name 'oak
of the oracle', 'oak of instruction' or even the present text),
which then passed over to the Israelite cult along with the city
(Richter**, 1963, 271).

(g) The second campaign and the destruction of Shechem (9.42–45)

9 [42]On the following day the people went out into the fields and the
matter was reported to Abimelech. [43]Then he took his troops, divided
them into three companies and hid them in the fields. As soon as he
saw the people coming out of the city, he attacked them and slaughtered them. [44]Then Abimelech and the company that was with him
rushed forward and spread themselves before the gate of the city,
whereas the two other companies rushed on those who had gone into
the field and massacred them as well. [45]Abimelech fought against the
city all that day and captured it; he killed the people who had remained
in it and rased it to the ground. Then he sowed it with salt.

---

[42] 'Following': this is missing from MT, but it has to be inserted
into any translation into a Western language. 'Was reported': MT has
the third person masculine plural, indicating an impersonal subject:
'referred the matter . . .'; 1Qb has *wygd*, hence *wayyuggād*, cf. LXX[A]
ἀπηγγέλη, which I have chosen here. The meaning remains the same.
[44] 'The company': the Hebrew has the plural, obviously a mistake;
read the singular with Vg and LXX MSS, cf. the commentaries, *BHK*[3]
and *BHS*. [45] Throwing salt on a place that has been destroyed is
an ancient rite of cursing which is also known in the West. It signifies
the irreversible character of the action which has been performed. The
rite is not attested in the Old Testament, but it appears in the curses
contained in some ancient Near Eastern treaties. There are examples
in T. H. Gaster**, 1969, 428ff.

(h) The destruction of the 'Tower of Shechem' (9.46–49)

9 [46]When the notables of the Tower of Shechem heard the news, they took refuge in the citadel of the temple of El Berith. [47]But it was reported to Abimelech that all the notables of the Tower of Shechem were gathered together. [48]Then he and his troops went up to Mount Zalmon. And he took an axe in his hand and cut down a bundle of wood and took it up and laid it on his shoulder. Then he said to all the troops, 'What you have seen me do, make haste to do also.' [49]So every one of the people cut down his bundle, and following Abimelech put it against the stronghold, and they set the stronghold on fire also. Thus all the men in the Tower of Shechem died, about a thousand men and women.

---

[46] 'Citadel': *ṣᵉrîyāh* is a term of unknown meaning which the ancient translations render in this way; others propose 'the crypt', on the basis of I Sam. 13.6, where the reference is to 'caves'. However, it seems more reasonable to follow the ancient translations (against Soggin, 1967, 195f.) in seeing this as the fortified part of the temple, cf. the commentary. [48] It is not clear what mountain is indicated by Zalmon: perhaps Ebal? 'An axe': the Hebrew has an inexplicable plural, perhaps influenced by the axes of the soldiers mentioned a little later on. Either the singular should be read, or *'aḥat*, 'one', should be inserted before 'axe'. 'On his shoulder': MT has *'al šikmō*, literally 'on his back', while one fragment with Palestinian vocalization[22] has *'al kᵉtēpō*, 'on his shoulder'. Although it is a later word, the latter could be the most relevant. [49] 'Against', in the sense of leaning it up against the citadel; for this and other analogous meanings of *'al*, cf. on 7.1.

The second expedition of Abimelech against Shechem, the destruction of the city and the massacre of the Tower of Shechem are two successive episodes which are very closely connected. [42–45] In the introduction (above, pp. 164f.), we have seen that these verses are sometimes thought to contradict vv. 30–41: however could the people have again gone into the fields 'the next morning' after the first defeat, as though nothing had happened? If Abimelech wanted to destroy Shechem and its dependencies, why did he not do it at the end of his first campaign? Quite apart from the fact that this kind of chronological indication is often conventional, and can indicate an indeterminate time, it is also probable that at the time of the vintage

---

[22]Cf. recently B. Chiesa, *L'Antico Testamento ebraico, secondo la tradizione palestinese*, Turin 1978, 164, 294.

and harvest these operations could not be delayed long without running the risk of the ruination of the crop and therefore of famine. And famine was certainly a greater danger than the uncertain perils of war. For the second feature, we have already alluded to the possibility that Abimelech had not wanted to attack a fortified place like Shechem, preferring to wait for a propitious occasion (p. 188). This presented itself with the departure of the citizens into the country to gather in the harvest. Given the season, this departure was predictable, and in these circumstances Abimelech had virtually a free hand: by a series of surprise attacks he first took possession of the gate (we do not know which), massacring those who were on the way out, and then fell upon those who were in the fields and the orchards, finally regrouping his troops to occupy the city, destroy it and kill the surviving inhabitants. And the excavations carried out by Drew University, McCormick Theological Seminary and ASOR have discovered the traces of a remarkable destruction dating from about the end of the twelfth century,[23] a destruction which the archaeologists concerned identify with this.

[46–49] Continuing his work of repression, Abimelech moved towards the Tower of Shechem, probably (against the views of the majority of scholars and the archaeologists) not a section or a quarter of the city but a quite distinct outpost of it, administratively autonomous. It had a temple, in the citadel of which the inhabitants took refuge; they were killed when it was set on fire.

That this was a separate place appears from a number of features.

(*i*) The place has a name of its own, and a temple dedicated to a different deity from that of Shechem: to El and not to Baal. *bēt millō'*, however, is an expression which goes well with the acropolis of Shechem, crowned with a temple dedicated to *ba'al b'rīt*; similarly already E. Täubler**, 1958, 276–82.

(*ii*) The notables of the Tower of Shechem *hear* what has happened to Shechem, i.e. either because of the uproar or because the news is reported to them. In any case they do not *see* anything, which would have been obvious if things had happened under their very eyes, a few yards away.

Thus the name Shechem seems to be connected with two places, with the capital of the city-state of the same name, and

[23]G. E. Wright, 1965, 101ff., 122.

the Tower. This duality seems to be reflected in some Egyptian texts and in the el 'Amarna letters. The stele of Ḥu-Sebek from the nineteenth century BC (*ANET*, 230) and an execration text from the nineteenth-eighteenth century BC (*ANET*, 329 n.1) speak of Shechem in the dual, and in *EA* 252 (Knudtzon, 807 and 1312; *ANET*, 486)[24] Lab'ayu laments that '. . . my two cities . . .' (or ' . . . two of my cities . . .') have been conquered by the invaders. Of course these are only pointers, and their significance is far from certain: for example, the Egyptian texts could refer to the two mountains which stand over Shechem, Ebal and Gerizim, while the text on Lab'ayu does not say what cities he is talking about. For further details see the articles cited above by Harrelson, 1957, and Soggin, 1967.

(*iii*) Is it possible to give a location to the Tower? In 1967 I suggested *tell ṣōfar*, situated on the western side of the valley of *nāblus*, a few yards from the end of the modern city (coord. 173–182, but on the map it is called *tell sufān*); that was on the basis of other studies and suggestions. However, for the moment this identification must remain hypothetical.

(*i–j*) The death of Abimelech (9.50–55)
Final comments (9.56f.)

9 [50]Then Abimelech went to Tebez, encamped there and destroyed it. [51]But in the middle of the city there was a fortified tower: the people fled there, men, women and all the inhabitants of the place, and shut themselves in. Then they went to the terrace of the tower. [52]As soon as Abimelech arrived at the tower he began to attack it. He went near to the gate to set fire to it, [53]but a woman threw a millstone on his head, shattering his skull. [54]Then he called to his shield-bearer who was carrying his arms, 'Draw your sword and kill me, so that it cannot be said of me that a woman has slain me.' And the young man thrust him through, so that he died. [55]When the men of Israel discovered that Abimelech was dead, they each returned to his own place.

56 So God requited the evil which Abimelech had done against his father, killing his seventy brothers. [57]And God made the evil committed by the men of Shechem rebound on their heads, and upon them came the curse of Jotham the son of Jerubbaal.

---

[50] 'Tebez', mentioned also in II Sam.11.21, but with an explicit reference to this text, has been identified from the time of Eusebius of

[24]This text is also cited by G. E. Wright, 1965, 195ff.

Caesarea (*Onomasticon* 262) with a place about thirteen Roman miles from 'Neapolis', in the direction of Beth-shean; there, about 16 km. north of Shechem, is present-day *ṭubas*, a place already pointed out by Edward Robinson (coord.173–182). However, this identification is uncertain for philological reasons also, so that A. Malamat**, 1971, and Y. Aharoni**, 1967, think in terms of a corruption of *tirṣāh*, generally identified with *tell el-far'ah* (coord.182–188). **[52]** Abimelech tries to set fire to the gate of the tower, in an attempt to repeat his achievement at the Tower of Shechem. **[53]** 'The millstone', i.e. the upper part which rotates; the base was fixed. **[54]** Death at the hand of a woman was considered a disgrace in the East as in the West; for a series of classic parallels see G. F. Moore*, 1895, and A. Penna*, 1963. **[55]** Here we find once again the pan-Israelite interpretation of v.22, which is as absurd here as it is there; this is a stratum which dates from a little before the Dtr history. According to this way of presenting the fact, Abimelech's army will have been no less than that of the 'tribal league', a theory which is obviously absurd. **[54]** It seems that we should follow J. Gray*, 1967, R. G. Boling*, 1975, and T. Veijola, 1977, in assigning these two verses to Dtr. Veijola speaks of DtrN. The reference that we have is to vv. 7–21, but without the apologue. The interpretation is a moralizing one; the comment hinges on the divine retribution on Abimelech and on the men of Shechem who were his instigators and accomplices. The unconditionally anti-monarchical attitude suggests the later N stratum of Dtr. For Jotham's fable as a 'curse' see on vv.7ff. above.

The conclusion which this chapter arrives at in these last two sections is twofold: what DtrN describes as a first attempt to institute the monarchy in Israel (in reality the earliest parts of the text speak only of Shechem) fails because of its intrinsic contradictions; on the death of the first sovereign, the institution collapses and the people go home. Furthermore, had Abimelech returned from his campaigns safe and well, there would have been little for him to rule over: Shechem and its acropolis, the Tower of Shechem and Tebez were in ruins, and a large part of the population had been exterminated.

Thus ended a Canaanite city-state whose attitude to the invaders had been ambivalent if not downright amicable; it was finished, but would soon rise again as an Israelite city (J. Wellhausen).

As F. Crüsemann (42) rightly remarks, the present setting seeks to make a contrast between the pious leader, Gideon, who refuses the kingship offered, and the wicked adventurer, who obtains the kingship and tries to hold on to it at any price.

CHAPTER 10.1–5

The First List of 'Minor' Judges

Bibliography: J. **van der Ploeg**, 'Šāfaṭ et Mišpāṭ', *OTS* 2, 1943, 144–55; id., 'Les chefs du peuple d'Israël et leurs noms', *RB* 57, 1950, 40–61; M. **Noth*******, 1950; H.-W. **Hertzberg**, 'Die kleinen Richter', *TLZ* 79, 1954, cols. 285–90 = *Beiträge zur Traditionsgeschichte des Alten Testaments*, Göttingen 1962, 118–25; H. C. **Thomson**, 'SHOPHEṬ and MISHPAṬ in the Book of Judges', *TGUOS* 19, 1961–62, 74–85; W. **Richter*********, 1963, 324–8; 1964, 13–23; J. **Dus**, 'Bethel und Mizpa in Jdc 19–21 und Jdc 10–12', *OrAnt* 3, 1964, 227–43; A. L. **Hauser**, 'The "Minor Judges" – A Revaluation', *JBL* 94, 1975, 190–200; J. A. **Soggin**, 'Das Amt der "Kleinen Richter" in Israel', *VT* 30, 1980, 245–8.

10 [1]After Abimelech there arose to save Israel Tola the son of Puah, son of Dodo, a man of Issachar; and he lived in Shamir on the 'Mountain of Ephraim'. [2]He acted as judge in Israel for twenty-three years, and when he died he was buried in Shamir.

3 After him arose Jair the Gileadite, who acted as judge in Israel for twenty-two years. [4]He had thirty sons who rode on thirty asses and had thirty cities (which are called Havvoth Jair, 'the encampments of Jair') to this day, in the region of Gilead. [5]When he died he was buried in Kamon.

[1] 'Dodo': in Hebrew, *dōd* is a paternal uncle; however, the root is also used to indicate 'the beloved', cf. *yādīd* in Isa. 5.1ff.; *yᵉdīd-yāh*, the name of Solomon in II Sam. 12.25. Probably the name *dāwīd* is also to be connected with this root. The name Dodo also appears in II Sam. 23.9 in the Q (K has *dōdī*)// I Chron. 11.12; II Sam. 23.24 // I Chron. 11.26; I Chron. 27.4 (var. *dōday*) and is known elsewhere in West Semitic, cf. *EA* 158, 164: *dudu*. However, the text is not without problems: LXX has the literal translation as though it were a noun and not a proper name. υἱὸς πατραδέλφου αὐτοῦ (of Abimelech!), similarly, Vg and Syr, and thus wants to relate the person in some

way to Abimelech, whom moreover MT makes a judge. 'Tola' and 'Puah' are clans of Issachar, Gen. 46.13f.; Num. 26.23; cf. I Chron 7.1f. 'Shamir' of Ephraim is of course different from the 'Shamir' of Judah mentioned in Josh. 15.48;[1] some would see it as a variant of *šōmᵉrōn*, 'Samaria', in which case we would have a *terminus post quem* for the dating of the text: Samaria was in fact purchased and built by Omri, king of Israel, I Kings 16.23–26, in the first quarter of the ninth century BC; otherwise its location is uncertain. 'The Mountain of Ephraim'; cf. on 3.27; this time we have a certain name connected with a date; besides, it is probable that the place had had this name before being made a district by Solomon. 'To save . . .': the text does not say from whom or what; therefore the current view is that the 'minor' judges were not classified as 'saviours'; cf also the commentary, p. 198.

[2] 'Twenty-three years': the figures given by the two lists of 'minor' judges are no longer stereotyped as they are in Dtr (forty or multiples or factors of forty).

[4] 'Asses': *'ayīr* is an ass (male) for riding, as opposed to a pack-ass. It is an animal held in high esteem in the Near East down to the present day and has always been the mount of the noble rather than the lowly; cf. Zech. 9.9 (where it is parallel to *hᵃmōr*), and variants in Judg. 5.10 (the feminine *'ātōn*) and I Kings 1.33ff. (the 'mule' in the royal procession). 'Cities': Hebrew *ᵃyārīm*, like the preceding 'asses', for *'ārīm*; is this a mistake which needs to be emended, or is it an exaggerated play on words? The second of these alternatives seems to be the more probable. *hawwōt yā'īr* (the first term is 'encampment', and is to be found only in the plural) is a region in Gilead in Trans-jordan, cf. Num. 32.39f., where Jair the Machirite had conquered the 'Amorites', and I Chron. 2.22; in I Kings 4.13 it is one of Solomon's districts. The location in Bashan, Deut. 3.14; Josh. 13.30, is usually considered to be late.[2] Note also the play on words between Jair and the other terms.

[5] 'Kamon': perhaps the present-day *qamm*, a ruin situated to the north-west of *qumēm*, about ten kilometres west of *irbid* (co-ord. 218–221).

This first list of 'minor' judges (for the second cf. on 12.8–15, pp. 223ff.) gives the names and the number of years of perma-nence in office of two of the so-called 'minor' judges. These are people whose functions are not yet clear; there is no information at all to help to solve the mystery, and attempts at explanation during the last forty years have confused the question rather

[1]Cf. *Joshua*, ad loc.
[2]Cf. *Joshua*, ad loc.

than clarified it. This is even true with regard to authors of undisputed authority like O. Grether, H. W. Hertzberg and M. Noth. However, where information is lacking it is logical to try to remedy the lack by means of conjecture. And the conjecture which has most attracted the interest of scholars over these decades is certainly the view that these will have been judges in the strictest sense of the term, performing judicial functions within the sphere of the tribal league or similar entities in Israel. This proposal is now a relatively old one; it was put forward for the first time by A. Klostermann,[3] a scholar who is chiefly distinguished for his work on Deuteronomy;[4] it was then taken up again by A. Alt[5] and developed by O. Grether, H.-W. Hertzberg and M. Noth; the second of this last group of scholars makes a completely arbitrary reconstruction of a list of these judges containing twelve names. No wonder, then, that practically all the commentaries appearing in the post-war years took it over, as did a number of other famous scholars.[6] In other words, in their capacity of judges in the strictly forensic sense of the term, these figures will have been entrusted with the apodeictic law of Israel and with the casuistically formulated law accepted throughout the ancient Near East; they will have been responsible for maintaining it, handing it down and, in specific instances, administering it. This function is also seen in contrast to that of the 'major' judges: they are essentially leaders and 'saviours' of Israel or groups within Israel from external enemies; these, however, are administrators of justice and therefore charged with defending Israel from dangers which come from inside.

For almost ten years now often harsh criticisms have been made of the hypothesis of the tribal league, the so-called amphictyony, the existence of which is presupposed by the reconstruction of the history of Israel in the period before the monarchy, as made essentially by Dtr. We cannot go into these criticisms in detail here, but they have removed the ground from under the hypothesis in question. In the case of the minor judges, however, the ground on which their identification with

[3]*Der Pentateuch*, Vol. II, Leipzig 1907, 419ff.
[4]Cf. my *Introduction to the Old Testament*, London and Philadelphia ²1980, 118ff.
[5]A. Alt, 'Die Ursprünge des israelitischen Rechts' (1934), *KlSchr* I, Munich 1953, 278–332; ET, 'The Origins of Israelite Law', *Essays in Old Testament History and Religion*, ET London and New York 1966, 79–132.
[6]R. de Vaux, *Les Institutions de l'Ancien Testament* I, Paris 1958, 233ff.; ET, *Ancient Israel*, London and New York 1961, 151ff.

the judges in the strictest ·sense of the word was made was
already very weak: in fact the texts do not attribute any functions
to these people, either in courts of law or elsewhere, whereas
they are clearly interested in the duration of the period during
which they exercised their functions and in certain distinctive
characteristics, usually picturesque, sometimes on the verge of
extravagance and connected with their family circumstances. So
how can we affirm, even hypothetically, that these will have
been judges in the forensic sense of the term? And on what basis
can we affirm that their ministry had an antithetical pattern to
that of the 'major' judges? In connection with this last question,
let me simply recall that v. 1 explicitly states that Tola arose
'to save Israel' (above, p. 196). Now we can certainly argue
(with Grether***, 1939, 110 n. 1, and Richter**, 1964, 12f. and
118) that this is an 'attempt to insert' their text in the general
context of the judges 'by means of the statement about the
saving work of 10.1'. In this case, however, it is evident that we
are eliminating the only dissentient voice from the theory proposed, and therefore doing away with a *lectio difficilior*. A me-
diating theory has been put forward by Boling*, 1975: Tola
saves Israel from the confusion and the disorder left by Abimelech. In this case, however, we are simply taking over the
pan-Israelite conception that inspires certain of the passages
which comment on the traditions of Gideon and Abimelech,
concepts which we have seen always to be late, if not directly
Deuteronomistic.

In any case, we may consider that we have acquired one
insight: with Noth and Richter we can say that these are independent traditions, traditions which the redactors have taken
over in an integral form, reporting them without any substantial
modifications. That presupposes that they wanted to insert these
traditions into their present context in pursuit of a particular
end. And this end cannot be separated from the social functions
of these people, given that there is no sign of a religious function.
Is it possible to establish any more than this?

Since we must necessarily resort to conjecture, we must
attempt at least to begin from incontrovertible evidence. We
have two points to note: the annalistic-type indication of the
length of the ministry of each 'minor' judge by means of figures
which are not stereotyped, as in the texts about the 'major'
judges (2.11, 30; 5.32; 8.28: always the number forty or multiples
or factors of it); these are figures which have every appearance

of being real. The other element is the picturesque indications
of the kinsmen of each judge.

The first element suggests a relative chronology (evidently
not an absolute one, seeing that we do not know the parameters
of reference), like that provided by the chronology of the kings
of Judah and Israel (the only difference is that the chronology
of each king is calculated on the basis of another king of the
other kingdom). The second feature seeks to provide information
the bizarre nature of which seems to be meant as an aid to the
memory. Who is there who does not remember the asses and
the cities, once they have been mentioned, and even the sons of
one or the other judge? So if we want to make a guess, we can
suppose that in Israel there was an institution not dissimilar to
that of the 'eponyms' in Mesopotamia or of the 'consuls' during
the Roman empire, which served as a reference point for official
chronological indications. It is, for example, as though we were
to say 'In year X of the judgeship of A', a person who was then
remembered for the strangeness of his children or his mounts or
both. This is confirmed by the existence of 'eponyms' in the
Punic world, though the confirmation is indirect and from a
distant area, and therefore only hypothetical. Here we find
phrases like *bšt špṭm X w-Y*, cf. *KAI* 66.2; 77.3; 80.2–3; 81.6 and
perhaps 101.2 (one name only).[7] And originally these *špṭm* had
no military power whatsoever.[8]

Even if we accept this hypothesis, there are still a number of
problems to resolve:

(*a*) The reference to the 'minor' judges is pan-Israelite, like
that of the redaction of the 'major' judges; each of them follows
his predecessor in succession. Furthermore, although the local
origin of each of them is stressed, it is also clear that, as I have
pointed out, they judge 'all Israel'. But here too it seems probable (as in the case of the 'major' judges) that their activity took
place within strict local limits, and was not universal, so that
we cannot rule out *a priori* the possibility that two or more of
them may have been contemporaneous.

(*b*) Another problem seems to be that of dating. Was this a
function existing before the monarchy, which came to an end
when the monarchy began, when the king was a sufficient point

[7]Cf. W. Richter***, 1965, 68ff.

[8]C. Krahmalkov, 'Notes on the Rule of the *Šōfṭīm* in Carthage', *Rivista di studi fenici*
4, Rome 1976, 153–7, and W. Huss, 'Vier Suffeten in Karthago?', *Le Muséon* 90, Louvain
1977, 427–33.

of reference, or was it a function which also continued in the period of the monarchy? The texts are unanimous in pointing to the first of these two theories; in favour of the second, however, are the mentions of the 'Mountain of Ephraim' and perhaps that of Samaria (vv. 1 and 2, above, p. 196).

*

Jephthah

Bibliography: M. **Noth**, 'Beiträge zur Geschichte des Ostjordanlandes III: Die Nachbaren der israelitischen Stämme im Ostjordanland', in *BBLAK* (= *ZDPV* 68), 1951, 1–50 = *ABLAK*, 434–75: 41 n. 1 = 467 n. 141; I. **Mendelssohn**, 'The Disinheritance of Jephthah in the Light of the Lipit-Ishtar Code', *IEJ* 4, 1954, 116–19; E. **Täubler****, 1958, 283ff.; A. **van Zyl**, *The Moabites*, Leiden 1960, 14f.; J. **Dus**, 'Bethel und Mizpa in Jdc. 19–21 und Jdc. 10–12', *OrAnt* 3, 1964, 227–43; R. **de Vaux**, *Studies in Old Testament Sacrifice*, Cardiff 1964, 65f.; R. G. **Boling**, 'Some Conflate Readings in Joshua-Judges', *VT* 16, 1966, 293–96: 295ff.; W. **Richter**, 'Die Überlieferungen um Jephtah, Ri 10, 17–12, 6', *Bibl* 47, 1966, 485–556 (a basic study, which continues ** 1963 and 1964); S. **Mittmann**, 'Aroer, Minnith und Abel Keramim (Jdc 11, 33)', *ZDPV* 85, 1969, 63–75; J. A. **Emerton**, 'Note on Two Proposed Emendations in the Book of Judges (11, 24 and 16, 28)', *ZAW* 85, 1973, 220–3; A. R. W. **Green**, *The Role of Human Sacrifice in the Ancient Near East*, ASOR Diss. Series 1, Missoula, Montana 1975, 161f.; M. **Wüst**, 'Die Einschaltungen in die Jiftachgeschichten, Ri. 11, 13–26', *Bibl* 56, 1975, 464–79 (another basic work); J. A. **Soggin**, 'Il galaadita Jefte, Giudici XI, 1–11', *Henoch* 1, Turin 1979, 332–6.

(a) Prologue: Deuteronomistic introduction (10.6–16)

10 [6]But the people of Israel returned to doing what Yahweh considered evil, and worshipped the Baals and the Astartes, the gods of Aram, of Sidon, of Moab, of Ammon and of the Philistines. They forsook Yahweh and no longer worshipped him. [7]Then the anger of Yahweh was kindled against Israel, and he delivered them into the hands of the Philistines and the Ammonites, [8]and they began to crush the Israelites from that year. For eighteen years they oppressed all the Israelites who lived in Transjordan, in the country of the Amorites who lived in Gilead.

9 The Amorites crossed the Jordan to make war on Judah, Benjamin and the house of Ephraim, so that these found themselves in a very difficult situation.

10 Then the Israelites cried out to Yahweh, 'We have sinned against you, since we have abandoned our God and worshipped Baal.' [11]But Yahweh replied to the Israelites, 'When the Egyptians, the Amorites, the Ammonites, the Philistines, [12]the Sidonians, Amalek and Midian oppressed you and you cried out to me, did I not deliver you from them? [13]But you have abandoned me and have worshipped strange gods, and because of this I will not help you any more. [14]Go and lament to the gods whom you have chosen! Let them deliver you in the time of your difficulties!' [15]But the Israelites replied to Yahweh, 'Yes, we have sinned; treat us as you think we deserve. But now deliver us.' [16]And they removed from their midst the strange gods, worshipping only Yahweh. And his heart felt sorry for the sufferings of Israel.

---

[6] For the deities see on 2.13. [7] The mention of the Philistines may be meant to be a prelude to the Samson traditions; otherwise it is out of place. [8] 'From that year' is in some tension with the following 'eighteen years', so some would delete it. It could be a reference to the oppression in general, whereas the 'eighteen years' refer only to the Ammonite period. [9] Perhaps the beginning of the ancient tradition which narrated the Ammonite invasions. I Sam. 11.1ff. seems to be a similar case. 'Who were': note the intransitive use of ṣārar. The verse is continued in vv. 17ff. [11] The syntax of this construction is suspect. First of all note the anacolouthon: contrary to Hebrew syntax, the verb appears only at the end, at v. 12, so that some modern traditions which keep MT have understood another one at the beginning (cf. W. Rudolph**, 1947, 204, and W. Richter**, 1965, 22). Note also the construction with a separate *min*, when in Judges we always have *miyad*. I have omitted the preposition, with LXX^A and MSS, Vg and Syr, following the majority of commentaries, *BHK*³ and *BHS*: only G. R. Driver**, 1964, and R. G. Boling*, 1975, keep MT, simply recognizing the corruption. 'Of the Amorites': it is not clear what they have to do with things, but this is probably a reminiscence of Num. 21.21–35; cf. Judg. 1.34: however, it is strange that the Moabites are not mentioned, cf. 3.12ff. These are probably just stereotyped references. 'His heart . . . felt sorry for ': literally 'his spirit was impatient . . .' [16] 'Removed from their midst . . .': the formula appears in Gen. 35.2 (E) and Josh. 24.23 (probably Dtr), and is a technical term for the removal of strange gods.

Once again we are faced with a formula which makes up the framework of the ancient narratives which are handed down. It is comparable with 2.11ff., and this passage should be consulted for detailed comment (pp. 41f. above).

The basic interpretation and formal aspect of the frameworks are always the same; however, there are remarkable differences in content: the formula here seems much broader as a result of the insertion of an important sequence of material. This comprises: (*a*) the list of deities in v. 6, long and prolix, but not very specific; (*b*) the pan-Israelite amplification of v. 9, which introduces Judah and Benjamin and which therefore seems to reflect the composition of the kingdom of Judah after the schism of 926/922, I Kings 12; (*c*) the introduction of the Philistines, perhaps a prelude to chs. 13–16 and to I Sam. 7; (*d*) the list of all the peoples conquered in the past (with the inexplicable omission of Moab), beginning with Egypt; (*e*) finally the discussion between Yahweh and the people on the problem of pardon for sin and confession of sin, where the confession does not seem to be enough for pardon: it is necessary to eliminate the strange gods and their cult. Thus Richter**, 1964, 13–23, is certainly right when he indicates that these elaborations are obviously meant to deepen the content of the 'frameworks' and take it to its extreme consequences. So rather than a Dtr framework, we have a real introduction to the rest of the book: in fact the characteristics of the Dtr 'frameworks' end with this book; we have a similar formula only in 13.1, where it is reduced to the minimum possible extent.

(*b*) The appointment of Jephthah (10.17–11.11)

10 [17]Then the Ammonites assembled for war and camped in Gilead. And the Israelites also came together and camped at Mizpah. [18]And the people, that is, the notables of Gilead, asked, 'Who is the man who will be able to fight against the Ammonites? He shall be head over all the inhabitants of Gilead.'

11 [1]Now Jephthah the Gileadite was a mighty warrior, but he was the son of a prostitute. Gilead was his father. [2]The wife of Gilead had given birth to other sons, and when they grew up, the sons of his wife threw Jephthah out and said to him, 'You shall not inherit anything in our father's house, for you are the son of another woman.' [3]Then Jephthah fled from his brothers and lived in the region of Tob. Some adventurers gathered around him, and went out on raids with him.

4 After a time the Ammonites began to make war on Israel. [5]And because the Ammonites made war on Israel, the elders of Gilead came to look for Jephthah in the country of Tob. [6]They proposed to him, 'You be our general, and let us fight against the Ammonites.' [7]But Jephthah replied to the elders of Gilead, 'Did you not dispossess me and drive me out of my father's house? Why have you come to me now that you are in trouble?' [8]But the elders of Gilead replied to

Jephthah, 'It is precisely because of this that we have turned to you, so that you fight against the Ammonites. We will appoint you commander of all the men of Gilead.' [9]Jephthah replied to the elders of Gilead, 'If you bring me home again to fight against the Ammonites, I will agree to being your commander: may the Lord give them over to me.'

10 Then the elders of Gilead said to Jephthah, 'The Lord be witness that we shall do as you say.' [11]And Jephthah went with the elders of Gilead and the people appointed him their commander and general. And Jephthah repeated all his words before the Lord, at Mizpah.

---

[17] 'Mizpah' of Gilead should evidently be distinguished from Mizpah of Benjamin, Josh. 18.26 and elsewhere, mentioned in Gen. 31.49; its location is uncertain. Some scholars see it as *ḫirbet eṣ-ṣār*, about 16 km. north of *ḥešbōn*, coord. 228–150 (Vincent*); others (Aharoni**, 1967, 189) see these ruins as the site of *ya'zēr*. [18] 'That is, the notables . . .'; the construction is heavy and the expression is perhaps a gloss; however, we should not follow C. F. Burney*, 1919, in deleting 'the notables of Gilead' and substituting 'of Israel': they are in fact mentioned many times in the following chapter. Furthermore, why should we introduce into this chapter a pan-Israelite view which we have seen in the previous chapters always to have been late? This is all the less likely since it seems clear that only the group in Gilead is threatened, as is evident from the subsequent verses. Thus, as I have said, the situation is similar to I Sam. 11.1ff. [11.1] 'Was his father . . .': not to be corrected (Noth**, 1943, 53 n. 5 and Rudolph**, 1947, 205) to 'a Gileadite'; given his mother's profession, Jephthah was 'of unknown parentage': it could have been anyone from Gilead (Vincent*, 1958, and Boling*, 1975). [2] This introduces a banal explanation which does not fit in well with the preceding verse and the one which follows, the implications of which were either no longer understood or, if they were understood, were considered inconvenient: the driving out of Jephthah, which vv. 7ff. explain as an official action, is here attributed to a family dispute over questions of inheritance, in which the illegitimate line was naturally at a disadvantage. Boling's* explanation that the woman, in each case the same, will have had other children, this time legitimate, is not at all convincing, seeing that the text does not say that this was the same woman. The verse can be deleted without affecting the context, all the more since, while Jephthah is later rehabilitated, nothing is said about his having received his family rights (but cf. against, Mendelssohn, 1954, and Richter, 1966, 496).[1] [3] 'Tob': probably present-day *eṭ-*

---

[1]E. L. Greenstein and D. Marcus, 'The Accadian Inscription of Idrimi', *JANESCU* 8, 1976, 59–96: 76, see a parallel between Judg. 11.2 and the flight of David in

ṭayibeh, east-south-east of *deraʿa* (coord. 266–218), then in Syria. 'Adventurers': for the expression see on 9.5; the situation of Jephthah recalls that of David in I Sam. 22.2 and 27.8. 'Brothers': in the wider sense, his clan. **[4]** Absent from LXX^B either because of homoioteleuton or because it is considered superfluous. 'After some time', Hebrew *miyāmīm*, literally, 'at a distance of days', but *yōm* often indicates an indeterminate length of time. Boling* suggests 'at the end of the year', but without giving any reasons. 'With Israel', again the pan-Israelite theory, or to be understood as 'that part of Israel to be found in Gilead'. **[7]** LXX adds: ' . . . and sent me away'; according to Boling this should be inserted into the text because it has fallen out through homoioteleuton. **[8]** 'Precisely because of this . . .': Hebrew *lākēn*: or should we read with LXX^A *loʾ kēn*, 'certainly not!' (Boling*, 1975)? **[11]** 'Mizpah'; cf. on 10.17. Jephthah must have had a house here, 11.34, but it is not said whether this is identical with that of 11.2 (which is hardly likely after what has been said).

1. As we have seen, this passage is preceded by a laborious introduction which repeats elements characteristic of the Dtr frameworks and which coherently takes forward their comments. Now we have the real narrative of Jephthah and his achievements.

It will not have escaped the notice of the attentive reader, however, that an element which distinguishes the other accounts is missing from between the introduction/Dtr prologue, 10.6–16, and the beginning of the account, 10.17ff. In 2.6, 33; 3.7–11, 12–30, cf. esp. 2.16; 3.9, 15, the people, oppressed by their enemies, cry out to the Lord who raises up a judge for them. This does not happen in 10.6–16; furthermore, in vv. 13ff. the Lord refuses to raise up a judge for Israel and only grows impatient at the end, though without raising up anyone. In other texts, 4.1–5, 32; 6.1–8, 35, cf. especially 4.3f. and 6.7–11, the change happens in a rather abrupt way: first Israel cries out to the Lord, then we are suddenly transported to the scene in which the future hero is found involved in his or her usual activities. Deborah is dispensing judgment under the palm-tree, Gideon is threshing the corn. Deborah is at the same time a prophetess, and in this capacity she announces to Barak the will and designation of the Lord, 4.6ff.: Gideon receives his investiture after the appearance

---

I Sam. 21.11 on the one hand, and the beginning of the autobiography of Idrimi, king of Alalah, who was forced to flee because of the hostility of his father's house, on the other. I cannot discern the 'clear parallels' seen by these writers, but see the 'parallels' rather as similar motifs.

of an angle, 6.12, and only on a second occasion, 6.14ff., does the calling become direct. This last pattern has every appearance of being typical of the original tradition of the account, a version which Dtr was able to use again without difficulty and without a great deal of change, given the deep theological content. In other traditions, however, he felt that he had to provide it himself, probably either because this item was absent or because it had a different content which could not be reconciled with his interpretation of the problems.

2. In the Jephthah narrative the situation seems to be substantially different. The introduction/prologue does not move at a stroke to the actual account. Jephthah does not receive any designation or divine vocation at a single moment. His calling to supreme command in Gilead (and this is the only instance throughout the book in which we do not find the pan-Israelite version, a version which is even inserted into the account of Abimelech, 9.22, 55) happens only after laborious negotiations with the elders of Gilead; furthermore, Jephthah too begins his mission with a negotiation, 11.12ff. Only at a second stage, 11.29, does Jephthah receive the 'spirit of the Lord' and pronounce the vow which then has such tragic consequences. Another obvious element is that the other judges come from other occupations, at least in those instances in which we have information in this respect, and are therefore not professionals; Jephthah, on the other hand, is chosen precisely because he is a professional and so that he can continue to be one. In this sense his figure is like that of David, who is also compelled to flee and is also involved with a band of people who go out on raids, who is also elected because of his capacity as a soldier and also because he is a skilled politician. No wonder, then, that the endowment of Jephthah with the spirit does not play any part in his career; we are given the impression that this did not belong to the original tradition, but to its later interpretation; the only case in which the spirit seems to have any part to play is in the brief notice 11.32b, which tries to make its war into a holy war, cf. v. 9aβ.

3. Another discordant element in the Jephthah story is the chronology, 12.7. It seems to be typical of the 'minor' judges, with a real figure instead of a stereotype (cf. above, pp. 6ff., 199f.) of the kind that appears with the 'major' judges; also, 12.8 presents the second list of 'minor' judges in explicit, direct succession to Jephthah.

Finally, Jephthah is the only figure apart from the 'minor' judges of whom it is explicitly said outside the Dtr redactional framework that he was a judge, cf. the expression *wayyišpōṭ X* in 12.7 and in 10.2, 3; 12.8, 11, 13.

We can therefore conclude with Richter**, 1963, 328, that the Jephthah narrative need not originally have belonged to the 'book of saviours'. We must also ask, as did M. Noth**, 1943, 48f., whether Jephthah was not in fact a 'minor' judge whom the redaction later wanted to turn into a major judge, into a saviour, bestowing on him the spirit and making him fight in the holy wars. Certainly, if this was the intention of the redactors, it is also necessary to recognize that the project did not succeed; it is difficult to see in him a charismatic hero, invested with dictatorial power over 'all Israel'.

4. In examining the text we have seen the problem of Jephthah's origins. Son of a prostitute (the text does not say whether the term *zōnāh* should be understood in a professional sense pure and simple, or in a sacral sense; the distinction was probably not very clear to begin with and in any case seems irrelevant to the redactors, who reject *all* forms of prostitution), his illegitimate birth made him suspect from many points of view. So he had been driven out of his own country and, if we accept the version of the event given in 11.7, this came about through a basically political act, which involved the responsible elements of the community, those who were later to enter into negotiations with him. This explanation is clearly difficult to reconcile with that of a family lawsuit with his own kinsmen (v. 2). In the meantime Jephthah had taken to acts of brigandry, which, if it could be described as a certain kind of war, did not make him more qualified either politically or socially. To recall him to his homeland, not only completely rehabilitated but also entrusted with supreme command, was therefore another more important political act, and not just an intervention of the authorities in a family dispute out of questions of self-interest, questions which would have had to be laid on one side in the name of the common good. In other words, the elders, hard pressed by the threat in the military sphere, 10.18, were constrained to make a choice in favour of the element which was more qualified from a technical point of view, even if their choice was doubtful, to say the least, in the political sphere. In fact they made their excuses to Jephthah and recognized the misguided character of their past actions.

5. Jephthah is presented by the account as a person who inspires sympathy. As Hertzberg has acutely pointed out, he appears as the positive antithesis to Abimelech: both are descended from parents who are considered doubtful or downright inadequate, both do not enjoy a high reputation from a political point of view, and both have a great political and military career. However, Abimelech is the man who insinuates himself into a position of power and exercises it with great and useless brutality and a lack of scruples; Jephthah, on the other hand, is the man who accepts only what is legitimately offered to him and exercises power in a wise way: confronted with enemies from the east, he first of all tries to enter into negotiations with them, 11.12ff. It is therefore not a matter of chance that Abimelech fails after a somewhat brief reign, whereas Jephthah succeeds in maintaining his position until his death, 12.7.

He enters into negotiations with the elders of Gilead which soon appear to have been somewhat laborious. There are two terms which indicate the functions offered to Jephthah: *qāṣīn*, something like our 'general', vv. 6, 11, and *rō'š*, probably our 'commander (in chief)', vv. 8b, 9b, 11; both refer to leadership of all the people of Gilead.[2] Part of any negotiation is to ask for a great deal and to offer very little. So first of all the elders offer him a temporary military command, which applies during the state of war; then they offer him a position which seems also to be political and not to be limited in time. In fact he holds power 'for six years', 12.7.

At all accounts, the newly-elected leader seems to have wanted to solemnize the pledges given and taken by means of a visit to the sanctuary. As we have seen, nothing is said of the restitution of his family rights.

(c) The delegation to the Ammonites (11.12–28)

11. [12] Then Jephthah sent messengers to the king of the Ammonites with the following message: 'What are the problems between me and you that you should come and fight against me in my country?' [13]The king of the Ammonites answered them, 'It is because when Israel came out of Egypt it conquered my country, from the Arnon to the Jabbok and to the Jordan. So restore this territory peacefully.'

14 And Jephthah again sent messengers to the king of the Ammon-

---

[2]H. Rösel, *Bibl* 61, 1980, 251–5, draws a distinction between *qāṣīn*, 'military commander' and major judge, and *rō'š*, 'civil governor', or the like.

ites [15]with the following message for him: 'Thus says Jephthah: Israel did not take away the country of Moab or the country of the Ammonites. [16]When it came out of Egypt, Israel marched through the desert as far as the "Red" Sea and arrived at Kadesh. [17]Then Israel sent messengers to the king of Edom, asking him for permission to cross through his country, but the king of Edom refused them. It also sent messengers to the king of Moab, but he too would not agree. And Israel had to remain at Kadesh. [18]Then they travelled through the desert and went around the countries of Edom and Moab; they passed to the east of the country of Moab and camped on the other side of the Arnon; they did not therefore enter the territory of Moab, which was bounded by the Arnon. [19]Then Israel sent messengers to Sihon, king of the Amorites, the ruler of Heshbon, asking him to let Israel cross through his country to reach its destination; [20]but Sihon did not give Israel permission to cross through its territory, and assembled all its troops, who camped at Yahas and fought against Israel. [21]But Yahweh, God of Israel, delivered Sihon and all his troops into the hands of Israel; they defeated him and took possession of all the region of the Amorites who lived. there. [22]They took possession of the whole territory of the Amorites, from the Arnon to the Jabbok, from the desert to the Jordan. [23]So if Yahweh, God of Israel, wanted to dispossess the Amorites in favour of his people Israel, do you think that you can deprive them of possession? [24]Will you not possess all that Chemosh your god has wanted to give to you? And that which Yahweh, our god, has wanted to give us to possess, that we shall possess. [25]Do you think that you are any better than Balak son of Sippor, king of Moab? Did he ever strive against Israel or did he ever go to war with them? [26]When Israel dwelt at Heshbon and its dependencies, and Aroer and its dependencies, and in all the other cities that are on the banks of the Arnon for three hundred years, why did you not recover them then? [27]I have not therefore committed any wrong against you, but you do an evil deed in making war on me. The Lord, the "judge", will judge this day between the Israelites and the Ammonites.' [28]But the king of the Ammonites would not heed the message which Jephthah had sent to him.

---

[12] In contrast to I Sam. 11.1, we are not given the name of the attacker. 'What are . . . the problems . . .' is the meaning of the formula 'What is there between you and me . . .', which translated literally would be of doubtful significance;[3] there are other instances in II Sam. 16.10; 19.23; I Kings 17.18; II Kings 3.13 etc.; we also have the same problem in John 2.3. 'Ammonites': even a cursory reading

[3]Cf. I. Lande, *Formelhafte Wendungen der Umgangssprache im Alten Testament*, Leiden 1949, 83–5; the thesis has been accepted by W. Richter, 1966, 528 n. 3.

of the text will immediately convince the reader that most of what is described, the territories, the people and the deities mentioned in what follows, are essentially part of Moab (mentioned only here in Judges) and not of Ammon. However, apart from *BHK*[3] and *BHS* no one has proposed the substitution of Moab for Ammon, though it has been suggested by G. F. Moore*, 1896; Burney*, 1919; and Richter, 1966, 524f.: the speech can in fact only be addressed to the Ammonites because it is they and not Moab who are threatening Israel; then, as Vincent*, 1958, and Boling* rightly suggest, Ammon had in fact partly taken Moabite territory, so that the references, like the problems, tend to be the same. O. Eissfeldt**, 1925, 26, made another proposal: that the narrative of the negotiations with Ammon had been artificially conflated at a later stage with additional material dealing with negotiations with Moab. **[13]** LXX[B] adds: 'and I shall go . . .' (καὶ πορεύσομαι); LXX[A]: 'and the messengers returned from Jephthah . . .' (καὶ ἀπέστρεψαν), while Vg confirms MT; Boling* wants to insert the last phrase, which he thinks has fallen out as a result of homoioteleuton. The 'Arnon' and the 'Jabbok' are the present-day *wādī muǧīb* and *wādī ez-zarqā*; the first runs into the Dead Sea and the second into the Jordan; it is the principal tributary of the Jordan on the left bank. In the Old Testament these are the classic frontiers of Ammon; it is about fifty miles as the crow flies from one river to the other. **[17]** Here, as in v. 19, I have translated as indirect speech: we already have two sets of direct speech, one inside the other. The reference is to Num. 20.14ff. **[19]** 'Sihon': cf. Num. 21.21–24; Deut. 2.26–35; Josh 12.2. Heshbon, present-day *ḥešbān* in Jordan (coord. 226–134). There have been excavations there since 1968. **[20]** 'Did not give permission'; with all the commentators, reading with LXX[A] (καὶ ἠθέλησαν . . . διελθεῖν . . .) the root *mā'an*, 'concede', 'allow', instead of *'āman*, with Num. 20.21; MT has 'did not trust Israel to pass', a construction whose syntax is difficult and whose sense is obscure. However, G. R. Driver**, 1964, indicated that here *'mn* could have the meaning that it sometimes has in Arabic, 'grant safe conduct', in which case the meaning which I have proposed would derive directly from the Hebrew text. 'Yahas' (with *he* locale, *yahṣāh*), a place which is also mentioned in Josh. 13.18; 21.36 and on the stele of Mesha of Moab, line 19 (*ANET*, 320f.; *KAI*, 181; *SSI* i, 71ff.); its location is uncertain, but some scholars identify it with *ḥirbet iskander* on the *wādī-el-wālī*, a tributary on the right bank of the Arnon, and others with *ḥirbet-el-medinīyeh*, on the edge of the desert (coordinates 240–089 and 236–110 respectively). **[24]** Chemosh is the national deity of Moab, in the Old Testament and on the stele of Mesha. **[25]** For Balak, see Num. 22.2f. **[26]** Aroer: here vocalized wrongly by MT as *'ar'ōr*: present-day *'arā'ir* (coord. 228–097). 'On the Arnon': LXX has *yāṣēr*; LXX[B] has 'Jordan' for Arnon, readings which Vincent considers to be better. Aroer is mentioned often in the Old Testament and on the Moabite stone. 'For three hundred years': the figure might seem to have been calculated on the basis of the total chronology of the book of Judges, which produces 301 years according to the calculations of G. F. Moore*, 1895; in this case it is to be taken as being late. On the other hand, Mesha, line 10, affirms: ' . . . the men of Gad had settled in the region of *'aṭārōt* from time immemorial . . .', which suggests that this is a round number, but not exaggerated. 'Did you not recover . . .': read *hiṣṣaltām* with LXX^B ἐρρύσω αὐτούς, for MT *hiṣṣaltem*. Note then how the king of Ammon becomes the direct heir of Moab over the territories conquered by him.

1. This text is generally recognized as being a long interpolation: only vv. 12 and 28 can belong to the original tradition: in fact it is by no means strange that Jephthah should have tried to prevent a war through timely treaties. From a historical point of view, however, the response of the king of Ammon to the first delegation and Jephthah's second delegation seem improbable. In their message, the latter are said to have retailed to the enemy king part of the history of salvation, changing it in some respect or adding whole sections which refer to Moab, deriving from this historical and theological construction a forensically valid right to the possession of the region. And as if this were not enough, the text has contradictions and tensions of its own. In vv. 15ff. it is said that Israel did not conquer any Ammonite or Moabite territory, as these are defined by the enemy in v. 13: 'from the Arnon to the Jabbok and to the Jordan'; the text also insists that Israel went round the boundaries of the two countries. However, in vv. 19ff. 'the region of the Amorites' seems to be for the most part identical with the Ammonite and Moabite territory just described, cf. vv. 22f.: 'From the Arnon to the Jabbok, from the desert to the Jordan', and 26. Furthermore these tensions already exist in the last section of the march across the desert (Num. 21.10–35, esp. v. 21),[4] where it is said that Sihon had conquered the territory in question for Moab, an evident attempt to harmonize two discordant traditions. However, this attempt at harmonization is absent from our text, for which the territories of Ammon and Moab and that of Sihon are in theory distinct, though in practice they coincide. If nothing else, this is a sign of a certain confusion in the redaction, which is evidently far re-

[4]For a detailed analysis of the relationships cf. W. Richter, 1966, 531ff.

moved from the redaction of Numbers, which could still see the incompatibility of the two statements in question and tried to harmonize them.

There is no need to go into further details here; for those the reader is referred to the studies by Richter, 1966, and Wüst, 1975, quoted above; it is enough to say that the latter recognizes the existence of three redactional strata by means of which the territory of Moab is attached to that of Ammon. In any case, we can be certain that the text as it is now cannot have made up the content of the message sent by Jephthah to the king of Ammon! Rather, it attempts in a general way, without any reference to a particular historical situation, to argue for the rights of Israel over Ammonite and Moabite Transjordan, a region also occupied by Gad and the eastern part of Manasseh (for this last see on Num. 32), possession of which was a cause of dispute between Israel and the two kingdoms of Transjordan.[5]

2. However, historical and theological syntheses of this kind, in which the theological element preponderates over the historical element, form a genre which is well known elsewhere in the Old Testament: Deut. 1–3; Josh. 2.9–11;[6] I Sam. 12.7–15; these seem to be essentially Dtn and Dtr passages. However, that does not appear to be the case in the present passage, where the historico-theological recapitulation does not seem to have any significance for the people and its spokesmen in the theological sphere. The importance lies in the political sphere: the disputed territory is Israelite, and for good legal reasons; if the God of Israel wanted to give it to his people, who could claim to be justified in taking it away from them? Nor is it the case, given the character of the text, that we have to look for complex harmonizing theories in the ethnic and historical sphere, following the attempt made by R. G. Boling*, 1975, who points out that there were only Edomites and Moabites in the region at the time, and that the Ammonites will have arrived only at a later stage; in this case the presentation would be historically and archaeologically correct. Even given this correspondence, it remains equally true that this text, presented as a letter to the king of Ammon, is not a diplomatic communication, nor is it addressed to the king of Ammon, leaving aside the point that

[5]Cf. my *Joshua*, 158, on 13.25–38.
[6]Cf. my *Joshua*, ad loc.

the mentions of Og king of Bashan (absent here) and of Sihon king of the Amorites are now usually thought to be legendary.

One solution has been proposed by M. Noth in 1951:[7] this is a late kind of insertion. However, as Richter pointed out in 1966 (540), it is an insertion which does not refer to any situation from the history of Israel known to us, so that it seems to be an independent writing, standing by itself. He compares it with Jer. 49.1f., an oracle against the Ammonites, with a theme similar to this one: for example, the theme of the conquest, expressed with the root *yāraš*, literally 'inherit'.

In any case, notwithstanding the difficulty of finding a historical and geographical context for the present text, it is the work of a cultured person who backs up his position with arguments taken from theology and international law: the territories belong to those who received them from their particular deity, and the fact of conquest is the most evident sign of this gift, which thus constitutes the element which makes it possible to affirm the legitimacy of the right of a people to a territory.

(d) Jephthah's vow (11.29–40)

11 [29] Then the spirit of Yahweh came upon Jephthah, and he crossed Gilead and Manasseh, so as to arrive at Mizpah in Gilead, and from Mizpah in Gilead he passed on in the direction of the Ammonites. [30]Then Jephthah made a vow before the Lord: 'If you will truly give the Ammonites into my hands, [31]then whoever first comes forth from the door of my house to meet me, when I return safe and sound from the Ammonites and from fighting with them, I will offer up in sacrifice.' [32]So Jephthah passed in the direction of the Ammonites to fight with them, and Yahweh gave them into his hand. [33]And he smote them from Aroer to the neighbourhood of Minnith, occupying twenty cities, and as far as Abel-keramim, a very great defeat. Thus the Ammonites were subdued by the Israelites.

34 And Jephthah returned to Mizpah, to his house, and behold his own daughter came out to meet him with tambourines, songs and dances; she was his only child, much loved: he did not have any other sons or daughters apart from her. [35]When he saw her, he rent his clothes and cried, 'Alas, my daughter, you have dealt me a deadly blow! You must be the cause of my misery! But now I have pronounced a vow before the face of the Lord and I can no longer take it back again.' [36]She replied to him, 'My father, if you have made a vow to Yahweh, do to me what you have pledged youself to do, since Yahweh

---

[7]M. Noth**, 1943, 53 n. 3 has suggested that this is a post-Dtr text.

has allowed you to annihilate your enemies, the Ammonites.' ³⁷Then she said to her father: 'Let this promise be fulfilled for me. But give me two months, and let me wander freely among the mountains and bewail my virginity, I and my companions.' ³⁸He replied to her, 'Go.' And he let her go for two months. She went, together with all her companions, to bewail her virginity on the mountains. ³⁹When two months had passed, she returned to her father, who fulfilled with her the vow that he had made. She had not yet had relations with any man. Thus it became a custom in Israel ⁴⁰that every year the Israelite women went to commemorate the daughter of Jephthah the Gileadite, for four days in the year.

[29] 'At Mizpah': many correct the *'et* of MT to *'el*, but G. F. Moore*, 1895, had already shown that *'ābar* with *'et* can have the sense of 'go towards a place'. [31] 'Whoever', literally, 'the one going out who goes out . . .', to which Vg adds an interpretative *primus*, cf. Josephus, *Antt.* V. vii. 10=§263, which is necessary in a Western language and which I have therefore adopted. Only in this passage is it said that Jephthah had a house of his own in Mizpah: this does not seem to be the same as the one which he was driven out of, according to 11.2f. [33] 'Aroer': is this the same as the one mentioned in v. 26 above, or another of the same name, of unknown location? However, the other places cannot be identified either, in the present state of research; in any case, this is the region around *rabbat 'ammōn*, capital of the Ammonite kingdom, present-day Amman, capital of the Hashemite Kingdom of Jordan (coord. 238–151). For details and valid attempts at solving the problem see the article by S. Mittmann, 1969: certainly the 'twenty cities' and 'from Aroer' are later additions, tending to magnify the victory; however, this produces a heavy text. [34] 'Apart from her . . .': MT has 'apart from him', but this is to be corrected to *s⁵bīrīn*, LXX^A, Σ, Θ, Syr and Tg in the feminine (*BHK*³ and *BHS*). 'You have dealt . . . you . . .' cf. the different reading of LXX^B followed by the Syriac: 'You have indeed ruined me and are the source of my ruin . . .': Vg has *'decepisti me et decepta es . . .'* (perhaps *b⁵'ōk⁵rāk?*). Note the difference between the real situation and the way in which it is presented by Jephthah, as though the fault were that of the girl; cf. the commentary, §1 (vi). [37] 'Wander . . .': read the root *rwd: w⁵rād⁵tī*, for the impossible 'descend on the mountains' (root *yārad*) of MT. [39] 'Became a custom . . .': note *hōq*, masculine, with a feminine verb: LXX and Vg therefore read, 'And that became a custom . . .' The reading is strange, to say the least: often a feminine term has the masculine verb, but not the contrary. The phrase belongs to the following verse, so that the *sōp pāsūq* had to be put after *'īš*. [40] 'Commemorate': root *tānāh*, 'sing', but in this sense, cf. on 5.11; however, the ancient translations have 'weep', i.e. *l⁵qōnēn*. MT could

give a euphemism for the rite, now only attested by LXX and Vg, cf. the commentary, §1 (iv).

1. (i) The episode of Jephthah's vow, considered by some to be rash (but cf. (ii) below), and of the sacrifice of his only daughter, is remarkably interesting not only for historians generally (in fact in the present context it is an anecdotal type of interpolation; and in any case, the historian is only rarely interested in details of a personal or sentimental kind), but also for the historian of religion. Here we have one of the very rare cases of human sacrifice attested in the Old Testament, which not only is nòt censured in any way, but is even considered necessary as the fulfilment of a vow. We have another case in Gen. 22.1ff., but there, as is well known, in the end Isaac is not sacrificed. Here, then, there is no kind of criticism, but the text does not give any possible alternative and the rite has to be performed. Elsewhere the Old Testament passes a severe judgment on the usage in question and condemns it outright, cf. Lev. 18.21; 20.2–5; Deut. 12.31; 18.10 and Micah 6.7, together with the texts which speak of acts of worship for '*mōlek*'.[8] Thus the exceptional character of this episode at an ideological level justifies a detailed study, which has partly been made by T. H. Gaster**, 1969, 430ff., who has collected a great many parallels from the history of religion.

(ii) First of all, we must clear some misunderstandings out of the way. This is a real human sacrifice, as is shown by the terminology used, cf. Num. 30.2ff.; furthermore, the vow clearly pledges a human sacrifice, without there being the possibility of something else, for example a domestic animal, as might seem to be implied, although by a formula ambiguous today, by H.W. Hertzberg*, 1958, and R. G. Boling*, 1975; this appears clearly from the terminology of the holocaust in Lev. 1.3ff. We find another conditional vow in I Sam 1.11ff., but without a fatal outcome, given that it provides only for the dedication of the son, so that it cannot be said, for example, that the sacrifice in question was part of a conditional vow. Nor can one diminish the gravity or the importance of the episode by speaking of Jephthah's rashness, or of his 'generosity and impulsiveness, in accordance with his character', as A. Penna*, 1963, would prefer: quite apart from the unsuitability of this terminology, this

[8]For '*mōlek*' cf. now D. Plataroti, 'Zum Gebrauch des Wortes *MLK* im Alten Testament', *VT* 28, 1978, 286–300.

generosity and impulsiveness do not seem to form any part of Jephthah's character; indeed, Jephthah seems to have been quite the opposite, if we consider all his negotiations with the elders or his delegation to the Ammonites. From the story presented here, Jephthah seems to have been a responsible man, calculating and particularly skilled at negotiations.

(iii) It is clear that the words must be interpreted in a different way. Vows and actions of this kind presuppose a state of emergency. The most obvious parallel, even if it is not a complete one, to this account is that of the king of Moab in II Kings 3.26ff.: unable to defeat the Israelites who were besieging him or to escape from them in any way, the monarch offered the prince his heir as a sacrifice on the walls of the city; 'this was a source of great anger against the Israelites. .' who had to give up the siege and go away. The text has to be translated in this way, and the anger is certainly that of Chemosh, the national deity of Moab. The situation must have seemed very much the same to Jephthah, even if these were only calculations and provisions, and not a specific emergency. Jephthah thus takes a risk the implications of which must have been clear; it is what we would normally call a calculated risk: few people apart from his daughter and possibly his wife could have come out from his house to meet him; however, we hear nothing of the wife, which evidently further reduces the scope of possible victims.

(iv) This narrative has remarkable parallels in ethnology and the history of religions, and the classical world provides some of the best known of them: Idomenaeus, king of Crete, caught up in a storm and on the point of being shipwrecked, makes a vow to offer up to Neptune the first being who comes out to meet him on his return, *Aeneid* (scholion) 11. 264, cf. 3.121; in Aulis, Agamemnon sacrifices his daughter Iphigenia, the theme of Euripides' tragedy of the same name (Moore*, 1895, ad loc., and T. H. Gaster**, 1969, loc. cit.). Classical and Christian authors attest the practice of human sacrifice, especially in Asia Minor, where however the victim (often a girl) is usually conveniently replaced by an animal.

(v) However, the episode is further complicated by the fact that it bears witness to the existence of a rite, celebrated every year by the 'daughters of Israel' on the mountains for a period of four days, a figure which is evidently independent of the months passed by the girl in the mountains, which number only two; the suspicion therefore arises that the rite and the story were combined at a later stage, the second now serving as the aetiology for the first. Furthermore, as we have seen, LXX and Vg speak of a rite of lament for the girl, a feature which, with its precision, is more likely to be authentic than the more generic commemoration. And rites of mourning are known in the Old Testament, even if they are not attested very often: in Ezek. 8.14 the women in the temple of Jerusalem between the two exiles 'lament Tammuz'. This is the Mesopotamian deity of vegetation, called 'Adōn in the West Semitic world (Graecized into Adonis), who died at the beginning of the summer, in the month named after him (June-July), indicating the death of vegetation which would rise again in the autumn. The parallel with Canaanite Baal as attested in Ugarit is obvious. Also in the postexilic period, in Zech. 12.11, 'the inhabitants of Jerusalem' lamented Hadad (a name for Baal)-Rimmon on the plain of Megiddo. This lament related specifically to the deity, who was either 'dead' or 'snatched away', as in the case of 'the maiden' Persephone in the Eleusinian mysteries.

(vi) Now G. F. Moore*, 1895, and C. F. Burney *, 1919, rightly pointed to the parallel which can be found between the narrative of Jephthah's daughter and the rite which follows, and these practices attested in both East and West; this is especially the case if we could accept the variant proposed by LXX and Vg, who speak of a lament instead of a commemoration. In other words, in the account of the sacrifice of Jephthah's daughter we would have an instance of the 'historicization' of a myth, a practice, which, as is well known,[9] is widespread in the Old Testament. This development of the material in the Old Testament would well explain the evident tensions existing within the narrative: Jephthah's exclamation, which seems to want to put the blame for what happens on the daughter (we do not find traces of any particular tenderness in Jephthah, a feature observed by some commentators, though otherwise irrelevant in the narrative); the girl's lack of resistance, which can be understood only if the sacrifice was part of a generally accepted practice (something like the human sacrifices among the Maya in pre-Columbian Mexico), perhaps directly honourable for the person involved; the tension between the two months which the girl is allowed to wait and the four days of the celebrations; and

[9]For the problem see my *Introduction to the Old Testament*, London and Philadelphia ²1980, 46ff.

finally the annual commemoration of an episode without historical importance, also attributed to a person living on the per-
iphery of civilization and Israelite faith, indeed who in all
probability was not even an Israelite, if his mother was a prostitute. Given this interpretation of the question, the redaction
succeeds in setting the only human sacrifice attested in the Old
Testament in a marginal context, making it appear 'not
Hebrew'.

(vii) Those who studied the episode before the discovery of
the Ugaritic texts in 1929 were able only to use the biblical,
classical and Christian material at their disposal. The Ugaritic
texts provide important parallels and further information. The
'virgin Anat' laments the dead Baal during the summer, when
nature languishes, and looks for him, running over 'every mountain in the heart of the country – every hill in the midst of the
fields. . .'; this is a rite connected with the fertility of the soil, as
Gray*, 1967, has indicated.[10] However, we must be careful not
to exaggerate such parallels, as Gray seems tempted to do; in
this case many elements of the Anat myth are missing and there
is no indication that they ever belonged to the narrative.

Thus there are remarkable parallels, but they are composed
of individual elements and do not come together in an organic
context.

(viii) However, if parallels of this kind serve to shed gleams
of light on the background of an episode like this, they still do
not explain how the Old Testament came to hand it on, making
it the aetiology for the celebration of a rite of dubious, indeed
improbable orthodoxy, practised in a peripheral area which was
unimportant for Israelite worship generally. As it is impossible
to arrive at any explanation in the present state of research, we
must be content with taking note of the phenomenon.

In any case, the episode allows us to have one of the few
possible glimpses of Israelite religion, albeit in a peripheral area,
as it was before the preaching of the great prophets and before
Josiah's reform, a religion which had much more in common
with that of Canaan and the other religions of the ancient Near
East than Israelites were able to record at a later stage or than
the revisions of the texts were disposed to admit: one need only
think that the rite for Hadad-Rimmon is attested in the post-
exilic period!

[10]The text (Gordon) 62: 1ff.; cf. C. H. Gordon, *Ugaritic Literature*, Rome 1949, 43.

2. At the beginning, this narrative presents Jephthah as a man possessed by the 'spirit of Yahweh', but it is not said in what way and with what characteristic elements this possession was manifested; nor is it said for what purpose Jephthah had been endowed with this gift. The fact that he had crossed the country is not very much justification for a possession of this kind! In any case, the text does not speak of a particular fury or of a warlike charisma, or of the other features through which this gift normally manifests itself in a tangible way. Nor is it said that he used this gift for his campaign: the information about it which the text gives is scanty, and the narrative is now completely governed by Jephthah's vow and its fulfilment. It takes place in an area of unknown localities (this could be because we have inadequate documentation, but that does not seem to be the case here) and ends with a note which seems as obvious to the redactors as it seems exaggerated to us and which constitutes the conditions for the fulfilling of the vow: the total defeat of Ammon and its subjection by Israel. Victories of this kind are rare in the Old Testament even during the time of David, but it is only under him that Ammon was effectively subjected to Israel (II Sam. 10.6–15; 12.26–31//I Chron. 19.6 – 20.3; the version in II Sam. has now been interrupted by the Bathsheba episode), but it appears clearly from the sources that the operation was far from simple. So if we accept the historicity of the campaign, it must have been extremely successful in teaching a lesson to the Ammonites, not in subjecting their country; they would still make things very hard for Israel, cf. I Sam. 11.1ff., in the time of Saul.

(e) The civil war between Gilead and Ephraim (12.1–7)

Bibliography on *šibbōlet*: J. **Marquart**, '*šibbolet* – ephraimitisch *sibbōlet–šibbōlet?*', *ZAW* 8, 1888, 151–5; R. **Marcus**, 'The Hebrew Sibilant ŚIN and the Name YIŚRA'EL', *JBL* 60, 1941, 141–50; E. A. **Speiser**, 'The Shibboleth Incident (Judges 12:6)', *BASOR* 85, 1942, 10–13 = *Oriental and Biblical Studies*, Philadelphia 1967, 143–50; R. **Marcus**, 'The Word *šibbolet* Again', *BASOR* 87, 1942, 39; W. **Baumgartner**, 'Was wir heute von der hebräischen Sprache und Ihrer Geschichte wissen', in *Das Alte Testament und seine Umwelt*, Leiden 1959, 208–39: 226 n. 2; F. **Willesen**, 'The *'efrātî* of the Shibbolet Incident', *VT* 8, 1958, 97; W. **Richter****, 1963, 324–8, and 1966, 517–22; T. H. **Gaster****, 1969, 433.

12 [1] The men of Ephraim mobilized, crossed to Zaphon and said to Jephthah, 'Why did you cross to make war on the Ammonites and did not invite us to come with you? We will set fire to your house over your head.' [2]But Jephthah replied to them, 'I and my people were all involved in the fight against the Ammonites, on whom they inflicted a heavy defeat; I called you to arms, but you did not come to deliver me from them. [3]And seeing that you did not come to my aid, I threw myself against the Ammonites at the risk of my life, and Yahweh gave them into my hands. Why then have you come out today in hostility against me?' [4]Then Jephthah gathered all the troops of Gilead and made war on Ephraim; because the latter had said, 'You are mere survivors of Ephraim, you Gileadites, half-way between Ephraim and Manasseh!' [5]Gilead captured the fords of the Jordan against the Ephraimites, and when an Ephraimite asked to be allowed to pass, the Gileadites replied, 'Are you by chance an Ephraimite?' When he said to them, 'No', [6]they asked him to say 'Shibboleth', but he would say 'Sibboleth', being incapable of pronouncing it correctly. Then they seized him and killed him by the ford of the Jordan. And on that occasion forty-two thousand Ephraimites fell.

7 Jephthah was judge over Israel for six years. When he died, Jephthah the Gileadite was buried in his city, in Mizpah of Gilead.

---

[1] 'Mobilized. . .'; for this meaning of *ṣā'aq*, cf. 4.10 and 7.23. 'Zaphon' in the valley of the Jordan, near to the left bank in the vicinity of Succoth (cf. on 8.5); mentioned in Josh. 13.27.[11] It is probably identical with *tell eṣ-ṣa'idīye* (coord. 204–186), cf. Y. Aharoni**, 1967, 115. For a different identification cf. R. O. Boling*, 1975. On the other hand, the meaning could simply be 'towards the north'. The reproach is identical to that directed by Ephraim to Gideon (8.1–3). [2] 'On whom they inflicted': added with LXX^A; it is absent from MT and Vg. [3] 'You did not come. . .': strangely, MT has the second person singular; LXX omits the pronominal suffix, having 'No one came. . ', a more generic formulation which some prefer. [4] The phrase is very much stronger and more offensive than it seems to be in translation; rather as if it were insinuating that Gilead was made up of throw-outs from the other tribes mentioned. [5] 'Against the Ephraimites': for this sense of *l'* cf. on 3.28b and 7.24, where we have an identical context. [6] *šibbōlet* means either 'ear (of grain)' or 'current, torrent of water', but the meaning of the word is not important, given that it serves as a test in pronunciation: in some dialects the initial sibilant cannot have been pronounced correctly. LXX (B στάχυς, A σύνθημα) wrongly see it as a password. Thus the Ephraimites are presented here as having a lisping pronunciation of

[11]Cf. *Joshua*, ad loc.

sibilants; this is a phonetic feature which is impossible to check. The passage recalls that on the Galilean accent of the apostle Peter (Matt. 26.69–75 par.). For details see the studies mentioned in the bibliography, especially that of Speiser. 'Incapable': Driver**, 1964, shows that this was an idiomatic expression, 'could not succeed in. . .', so it should not be either corrected or deleted.

1. In his 1966 study, W. Richter has shown that there are some tensions in this brief section. For example, was the war caused by the charge made by Ephraim against Jephthah that he had acted without consulting with them, or by the insult given by the Ephraimites (vv. 1,4)? Is Zaphon a place, or does it simply mean 'northwards'? What is the connection between the term *'eprātī* in v. 5c and Ephraim in v. 5ab and elsewhere? The beginning of the chapter, moreover, has evident connections with 8.1ff. and 7.24ff., which raises the question whether this text might be dependent on these other passages, a view which is accepted by the majority of scholars.

Thus Richter rightly points out that although some features do not appear sufficient to point to the existence of sources, it is not possible to consider the present text a unity. He makes a distinction between vv. 1–4a, where the discursive and theoretical element is more dominant than the action (and this section depends on chs. 7 and 8), and vv. 5–6abα, which by contrast present specific situations, sometimes quite brutal, with an indispensable minimum of dialogue; Jephthah is not even mentioned in them. Verse 4b and 6bβ would be additions, especially the exaggerated figure.

It is probable that the second of these two sections, now precariously added to the account of Jephthah, preserves the remembrance of small frontier conflicts which took place between Gilead and Ephraim, conflicts which often arose for more or less pointless reasons and which sometimes resulted in bloodshed. These are conflicts which have nothing to do with Jephthah, though the account has now been added to his cycle. Rather, the first section rests on chs. 7 and 8, in an attempt to make Jephthah a 'major' judge and to insert him into the group of 'saviours'.

2. It is difficult to evaluate the *šibbōlet* episode on a linguistic and particularly on a phonetic level. We do not in fact know the precise pronunciation of the two consonants, the *šin* and the *śin/samek*. Moreover, a phonetic phenomenon is not necessarily

identical with the orthographical elements which reproduce it, as has rightly been observed by Richter, 1966, 521 n.1, against W. Baumgartner and H. -W. Hertzberg, who both seem to be too optimistic about the conclusions they feel they can draw from it. It is possible[12] that the episode reflects the phonetic changes of *šin* and *ṯa* so that they virtually coincide. In any case, according to the note, the Ephraimites pronounced *šin* as *śin/samek* (and probably, though this is not stated, *śin/samek* as *šin*): moreover, this is one of the constant phonetic differences between Hebrew and Ugaritic then, Arabic today. However, we cannot draw any other conclusions except that in Ephraim the consonants were pronounced as in the north, and not as in Judah.

3. The clearly legendary episode contains a theme which appears later in medieval Europe: the pronunciation of French in Sicily during the Sicilian Vespers of 1282; the Flemish pronunciation in the course of the revolt against the French in Flanders in 1302, and also, in our day, when at the end of the Second World War the Dutch resistance made fleeing Germans who were trying to pass themselves off as Dutchmen pronounce the word 'Scheveningen', recognizing who they were from their faulty pronunciation of the combination of sibilant and guttural.[13] This generalized use of the theme also shows the limits of its historicity; within the sphere of popular tradition it codifies aversion to the stranger, the stranger who of necessity never succeeds in speaking the language of his surroundings well, or at least without showing himself to be what he is. That in the cases cited we always have an invader or a member of the occupation notably weakens the xenophobic character of the theme: this is not the stranger in himself, but only the stranger who turns out to be the invader and the oppressor.

4. The passage ends by presenting Jephthah as if he were a 'minor' judge, a theme which is accepted by a number of certainly authoritative authors, as we have seen above, pp. 206f.

[12]As Speiser would prefer, but cf., against, R. Marcus, 1942.
[13]For details see the commentaries by G. F. Moore*, 1895, and R. G. Boling*, 1975, and also T. H. Gaster**, 1969, ad loc.

Second List of 'Minor' Judges

12 ⁸After him Ibzan of Bethlehem was judge in Israel. ⁹He had thirty sons, and thirty daughters he gave in marriage outside his clan; he also brought in thirty wives from outside for his sons. He was judge in Israel for seven years. ¹⁰When he died, Ibzan was buried in Bethlehem.

11 After him, Elon the Zebulonite was judge in Israel; he was judge in Israel for ten years. ¹²When he died, Elon the Zebulonite was buried in Aijalon, in the land of Zebulon.

13 After him, Abdon the son of Hillel the Pirathonite was judge in Israel. ¹⁴He had forty sons and thirty grandsons, who rode on seventy asses. He was judge in Israel for eight years. ¹⁵When he died, Abdon, son of Hillel, the Pirathonite, was buried at Pirathon, in the territory of Ephraim, in the mountain of Amalek.

---

[8] 'After him . . .': does the text consider Jephthah to be one of the 'minor' judges, or does it connect with 10.5? 'Bethlehem': we know two Bethlehems: the best known is Bethlehem of Judah; there is another one in the north, about ten kilometres west-north-west of Nazareth (coord. 168–238), mentioned in Josh. 19.15.[1] The majority prefer the latter. ' 'Ibzan': for the various interpretations of the name cf. the texts of LXX and Vg. [9] 'Wives': the Hebrew has 'daughters', which, if clear, is incorrect unless we suppose that the term could also have the precise meaning of 'wives', which I read with LXX^A and Vg, which has 'wives' (*uxores*). [12] 'Aijalon': LXX has Αἰλώμ or Αἰλόν; Vg omits the place and calls the judge *Ahialon*. It is probable that the two names, that of the judge and that of the place, similar as they are on the phonetic level, also coincided in other respects. Now if we have here the place Aijalon, this would be present-day *yālō* (coord. 153–138), situated a few yards from the demarcation line between Israel and Jordan up to 1967, one of the places in the area destroyed during

<hr style="width:30%">

[1]Cf. *Joshua*, ad loc.

the Six-Day War.[2] [**13**] 'Hillel': cf. the variants of the name in LXX^A and VetLat: Σελλήμ and *Ellen*. 'Pirathon': probably present-day Arab *far'āta*, about ten kilometres south-west of *nāblus* (coord. 165–177). [**15**] The final topographical description is now sometimes thought to be doubtful, cf. J. Gray*, 1967, on the basis of a number of Greek MSS (cf. the details in C. F. Burney*, 1919, ad loc.), which invert the order of the phrase, reading ἐν ὄρει Ἐφραίμ, ἐν γῇ Σελλήμ. The 'Mountain of Ephraim' is in fact, as we have seen at 3.37 and elsewhere, one of the districts of Solomon (I Kings 4.8b), of which the 'region of Sellem' would then have been a department. The mention of Amalek, here as in 5.14, cannot be explained on the basis of the information now in our possession, and appears at least to be a doubtful reading.[3] The Greek seems to support a Hebrew *ša^{a}līm* or *š^e'ālīm*, cf. I Sam. 9.4, though there some scholars think that it is doubtful; however, the reading is accepted by Vincent*, 1958. Besides, this is again an unknown area, cf. Y. Aharoni**, 1967, 223. Only here and in 5.14 do we hear mention of a possible relationship between the 'Mountain of Ephraim' and the Amalekites (and it is not clear whether this is the group mentioned in the desert narratives or another of the same name situated further north, given that this is a group at all, which is far from certain).

For the problems connected with the history and the functions of the 'minor' judges see what has been said in connection with the first list, pp. 195f. above.

---

[2] *Joshua*, 126.
[3] I too have also suggested another, cf. above, pp. 88f., on 5.14.

frontier points and we know only the names of the principal places there; but then, we are told that Dan did not succeed in remaining here, v. 47.[1]

Now we have sufficient knowledge of the northern frontier of Judah as far as Benjamin and a little beyond; further west, the frontier is more obscure (Josh. 15.5–11 and 18.11–20). We know less well, only fragmentarily, the southern frontier of Ephraim (Josh. 16.1ff.; cf. 18.12f.). The western frontier of Benjamin, which, as we have seen, is the eastern frontier of Dan, is made up simply of a more or less straight line drawn from the north-east towards the south-east (Josh. 18.14),[2] whereas the western frontier of Dan is almost unknown: it could have been the Mediterranean, but we simply have no information. Therefore it is only thanks to the list of cities in the passage from Joshua cited above that we can reconstruct the essential contours of the territory which the tradition assigns to Dan before its migration in chs. 17 and 18 (see pp. 269ff.).

However, as we have seen in Joshua, this list of places also proves to be problematical: in fact it is a combination of the cities of Judah in 'the foothills', Josh. 15.33–36, that is, the second district, and Judg. 1:34f. (cf. p. 30 above); and in the last passage the localities of Har-heres (or *ʿīr/bēt šemeš*), Aijalon and Shaalbim remain in the hands of the 'Amorites', while 'Joseph' (NB: not Dan!) does not succeed in making it subject and exacting tribute. Ekron, however (Josh. 19.43), was never an Israelite settlement; it was Philistine (cf. also the commentary on 14.1).

2. As I have indicated elsewhere,[3] there is not the slightest certainty about the authenticity of the traditions which assign this territory to Dan; this is even more the case because in 15.10 (cf. pp. 246f.) it is the men of Judah who move against Samson and capture him, whereas 18.1ff. (cf. p. 271) explicitly affirms that Dan did *not* receive a territory, as a result of which it went to look for one in the north. It is therefore not surprising that M. Noth[4] attributes this assignation to a later artificial construction which is concerned to find a place in the traditions which locate Dan in this area. For all these reasons, it is not easy to make a decision, and we have to recognize that the elements

[1]Cf. my *Joshua*, ad loc., for details.
[2]Ibid., ad loc.
[3]Ibid., 195.
[4]M. Noth, *Das Buch Josua*, HAT I.7, ²1953, 14 and ad loc.

CHAPTERS 13–16

Samson

Bibliography: A. **van Selms**, 'The Best Man and Bride – From Sumer to St John, with a New Interpretation of Judges, Chapters 14 and 15', *JNES* 9, 1950, 65–75; E. **Täubler****, 1958, 63–6, 85–9; F. C. **Fensham**, 'The Shaving of Samson: a Note on Judges 16:19', *Evangelical Quarterly* 31, London 1959, 97ff.; A. **Schreiber**, 'Samson, the Tree Uprooter', *JQR* 50, 1959–60, 176–80; id., 'Further Parallels to Samson, the Tree Uprooter', *JQR* 51, 1961–62, 35–40; J. **Blenkinsopp**, 'Structure and Style in Judges 13–16', *JBL* 82, 1963, 65–76; P. **Kübel**, 'Epiphanie und Altarbau', *ZAW* 83, 1971, 225–31; J. R. **Porter**, 'Samson's Riddle: Judges XIV 14,18', *JTS* NS 13, 1962, 106–9; R. **Yaron**, '*Duobus Sororibus Coniunctio*', *RIDA* III, 10, 1963, 115–36; A. G. **van Daalen**, *Simson*, Assen 1966; T. H. **Gaster****, 1969, 433ff.; D. N. **Freedman**, 'A Note on Judges 15,5', *Bibl* 52, 1971, 535; J. A. **Emerton**, 'Notes on Two Proposed Emendations in the Book of Judges (11, 24 and 16, 28)', *ZAW* 85, 1973, 220–3; J. A. **Wharton**, 'The Secret of Yahweh: Story and Affirmations in Judges 13–16', *Interp* 27, 1973, 48–66; H. **Margulies**, 'Das Rätsel der Biene im Alten Testament', *VT* 24, 1974, 56–76; J. L. **Crenshaw**, 'The Samson Saga: Filial Devotion or Erotic Attachment?', *ZAW* 86, 1974, 470–504; S. **Carmy**, 'The Sphinx as Leader: a Reading of Judges 13–16', *Tradition* 14. 3, New York 1974, 66–79 (which I have not consulted since it was not available to me); G. **von Rad**, 'Die Geschichte von Simson', in *Gottes Wirken in Israel*, Neukirchen 1974, 49–52; C. **Grottanelli**, 'Motivi escatologici nell' iconografia di un rasoio cartaginese', *RSF* 5, 1977, 13–22: 19ff.; J. L. **Crenshaw**, *Samson*, Atlanta and London 1978.

1. The cycle of Samson traditions is set in territory which, according to the traditional tribal geography of Israel, should have been occupied by Dan before its move to the extreme north of Palestine. This region is located between Ephraim in the north, Judah in the south and Benjamin in the east. Joshua 19.40–48 describes the area, but without the details that we would have liked; for example, there is no information about

which militate against the authenticity of this attribution are
stronger than those which argue in its favour.

In my commentary on *Joshua* I was more optimistic: I thought
it probable that Josh. 19. 40–49 should be taken to be substantially historical; therefore the territories listed would originally
have belonged to Dan. However, after a number of years my
relative assurance of that time is considerably diminished, given
the lack of certain information about the frontiers of Dan and
the vagueness of the western frontier of Benjamin. Furthermore,
the cities which the text in question assigns to Dan are elsewhere, and with greater probability, attributed to others. Certainly, there is information which allows other interpretations:
for example, that of a reconquest of the region by local elements
after the departure of Dan, and that of a new conquest by Judah
and Ephraim in the time of David. But in this case the local
elements are evidently the Philistines, and not the phantom
'Amorites'. This last designation is in fact so imprecise that we
never really know its specific reference (granted that it has any
specific reference at all); however, it is certain that in the E and
Dtr tradition it always indicates the autochthonous inhabitants
of Palestine, and never the Philistines.[5]

Thus on the one hand there are objective data, and on the
other considerations which certainly do not tell in favour of the
historicity of the theory which seeks to put a settlement by Dan
in that region, unless it is a somewhat precarious stay, without
a proper territory, limited to a group of semi-nomads; but in
that case one cannot talk of a settlement within tribal boundaries. In favour of the traditional theory, though, is the account
of the adventures of the Danite Samson, and the report in
chs. 17–18, which makes Dan emigrate from this region to its
definitive location in the north of the country, cf. also
Josh. 19.47. This could also fit in with the theory that Dan led
a semi-nomadic existence in this area. In that case it is possible
that the migration of the group is completely independent of the
Samson cycle, and could even have happened beforehand, leaving in the region to the west of Benjamin some non-sedentary
groups without a tribal organization. This could well explain

---

[5]J. J. Bimson, *Redating the Exodus and Conquest*, *JSOT*, SS 5 1978, 208ff., maintains that
the Amorites, and not the Philistines, 'caused problems for the Danites' within the more
general framework of his redating the conquest at the end of the Middle Bronze Age
rather than of the Late Bronze Age. For this proposal see my forthcoming review of the
book in *VT*.

why Samson is handed over to the Philistines by people from Judah, and would add verisimilitude to the fame of being mighty warriors acquired by Dan in circumstances unknown to us, but probably connected with the exploits of Samson and with equally unknown episodes ˙from their migration northwards, cf. Gen. 49.16f.; Deut. 33.22. The only piece of information that we have independent of the Samson cycle and the march northwards, Judg. 5.17, makes Dan dwell 'among the ships', or 'in security', and thus is necessarily ambiguous (cf. p. 90).

3. On first reading, the Samson traditions do not seem to be very different from those of the other 'major' judges: we have the Dtr framework, albeit reduced to the minimum, the spirit which takes possession of the hero and the hero's achievements. However, closer examination reveals that a large proportion of the elements present in the cycle do not fit in with this first impression.

(i) The Dtr framework is reduced simply to the first element and gives the impression of having been put at the beginning for reasons which have nothing to do with the purpose of the 'frameworks' of the traditions on the 'major' judges: in fact it does not provide the hermeneutical key to the episodes which follow.

(ii) Samson appears as a judge only in a manner of speaking; it is a conventional designation. The texts, 13.5b; 15.20 and 16.31 say this, but without very much conviction. He did not liberate Israel either from the power of the Philistines or from that of any other oppressor; if anything, he initiated this work, but independently of Israel.

(iii) The chronology seems confused: 13.1 talks of 'forty years' and 16.31 of 'twenty years': the last date indicates the duration of Samson's office, i.e. of his supposed 'judgeship'. But what about the other twenty years? In I Sam. 7.2 Samuel 'judges' Israel for 'twenty years', until the victory over the Philistines attributed to him in the Dtr framework of I Sam. 7, assuming that this is not a reference to the whole of his life (I Sam. 7.15). However, it is also necessary to take account of the years of Eli, who died at the age of ninety-eight (I Sam. 4.15), having 'judged' Israel also for forty years (I Sam. 4.18). So it is by no means easy to square the accounts here, given that we do not know the function of the figures in question. Perhaps this is evidence of two different Dtr redactions: DtrH and DtrN? It is difficult to say anything with any degree of certainty.

(iv) Samson never commanded an army, whether local or consisting of all Israel; he is the typical individualistic hero of popular fantasy. The story is really interested only in his actions,, a mixture of extravaganza, of provoked sexuality, of historically irrelevant anecdotal elements, pervaded with a rigid sense of retribution, of the *lex talionis* (Crenshaw, 122). Their folk-tale character was already commented on by St Jerome (PL 26, col. 609), and has been noted by E. Täubler**, 74f., who speaks of a 'narrative verging on the *Novelle*'.

(v) The pan-Israelite ideal which characterizes the pre-Dtr redactional phase and the Dtr redaction of the material concerned with the 'major' judges is here conspicuous by its absence, as I have already pointed out – apart, that is, from the few passages which see Samson as a judge 'of Israel'.

(vi) The spirit of Yahweh takes possession of him in 13.25, but as in the case of Jephthah (above, p. 206) we are left unsure about the effects it produces, except to endow Samson with extraordinary physical strength (14.6, 19; 15.14). However, apart from the fact that this strength is used only in Samson's personal exploits, and does not have any political or social function, it also exists without the spirit (16.3, 38), and seems to depend on his hair and therefore, in the better instances, on his Nazirate. And it is in fact as a Nazirite that Samson appears in the story of his birth (13.3ff.); Nazirite features are his consecration and purity (essentially negative elements, based as they are on abstinence, but which begin even before birth, from the moment of conception). Implicit in the text seems to be the theory that Samson was obliged to maintain these marks of purity all through his life: keeping away from corpses, abstaining from alcoholic drinks, refusing to cut his hair; thus, not to have observed these obligations seems to have been the chief cause of his fall and of his end. This is particularly evident in 16.13, where Samson explicitly declares that without long hair he would have been a man like everyone else. However, in ancient Israel the office of the charismatic and that of the Nazirite are distinct, even if many points of detail escape us today. It is certain that every charismatic office was only temporary, whereas the Nazirate could be lifelong; the first arises from the gift of the divine spirit with a view to a particular task or to deal with a particular situation; the second does not have temporal limits and derives from the vow: it arises, therefore, from the Nazirite himself or the person who makes a pledge on his behalf. If we want to compare the Nazirite with anyone else, we should think of the sect of the Rechabites described in Jer. 34: these were a group which tried to maintain the ideals of semi-nomadic life in Palestine, viewing them as a privileged condition for a relationship with God. They therefore rejected agricultural produce which came from sedentary farming, especially wine, and permanent buildings, except when the latter provided places of refuge in case of danger, usually in fortified places.

Now the combination of two such diverse offices in one and the same person is the more suspect,[6] the more we fail to see what this combination implies.

(vii) Finally – and I have listed only some of the more important features – the account of his calling, ch. 13, is a combination and concentration of themes which appear separated in other Old Testament narratives and are typical of the narratives in which they appear: the promise of a son (vv. 3f., 6ff.); birth from a barren woman (vv. 2f.); the *theoxenia* (vv. 15f.); the recognition of the deity or his envoy (v. 21) and his refusal to reveal his own name (cf. Gen. 32.30 (EVV 29) and Ex. 3.1ff.); the fear which follows the meeting (v. 22), cf. Isa. 6.1ff. Richter**, 1963, 142ff., has rightly concluded from these features that this narrative was originally composed of a number of accounts which had the birth of Samson as their theme, to which ch. 13 has been prefixed, composed *ad hoc* to serve as an introduction, on the basis of other relevant material attested elsewhere. This is material which, used as it is abundantly elsewhere, bears witness to what would be called in the language of the media a high audience rating. This is also true for the figures: Abraham, the hero of faith; Gideon, the immaculate and fearless leader; Samson, the attractive though coarse knave, author of heavy-handed jokes played on the classic enemies of Israel, rather than a religious figure.

4. The Samson traditions can easily be divided up in accordance with the chapters in which they are arranged: (*a*) the miraculous birth (ch. 13); (*b*) Samson's first wedding (ch. 14); (*c*) Samson the incendiary and warrior (ch. 15); (*d*) the capture and death of Samson (ch. 16). This is a literary construction, fragmentary, but organized in a coherent way. It is fragmentary because it is obvious to the attentive reader that each episode

---

[6]R. de Vaux, *Les Institutions de l'Ancien Testament* II, Paris 1960, 360–2; ET, *Ancient Israel*, London and New York 1961, 466f.

has an existence of its own which does not presuppose that of the others, apart from ch. 13, which has been composed, as we have seen, with the purpose of providing an introduction to the rest of the narratives. However, this fragmentary character should not deceive us: in fact the fragments have been connected artistically and logically, giving rise to a unitary narrative. We cannot spend time on this; the reader is therefore referred to the studies by Blenkinsopp (1963) and Crenshaw (1974 and 1978) quoted above, which among other things are concerned with precisely this problem. The first of them even goes so far as to speak in terms of a plot.

5. I have already spoken of the problems connected with the historicity of the stay of Dan in this area (above, §1, pp. 225f.); we must now see whether there is a historical background to these narratives. That is certainly not an easy undertaking; it is obvious that if it proves impossible to demonstrate the presence of Dan in the region, we could nevertheless consider the possibility of a cycle of legends which were partly aetiological (cf. 13.9ff.; 15.9–17, 18–20, and perhaps 16.1–3) going back to the time of the first encounters between Israel and the Philistines, who had just arrived in the southern coastal region. In that case we would have an Israel which was trying to come down to the fertile plain, which was important economically, and the Philistines, who were trying to settle in the mountains, strategically important, one of the key themes of ch. 1. However, this is the most that the historiographical poverty of the texts allows us to do.

6. There are, however, other elements which do not tell in favour of the historicity of these accounts. As has been recognized for some time (cf. C. F. Burney*, 1919, 391–408; J. Gray*, 1967, 234ff.; and T. H. Gaster**, 1969, ad loc.), it is difficult to dissociate the stories of Samson, the hero with the solar name (cf. below on 13.24), coming moreover from an area situated not very far away from the 'temple of the sun', from various solar myths which were in existence in the ancient Near East and in the West. Here the sun appears as the guarantor of the cosmos against the adversaries of chaos, a theme attested in ancient Egypt, in Ugarit in the text (Gordon) 62:42–52, and also in the Old Testament, cf. Ps. 19.1–6. Solar myths are also involved in the labours of Hercules, in whose achievements we have some analogous to those of Samson: the killing of the lion, the 'descent into darkness' in ch. 16 (where the connection between blindness

and the underworld is quite significant), forced labour, and so on. However, it is doubtful whether Israel used this religious material consciously in the sense which was originally attached to it in constructing the story of Samson; it seems more probable that Israel had an essentially literary rapport with this material; it will have come into Israel as part of the culture of the time, perhaps through such universal vehicles of narrative as could be found in the ancient Near East in the epic of Gilgamesh.[7] We now know that this was also a well-known text in the area of Palestine. In particular, the negative part assigned to the women outside the prologue in ch. 13 could originate from this source, as Gray*, 1967, noted.

(a) The miraculous birth (ch. 13)

13 [1]The Israelites returned to doing what Yahweh thought to be evil, and he delivered them into the hands of the Philistines for forty years.

2 There was once a man of Zorah, of a Danite family, Manoah by name; his wife was barren and had had no children. [3]An angel appeared to the woman and said to her, 'Behold, you are barren and childless, but you shall conceive and bear a son. [4]But pay heed: do not drink wine or any other alcoholic drink, nor eat anything unclean, because [5]you shall conceive and bear a son. No razor shall come upon his head, because the boy shall be a Nazirite to God from birth. He will be the one who will begin to save Israel from the hands of the Philistines.'

6 The woman went back and told this to her husband: 'A man came to me and his countenance was like that of an angel: terrible! So much so that I did not dare to ask him where he came from and he did not tell me his name. [7]He said to me, "Behold, you shall conceive and bear a son. But you must not drink wine or any alcoholic drink nor eat anything unclean, because the boy will be a Nazirite to God from birth until the day of his death." ' [8]Then Manoah turned to Yahweh in prayer: 'I pray you, Lord, let the man whom you sent come again to us and teach us what we must do for the boy who is to be born.' [9]And God heard the prayer of Manoah: the angel came again to the woman while she was sitting in the field, but Manoah, her husband, was not with her. [10]The woman hastened to tell the news to her husband: 'The man who came to me the other day has appeared to me again.' [11]Then Manoah arose and followed his wife and came to the man and said to him, 'Are you the man who spoke with my wife?'

[7]Cf. A Goetze and S. Levy, 'A Fragment of the Gilgameš Epic from Megiddo', *Atiqot* 2, Jerusalem 1959, 121–8.

He replied, 'Yes, I am.' [12]Then Manoah said: 'Now when your announcement comes true, what will be the boy's manner of life and what is he to do?' [13]The angel replied, 'Do everything that I said to your wife: [14]she must not eat anything that comes from the vine; she must not drink wine or any alcoholic drink nor eat any unclean food. Observe everything that I have commanded her.' [15]Then Manoah said to the angel: 'Let us detain you a little further; we will prepare a kid for you.' [16]But the angel replied to Manoah, 'Even if you detain me, I will not eat of your food; but if you want to offer a holocaust, offer it to Yahweh.' In fact, Manoah was not yet aware that he was an angel. [17]Then Manoah said to the angel, 'What is your name, so that we can invoke you when your message comes true?' [18]But the angel replied to him, 'Why do you ask me my name? It is wonderful.' [19]Then Manoah took the kid and the offering and offered it on a rock to Yahweh who works wonders. [20]And when the flame leapt up from the altar towards heaven, the angel also ascended among the flames of the altar; and Manoah and his wife who were standing watching prostrated themselves with their faces to the ground. [21]The angel did not appear a second time to Manoah and his wife. And only then did Manoah know that it had been an angel.

22 Then he said to his wife. 'We deserve to die because we have seen a divine being.' [23]But his wife replied, 'The Lord certainly will not make us die: otherwise he would not have accepted the sacrifice and the offering from our hands and would not have shown us or told us all these things.'

24 And the woman bore a son, and he was given the name Samson. The boy grew and Yahweh blessed him. [25]The spirit of Yahweh began to move him in the 'Field of Dan', between Zorah and Eshtaol.

[13.1] A very reduced Dtr framework, perhaps DtrN, cf. further on 14.4. For the chronology cf. the introduction, § 3(iii). There is no trace of the themes of the penitence of the people, their cry of anguish and the hearing of it, but cf. above on 10.6–18, pp. 202f. Before chs. 13–16 'the Philistines' appear only in Dtr contexts or in passages related to them; only in 3.31 (cf. there) are they mentioned outside such a context. The name 'Palestine' already attested by Herodotus (II. 104; VII. 89), derives from them. [2] Reminiscent of 6.11. For the opening 'There was once' (*way⁽ᵉʰī*) cf. I Sam. 1.1. For Zorah cf. also on v. 25. 'Family', literally clan. 'Danite': this was the period when Dan was still settled west of Benjamin, cf. the introduction, § 1. Although the wife is the protagonist in this episode, her name does not appear; instead, we have that of her husband, an unimportant figure, Manoah. The name is not attested outside this context, except in a reference in I Chron. 2.54, where there is mention of 'the Manahathites of Zorah'. The theme of barrenness, considered to be a disgrace and always attributed to the woman (here the theme of disgrace does not appear explicitly, but seems to be implied in the words of the angel) is frequent in the Old Testament and in the New: Gen. 11.30; I Sam. 1.2ff.; Luke 1.7f., etc. In all these instances it forms the occasion for a divine miraculous intervention. **[3]** 'An angel', literally 'a messenger from Yahweh' (other times 'from God'); for my rendering cf. on 2.1 and 6.11. The conclusion of the verse anticipates 5a and the two are evidently duplicates; it is not, however, easy to decide which of the two is superfluous: for Vincent*, 1958, it is this one; for others, v. 5; the possibility is also considered that both should remain, Boling *1975. **[5]** 'Bear'; for the form cf. *GesK* § 80d. 'Nazirite': Num. 6.1ff.; cf. Amos 2.1f. In the New Testament we find analogous language for John the Baptist, Luke 1.13–17, esp. v. 15. **[6]** 'A man . . .': MT says specifically 'of God', which, however, anticipates something that the woman cannot yet know, cf. also v. 21b, but at most guess. Still, Hebrew narrative sometimes anticipates elements which are considered relevant in a speech, giving rise to what would seem to us to be chronological confusion or even anachronism. In a Western translation the mention is to be deleted, cf. Burney* and others. **[8]** Manoah seems to realize the possibility that the 'man' is a messenger from God, contrary to what is said in v. 21. **[9]** Many scholars, with some minor translations, substitute Yahweh for 'God', for better coherence in the text. However, this substitution is not indispensable. **[10]** 'The other day': *bayyōm* sometimes refers to the period of the basic event, but usually means 'today', cf. LXX^A, which adds ἐκείνῃ. **[12]** 'Your announcement': here as in v. 17 I read the singular with LXX, Θ, Vg and others, for 'your words' of MT, cf. the verb in the singular. The Hebrew construction may be understood as a collective concept, but in any case the translation should be in the singular. 'The manner of life . . .' thus Gray*, 1967, cf. Deut. 18.3: *mišpaṭ hakkoh°nīm*, or I Sam. 8.11; *mišpaṭ hammelek*, etc. **[13f.]** Here some scholars find a certain lack of clarity in the persons of the verbs: it is not clear whether the commandment in question refers to the father, the mother or the child to be born. At the beginning of v. 13, *tiššāmēr* could be third person feminine singular or second person masculine singular, but the speech is evidently addressed to the father: in v. 14, it refers to what the wife must or must not do (here too the verb can be either third person feminine singular or second person masculine singular), cf. vv. 4f., 7. Thus the theory seems to be that the purity of the Nazirite must begin at his conception, and therefore with the mother. It does not therefore seem admissible to emend the text on the basis of LXX^B and Vg, which read the third person, with the boy as subject, against Vincent*, 1958, and Penna*, 1963. **[15]** For the theme of *theoxenia*, cf. on v. 16.

[16] In Gen. 18 the visitors accept the food which is offered to them, maintaining their human attitude to the end; in Judg. 6.21 the angel transforms it into a sacrifice; here we have the refusal of the food and the invitation, somewhat prosaic, to offer it directly as a sacrifice. **[17]** Literally, 'Who is your name?'; at other times we have 'What . . .' The phrase is equivalent to 'Who are you . . .?' 'When . . . comes true': The Q also attests the singular, but cf. the discussion at v. 12. The construction of the phrase is not completely clear, cf. the discussion in C. F. Burney*, 1919. **[18]** 'Wonderful': Hebrew *pil'ī*, attested only in the feminine in Ps. 139.6; K *pil'iyāh*, Q *peliyāh*; in the Psalm it refers to divine knowledge, marvellous in a way that the Psalmist is unable to understand. Here the meaning is similar: 'You cannot understand'. *pele'* is a 'wonder'. Note how the *massōrāh* proposes the deletion of an *aleph* here. **[19]** 'The offering': in ancient times *minḥāh* is a generic term for any kind of offering, religious or secular, cf. above on 3.15, 17f.; it therefore also includes the holocaust. Later, from P onwards, it always tends to assume the meaning of a 'bloodless offering'. Given that the offering is contrasted with the holocaust here, we have the late use of the term. 'On a rock': cf. 6.20, where we have *sela'* and *ṣūr*. LXX and Vg have an unnecessary addition: 'and Manoah and his wife stood watching'. **[20]** 'The rock' has now become 'the altar'. **[21]** The majority of scholars would prefer to invert the order of the two parts of the verse: the father becomes aware that this is an angel (but cf. v. 8) after he has seen him ascend into heaven, and only after that speaks to his wife. **[22]** 'We deserve . . .': cf. on 6.22, where the danger is implicit. I have translated 'divine being' in general here, and not 'god' or 'God'. In I Sam. 28.13, Samuel's ghost is described by the same title. **[23]** 'Will not make . . .': MT is heavy; for a discussion cf. C. F. Burney*. We should probably delete *wekā'ēt*, 'now', not attested in LXX and Vg, but G. R. Driver**, 1964, suggests that it should be shifted: 'He would not now have accepted . . .' **[24]** 'Samson': Hebrew *šimšōn*; LXX and Vg keep the original *a* of the segholate of the *qatl* type, cf. *šemeš*, but *šamšī*, 'sun'. Theophoric names with sun are common in the ancient Near East, cf. for the Old Testament Ezra 4.8ff. Other etymologies have been put forward, but only to be rejected: Josephus, *Antt.* V. vii.4 = § 285, suggests ἰσχυρός, Heb. *šāmēn*, 'fat', but used also in a figurative sense to mean 'rich', 'fertile', 'robust', cf. also the Arabic *sumsūmu(n)*, 'active, vigorous' (Driver**, 1964, 17), and other more recent commentators. However, the fact that Samson's place of origin is a short way from Beth-shemesh (about 4 kilometres, coord. 147–128), i.e. the 'temple of the sun', does not seem to be irrelevant, even if it is impossible to establish a precise connection; cf. also on Josh. 19.41, where it is called *'īr šemeš*, 'city of the sun'. **[25]** 'The spirit': whereas according to our text the Nazirate begins in Samson at the moment he is conceived, the spirit takes possession of his person later. We are no longer in a position to be able to locate the 'Field of Dan'; in 18.12 (cf. there) it is to the east of Kiriath-jearim, present-day *dīr el-ʿāzar* (coord. 159–135), but this place is too far away from the scene of Samson's exploits, about 12 kilometres to the north-east. S. A. Cooke*, 1913, has suggested that the text should be emended to Manahat-dan: according to the quotation in I Chron 2.52, 54, the group of Manahathites lived here; but we have seen on v. 2 that this name is connected, rather, with Manoah. It seems evident that there must have been at least two places with this name, which is understandable if we think of the traditions which make Dan live in, or at least move from, this area. 'Move': root *ḥyl*$_\mathrm{I}$, 'agitate', often 'have the pains of childbirth': probably a reference to ecstatic phenomena connected with the possession of the divine spirit. 'Zorah': present-day *ṣarʿāh* in the Vale of Zorek, through which the railway begins its ascent towards Jerusalem about 20 kilometres from the capital (coord. 148–131), cf. Josh 15.33. 'Eshtaol': present-day *išwāʿ* (coord. 151–132).

As we saw in the introduction to the cycle as a whole this chapter seems to be suitably composed to introduce the acts of Samson, and is the only active theological element in the narrative (cf. § 3[vii] above). By means of this introduction the story of the exploits of Samson is transformed into the narrative of 'the violation of the Nazirite's vow' (cf. the introduction, § 3[vi]): the Nazirite must not have any contact with corpses, but cf. 14.5–9 and 15.15ff.; he must not drink wine or other alcoholic drinks, but cf. the 'festival' in 14.10–20, where, as we shall see, the Hebrew term means something like 'symposium', in the etymological sense of the word; he must not cut his hair, but cf. 16.13ff. These are prohibitions which remain fully in force during the period of the vow, and in the successive stories nothing is said about the vow being terminated. It is more probable to assume that in the later stories the question of the Nazirite's vow was not known, but belonged to the prologue, which was composed *ad hoc*. However, in the present form of the story the image which we get of Samson is no longer that of the attractive, albeit somewhat coarse popular hero, but rather that of a feckless and easy-going character: the only virtue which the spirit seems to have given Samson is physical strength pure and simple – certainly not wisdom or ethical consistency (cf. § 3[vi] above).

This somewhat negative image contrasts with the family setting: the Israelite family portrayed here is somewhat idealized, the home of ancient virtues in sharp contrast with the general sexual and ethical disorder of the protagonist. That explains the importance assumed in it by the mother of Samson, a real contrast with the erotic adventures in which the narrative abounds. Evidence of the seriousness of the surroundings can be found in a feature which we shall examine in due course (14.3ff.), the refusal of Samson's pious parents to have anything to do with his first wife; this is therefore the ideal framework of a believing and practising family.

The erotic adventures of the hero are simply the exemplification of the theme of the foreign woman who brings shame, deception and death, a theme dear to Israelite wisdom. Thus the speech tends to have the character of wisdom, and there are other genres of wisdom, like the riddle in 14.14ff. If this is the interpretation, it is no wonder that the text does not have any theology in the traditional Israelite sense.

(b) Samson's first wedding (ch. 14)

14 ¹One day Samson went down to Timnah; there he saw a woman of Philistine descent. ²When he came back he told his father and his mother, 'In Timnah I saw a Philistine woman; go and get her for me as a wife.' ³His father and his mother replied: 'Is there not perhaps a woman among the daughers of your kinsmen and among all my people, that you have to go to take a wife from among these uncircumcised Philistines?' Samson replied to his father, 'Get her for me: she is the one who pleases me.' ⁴His father and his mother did not know that the matter came from Yahweh: in fact he was looking for a pretext against the Philistines. At that time the Philistines dominated Israel.

5 So Samson went down to Timnah, but when he came to the 'Vineyards of Timnah', a lion came out to him, roaring. ⁶Then the spirit of Yahweh took possession of him and he tore the lion in pieces as one tears a kid, with his bare hands, but he did not tell his father and his mother what he had done.

7 Then he went down and talked with the woman and she pleased him.

8 After some time he returned, to take her with him, but went aside to examine the carcass of the lion. And behold, there was a swarm of bees and honey in the carcass. ⁹He took a little into his hand, scraping it out from the honeycomb, and ate it while he was going along. When he got back to his parents, he gave them some of it to eat as well, but without telling them that he had scraped the honey out of the corpse of the lion.

10 Then Samson went down to the woman and had a feast there: this was in fact the custom of the young men. ¹¹And when the people saw him, they brought thirty companions to be with him. ¹²Then

Samson said to them: 'Let me put a riddle to you. If you can explain it within the seven days of the feast, I will give you thirty festal garments and thirty changes of clothing. [13]But if you fail, you shall give me thirty festal garments and thirty changes of clothing.' [14]Then he said to them:

'Out of the eater came forth something to eat,
out of the strong came forth something sweet.'

And in $\left\{ \begin{array}{c} \text{three} \\ \text{six} \end{array} \right\}$ days they could not tell what the riddle was.

[15]On the $\left\{ \begin{array}{c} \text{fourth} \\ \text{sevénth} \end{array} \right\}$ day they said to Samson's wife, 'Try to seduce Samson into telling what the riddle is; otherwise we shall set fire to you and your father's house! Have you invited us here to impoverish us?'

16 Then Samson's wife began to weep beside him, and said to him, 'You only hate me, and it is not true that you wish me well: you have told my countrymen a riddle, and you have not explained it to me.' He replied to her, 'I did not tell even my father and my mother, so why should I tell it to you?' But she went on [17]weeping at his side for the seven days of the feast, and on the seventh day he told her because she tormented him so much. And she was able to communicate the riddle to her compatriots.

18 Then the men of the city said to him on the seventh day, before the sun went down:

'What is sweeter than honey –
and what is stronger than the lion?'

But he said to them,

'If you had not ploughed with my cow,
you would not have solved the riddle.'

19 And the spirit of Yahweh took possession of him; he went down to Ashkelon, and there killed thirty people, spoiled them of their garments and gave the festal robes to those who had solved the riddle. Then, full of fury, he went back to his father's house. [20]Samson's wife was given to the companion who had been his best man.

---

[1] 'Timnah': mentioned in Josh. 19.43: here Y. Aharoni**, 1967, 266ff., wants to read Timnath-ekron, perhaps *ḥirbet taḥuna* (coord. 148–131), given that Ekron was never Israelite (cf. above, 226); otherwise, the most probable identification is with present-day Tibneh, or better, with *tell batasi*, both about half-way between Zorah and Ekron, a little to the north (coord. 141–132). One goes down from places in the hill country into the plain where the Philistines are. 'Timnah': the name is not transmitted coherently: sometimes (vv. 1b, 2, 5b) it ends in -*ātāh*, even where there is no movement from place to place. 'A

woman': *'iššāh*; an unusual expression: in cases like this the Hebrew uses *na'ªrah*, 'girl', or *bᵉtūlāh*, 'virgin', or analogous expressions. Perhaps the text implies that she was widowed or divorced, or, more probably, wants to convey a derogatory note to the reader, Burney*, 1919, cf. the case of Delilah in 16.4. At the end, LXX^A adds, 'and she pleased him', cf. vv. 3, 7. **[2]** The negotiations over a marriage are carried on (as in part they still are in traditional Arab circles) by the father of the bridegroom, so that some authors (cf. *BHK*³ and *BHS*) delete the mother, who has perhaps come in under the influence of ch. 13, where she has the principal part. However, the construction of the cycle as a whole presupposes her presence, together with that of the father. **[3]** 'My people': thus MT, LXX^B and Vg; by contrast LXX^A has 'in all the people'; Syr has 'your people'. It does not seem necessary to correct. 'Uncircumcised': a term used only for Philistines in the Old Testament, perhaps because they were the only people in the region who did not practise circumcision. In Israel from time immemorial it was the mother who determined the religion and therefore the nationality of the child, as well as educating him when he was smaller. Thus even now an Israeli is one who, among other things, is born of a Hebrew mother and has not committed any acts incompatible with being a Hebrew. The problem, which is of an eminently religious kind, should not therefore be confused with nationalistic or, even worse, racist interpretations of the problem. We know that the problem had become acute in post-exilic times, cf. the preaching of Malachi and the problems of Ezra-Nehemiah.[8] **[4]** This provides a short and isolated theological interlude, which at the same time is the interpretative key for the events narrated: what is narrated here is happening because that is what God wants. However, it is not clear what his plan is (inflicting blows on the Philistines by means of Samson?). The reference to Philistine dominion is older than 13.1ff. and is evidently a duplicate; however, like 17.6; 18.1; 19.1; 21.25, it is a positive evaluation, albeit purely implicit, of the monarchy, an element characteristic of DtrH:[9] this dominion can be eliminated only through the monarchy. In that case 13.1, the duplicate, could be part of DtrN. We would then have an indirect allusion, albeit of a very subtle kind, in 14.4 to the benefits which would accrue to Israel from the monarchy: the struggle against the Philistines (Saul and David) and their definitive defeat and submission (David). **[5]** 'Samson': MT and the ancient translations all expand: ' . . . his father and his mother', cf. 10a. However, LXX has the verb in the singular. Thus as the text now stands, the idea is that the parents (or perhaps only the father) would have initiated the

[8]For the problem see my *Introduction to the Old Testament*, London and Philadelphia ²1980, 472ff.
[9]Cf. T. Veijola, *Das Königtum in der Beurteilung der deuteronomistischen Historiographie*, AASF B–198, 1977, 15–29.

negotiations with the parents of the woman, notwithstanding their recent refusal. However, Samson met the lion by himself, on his way towards the woman (v. 6), and the parents must have known about it, but they do not. Hence they cannot all have gone to Timnah. Here the original text of the narrative seems to have been modified in the sense that the affectionate relationship between parents and child is continued, but with little coherence and a good deal of confusion. Samson will have emerged as the victim of such a version of the story; the reality of the text in its original form seems to have been more prosaic: confronted with his parents' refusal to have anything to do with the girl and her family, Samson took things into his own hands without involving his parents. That explains how the feast was celebrated at his wife's home and Samson had Philistine companions and a Philistine best man (cf. below), instead of his own people, while the wife continued to live at home with her father. This is what in Arab society today is called a *ṣadīqa* marriage, arranged directly by the groom with the family of his wife, without the involvement of his own family, and with the wife herself (here v.7); the wife continued to live at her own home, where the husband would come to visit her at more or less regular intervals. **[6]** It is a practice even today in Arab countries to tear a kid or a lamb to pieces with the hands; though of course this is when the animal has already been cooked. The paragon demonstrates the ease of the operation, proof of his heroic strength. **[8]** 'After some time': cf. the same expression in 11.4 and the comments made on it there. 'To take her with him': another redactional element out of context: in fact Samson is returning from his parents and not from the girl, cf. v.9; this last feature has not always been understood by commentators, resulting in some degree of confusion over the various journeys. 'Bee . . . honey . . .': it is strange, not to say impossible, that bees should have settled in a carcass (in his study, H. Margulies, 1974, makes a series of very useful remarks about apiculture, connected with our text and more generally); however, the whole thing seems less strange if we suppose either that the summer sun and the dry climate had rapidly dried out the carcass, eliminating the putrefaction, or that the narrative presupposes the ancient belief that a cadaver 'generates' the insects which swarm in it. In any case it is an integral part of a story in which extraordinary events continually happen: cf. C. F. Burney*, 1919, 360, for the discussion. **[9]** 'Took it . . . from the honeycomb': root *rādāh*, which seems to have been used in instances of this kind. There is no evidence of apiculture in the Old Testament, but there are instances of gathering wild honey. For the Nazirite this action is doubly sinful: Num. 6.6 ordains: 'All the days that he separates himself to the Lord, he shall not go near a dead body' (*nepeš mēt*: 'corpse' in general); however, even for someone who was not a Nazirite, this honey would have been impure, since it came from a corpse (Lev. 11.24f., 39, etc.). Silence about this episode even to his parents, cf. below, v. 16b, prepares for the riddle; no one will be able to solve it. [10] 'Samson': MT and the ancient translations all have the absurd 'his father', which has not appeared by accident: the phrase is part of the revision discussed in connection with v.5. 'The custom': clearly this custom was not practised at the time and in the social milieu of the person writing, for whom it was normal that the feast should be held in the bridegroom's house, probably evidence that the *ṣadīqa* marriage mentioned above was not practised in Israel. 'Feast': the Hebrew *mišteh*, literally 'symposium', with stress on the fact that there was lots to drink, root *šātāh*. So here was the second way in which Samson violated his vows: Num. 6.2ff. says of those who have made a Nazirite's vow, 'he shall separate himself from wine and strong drink . . .'; the mother of Samson, too, had been ordered to abstain from any produce of the vine, even non-alcoholic (cf. 13.14). For Samson, as we have seen, the vow begins with the act of conception. [11] 'Saw him . . .': LXX^A has ἐν τῷ φοβεῖσθαι, i.e. *b*ᵉ*yir'ātām*, root *yārē*, instead of *rā'āh*; the confusion between the two roots, which often have phonetically similar forms, is quite frequent; here the choice is not easy: according to MT, given that the feast was not in the bridegroom's house and that the bridegroom had arrived at the bride's house without an escort, the bride's parents gave him one; according to LXX^A, however, the thirty youths were provided as a bodyguard for Samson because the Philistines were afraid of him: they did not know what might happen. The theory of MT seems to fit in better with the general pattern of the text, provided that it is corrected in accordance with my earlier suggestion. 'Riddle': Hebrew *ḥīdāh*. The text seems to have a phonetic play on words, through the frequent repetition of the letter *mem*. [14] 'Strong . . . sweet': the term *'az* normally means 'strong', first of all in a physical sense, but also in a moral and spiritual one: here it evidently refers to 'strong' taste. In the translation I have tried to reproduce as far as possible the original play on words: this is what we have here, a well known genre throughout the ancient Near East. In Ugarit we have the mythical 'eaters' (*'aklm*) in text (Gordon) 75.I: 26,36, while in Arabic *'akīl* is one of the many epithets for the lion, Gaster**, 1969, 536. Moreover, it could be noted that the precise solution of the riddle presupposes knowledge of the episode of the lion: because that is impossible, the riddle is an unfair one. This does not seem to have troubled the ancient narrators overmuch, cf. the commentary. 'Three/six days': cf. on the next verse. [15] 'On the fourth/seventh day . . .': LXX read 'on the fourth . . .', MT 'on the seventh', cf. the preceding verse, where we have the same problem. It is difficult to choose: the chronology of the episode is somewhat confused. The desperation of the thirty could indicate that the period was drawing to an end, but according to v. 17 we get the impression that it was only beginning, and the work of seducing Samson by his wife needed time. The words of his companions are not completely clear, though the general sense is evident: *hal'yoršēnī* is an anomalous conjugation of the infinitive construct of *yāraš*, normally *rešet*, *GesK* §69m; a variant of it is the probable piel *hal'yaršēnī*. Among other things, the verb means 'drive out', 'deprive of one's own possession', and as such is characteristic of the Israelite conquest of Palestine: the other sense, 'inherit', does not arise here. But LXX^A has πτωχεῦσαι ἐκαλέσατε ἡμᾶς: 'Did you invite us to make beggars of us?' 'Here': read *h^{a}lōm* for *h^{a}lō'*, 'Is it not . . .?' 'It is certain that . . .' (for this last meaning cf. on 4.6). We do not know whether here and in 15.6 the threat is to be taken literally or is only a manner of speaking. **[16]** 'Beside': for this meaning of *'al* cf. on 7.1. **[18]** 'The sun . . .': the Hebrew has the rare *ḥeres*, sometimes used in geographical contexts, cf. on 8.18, perhaps Horus. It is not necessary to correct it, as some commentators would prefer, to *haḥadrāh*, 'in the bridal chamber': with the setting of the sun the seventh day ended and the period of time set by Samson ran out. The reading is confirmed by LXX and Vg. The people of Timnah reply to Samson's riddle with another one, to which Samson replies with a third, a real conversation in riddles, which also forms a violent interruption to the consummation of Samson's marriage. 'Cow': the term probably had the same disparaging sense in Hebrew as it does in modern English. **[20]** 'To the companion . . .': A. van Selms, 1950, taken up passim by Crenshaw, 1978, argues with good reasons that this is what we would call the best man, and therefore the one closest to the bridegroom, cf. John 3.29 in the New Testament. I accept this version. Giving the woman to him is a grave insult to Samson, even if he was closer to her than to him, for reasons which we have examined.

1. After the idyllic family scene presented in ch. 13, we now have the first of Samson's erotic escapades with a foreign woman who, moreover, is an enemy. This time appearances are more or less kept up, because this is a proper wedding; however, Samson's family and people are remarkable for their absence. The downright condemnation implied in this absence is clearly shared by those who originally handed down the story: the only thing that the two have in common is that she pleased him, vv. 3b, 7b; the repetition probably accentuates the importance of the note. Again, the marriage takes place in deliberate disregard of any family, tribal or ethnic loyalty; therefore it can only have been the *ṣadiqā* marriage which we looked at earlier, clearly a kind of second-class marriage. Perhaps it is similar to the relationship expressed with the term *pīlegeš* for the woman, cf. 8.31;

19.1ff. And in the context of the celebration of this marriage, Samson violates his vow twice: touching a corpse and drinking wine: does the text know nothing of ch. 13?

2. But we have a second feature which is characteristic of this chapter: the various riddles or conundrums put forward by the people involved. This genre is well known in the ancient Near East and in the West, cf. the stories of Oedipus and the Sphinx, and we cannot go into too much detail here: it is enough to refer to the exhaustive treatment of the theme by Crenshaw, 1978, ch. III, 99ff.

Characteristic of the Hebrew *ḥīdāh* is the play on semantic ambiguity which can be found in any language. The person who solves it must therefore discover, alongside the current and therefore obvious meaning of the words or phrase, meanings which are less obvious because they are little used or because they are even codified in word-plays. For example, certain euphemistic usages in connection with hygienic or sexual matters can be enigmatic even now for people who do not know a language well or are unaware of different regional usages. In other instances the riddle can deliberately reproduce in cipher what is meant to be understood only by certain people in particular circumstances.

So if it is true that the riddle posed by Samson to his companions is unfair, because they could not know the episode apart from which the riddle is meaningless (which in our eyes would justify the use of somewhat unfair means on the part of the Philistines), it should be remembered that the case of the impossible riddle is not unknown in antiquity and is therefore part of the rules of the game. Grottanelli offers several examples of the belief that bees can be born from corpses. So according to the criteria of the time, Samson's saying should not be considered unfair. Crenshaw, 114, cites the story of 'the princess who could not solve the riddle': the hero, on his way to take part in a riddle contest, the chief prize of which was the hand of a princess in marriage, sees in succession a horse dying from some sort of poisoning, a crow feeding on the corpse and twelve men dying from poisoning having eaten the crow. The hero sums it all up in a riddle: 'One did not kill anyone, but killed twelve.' The princess did not succeed in solving the riddle and was married to the hero. Here, then, is another instance of an 'unfair' riddle, though from a much later date. However, these are extreme cases: the normal situation, well attested in the Old

Testament, is a contest based on the subtlety of the formulations and also, of course, of the solutions put forward, as is shown by Grottanelli and Crenshaw. The biblical tradition presents Solomon as being particularly skilful in posing riddles and solving them. in I Kings 10.1ff./II Chron 9.1ff., the queen of Sheba comes 'to test Solomon with hard questions', and she is not the only one; others also came from afar to hear him, I Kings 5.14 (EVV 4.34); 10.24 and parallels.

Quite apart from the impossibility of solving the riddle posed by Samson unless someone were aware of the private actions of the hero (and no one was, as we have seen, not even his parents), one of its features is that it is a play on ambiguity: the most obvious meaning seems to border on pornography, sheer ribaldry in an exclusively masculine company of equals, the kind of humour that can be found all round the Mediterranean even today. However, this first and scurrilous meaning is not the 'true' one, as the thirty soon find out when the episode seems to end at their expense, and general merriment gives way in the end to embarrassment.

(c) Samson – incendiary and warrior (ch. 15)

15 [1]After a while, at the time of the wheat harvest, Samson went to visit his wife, taking with him a kid, and he asked to be allowed to enter his wife's room. But her father would not allow him to go in. [2]He said, 'I thought that you must now hate her and so I gave her to your companion. Her younger sister is even more beautiful; take her instead.' [3]But Samson said to them, 'This time I shall be completely blameless in regard to the Philistines, if I do them mischief.'

4 Then he caught three hundred foxes, and took torches. He bound the foxes together, two by two, by the tail, and put a torch between each pair of tails. [5]Then he set fire to the torches and sent the animals into the standing grain of the Philistines. They burnt up the sheaves and the grain which had not yet been harvested, and even the vines and the olive orchards.

6 Then the Philistines asked themselves, 'Who has done this?' They received the reply, 'It was Samson, the son-in-law of the Timnathite, because he has taken away his wife and given her to his companion.' Then the Philistines went and burned her and her father's house.

7 But Samson said to them, 'Since you have acted in this way, I will be avenged upon you; only then will I be satisfied.' [8]And he smote them, hip and thigh, making a great slaughter. Then he went down to stay in a cleft of the 'Rock of Etam'.

9 One day the Philistines went out on an expedition and encamped

in the territory of Judah, making a raid on Lehi. [10]But the men of Judah protested. 'Why have you come against us?' They replied, 'We have come to take Samson prisoner and to treat him as he deserves.' [11]Then three companies of men of Judah went down towards the cleft in the 'Rock of Etam' and said to Samson, 'Do you not know that we are under the dominion of the Philistines? What, then, have you done?' But he replied, 'I have only repaid them for what they have done to me.' [12]Then they said to him, 'We must capture you, take you with us and deliver you to the Philistines.' But he said, 'Swear to me that you will not do me evil.' [13]They replied, 'We will not harm you, but we must capture you and deliver you to the Philistines. As for killing you, we certainly will not do that.' And they bound him with two new ropes and made him come up from the Rock.

14 When he came to Lehi, the Philistines came to meet him, shouting for joy. But the spirit of Yahweh took possession of him, and the ropes which bound his arms became weak as though they were burnt flax; and his bonds melted from his arms. [15]He found a jawbone of an ass that was still fresh, seized it, and with it he slew a thousand men. [16]Then Samson said,

'With the jawbone of an ass,
I have given them a thrashing!
With the jawbone of an ass
I have slain a thousand men.'

17 When he had finished speaking, he threw away the jawbone and called the place Ramath-lehi ('the Hill of the Jawbone').

18 Then he was seized with a great thirst and cried out to Yahweh, 'You have granted your servant this great victory. But now I am dying of thirst and I shall fall into the hands of the uncircumcised!' [19]Then God split the 'Mortar' that can be found in Lehi and from it he drew water. He drank of it, his strength revived and he was refreshed. For that reason its place is En-hakkore ('The spring of the one who calls'), which is at Lehi to this very day.

20 He was judge in Israel for twenty years, in the days of the Philistines.

---

[1] 'After a while': cf. on 11.4 and 14.8. Samson left in a fury, but without breaking with his wife; however, his action had been interpreted as a divorce by her family. 'With a kid': the ancient Near Eastern alternative to our box of chocolates (Boling*, 1975). [2] 'Hate her. . .': the expression is part of the Israelite formula of repudiation, cf. Deut. 22.13,16 and 24.3. The father-in-law therefore thinks that Samson has repudiated the wife and finds himself in difficulties because Deut. 24.1, cf. Jer. 3.1, expressly prohibits the return of the wife to her first husband if she has married again. He therefore proposes an alternative which might seem suitable in the context of sexual exas-

peration to be found in this story. The verb 'hate' here has a legal meaning which it does not have in 14.16, where it is put on the lips of the woman.[10] **[3]** 'Them': LXX^A and Vg read the singular *lō* instead of *lāhem*; however an emendation is unnecessary: the father is the spokesman of the nuclear family. 'Blameless' in the sense that no one can accuse him of anything or claim anything from him, even if in reality he has done mischief to the Philistines: this is simply a matter of reprisal. **[4]** 'Foxes': Hebrew *šū'āl*, or perhaps better, 'jackal', cf. recently G. R. Driver**, 1964, and R. G. Boling*, 1975: foxes are solitary animals and would be virtually impossible to tie together. Furthermore, they are very rare in Palestine; by contrast, jackals go in packs and have always been numerous. In any case, it is not easy to visualize the scene: it seems more to be the product of a good idea than to draw on an effective knowledge of the animal world. **[5]** 'Into the grain. . .': *qāmōt* is the term for standing grain before it has been cut, but the plural appears only in this text and is strange, as it is a collective term; it is probably better to read *qāmat* (a singular with the archaic termination in *–t*, confused rather later with a plural), cf. G. R. Driver**, 1964, and R. G. Boling*, 1975, so that there is no real need to emend. 'Vines and olive orchards' is probably a later addition, too exaggerated even for a Samson story, where exaggeration seems to be a matter of course. Besides, the point of the story is that Samson sets fire to objects which will in any case burn because they are dry: this is not the case with trees. For the construction, D. N. Freedman has suggested that we should take the final *mem* of *kerem* as a prefix of *zayit*, to give 'from the vine to the olive'. **[6]** 'House. . .': added with LXX^A and Syr, and necessary here; LXX^B and Vg confirm MT. It is the very threat pronounced in 14.15, see there. **[8]** 'Hip and thigh': it is not clear whether this is a technical military expression or fighting slang (Burney*, 1919) whose implications escape us, or whether it is an idiomatic way of indicating total defeat. The place where Samson withdraws is unknown: there are rocks, caves and clefts by the score in the mountains of Judah. II Chron. 11.6 mentions a place by the same name (coord. 166–121), but this is too far from the scene of this story for it to be able to be the same. **[9]** *leḥī*, 'jawbone', is another unknown place; in II Sam. 23.11f. (emended text), Shammah, one of David's heroes, fights against the Philistines who are massed at Lehi. The mention of the place is in any case necessary here for the play on words in v. 17, but one has to note the similarity in the names of the protagonists and the identity of the place and of the enemy. **[10]** The presence of the men of Judah in the region shows that the Danites

---

[10]For the theme cf. R. Yaron, 'On Divorce in Old Testament Times' *RIDA* III. 4, 1957, 117–28, and R. de Vaux, *Les Institutions* . . . I, 1958, 60–62; ET, *Ancient Israel*, 34–6. It is better in these cases to speak of the 'repudiation' of the wife by her husband and not of 'divorce'.

were not around (any longer?), cf. my remarks in §1, pp. 225ff. As we saw there, at a later stage, as well as being Philistine, the region would be part Judahite, and part Ephraimite. 'As he deserves': literally, 'as he has treated us'. **[11]** For the Philistine 'dominion' cf. above on 14.4; the phrase could imply praise of the monarchy, which puts an end to this state of things. The words of the Philistines mean, 'Deliver him up, otherwise we will see about capturing you and you will suffer the consequences!' 'Companies': literally 'three thousand': here the term *'elep* probably has a military sense, cf. on 4.6. Note the promptness with which the men of Judah 'collaborate' with the Philistines, recognizing not only their sovereignty but also the legitimacy and reasonableness of their request: perhaps a dig at Judah? **[12]** 'That you will not do. . .': literally 'That you will not fall on me (sc. to kill me)'.

[15] 'Jawbone' : again Samson touches a cadaver or part of it, violating his Nazirite's vow; it is 'fresh', and therefore not fragile, but not in such a condition as not to be considered part of a corpse either.

[16] 'I have given them. . .': it is impossible to reproduce even approximately the play on words in the text which, moreover, seems to be corrupt: I have read, for the two nouns in MT, the absolute infinitive *ḥᵃmōr* and the perfect *ḥᵃmartīm*: 'have totally piled up' or 'have made a heap of them'; i.e. 'I have done away with them', cf. Vg *delevi* and LXX ἐξέλειψα αὐτούς, thus Targ. The play on words revolves around the different possibilities of the root *ḥāmar*: 'ass', 'pile up', 'be ruddy'. **[18]** 'Dying': an obvious exaggeration, but cf. Esau in Gen. 25.32. **[19]** 'The "Mortar"', Hebrew *maktēš*, is a depression with a circular shape, large or small, see the name of such areas in the Negeb today: *maktēš qātān, maktēš rāmōn,* etc. 'Of the one who calls', active *qal* participle of *qārā'*, but *qōre'* is also the 'partridge'; this last is probably the original name, which was then aetiologically connected with this episode.

The second episode in the deeds of Samson is made up of two, perhaps three sections, now connected together by means of links with what has gone before, just as ch. 15 is connected to ch. 14 by Samson's attempt to return to his wife. In fact these are self-sufficient stories which do not need one to come first or another to follow. All that they have in common is that the protagonist is Samson.

Thus the note about Samson who sets fire to the Philistine crops, the note about the slaughter made among the Philistines with the skilful use of an ass's jawbone, and finally the aetiological note about the 'spring of the partridge' or 'the spring of the one who calls' are all features which have logical and literary autonomy, organically bound up by the collector, but without having a particular place in the structure of the collection. None of them in fact presupposes the existence of the previous episode nor is presupposed by the one which follows.

Although it has been done skilfully, the redactional connection does not succeed in avoiding a notable lack of logic between one passage and another: it seems strange, to say the least, that Samson should have returned to his wife having apparently repudiated her; if he had not given this impression, no one, knowing his character, would have dared to have insulted him by giving his wife to someone else. Nor does it seem logical to burn all the Philistine crop if only the one family had dealt somewhat improperly with him, or to exact savage revenge for the reprisals taken by the Philistines on the family of his wife whose attitude had been the cause of his anger and therefore of the loss of the crop. And if Samson had hidden himself, it was not a matter of going to look for him, far less of entrusting this task to the men of Judah, over whose capacity for action and indeed over whose fidelity there must have been considerable doubts. And at the end of the narrative, why all this fear of falling into the hands of the Philistines after having defeated them, and how was he suddenly overcome with thirst? It is not certain that he was in the desert. In any case, it seems legitimate to treat each section separately.

[1–8] The first episode is that of the foxes. This is a theme which has a number of analogies in the history of religion and in popular tradition.

(i) To the former category belongs the Roman custom during the feast of Ceres (*cerealia*), every 19 April, of loosing and then chasing, in the circus or in the fields, foxes which had had lighted torches attached to their tails. The rite is described and explained by Ovid, *Fasti* IV, 679ff.; it seems to have been connected with the celebration, immediately after (25 April), of the *Robigalia*, a festival during which puppies with a rust colour (reddish) were sacrificed. This ceremony was meant to ensure that the crops would not be infected with rust before the harvest, cf. *Fasti* IV, 901ff. The two rites, of different origins, tended increasingly to come together because of the nearness of the dates, the similarity of the animals even in colour, and the agricultural basis of the two. However, it should immediately be noted that the date of the two feasts, in the second half of April, is connected with harvesting where the rite originated, not in Italy, where it takes place a couple of months later. And this area seems very likely to be Syria-Palestine. This discovery could be an important element in explaining the origin and significance of the two celebrations: an original rite transplanted to Rome from time immemorial. Similar rites are attested among country-dwelling Arabs, though they are now connected with the rain and with fertility, and were still known of in continental Europe at the end of the last century; however, their content does not seem to be more clearly defined. For a detailed examination of these parallels see C. F. Burney*, 1919, 393–5, and T. H. Gaster**, 1969, 434f.

Thus this text historicizes a rite also known elsewhere, at the same time attributing farcical connotations to it: in this way it is polemic against pagan or syncretistic customs. For the analogy between these rites and our text cf. J. Gray*, 1967.

(ii) However, there are also other explanations, one of a military kind, cf. Gaster, ibid. According to this view these would be typical guerilla tactics, and in this connection mention is made of the stratagem of Hannibal during the battle of Lake Trasimene (217 BC, cf. Livy XXII. 16ff.): he sent into the fields oxen with burning torches between their horns, causing panic among the Romans; we have similar instances among the Arabs, the Mongols, the Icelanders and yet others. In this case the practice would be part of military folklore and would not have any originally mythical base. Boling*, 1975, and some Israeli authors who have studied the technique of ancient military campaigns also support this theory. Obviously one of the explanations need not exclude the other.

[9–17] By contrast, the episode of the jawbone of the ass is not notable for its mythical-religious and popular basis, which is absent, but for the almost grotesque insistence on the extraordinary physical strength of Samson, especially when the spirit takes possession of him. The term grotesque does not seem rash: this narrative has an obviously humorous tone, as does the one which precedes it. Here the Philistines are not only implacable enemies: they are also ridiculous, and the men of Judah, with their prompt submission and obedience, are not less so. The men of Judah also introduce a despicable note into this passage: not only are they submissive as can be, but they are critical of the rash exploits of their neighbour, whom they consider to be a danger to the general peace. Futhermore, well aware of Samson's might, they move against him with three whole platoons, only to find him ready to surrender! Their servility towards the enemy is thus turned into a real collaboration, in which they carried out a strict piece of police work on behalf of their enemies. This attitude is also criticized implicitly at the end of the episode, when the men of Judah disappear in silence, instead of siding to a man with the one who could have led them to victory (cf. 13.5).

The character of the exploit seems extraordinary, and the narrative brings it out both by describing it in detail and by a song of victory which Samson sings at the end, a song which is somewhat obscure because of the lack of clarity and perhaps the corruption in the second line. What the text does not show, but which appears from the premises of ch. 13, is that for the second time (even if this time he could have justified the action by his need) Samson violated that part of the Nazirite rule which prohibited their touching corpses.

It is difficult to establish here whether we have a recollection of a genuine submission by Judah to the Philistines, a submission which will have driven them to the point of collaborating with the Philistines against the last areas of resistance in Israel, or whether we have simply one of those caricatures which the inhabitants of various regions in any country are accustomed to pass round. Given the minimally historical character of the whole cycle, it is probable that we have the latter alternative.

[18–19] The place had another tradition, connected with 'the spring of the partridge': really, as tradition says, the word means 'the one who calls', in form both the active qal participles of *qārā'*; this is the more frequent root, whereas the Deuteronomistic 'framework' prefers to use *ṣā'aq/zā'aq*.

[20] The chapter ends with a note about Samson's 'judgeship', cf. also 16.31; once again we find a very brief formula indeed, without the addition that from then on there was peace between Israel and their enemies; perhaps, though, this was also because the redactors knew that there were still many years of war to come before the Philistines finally submitted under David. With Samson, the texts convey, the victory only began; this is perhaps the reason why these narratives were included in Dtr.

(d) Other exploits and the death of Samson (ch. 16)

16 [1]Then Samson went to Gaza and saw there a prostitute; and he went in to her. [2]The news was passed on to the inhabitants, 'Samson has come here.' They surrounded the place and prepared a watch for him all day at the gate of the city. Then they kept quiet all night, thinking, 'At daybreak we will kill him.' [3]But Samson stayed with the woman until the middle of the night, and then, after midnight, he arose and took hold of the two doors of the gate of the city together with the bolts, put them on his shoulder and carried them up to the summit of the mountain which is before Hebron, where he left them.

4 After this exploit he fell in love with a woman in the valley of Sorek, whose name was Delilah. [5]Then the 'tyrants' of the Philistines went in to her and said, 'Entice him, and try to discover wherein his great strength lies, and how we can overcome him, capture him and make him helpless. We are ready each to give you eleven hundred shekels of silver.' [6]And Delilah said to Samson, 'Tell me wherein your great strength lies and how someone could capture you and make you helpless.' [7]Samson replied, 'If they were to bind me with seven fresh bowstrings which have not yet been dried, then I should become weak and be like any other man.' [8]The 'tyrants' of the Philistines brought her seven fresh bowstrings which had not been dried, and she bound him with them. [9]She had prepared an ambush in her room. Then she said, 'The Philistines are upon you, Samson!' But he snapped the bowstrings as a string of tow snaps when it feels the fire. So the secret of his strength was not revealed.

10 But Delilah said to Samson, 'You have deceived me and told me lies. Tell me how someone might capture you.' [11]He replied, 'If they were to bind me with new ropes which had not been used, I should become weak and be like any other man.' [12]Then Delilah took new ropes, bound him with them and said, 'The Philistines are upon you, Samson!' And an ambush had been prepared in the room. But he snapped the ropes with his arms as though they were thread. [13]Then Delilah said to Samson, 'How long will you go on deceiving me and telling me lies? Tell me how someone might capture you.' He replied, 'If you wove the seven locks of my head with the web and made it tight with the pin, I should become weak and be like any other man.' [14]Then while he was asleep, Delilah took the seven locks of his head and wove them into the web, made them tight with the pin, and said, 'The Philistines are upon you, Samson!' He awoke from his sleep and pulled away the web and the pin. [15]Then she said to him, 'Why do you say that you wish me well when your mind is not with me? You have deceived me three times and have not told me wherein your great strength lies.' [16]And she tormented him every day with her words and troubled him, so that his soul became sad to the point of death. [17]Finally he told her all that was in his mind: 'A razor has never come upon my head, for I have been a Nazirite to God from my mother's womb. If I should be shaved, my strength would leave me, and I would become weak like any other man.' [18]Delilah noted that this time he had opened his mind to her; then she sent and called the 'tyrants'

of the Philistines and said to them, 'This time he has told me all his mind.' And they came up to her with the money in their hands. [19]She made him sleep on her knees, and then she called a man who shaved the seven locks from his head. And immediately he began to grow weak, and his strength left him. [20]She said, 'The Philistines are upon you, Samson!' He awoke from sleep, thinking, 'This time, too, as at other times, I shall go out and shake myself free,' without realizing that Yahweh had left him.

21 The Philistines captured him, gouged out his eyes and took him with them to Gaza, where they bound him with a double chain of bronze. Then they put him on the treadmill, in prison. [22]But the hair on his head began to grow again, after it had been shaved.

23 One day the 'tyrants' of the Philistines gathered to offer a huge sacrifice to Dagon, their god, with great festivity. They said,

'Our god has given into our hands
Samson, our great enemy.'

24 And when the people saw him, they praised their god in these words:

'Our god has given
our enemy into our hands;
the one who ravaged our country,
who has multiplied the corpses among us.'

25 Glad in heart, they made a suggestion, 'Call Samson so that he may entertain us.' They called him from prison and made fun of him before them; then they made him stand between the pillars. [26]Then Samson said to the youth who was guarding him and holding his hand, 'Let me touch the pillars which hold up the building, and let me rest on them.' [27]The building was full of men and women; all the 'tyrants' of the Philistines were also there; on the roof there were about three thousand men and women who were spectators at Samson's entertainment. [28]Then Samson called to Yahweh, 'O Lord Yahweh, remember me and give me strength just once again, O God! With one blow let me be avenged of the Philistines for my two eyes.'

29 And Samson pressed against the two central pillars which held up the building, leaning on them with his right hand and with his left; [30]then he cried out, 'Only let me die, but with the Philistines.' He leant with all his might and the building collapsed upon the 'tyrants' and on all the people who were in it. So the people whom he killed with his death were more than those whom he killed in his life.

31 His brothers and all his father's house came down and took him and carried him to bury him between Zorah and Eshtaol, in the tomb of his father Manoah. He had been judge of Israel for twenty years.

---

[1] 'Prostitute': cf. on 13.1. LXX[A] adds ἐκεῖθεν, miššām, 'from

there', which some people want to insert in the text. **[2]** 'Passed on
. . .' is missing from MT, but it is attested by LXX, Vg, Targ and Syr
MSS. The verb (or some other equivalent) is needed, and I have
added it. 'All day' is a substitute for a first 'all night', which anticipates
the immediate sequel. Some scholars find it contradictory that Samson
should be able to unhinge the gates of a city while the Philistines were
standing guard; in fact down to the end of the second half of the second
millennium BC the gate of a Palestinian city was a very complex
construction[11] and anyone lying in wait in one of the rooms, instead
of watching the way through, would not always succeed in maintaining
control of the latter (Boling*, 1975). **[3]** 'The mountain': between
Gaza (coord. 099–101) and Hebron, present-day *el-ḥalīl* (coord. 160–
103) is a distance of about 60 kilometres as the crow flies, with a
difference in height of rather less than 1000 metres; according to
Hebrew style, the mountain must be a little to the east of the place
and is probably *ğebel ğālis*, 987 metres above sea level (coord. 162–
104). In reality, the text does not set out to give topographical details,
but to underline the magnitude of the exploit. 'The gate': this did not
have hinges like modern or mediaeval gates, but turned on upper and
lower pivots, each fixed into a socket; removed from one of the sockets
the gate would automatically come away. 'Where he left them': with
LXX; an indication of the insult shown to the Philistines. **[4]** 'The
valley of Sorek' is the one which begins the ascent towards Jerusalem,
starting from near Zorah (see on 13.25 for the details). The name also
denotes a highly prized vine, cf. Isa. 5.2 and Jer. 2.21, though we
cannot establish whether there was any connection between the two.
Thus the woman lived near to Samson's family.

'Delilah': Hebrew *dᵉlīlāh* apparently means either 'falling curl', root
*dālal*I, in which case it would refer to her hairstyle,[12] or it should be
connected with *dālal*II, 'be humble, submissive'; however,
G. F. Moore*, 1895, already found all these etymologies 'hideously
inapt'; so Crenshaw 1978, 92, against R. G. Boling*, 1975. Others
think of an Arabic root which means 'beloved'. However, C. F. Burney*, 1919, 407, pointed out how the name appears in Akkadian,
especially in theophoric names compounded with Ishtar, so that it
means 'dedicated to the (deity) X'. Therefore it is probable that even
if the text says nothing to that effect, the woman was Canaanite, or
given Samson's preferences, perhaps even Philistine. Perhaps the text
wants to produce a play on words with the demon Lilith, but it is
difficult to say that with precision. **[5]** 'Tyrants': cf. on 3.3. The
problem of Samson seems to have been very serious if the narrators

[11]For pictures and plans cf. *ANEP* nos. 712, 713, 721; for the gates of Shechem cf.
above on ch. 9.
[12]M. Noth, *Die israelitischen Personennamen im Rahmen der gemeinsemitischen Namengebung*,
BWANT III. 10, Stuttgart 1928, 227.

bring the supreme commanders of the Philistines against him. However, this feature, too, is characteristic of the fable, in which king and princes have positions of pre-eminence. For the 'shekel' cf. on 8.26. The sum is exorbitant, another typical feature of the fable, and the figure offered by each one is equal to the total in 17.1ff.; however, in this text that is not important, though it is in 17.1ff., cf. J. L. Crenshaw, 1978, 93, with bibliography. 'Entice him': as in 14.15.   [7] The 'bowstrings' were made from the tendons of slaughtered animals; with tanning they underwent a process of dessication and shrinking. I do not see how the request can be connected with cursing in the ancient Near East, far less with a dishonourable discharge of Samson from military service (thus Boling). Once again Samson touches elements belonging to a corpse.   [9] 'Feels': root *rwḥ*, hiphil, unusual in contexts of this kind. The expression recalls that of 15.14, but is not the same.   [10] 'Deceived': cf. 14.15: root *tālal*$_{II}$.   [11] 'New ropes' as in 15.13.   [13f.] The last part of v.13 and the beginning of v. 14 are missing in MT; this section, which is indispensable for understanding the text, has fallen out by homoioteleuton between the first and second *hammasseket*; I have restored it with LXX and Vg, and it is reproduced in its entirety in *BHK*^{3} and *BHS*.   [14] *hay^{e}tad hā'ereg*: a corrupt expression: the first term appears in the construct state, but has the article, a form attested very rarely and of unknown meaning: it was earlier thought to be a textual error, but the problem is more complex. Usually the second term is deleted, but it could be that the first term is a gloss on the second, which was then misunderstood and vocalized as though it were a construct. Samson has 'locks', cf. v. 19, because he never has his hair cut and keeps it unkempt.[13]   [15] 'Mind': here and in vv. 17, 18 and 25; I have chosen this translation for the Hebrew 'heart', which here is not the seat of the affections (as with us) but of the intellect. [16] 'Tormented': cf. on 14.17b. The technique of seduction is very similar.   [18] K read *lāh*, 'to her' (indirect speech, rare in biblical Hebrew), Q has *lī*, 'to me' (direct speech, normal in biblical Hebrew). 'Came up': the Hebrew has the perfect with *waw* consecutive, presupposed by the ancient translations. The bringing of the money, confirmed in the Hebrew, is a rhetorical anticipation of what is about to happen, a form frequent in the Old Testament but impossible for us, so I have translated it 'in their hands'.   [19] 'On her': some read 'between her knees' with the ancient translations. 'Who shaved . . .': reading the masculine, with the man as subject, and not the feminine, with Delilah as subject: why bring a man to shave Samson if it is then Delilah who shaves him? The confusion arises from the fact that it is Delilah who is acting, but through the intermediary of the barber. [23] 'Dagon': An ancient agricultural deity of the West Semitic world

---

[13]For the technique of weaving presupposed by the remarks cf. G. F. Moore*, 1895, and G. Dalman, *Arbeit und Sitte in Palästina* V, Gütersloh 1937, 100ff.

already known at Ebla (end of the third millennium BC) and Mari (eighteenth to seventeenth centuries BC) as *dāgān* and also known in Ugarit and Phoenicia. He is either the father of Baal or identified with him. The term means 'wheat', so he is the god of harvests; by contrast Baal is essentially a weather god. In the biblical texts he appears exclusively as a deity of the Philistines, here and In I Sam. 5. The West Semitic character of the deity shows how far the Philistines in the Bible had become Canaanized, unless we postulate for Israel the existence of a custom which is also attested among classical authors, of assigning to foreign gods the names of their own, in accordance with their functions. We should therefore reject an etymology from *dāg*, 'fish', which is attested in the rabbinic texts. **[24]** According to some scholars this should be transposed to after v. 25: first Samson is introduced into the room and only then do the people see him and praise God; only a few authorized persons had been admitted to the prison. Some scholars prefer to insert 'Samson' here, but that is unnecessary; it could well be understood. **[25]** 'Glad': K has *kī ṭōb* (perfect), Q *kᵉṭōb* (infinitive construct), forms which are semantically equivalent here. **[26]** 'Touch': K *wᵉhēmīšēnī*, root either *yāmaš* (unknown), or better *māšaš*, 'touch'; Q has *wāhᵃmīšēnī*, root *mwš*, identical in meaning. The confusion between verbs in median *y/w* and geminates is frequent in West Semitic. 'The pillars': the excavations on *tell qaṣīle*[14] at the beginning of the 1970s have brought to light a building which seems to correspond to the description in this text: a room with a ceiling held up by two columns and which the excavators interpret as a temple. The theory evidently presupposes that the Samson scene took place in the temple of Gaza, as the context seems to make probable; however, one could also think of a large room along the lines of the Homeric *megaron*, cf. J. Gray, 1967. **[27]**: 'Three thousand' on the terrace (incidentally, it is not easy to understand how from there they could see Samson in the room below) is an obvious exaggeration, as well as being a later addition. LXX read 'seven hundred', also too much. **[28]** The meaning is: one vengeance for two offences. **[31]** The return to an idyllic family setting, as in ch. 13. The text does not say where these brothers come from: in ch. 13 it is not in fact said that the wife of Manoah had other children, once the barrenness had been removed; perhaps it simply means 'members of his tribe', i.e. the Danites, cf. 18.8. In this last instance we would have the theme of the reconciliation of the bandit with his own people after his heroic death.

1. Chapter 16 is composed of at least two episodes connected only in a very precarious way: a third episode could be considered to be that of the death of Samson, which in turn is

---

[14]Cf. A. Mazar, 'A Philistine Temple at Tell Qasîle', *BA* 36, 1973, 43–8.

logically and chronologically connected with the second of the two which precede it. In the first episode a woman plays an important part, and in the second another woman is the protagonist: she betrays him and sells him to the Philistines, thus making possible his capture. No women, however, appear in the episode of his death.

The visit to a prostitute in the city of Gaza is the theme of the first account. It is reasonably well placed in its present context: after his disappointments in chs. 14 and 15, Samson will have tried to avoid any form of sentimental involvement, any circumstances in which he could be again persuaded to supply a proof of his love, a theme which reappears again in 16.4ff. with almost obsessive abundance; he is therefore content with a transaction of a commercial kind. However, although he is freed of any danger to his affections, he is now confronted with the trap laid by his enemies in the city. Strangely, however, nis enemies either do not know that Samson is staying in the woman's house, or if they do, they do not attack him there, for reasons which are obscure: is it for fear of his strength? Is it out of respect for the laws of hospitality, although this is the house of a prostitute? Do they want to act without any risks, as is shown by the ambush that they lay, however inadequate it may be? We are not told here, nor do we know from other sources. In any case, they are content to patrol the streets of the city and to guard its gate, through which anyone wanting to leave the place would have to pass, provided that we accept, as the text seems to presuppose, that the city had only one gate.

However, Samson succeeds in getting away, leaving the woman at an unexpected time and thus taking them by surprise. The action which follows is a joke pure and simple, meant to make the inhabitants of Gaza seems utterly ridiculous and robbing them of the last shreds of their reputation. Contrary to all warlike actions or incendiary exploits, here we have a piece of bravado which is clearly an end in itself.

2. The theme of the second narrative is again a secret extracted from Samson by a woman: this time our hero is truly in love, and not just attracted by the physical beauty of the woman, as in 14.3b and 7b, or by an uncommitted relationship as in 16.1ff. This time, however, the secret extracted from Samson is something much more serious: it does not simply concern victory in a contest or a wager, but his very liberty and, in the last analysis, his life. However, whereas the seduction scene in 14.16f. has

some highly probable features, among other things the fact that the scene happens only once and is not repeated, in this case we have a somewhat improbable sequence of reciprocal deceptions, that on the part of Samson, however, being justified by the woman's intentions. This leads to a series of stereotyped scenes with a somewhat crude psychology, and utterly lacking in any logic. Samson, who is presented elsewhere as being skilled at riddles, here appears so ingenuous and absurdly infatuated that his behaviour smacks of stupidity or even mental abnormality. Despite this, however, the story provides a good and emotive narrative, and probably finds its particular *raison d'être* here.

The Philistines seem now to have given up any attempt to kill Samson, if they are content to capture him and put him to forced labour; if they are to do this, however, they need to know what makes Samson invincible. They therefore help the woman with all her plans over Samson, the first at the expense of the people of Gaza, so that in the end, by dint of insisting, she succeeds in extracting his secret. Now the Philistines can act with an easy mind: all they need is a barber; so certain are they of their victory that they bring with them the sum agreed with the woman.

3. The theme of the strength which resides in hair is well known in the history of religions and in popular traditions. The reason for its presence here seems to be somewhat obscure, unless it is the faintest echo of the solar myth (hair like rays, van Daalen): first of all it has never been mentioned before, and then it does not appear in the texts about Samson's Nazirate. In fact, in the texts about the Nazirate it is never said that abstention from certain foods and length of hair produces a particular strength, all the more since Samson never took very seriously the vows mentioned in ch. 13.[15] The redactors were also evidently aware of the problem, since in v. 20b they explain that in reality it was the Lord who had abandoned Samson, whereas in v. 28 the return of his extraordinary strength is connected implicitly with the hearing of his prayer, notwithstanding the ominous allusion of v. 22. Again, as we saw in the introduction to these chapters, the theme of Samson's strength

[15]Against A. Penna*, 1963, 212, for whom 'the Nazirate explains the exploits of Samson described in chs. 14; 15 which in turn are connected with ch. 16 . . .' Samson's 'locks' are simply a particular kind of hair-style attested elsewhere in the Ancient Near East. Cf. the convincing study by R. Mayer-Opificius, 'Simson, der sechslockige Held?', *UF* 14, 1982, 149–51, with numerous illustrations.

hand, the theme of the strength residing in Samson's hair seems basic to the present narrative, cf. v. 22, which has already been mentioned, and cannot in any way be eliminated (Crenshaw, 1978, 95f.).

For the theme and the way in which it has been diffused, cf. Gaster**, 1969, 436–63; I shall only list a few parallels. In mediaeval Europe, in some trials for witchcraft, the threat of cutting the hair could sometimes achieve more than torture: the strength of the person in question was thought to reside in the hair. Similar cases are also attested in ancient India. In ancient Greece we have the case of Nisus, king of Megara, whose life, or according to another tradition, whose strength, resided in a lock of gold and purple. If this were torn out or cut, the life or the strength of Nisus would become less and he could be killed. The diffusion of the theme could be a sufficient reason to explain why it had not been mentioned before and why it appears here, in an essentially narrative context.

4. With the third deception Samson is dangerously near to the truth, in that he has at least partly revealed the function of his hair. Now he is put in a situation in which it is difficult to refuse to reveal all (Crenshaw, 1978, 93ff.).

The result is that he is captured, blinded and put to forced labour. A rabbinic source tells us that it was at Gaza that he 'followed the desire of his eyes', and so it was there that they were gouged out (*bab. Sotah* 9b, Crenshaw, 96 and 162 n. 26): however, in the present narrative this is also the place of his success, victory and reconciliation with his own people, albeit at the cost of his life.

5. It is not possible to make a general evaluation of the person of Samson in the context of the biblical narratives. As we have them now, a tenuous theological thread has been woven into the general pattern where it was clearly originally absent: all of ch. 13, then 14.4; 15.19; 16.28 and also those texts which present his strength as the product of the work of the spirit. But is it possible to give a general evaluation which leaves aside these superimposed elements, sometimes only precariously attached to the narrative? Many people have made the attempt; by and large there are two lines of approach: those who see in Samson a religious hero with tragic elements, and others who make an essentially negative evaluation of him, as an example not to be imitated, the opposite of the true hero.

We find that Josephus already takes the first line, cf. *Antt.* V.

viii. 12=§317, though he passes a severe judgment on his weaknesses towards the other sex; Hebrews 11.32f. places him in the line of the judges and the other great personages of antiquity without further comment, thus demonstrating its views of Samson. This line has been followed by the Christian patristic tradition, which in some instances has in fact made him virtually a kind of saint; some have even gone so far as to see him as the 'type' of Christ (as H. W. Hertzberg*, 1958, still does today, though rather as his opposite: Jesus dies to save, Samson to kill). He is again presented as a tragically positive figure by John Milton in his *Samson Agonistes* of 1671; for Milton, the tragedy of Samson develops into a catharsis (cf. Crenshaw, 1978, 121–51).

He appears as a negative figure in the study of G. von Rad, 1974: von Rad continues here a line begun by Martin Luther, cf. for details most recently Crenshaw, esp. 137ff.

PART THREE

APPENDIX ON VARIOUS THEMES
17–21

*

CHAPTERS 17–18

The Migration of Dan and the Origins of its Sanctuary

Bibliography: **Täubler****, 1958, 43–99; R. **de Vaux**, *Les Institutions de l'Ancien Testament* II, Paris 1960, 213–31; ET, *Ancient Israel*, London and New York 1961, 307f., 359; M. **Noth**, 'The Background of Judges 17–18', in *Israel's Prophetic Heritage. Essays in honor of J. Muilenburg*, New York and London 1962, 68–85; A. H. J. **Gunneweg**, *Leviten und Priester*, FRLANT 89, 1965, 14–26; A. **Cody**, *A History of Old Testament Priesthood*, AnBibl 35, 1969; S. **Talmon**, 'In Those Days there was no King in Israel', in *Proceedings of the Fifth World Congress of Jewish Studies, Jerusalem 1969*, I, Jerusalem 1971, 135–43 (in Hebrew, with an English summary); A. **Malamat**, 'The Danite Migration and the Pan-Israelite Exodus-Conquest: A Biblical Narrative Pattern', *Bibl* 51, 1970, 1–16; T. **Veijola**, *Das Königtum in der Beurteilung der deuteronomistischen historiographie*, AASF B–198, 1977, 24–29; F. A. **Spina**, 'The Dan Story Historically Reconsidered', *JSOT* 1.4, 1977, 60–71; F. **Crüsemann**, *Der Widerstand gegen das Königtum*, WMANT 49, 1978, 155ff.

(a) Micah's idol (17.1–6)

17 [1]Once upon a time, in the Mountain of Ephraim, there was a man whose name was Micah. [2,3]One day he said to his mother: 'The eleven hundred shekels of silver which were taken from you and about which you uttered a curse, speaking in such a way that I heard you, "I mean to consecrate this money to Yahweh personally for my son, to make a statue, a metal image," this money is with me; I took it, and now I will restore it to you.' And his mother replied, 'Be blessed by the Lord, my son.' And he restored the eleven hundred shekels of silver to his mother. [4]And she took two hundred shekels, gave them to a founder, and he made them into a statue, a metal image, which was put in Micah's house. [5]This man, Micah, had a shrine and he made an ephod and teraphim; then he consecrated one of his sons to function as priest. [6]In those days, when there was no king in Israel, everyone did what seemed to him to be right.

The Migration of Dan and the Origins of its Sanctuary

Bibliography: **Täubler****, 1958, 43–99; R. **de Vaux**, *Les Institutions de l'Ancien Testament* II, Paris 1960, 213–31; ET, *Ancient Israel*, London and New York 1961, 307f., 359; M. **Noth**, 'The Background of Judges 17–18', in *Israel's Prophetic Heritage. Essays in honor of J. Muilenburg*, New York and London 1962, 68–85; A. H. J. **Gunneweg**, *Leviten und Priester*, FRLANT 89, 1965, 14–26; A. **Cody**, *A History of Old Testament Priesthood*, AnBibl 35, 1969; S. **Talmon**, 'In Those Days there was no King in Israel', in *Proceedings of the Fifth World Congress of Jewish Studies, Jerusalem 1969*, I, Jerusalem 1971, 135–43 (in Hebrew, with an English summary); A. **Malamat**, 'The Danite Migration and the Pan-Israelite Exodus-Conquest: A Biblical Narrative Pattern', *Bibl* 51, 1970, 1–16; T. **Veijola**, *Das Königtum in der Beurteilung der deuteronomistischen historiographie*, AASF B–198, 1977, 24–29; F. A. **Spina**, 'The Dan Story Historically Reconsidered', *JSOT* 1.4, 1977, 60–71; F. **Crüsemann**, *Der Widerstand gegen das Königtum*, WMANT 49, 1978, 155ff.

(a) Micah's idol (17.1–6)

17 [1]Once upon a time, in the Mountain of Ephraim, there was a man whose name was Micah. [2,3]One day he said to his mother: 'The eleven hundred shekels of silver which were taken from you and about which you uttered a curse, speaking in such a way that I heard you, "I mean to consecrate this money to Yahweh personally for my son, to make a statue, a metal image," this money is with me; I took it, and now I will restore it to you.' And his mother replied, 'Be blessed by the Lord, my son.' And he restored the eleven hundred shekels of silver to his mother. [4]And she took two hundred shekels, gave them to a founder, and he made them into a statue, a metal image, which was put in Micah's house. [5]This man, Micah, had a shrine and he made an ephod and teraphim; then he consecrated one of his sons to function as priest. [6]In those days, when there was no king in Israel, everyone did what seemed to him to be right.

[1] 'Mountain of Ephraim': cf. on 3.27. For the 'shekel' see on 8.26. The name of the hero is transmitted in its short form, 'Micah', and a longer one, 'Micah-yahu', as here. It means 'Who (is) like Yahweh?' [2–3] The order of these two verses, although it is confirmed by the ancient translations, will not do. With the majority of commentators (cf. G. F. Moore*, 1895, for the earliest ones) I read 2aα, 3bα, 2aβ, 3bβ, 2b, 3a, thus restoring the text to a logical and probable sequence. Others suggest other possible combinations, while R. G. Boling*, 1975, leaves the text as it is: ". . . about which you swore an oath, and said it in my hearing – look, I have the money. I took it.' And his mother said, 'My son is blessed by Yahweh.' ³He returned . . .' One of the two phrases which indicate that it is restored should certainly be deleted; with Rudolph**, 1947, I choose v. 4a. The consecration of the money is the condition for its restitution: it puts the thief, here the son, in the embarrassing situation of also committing sacrilege. For the double term 'statue-image': the second expression seems to be an explanation of the first (hendiadys), notwithstanding 18.17, cf. there; this seems to be a feature which was misunderstood later (Boling). [5] The inventory of the sacred elements in the verse, cf. v. 4, is excessive and confused (Moore): this is an artificial archaism rather than a genuine memory of antiquity. For the ephod see 8.24–27; the teraphim must have been a kind of household deity, cf. Gen. 31.19–35 and elsewhere. 'A shrine . . .': literally, 'a house of God'. 'Consecrated': *mālē' yād* indicates the investiture, if not the consecration of the priest, connected with his endowment with the means of livelihood; the literal meaning is 'fill the hand'. [6] One of the pro-monarchical phrases, complete here and in 21.25, partial in 18.1; 19.1. The study by T. Veijola, 1977, has made it probable that these originally derive from DtrH: a similar phrase in fact appears in Deut. 12.8–12 in the context of one of the laws about the centralization of the cult. The earlier period is here described as that in which 'everyone did what seemed to him to be right', and is contrasted with the time of centralization. In our texts the figure of the monarch appears in place of the centralization of the cult; furthermore, with a sovereign like Josiah, the monarchy will in fact have been the driving force behind the centralization of the cult. On the other hand, H.-W. Jüngling's theory (140) rejects any connection between the phrase and Dtn, Dtr in this context; in his forthcoming publication (see p. 279 below) he will affirm this in a specific way. In any case, I accept his translation (133). It does not seem probable that *melek* here is synonymous with *šōpēṭ*, as Talmon suggests; he would prefer the phrase to mean: 'At that time there were not yet judges in Israel . . .', so that the episode would be dated after 1.1–2.5.

(b) The levite, Micah's priest (17.7–13)

17 [7]Once there was a young man of Bethlehem in Judah, of a Judahite family; but he was a levite who was settled there as a stranger. [8]The man left the place of Bethlehem in Judah to live where he could find a place; in this way, as he travelled, he came to the Mountain of Ephraim, to the house of Micah. [9]And Micah said to him, 'Where do you come from?' He replied, 'I am a levite of Bethlehem in Judah and I am going to settle wherever I can.' [10]Then Micah proposed to him, 'Settle here with me: you will be to me a father and a priest, and I will give you ten shekels of silver a year, and a change of clothing, and food.' He hesitated, [11]and then agreed to live with the man, for whom the young man was like one of his own sons. [12]Micah consecrated the levite and the young man served as his priest, staying in Micah's house. [13]And Micah said, 'Now I am sure that Yahweh is gracious to me, because I have a levite as priest.'

---

[7] 'Settled . . .': *gēr* is the resident stranger who does not have land of his own; that does not necessarily imply poverty, though the person in question can hardly have been rich. The Hebrew has *gār šām*, but should we not perhaps read *gersōm*, the name of Moses' son, attested later in 18.30 as the ancestor of the priest in question? As well as corresponding with an assured piece of later information, this reading reduces the difficulty presented by the fact that the 'levite' was 'of a Judahite family', cf. the commentary; however, the phrase seems improbable from a stylistic point of view (Gunneweg, 20 n. 3, and Cody, 54 n. 56), and all the probabilities are that 'of a Judahite family' should be deleted, although it is the *lectio difficilior*. According to 18.3, the Danites recognize the levite, so he must have been in touch with Dan. [10] At the end of the verse MT reads, 'The levite went away', *wayyēlek hallēwī*, which does not make sense here. However, LXX[L] and VetLat render, 'He pressed the levite', i.e. *wayyā'eṣ ballēwī*. G. R. Driver**, 1964, 18, proposes a derivation from *lākak* (instead of from *hālak*), a root not attested in Hebrew, but which in Arabic means 'hesitate'; this would produce *wayillāk hallēwī*, which I adopt. 'Father': the term is widespread in the Christian confessions; but cf. especially Arabic-speaking Christians who call their priests *'abbūna*. '. . . a year': for this meaning of *yāmīm*, days, see I Sam. 27.7.[3]

1. The narrative of the migration of Dan towards its own place in the north of the country and the foundation of its sanctuary has been modelled on the pattern of the journey across

---

[3]Cf. among others S. R. Driver, *Notes on the Hebrew Text and the Topography of the Books of Samuel*, Oxford [2]1913, 210, and *KB*[3], s.v. *yōm*, § 7.

the desert and the conquest, of which it forms 'a sort of diminutive model', as A. Malamat has recently noted with some acuteness. It begins with an apparently anecdotal and trivial episode which takes place at the family sanctuary of a certain Micah who lives in an unknown locality in the Mountain of Ephraim, and concerns a levite who is soon employed by him to serve at the sanctuary in question. However, the episode is trivial only in appearance, given that this narrative provides the key for understanding the whole account. In fact this account does not set out to give a chapter of tribal history, but information about the origins, nature and purpose of the sanctuary in question. It is therefore not surprising that we have generic or conventional geographical and topographical indications (cf. 17.1, 8; 18.2), somewhat lightweight figures, and other features of this kind.

The sanctuary of Dan enjoyed a kind of revival and renaissance when on the break-up of the personal union between Israel and Judah which formed the foundation of the empire of David and Solomon, in 926 or 922, it became the national sanctuary of the north, along with that at Bethel. The biblical tradition reports that an artefact was put in the two sanctuaries which the texts disparagingly call a 'golden calf', i.e. an image of a bull, probably of Canaanite origin; in Ugarit, Baal often appears with characteristics of this kind. In I Kings 12.26–33 we find an account of the operation and of the motives which inspired it. The 'calves' in question were probably not representations of the deity: animal statues are attested throughout the ancient Near East (bulls, and others as well), carrying the statue of a deity on their back,[4] and it seems likely enough that we should suppose that at Bethel and Dan, too, the statues were the pedestal on which the God of Israel was raised, though this time invisibly, just as the ark in the Temple at Jerusalem was his throne.[5]

The introduction of these images into the worship of Yahweh

[4]Cf. *ANEP*, nos. 500, 501, 531, 534, 537.
[5]Cf. my study, 'Der offiziell geförderte Synkretismus im Israel während des 10. Jahrhunderts', *ZAW* 78, 1966, 179–203; with some modifications of detail and some necessary updating after twelve years, I still regard this work as valid. The text does not tell us that the image was one of a bull, but this is assumed, and with good reasons, by many authors, cf. among others W. Beyerlin, *Herkunft und Geschichte der ältesten Sinaitraditionen*, Tübingen 1961, 147; ET, *Origins and History of the Earliest Sinaitic Traditions*, Oxford 1965, 156; W. Zimmerli, 'Das Bildverbot in der Geschichte des alten Israel', *Schalom. Studien zu Glaube und Geschichte Israels A. Jepsen . . . dargebracht*, Stuttgart and Berlin 1971, 86–96: 89; cf. the discussion in H. Valentin, *Aaron*, OBO 18, Freiburg CH – Göttingen 1978, 291ff.

is presented by the texts as an innovation due to Jeroboam I
and his advisers. However, Ex. 32.1ff. suggests that the first
'golden calf' had been made in the desert, under Sinai, at the
request of the people, by Aaron, brother of Moses and his
substitute while Moses was on the mountain. Later Aaron would
become the ancestor of the Jerusalem priesthood, cf. P and
Chronicles. Now in Ex. 32.1–6 the narrative seems to be essentially neutral to a cult which Jerusalem later condemned out of
hand.[6] It is therefore not surprising that A. Penna*, 1963, 217,
considered it 'probable that the *pesel* (or statue) of Micah took
the form of a bull . . .'

2. Now the attitude of the present text towards the Danite
sanctuary and what it contains is essentially negative, with
marked ironical thrusts, even if they are sometimes ambiguous
(against J. Gray*, 1967, 237ff. and ad loc.). 17.2f. explicitly
indicates that the silver used for making the sacred objects was
originally stolen and stresses that only a tiny part of the money
when it had been restored was used for these sacred functions:
that implies that the rest of the money was simply pocketed,
though all of it had been consecrated. Again, the account leaves
the door wide open to pejorative ideas about the ultimate origin
of the silver. 17.4f. then lists a series of objects the presence of
which in Israelite worship had been explicitly prohibited: it is
enough to recall that the term *pesel* stands for the idolatrous
image *par excellence* mentioned in the Decalogue, Ex. 20.4–6//
Deut. 5.8–10, and Deutero-Isaiah, cf. Isa. 40.18–20; 44.14–20.
And if it is the case that the priest was a levite, he was completely
dependent on ˏthe patronage first of Micah and then of the
Danites, 17.5, 10ff.; 18.9ff. The framework thus sketched out is
certainly a contrast with the clearly Yahwistic interpretation of
the two chapters, and shows that even under the most favourable
interpretation what we have here is a syncretistic cult. Another
positive element is the mention in 18.30 of the genealogy of the
levite, who unexpectedly is given a name (probably a sign of
the combination of two traditions): Jonathan ben Gershom ben
Manasseh. However, the last name has been written with the
'suspended' *nun* (Hebrew *tᵉlūyāh*) which indicates its precarious
character in the tradition: *mⁿsh*; Gershom appears to be the son

---

[6]On this problem, which I cannot deal with in detail here, cf. the commentaries on
Exodus and recently H. Valentin, op. cit., 205–303.

of Moses, a reading attested by some LXX Mss (but not by LXX^BAL) and by Vg, and confirmed by Rashi.

At the end, 18.30, we find the note about the deportation from the region which took place, as we know, during the campaign of Tiglath-pileser III in 734–732, II Kings 15.29, which provides a *terminus post quem* for the dating of the text.

The account ends by adding some elements to the complex of problems connected with the migration of Dan towards the north, a theme which we considered above, pp. 226ff. The date indicated by 18.30, the conventional character of the narrative (the spies and what they say), the topographical vagueness, the confused and exaggerated list of objects in 17.4f. and the generally ironical tone show that we do not have an ancient tradition here (against A. Vincent*, 1958, who says that the text is 'indisputably old', and others): as M. Noth, art. cit., and A. Cody, op. cit., 52, have rightly pointed out, we can at best suppose that the late redactors used traditional material of Danite origin, but twisted it polemically against Dan and its sanctuary. The composition tries, rather, to answer the question, 'How could the sanctuary of Dan, which boasted a priesthood directly descended from Moses, have been destroyed in the context of the deportation from that region?' The reply does not yet seem to have been that of Dtr (against Veijola, 24ff.): Dtr had in fact spoken decisively of the 'sin of Jeroboam' (I), as it does with any sanctuary in the north; cf. also the fact that here, in contrast to what is said about the north in I Kings 12.31, we have at least a priesthood which is truly levitical. If, then, this were Dtr polemic, the characteristic features of this source would have been more clearly brought out. Here, rather, we have a polemic against this sanctuary which dates from a little before Josiah's reform. And in this polemic it is said that the premises of the sanctuary in question had been false from the beginning: its cult was syncretistic, the money which served to maintain it derived from a theft, and its priesthood, though it boasted a most noble descent, was not free, but subject to patronage.

3. Another problem connected with chs. 17–18 and which reappears in 19–21 is that of the position of the levites in this context: in the first instances we are confronted with a levite 'of a Judahite family' (17.7a), who lived in Judah as a stranger; in the second instance we find a levite who lived as a stranger in the Mountain of Ephraim (19.1). In the first instance I have

rejected a reading 'Gershom'. The problem cannot be resolved at this point, but we can at least try to state it.

In our texts the levites appear as a priestly class, a caste all of whose members are at least potentially capable of acting as priests: furthermore, the first is called to exercise his priesthood because he is particularly qualified; we know nothing of the second, and his qualification as a levite is irrelevant for the purposes of the narrative. Furthermore, the fact that Micah consecrates one of his own sons to function as priest (17.5) in his domestic sanctuary shows that the qualification as a levite was not necessary, although it was something highly to be desired.

Thus we find here an important feature in favour of the theory which would seek to dissociate the levitical priesthood from the tribe of Levi, a tribe which broke up in prehistoric times and in circumstances about which we are ignorant:[7] a levite could thus very well have been a member of another tribe, a feature which the sources later censored because it contradicted the traditional system of biblical tribes which saw Levi as an ethnic group, and it was of course impossible to be a member of more than one tribe. On the other hand, the theory which sees the levites as distinct from the tribe of the same name would also explain why they did not receive a territory of their own but only cities, whose revenue was to serve as their sustenance, cf. Josh. 21.[8] However, the theory leaves at least one important problem open: how did the levites, as a priestly caste and class (a position attested with certainty only from Deut. 18.1–8 onwards, and therefore apparently Dtn or Dtr), come to claim descent from a tribe which was broken up and dispersed even in the prehistoric period? That seems to be the view of the ancient song Gen. 49.5–7: there this dispersion is explicitly claimed as a consequence of their violence, cf. A. Cody, op. cit., 56f., who points this out, affirming, however, that we do not know either the reasons or the circumstances, and Veijola, op. cit., 18ff.

(c) The Danites explore (18.1–7)

18 [1]In those times there was no king in Israel; and in those times the tribe of Dan was looking for a territory in which to settle, because

[7]For example E. Nielsen, *Shechem, a Traditio-Historical Investigation*, Copenhagen 1955, 28, and A. H. J. Gunneweg, op. cit., 16ff., 28, 33f.
[8]Cf. my *Joshua*, ad loc.

up to that time they had not received a territory among the tribes of Israel. [2]The Danites sent five men, mighty warriors, from their group, from their borders, from Zorah and Eshtaol, to explore, to spy out the country. And they gave them the following instructions: 'Go and spy out the country.' And they arrived at the Mountain of Ephraim, at Micah's house, and there they spent the night. [3]When they were near Micah's house, they recognized the voice of the young levite. They turned aside towards the place and asked him, 'Who made you come here? What are you doing here and what is your business?' [4]He replied to them, 'Micah has done this and that for me; he has hired me and so I have become his priest.' [5]Then they said, 'Inquire of God so that he will show if he will give success on the journey on which we are engaged.' [6]The priest said to them, 'Go in peace. The journey on which you go is under the watch of Yahweh.' [7]The five men then continued their journey and arrived at Laish, a place which dwelt in security, and they saw the people who lived there, peaceful and trusting, according to the custom of the Sidonians; in that region with its rich produce they lacked nothing. They were far from the Sidonians and did not have dealings with Aram.

---

[1] It is difficult to say whether this verse means to indicate that in fact Dan had not received any territory; however, this hypothesis must be taken seriously in view of the inadequate descriptions of the territories in question, descriptions which exist in this way only because the theory of the tribal league wanted all the tribes but one, Levi (and therefore even those tribes which had already disappeared by historical times, Reuben and Simon), along with certain allied groups, to have received a territory (cf. above, pp. 26ff.). If this theory is valid, then the settlement of the group to the west of Benjamin will not have been on a territory of its own; in the most favourable of cases it will have been leading a semi-nomadic existence in the region in question. 'A territory': preceded the second time by a *b'-* which does not make sense and which I have therefore deleted with all the ancient translations. For the expressions used cf. G. R. Driver**, 1964, 18. [2] The theme of the spies (here sent out with two verbs which duplicate each other, a fact which some scholars have understood as evidence of the existence of two sources: one which speaks of five spies from two places, the other with warriors from the whole of one tribe, cf. G. F. Moore*, 1897, and others) is common to many stories, ancient and less ancient, in the Old Testament, cf. Num. 13; Josh. 2; and, outside the Old Testament, *Odyss.* IX. 85–102 (the

Lotus Eaters). In the Old Testament the genre has the aim of
creating trust or blaming someone who does not have it. 'From
their borders': this redundant phrase is missing in LXX and
some scholars want to delete it; others consider it part of the
second, parallel version. In Judges, 'Zorah and Eshtaol' are
connected with the figure of Samson, but in the phase of the
theological redaction of its traditions; cf. also the generic and
conventional character of the topographical indications in this
text. Typical of this interpretation is also the fact that the text
does not say where Micah had his house, but that the spies
immediately find the place. **[3]** 'Recognized': they must therefore have known him well, for reasons which are not given. He
lived in the sanctuary, a building near to Micah's house (within
calling distance), but not identical with it and not situated on
the main road. **[5]** 'If he will give success': MT has the causative, but either the third person feminine or the second person
masculine, with the deity as subject, which does not make much
sense: either the subject is the journey, in which case we must
read $h^a ti\d{s}la\d{h}$ (qal), or if we want to keep the deity as subject (as
I do), we must read $hi\d{s}l\bar{\imath}^a\d{h}$. 'Inquire': the formula $\check{s}\bar{a}'al\ b^e\text{-}X$
(the name of the deity) is a technical term for inquiring by
means of an oracle; here probably the ephod and teraphim
which are mentioned. Note how the Danites talk of *$^*l\bar{o}h\bar{\imath}m$* and
the priest of Yahweh. **[7]** A difficult verse, either because it is
full of technical expressions unknown to us or because it is
corrupt. 'Dwelt in security' is to be transposed after Laish as it
is in the feminine; or the feminine must be emended. 'According
to the custom of the Sidonians' seems to indicate that this was
a place with Phoenician customs, whose inhabitants were un-
interested in war, being concerned, rather, with agriculture and
commerce. 'Laish', then Dan: present-day *tell el-qādi* or *tell dan*
(the two terms have the same meaning in Arabic and in Hebrew,
'judge') is the Leshem of Josh. 19.47,[9] the latter with a final
mem, the former with a diphthong which has not been contracted
(coord. 211–294). From the beginning of the 1960s it has been
the object of excavations by an Israeli expedition directed by A.
Biran. 'Lacked nothing': with v. 10 and some commentaries I
have corrected w^e'ēn maḥsōr kōl dābār; MT has a strange
expression which is, however, defended by Boling*, 1975: 'With-

---

[9]*Joshua*, ad loc. For the excavations at Tell Dan see the provisional report by A. Biran,
'Tel Dan', *BA* 37, 1974, 26–51.

out anyone usurping the power to make them ashamed', with the root *nākal*, never used elsewhere as it is here. 'Aram': the mention of the Phoenicians to the west makes a mention of the Aramaeans to the north and east probable, cf. LXX^A: μετὰ Συρίας, rather than *'ādām* ('did not have dealings with any human being'). The confusion between *reš* and *dālet* is frequent in a manuscript text. Thus there are two factors in the prosperity of Laish: the fertility of the soil and its distance both from enemies and from friends who might claim some sort of tribute from the place, and therefore the fact that nothing had to be expended on military affairs. The two factors will be the reason for the fall of the city.

(d) The beginning of the Danite migration (18.8–13)

18 [8]The spies returned to their brothers at Zorah and Eshtaol and these asked, 'So what . . .?' [9]They replied, 'We went and passed through the country as far as Laish. We saw that the people who lived there dwelt in security, according to the customs of the Sidonians, and did not have dealings with Aram. Arise, let us march against them: we have seen that their land is very fertile. Do you hesitate? Do not delay when leaving to enter and take possession of the country. [10]When you arrive, you will come upon a trusting people; the land is broad and God has intended it for you. It is a place which does not lack anything that exists on earth.'

11 Then they set out from there, from the Danite region, from Zorah and Eshtaol, six hundred men, each armed with his weapons of war. [12]They went up and encamped at Kiriath-jearim in Judah, because of which the place is called 'the camp of Dan' to this day: it is to the east of Kiriath-jearim. [13]From there they went to the Mountain of Ephraim, arriving at Micah's house.

---

[8] 'What . . .?': the phrase, literally, 'What do you . . .?' has sometimes been thought to be incomplete, cf. Burney*, 1919, who suggests adding *'ittem*, 'What (have you brought) with you?', others *mah m'šībīm dābār*, 'What news have you brought back?' (Moore*, 1897); LXX has τί ὑμεῖς καθήσθε, i.e. *mahšīm* or *yōš'bīm*, wrongly read for *m'šībīm*. However, as W. Rudolph**, 1947, and G. R. Driver**, 1964, point out, cf. *BHS*, in Ruth 3.16 we have the expression *mī 'att*, 'What news?', or 'How did it go?', which also gives the best sense here, cf. Vg *quid egissent*. [9] 'Arise!', Hebrew *qūmāh*, not to be emended: it is a stereotyped interjection (Burney*, 1919), like our 'Come on'. 'Let us march against them . . .': not to be emended; a whole phrase has fallen out which we can restore with LXX^AL, Vincent*, 1958: 'We

went ... Aram'. C. F. Burney*, 1919, brings out the phrase in extended form, thinking it probable that it is the original. In this case there is no problem. **[12]** 'Kiriath-jearim': present-day *dēr el ʿazar*, near *abu-ḡōš*, in the vicinity of the modern motorway to Jerusalem (coord. 159–135, cf. Josh. 9.17; 15.8).[10]

(e) The capture of Micah's image (18.14–21)

18 [14]Then the five men who had gone to spy out the country explained to their brothers, 'Do you know that in these buildings there are an ephod and teraphim, a statue and a metal image? Now think what you should do!' [15]They turned aside from the way in that direction and arrived at the house of the young levite, at the house of Micah, and asked him how he was. [16]The six hundred men of the Danites, armed with their weapons of war, stood guard at the entrance to the gate. [17]And the five men who had gone to explore the region went up and entered and took the statue of the ephod and the teraphim and the metal image, while the priest stood at the entrance of the gate together with the six hundred men armed with their weapons of war. [18]Then they entered Micah's house and took the statue of the ephod, the teraphim and the metal image. But the priest said to them, 'What are you doing?' [19]They replied, 'Keep quiet, put your hand on your mouth, and come with us: you shall be to us a father and a priest. Is it better for you to be the priest of the house of one man, or to be one for a tribe and a clan of Israel?' [20]This thing pleased the priest, who took the ephod, the teraphim and the statue and went along with the people. [21]They resumed their journey and left, taking the women, the children, the animals and the baggage with them.

---

[14] 'Explained': *ʿānāh*ı always means 'reply' to a question, but here there is no question. We must therefore assume either that the original question has fallen out, which is improbable, or that in some circumstances the verb can mean 'explain', 'clarify'. 'The country': in MT, in LXX and Vg it is followed by 'Laish', an obvious mistaken gloss which was meant to explain which country. I have deleted it, with some LXX MSS. **[15]** 'At the house of Micah': above, at v. 3, the house of the levite and the temple seem to be separate from Micah's house, though they form a single complex: one is on the road, and the other is off it, cf. here vv. 21f. It may be a secondary gloss, also wrong, now attested by all translations. **[16]** 'The Danites' is at the end of the verse, but is to be transposed here. **[17]** 'Went up': we do not know the topography of the house and the sanctuary, so we cannot

[10] *Joshua*, ad loc.

know if they were on a height, or if the sanctuary was situated on the upper floor of a building with the levite living on the lower floor. It is therefore wiser to follow some scholars (W. Rudolph**, 1947, cf. *BHK*³ and *BHS*) in correcting it to *wayyō'ilū*, 'approached . . .' 'And entered . . . took': the conjunction is absent in Hebrew, giving rise to what some scholars call a heavy asyndeton: therefore some suggest reading *laqaḥat* . . . 'to take'. 'The statue . . . the image' appear here and in v. 18 as two distinct objects, probably because the hendiadys (cf. above, 17.2f.) has been completely misunderstood here (Boling*, 1975) and unusual terms have therefore been repeated. MT seems to want to remedy things by reading ' . . . the statue of the ephod', an expression which seems absurd. LXX has a shorter text with few repetitions, another attempt to remedy the confused and repetitive character of the text. **[21]** 'The women': added with Vincent*, 1958, and Penna*, 1963; for the tactics cf. on Gen. 33.2; the other passages cited by Vincent, Deut. 2.34 and 3.6, are not relevant because they refer to the ban. 'Baggage': Hebrew *kᵉbûddāh* (sic); the masculine, 'riches', appears in Gen. 31.1; Isa. 10.3 and 61.6: the literal meaning is 'what is heavy'.

(f) Micah's reaction (18.22–26)

18 ²²When they were some way from Micah's house, the men who were in the buildings near the house gave the alarm and set off in pursuit of the Danites. ²³They shouted at them, and they simply turned round and said to Micah, 'What has happened for you to make so much noise?' ²⁴He replied to them: 'You have taken the gods which I have made and the priest and have gone away, and what do I have left? And then you can ask, "What has happened?"' ²⁵The Danites replied, 'Do not make too much of a fuss near us; there may be impulsive people who will fall upon you so that you lose your life and the lives of your people!' ²⁶So the Danites continued on their way, and when Micah saw that they were too strong for him, he turned back and went home.

---

[22] 'Gave the alarm' or 'called each other out', cf. on 4.12. **[25]** 'Impulsive men . . .': literally 'bitter in spirit'. The phrase is sarcastic and recalls the reply which malefactors of all times and all places have given to their victims.

(g) The conquest of Laish (18.27–31)

18 ²⁷So they took what Micah had made and the priest whom he had employed and came near to Laish, the place of the quiet and trusting people; they put them to the edge of the sword and set fire to the city. [28]No one succeeded in escaping because it was far from Sidon and had no dealings with the Aramaeans. It was situated in the valley belonging to Beth-rehob. Here they rebuilt the city and lived in it. [29]They called the city Dan after the name of Dan, their eponymous ancestor who was a son of Israel; once, however, in ancient days, the city was called Laish. [30]There the Danites set up the statue and Jonathan, sone of Gershom, son of M-(n)-s-h, he and his descendants, were the priests for the tribe of Dan until the time when people were deported from the region. [31]Thus they set up for their own use the statue which Micah had made, for all the time that there was a sanctuary in Shiloh.

---

[27] What . . .': for some the object is too indeterminate, and they suggest inserting *hā'ᵉlōhīm* or *happesel*; however, it seems to be a comprehensive expression. 'Near': for this meaning of *'al* cf. on 7.1. It is not necessary to emend, as is already done by some fragments with Palestinian vocalization.[11] [28] 'Aramaeans' instead of 'humanity', cf. on 18.7. *bēt rᵉhōb*: an Aramaean state mentioned in I Sam. 14.47 (LXX); II Sam. 10.8, cf. Num. 13.21 (which, however, puts it further north: might that be another one?). The place has not yet been identified with certainty, but it is possible, hypothetically, to connect it with present-day *banyas* (coord. 295–214) on the north-western Golan, from 1967 under Israeli military administration. 'Belonging to . . .' (*'ᵃšer lᵉ-*) seems to indicate the existence of the state in question. In the tenth century BC it was defeated and subjected by David (II Sam. 10.6ff.). [29] 'After the name . . .': it is unnecessary to emend *bᵉšēm*: the preposition sometimes has this meaning, as in Ugaritic. 'Israel': cf. Gen. 30.6 and other passages. [30] For the patronym of the priests and the events referred to here cf. on 17.7–13, § 2, pp. 268f. Unexpectedly, the levite has a name, a fact noted for a long time and which Veijola, 19ff., says is 'surprising'; is this perhaps DtrH? [31] The mention of Shiloh has always been a *crux interpretum* for scholars, who have proposed either the metathesis ŠL(H) – LŠ, or the vocalization *bᵉšalwāh*, 'while it was intact', Rudolph**, 1947, *BHK³*, and *BHS*. The difficulty lies in the fact that it is generally believed that Shiloh was destroyed following the events described in I Sam. 4, events referred to in Jer. 7.12//26.9. Reports of the excavations which came out a few years ago,[12] however, show that there is no sign that the place and its temple were destroyed at the end of the eleventh century BC, and if in I Kings 11.29 we have a prophet called Ahijah of Shiloh it is a sign that the place existed and was inhabited and that its

[11]Cf. B. Chiesa, *L'Antico Testamento ebraico secondo la tradizione palestinese*, Turin 1978, 165.

[12]M.-L. Buhl, S. Holm-Nielsen, *Shilo*, Copenhagen 1969, 56–9.

sanctuary was in use; furthermore, it is never said in I Sam. 4 that the place or its sanctuary had been destroyed. No correction of the text is therefore necessary.

1. Above, pp. 266ff., we examined the problems connected with a stay of Dan in a tribal territory situated to the west of Benjamin and its migration from there northwards: in the best of circumstances, as we have seen, this will have been a precarious stay and will have been connected with the semi-nomadic period of the group; cf. also 18.1, which seems to affirm that Dan never had a territory of its own among the tribes of Israel.[13] However, the purpose of this text is to describe the sanctuary of Dan in the north of the region and to explain why it fell and the people were deported. These explanations clearly want to show the theologically syncretistic character of the sanctuary in question and hence its invalidity, along with the doubtful moral basis on which it was founded (theft, sacrilege, broken promises, physical violence, etc.). It was therefore a sanctuary which our text does not condemn in general terms because it was situated outside Jerusalem, but which it condemns because of the irremediable vices connected with its origins. Thus its destruction and the deportation of its unworthy priesthood along with the inhabitants of the region were fully deserved (G. W. Ahlström). This theory emerges from the text with remarkable force and with clearly humorous touches; the dialogue between Micah and the Danites is a good example of this, cf. 18.24–26; the scene with the unanswerable argument, 'the argument which cannot be refuted', put to the levite in almost Mafia-like terms (18.19), is also humorous, as is the phrase, 'Keep quiet . . .' However, the effectiveness of the account is lessened by the confusion in the text, which is full of redundancies and repetitions. Still, the general lines of the story run well, given its basic premise: what else could the Danites expect but divine judgment? Although this theory may be Dtn or date from a little before that, it seems to be typical of the great historical synthesis of the Old Testament.

2. However, there are some missing links between the account and the description of the foundation of the sanctuary which the redactors have had some difficulty in remedying. We have seen how the levite, who is at first anonymous, is suddenly given a

name, and not just any old name at that. In addition, the *pesel*
which the Danites put up in their sanctuary does not seem to
be completely identical with that of the narrative (vv. 30f.): it
is not a metal image; there are no ephod and teraphim, although
18.18f. says expressly that 'they took them'. Therefore there is
some degree of tension between the narrative and the conclusion
which shows, if nothing else, the way in which the whole complex is a compilation. It is a complex which has come into being
as a kind of *hieros logos* of the overthrow: instead of legitimating
the existence of a sanctuary, telling its origin in miraculous
circumstances, it serves to disqualify a sanctuary, describing its
pagan and morally perverse origins which provides the reason
for its destruction in 734–732.[14]

[14]The shakiness of this information from the historical point of view has been remarked
by N. H. Tur-Sinai, *Pᵉšūtō šel miqrā'* II, Jerusalem 1964, 97.

The Civil War against Benjamin

Bibliography: M. **Noth**, *Das System der zwölf Stämme Israels*, BWANT IV.1, 1930, 162ff.; O. **Eissfeldt**, 'Der geschichtliche Hintergrund der Erzählung von Gibeas Schandtat (Richter 19–21)', in *Festschrift Georg Beer zum 70. Geburstag*, Stuttgart 1935, 19–40 = *KlSchr* II, 1963, 64–80; G. **Wallis**, 'Eine Parallele zu Richter 19,29ff. und I Sam. 11,5ff. aus dem Briefarchiv von Mari', *ZAW* 64, 1952, 57–61; G. **Fohrer**, 'Tradition und Interpretation im Alten Testament', *ZAW* 73, 1961, 1–30:17; H.-J. **Kraus**, *Gottesdienst in Israel*, Munich ²1962; ET *Worship in Israel*, Oxford and Richmond, Va. 1966, 173–7; G. **Wallis**, 'Die Anfänge des Königtums in Israel', *WZ(H)* 12, 1962-63, 239–47 = *Geschichte und Überlieferung*, Berlin and Stuttgart 1968, 45–65; K.-D. **Schunck**, *Benjamin*, BZAW 86, 1963, 57–79; H. **Reventlow**, 'Kultisches Recht im Alten Testament', *ZTK* 60, 1963, 267–304, esp. 291ff.; A. **Besters**, 'Le sanctuaire central dans Jud. XIX-XXI', *EThL* 41, 1965, 20–41; J. **Dus**, 'Bethel und Mispa in Jdc. 19–21 und Jdc. 10–12', *OrAnt* 3, 1964, 227–43; H. **Rösel****, 1976, 31ff.; S. **Springer**, *Neuinterpretationen im Alten Testament*, Stuttgart 1979, 19ff; W. Jüngling, *Richter 19 – Ein Plädoyer für das Königtum*, AnBibl 84, Rome 1981; F. **Crüsemann**, *Der Widerstand gegen das Königtum*, WMANT 49, Neukirchen 1978, 155ff.; M. **Liverani**, 'Messaggi, donne, ospitalità; communicazione intertribale in Giud. 19–21', *Studi storico-religiosi* (formerly *SMSH*), 3, 1979, 303–41

1. Leaving aside a few odd features here and there, at first sight this text gives an impression of unity and coherence; it could be considered a source of prime importance for the historian, and in fact has been evaluated at such even by those who recognize the existence of material of a novelistic or anecdotal type, for example the quarrel between husband and wife and their reconciliation, the courage of the man who entertains strangers in difficulty, the good proposals and feelings of justice infringed shown by the assembly, and the stratagems used to renew the tribe of Benjamin after its severe losses in war. In fact

the narrative runs very well except in 20.29–46 (where, however, as we shall see, two narratives have been combined into one): a young couple on the way home is assaulted by a group of toughs in the place where they are staying the night; the husband manages to escape, but the wife dies as a result of the maltreatment that she receives. The case is put before the inter-tribal authority (and here we would have a notable feature in favour of the theory of the sacral alliance of the tribes of Israel), which after having expressed its condemnation of the act with harsh words, invites the inhabitants of the place, or otherwise the tribe to which they belong, to hand over those responsible to the tribunal, so that they can be judged and condemned in accordance with the current inter-tribal law. When the responsible ruling groups refuse, a punitive expedition is launched against the tribe which showed its solidarity with the authors of such a crime, as a result of which a few survivors of the tribe are all that remain. That could happen because here, as in chs. 17–18, there was not yet a king and each one did what he thought to be right.

However, a closer inspection soon shows the presence of some contradictory features. The chief of these is certainly the pro-monarchical formula, complete in 17.6 and 21.25, partial in 18.1 and 19.1 (cf. above on 17.6). This is a phrase which, as we have seen, has recently and authoritatively been attributed to DtrH, the earliest, pro-monarchical phase of the Dtr redaction. However, while the phrase fits well with the situation existing in chs. 17–18, where in fact we find examples of political and religious licence, it seems to be particularly ill-chosen for chs. 19–21: here the existence of an inter-tribal assembly is actually affirmed, an assembly which judges controversies that have broken out among the various members and whose decisions appear to be binding on all, so much so that if necessary they are implemented by force of arms. Thus the phrase 'in those days . . . everyone did what seemed to him to be right' seems somewhat inappropriate to indicate what happened in that era, at least according to the different opinion of the pro-monarchical redaction. Anyone who violated certain legal norms applying in the sphere of the tribal league was severely punished, and the severest penalties were meted out on those who gave refuge to the malefactors and impeded their extradition: in this particular case they amounted to the virtual extermination of a whole tribe and, moreover, during the critical period of the conquest. And from the phrase reported in 19.30 and 20.6, it appears that this was an ancient and accepted custom. So not only were there severe laws, but there was also an institution which passed judgment and secured respect for the law, if necessary by force, 20.11.

On the other hand, as Veijola has shown to be probable (for doubts and opposition cf. above on 17.6), the pro-monarchical remark given here, as in the preceding chapters, reflects the earliest, pro-monarchical phase of Dtr, DtrH; if this theory proves to be valid, it would then seem to be a logical deduction that the texts which presuppose an alternative institution to the monarchy, the tribal league (which M. Noth used to refer to as the 'amphictyony'), and contradict what has gone before, could belong to the late and anti-monarchical phase of the Dtr redaction, DtrN, which would evidently have used earlier material for its elaborations. We cannot follow this interesting problem in detail here; it is enough to point to its existence and to hope that a monograph or a thesis will produce the necessary clarity in this area. I accept that in the two instances we are faced with a relatively late phase of the tradition in comparison with the period in which the events described took place; this is therefore a different situation from the one which we find in connection with the narratives contained in the second part of the book, which now have a Dtr framework.

2. However, there are other features. First of all there is the utter disproportion between the crime and the punishment, a feature which was already noted, not without irony, by J. Wellhausen.[1] Then, the historian will automatically make a distinction between the account of the personal misfortunes of the young levite and his wife (ch. 19), and that of the expedition against the Benjaminites, followed by the extermination of the majority of the tribe: the former is a family-type anecdotal account followed by a tragic ending, which is probably early, as it is already noted in Hos. 9.9; 10.9; the latter is concerned with an essentially political problem, that of the civil war between Benjamin and its neighbours. There are other features: the summoning of the assembly (19.29f.; 20.1–11); the first battles (20.18–28); and finally the two parallel attempts (which is what

[1]F. ʾBleek, *Einleitung in das Alte Testament,* ed. J. Wellhausen, Berlin ⁴1878, 201; O. Kaiser, *Einleitung in das Alte Testament,* Wiesbaden ³1975, 141; ET, *Introduction to the Old Testament,* Oxford and Minneapolis 1975, 150; the theory is discussed in detail by H.W. Jüngling in his dissertation (see above, p. 279), p. 314 n. 1044 (p. 189).

they are, cf. ad loc.) to provide women for the Benjaminites so that the tribe does not become completely extinct (21.1–14, 15–26). These are features which in essence are purely narrative; they satisfy what in German is referred to as the *Lust zum fabulieren*,[2] and partly serve to establish a logical network, composed, especially in 20.1–17, of essentially Dtr elements (Jüngling, 329–35), between two narratives which originally had nothing to do with one another.

3. Now there can be no doubt that the first of the two narratives seems somewhat irrelevant from the point of view of the historian and is, rather, a literary 'novel'; furthermore, the narrator has drawn considerably on Gen. 19 (for a synopsis cf. C. F. Burney*, 1919, 444f.), but without much coherence. For example, the theme of homosexual violence, basic to Gen. 19 and therefore developed coherently, cf. vv. 5–7, from which only a miraculous intervention can rescue the destined victim, vv. 10f., appears only briefly in Judg. 19, but is irrelevant and does not produce any effect, given that the toughs are content to rape the woman (v. 25), leaving the levite and his servant alone. The narrator has also drawn on I Sam. 11.9, cf. Judg. 19.29, as has been noted for some time (see again the synopsis in Burney, 445); however, in I Sam. the rite has an obvious symbolism: woe to those who do not respond to Saul's call to arms! However, in this instance the symbolism seems to be missing: the quartered limbs of the concubine are not a summons to arms, nor do they threaten the reluctant; they simply arouse horror. Such a macabre gesture is not only unnecessary for summoning the assembly; it does not even seem to serve a useful purpose. In any case, after their condemnation by the assembly, the Benjaminites could have handed over the guilty ones and justice could have taken its course. In the case of Judg. 19 the rite therefore seems to be connected with the assembly and that could point to the latest redactional phase, DtrN.

4. On the other hand, the passage about the civil war could be historically important; not so much for the details reported here, as we shall see, as for the event in itself. In fact it is connected with the tradition which sees Benjamin as having been a group which at the same time was reduced, but warlike and valiant. Furthermore, the episode of the campaign against Jabesh, 21.2ff., refers to an element which is also attested else-

---

[2]Cf. my *Introduction to the Old Testament*, London and Philadelphia ²1980, 52.

where: that there were friendly and supportive relations between Benjamin and Jabesh. In I Sam. 11.1–14, esp. 4ff., the men of Jabesh send a delegation first of all the Gibeah of Saul, whereas in 31.11–13 it is they who recover the desecrated remains of Saul and his sons who had fallen in battle and give them honourable burial; cf. again II Sam. 2.4b-7, where this feature is connected with a letter of praise which David is said to have written to them. Nor does it seem to be a coincidence that Saul's successor, Ishbaal, and his commander Abner, took refuge in Transjordan, about twenty kilometres further south, II Sam. 2.8. And the bones of Saul and his sons remained at Jabesh until David had them brought home (II Sam. 21.12–14), a passage which is now connected with the preceding context in a somewhat precarious way.

5. The problem of the war between Benjamin and its neighbours is more complex. Here we have the study of O. Eissfeldt, published in the middle of the 1930s and still accepted by a number of writers; his theory seems quite plausible. The narrative is based on an essentially political feature: the need for Benjamin to assert its own independence, situated as it was between Joseph (Ephraim) and Judah. These attempts will have ended with a national catastrophe: the destruction of the greater part of the tribe. If we accept that it prefaced the narrative even in ancient times, the outrage at Gibeah will have simply had the function of concealing the political motives inherent in the event and of translating it into a mere question of crime and punishment: facts of this kind do not cause war, but they can justify it on an ethical level.

(a) The levite and his concubine (19.1–9)

19 [1]In those days, when there was no king in Israel, there was a levite who had settled as a stranger in the most remote area of the Mountain of Ephraim. He had taken as concubine a woman from Bethlehem in Judah. [2]But the concubine quarrelled with him and left him, to return home to her father's house in Bethlehem; and there she stayed for a certain length of time: four months. [3]One day her husband went to see her, to speak reasonably with her and to persude her to return home with him. He had with him a young servant and a couple of asses. As soon as he arrived at her father's house, he saw him and came out with joy to meet him. [4]And his father-in-law, the girl's father, made him stay, and he stayed with him for three days. They ate there, drank and spent the night there. [5]On the fourth day they got up early and prepared to leave, but the father of the girl said to his son-in-law, 'Refresh yourself with a bite of food before you go your way.' [6]So the two men sat down and ate and drank; then the father of the girl said to the man, 'Come, spend the night here and enjoy yourself.' [7]The man was all ready to leave, but his father-in-law insisted so much that he sat down again and spent the night there. [8]At dawn on the fifth day they got up to leave, but the father of the girl said, 'Stay again.' And they remained until the end of the day; they both ate and drank. [9]Then the man, the concubine and the young servant got up to go, but the father-in-law, the girl's father, said to them, 'Look, the day is waning and it is late; please stay this time also and spend the night here and enjoy yourselves; then tomorrow you can get up, leave and return home.'

---

[1] For the phrase about the monarchy cf. on 17.6: the slightly different wording serves as a connecting link between chs. 17–18 and chs. 19–21. ' . . . a levite': Hebrew *'îš lēwî*: the fact that the young man is a levite is unimportant for the purpose of the narrative, so much so that K. Budde*, 1897 and others, following him, suggest deleting it (Jüngling, 1976, is the most recent to favour this). 'Concubine': Hebrew *pîlegeš*, for which cf. on 8.21. 'Stranger': in the construct state before the *nomen regens*, an emphatic form, cf. Jüngling, 134. This is a piece of stylistic finesse which exploits the potentiality of the language to the full. Note the general anonymity. [2] 'Quarrelled': Hebrew *zānāh*II, cf. the Accadian *zenū* (*KB*[3], s.v.), LXX[A] ὠργίσθη and Tg 'scorned him'; LXX[B] has ἐπορεύθη, 'he went away'; medieval Hebrew exegesis also took it in this sense (Moore*, 1897). In no way can this be *zānāh*I, 'practise prostitution', in the sense of 'betrayed him'. A. Vincent*, 1958, puts it well: 'Dans un moment de colère . . . le quitta . . .' The responsibility for the matrimonial crisis, on which the text gives us no information, must have lain with the husband, at least in view of his later behaviour; however, the cause of the quarrel cannot have been very serious, if the wife and the father-in-law are so glad to be reconciled. Jüngling, 153, provides a very interesting piece of information: the initiative for the separation begins with the woman, a singular instance in the Old Testament where it is only the man who has the right to repudiate her; however, similar norms exist in Codex Hammurabi, art. 142, cf. *ANET*, 172. 'A certain length of time: four months': syntactically rather a clumsy sentence. However, in some ancient manuscripts with Palestinian vocalization we read . . . *yāmîm w'arbā'āh ḥŏdāšîm*,[3] i.e., ' . . . and here she stayed for one year and four months' (for this meaning of *yāmîm* see on

---

[3]See recently B. Chiesa, *L'Antico Testamento ebraico secondo la tradizione palestinese*, Turin 1978, 166, 315ff.

17.10). This is certainly a much better phrase syntactically; perhaps it should replace MT. [3] 'Reasonably': literally, 'to his heart', which in the metaphorical usage of the context in the Semitic languages is the seat of the reason and not the emotions, cf. Hos. 2.16; Isa. 40.2 and other passages. 'Persuade her to return . . .'; with Q *lah*ᵃ*šībāh*; K has *lah*ᵃ*šibō*, referring to the heart. The sense is the same. 'Arrived': I read *wayyābō'* with LXX^A instead of 'and she introduced him . . .' an improbable formulation (despite the arguments put forward by Jüngling, 166), in view of what follows. [4] 'His father-in-law': as we have seen at 1.16 and elsewhere, *ḥōtēn* is an ambiguous term and needs to be made more precise. There is therefore no duplication or repetition here. Note the particularly affectionate atmosphere. 'Made him . . .': root *ḥāzaq*; for the expression cf. Jüngling, 171. 'Spent the night': meaning the man and the concubine, together again: the expression seems to be a euphemism for the resumption of matrimonial relations, cf. also vv. 6b, 9b. Thus the reconciliation is complete, as is also shown by the cordial and hospital attitude of the father-in-law, vv. 5f. [5] 'Refresh': root *sāʿad* (probably read *sᵉʿod*, cf. Gen. 18.5, with Burncy, ad loc.). The change in number should not cause difficulties: the invitation is addressed to the woman and her husband, and everyone is prepared to leave, including the animals. [7] 'Sat': read *wayyāšeb*, from *yašab*, for *wayyāšōb*, from *šwb*. But cf. the discussion and the alternatives proposed in the commentaries and in Jüngling, 200ff. [8] 'They remained': with LXX^B and all the commentaries; MT has the imperative 'remain', but the father cannot invite the son-in-law and the daughter to remain until the evening, given that this was no longer the time of departure. [9] 'Please . . .': with LXX^AL: κατάλυσον (δὴᴸ) ὧδε ἐπὶ σήμερον; LXX^B, on the other hands, omits the second reference to staying the night and to the end of the day; for this last reading cf. W. Rudolph**, 1947; G. R. Driver**, 1964 (who, moreover, considers the expression here, as elsewhere, to be a gloss), and now H.-W. Jüngling, 206f. 'Home': literally, 'to your tent'.

(*b*) The arrival at Gibeah (19.10–21)

19 ¹⁰The man would not pass another night there, but got up and went, arriving opposite Jebus (which is Jerusalem); he had with him the couple of saddled asses and also his concubine. ¹¹So they were near Jebus, and the day was almost over. Then the young servant said to his master. 'Come now, let us turn aside towards this Jebusite city to spend the night.' ¹²But his master replied, 'We will not turn aside to a foreign city, of people who have nothing to do with the Israelites. Instead, we will try to get as far as Gibeah.' ¹³Then he said to his servant, 'Come, and let us try to arrive at one of these places where we can spend the night, Gibeah or Ramah.' ¹⁴So they continued their journey while the sun had set, and arrived at Gibeah which belongs to Benjamin. [15]They turned aside to the place to spend the night there. The levite went and sat in the square of the city, but no one invited them home to spend the night. [16]And behold, coming back from his work in the fields, late, there was an old man: he was a native of the Mountain of Ephraim and had settled as a stranger in Gibeah (the inhabitants of the place were Benjaminites). [17]No sooner had the old man seen a wayfarer in the square than he said to him, 'Where are you going and where do you come from?' [18]He replied: 'We come from Bethlehem in Judah and we are going to the furthest part of the Mountain of Ephraim. I come from there, but I have been to Bethlehem in Judah. [19]I have straw and fodder for our asses and food and drink for me, for your maidservant and for the boy who is with your servant; we do not lack anything.'[20] Then the old man said, 'Welcome. I will care for all your needs. Only do not spend the night in the square.' [21]And he brought him into his house and gave him fodder for the asses. They washed their feet, ate and drank.

---

[10] 'And also. . .': LXX[L] and other versions add, 'and his young servant', probably rightly. [11] 'Over': Hebrew *rad*, root *rādad*, 'finish', 'extinguish, be extinguished'; or should we read *yārad*, 'had declined, waned'? However, this is a verb which is never used to indicate sunset. 'Jebus': the term used by the biblical tradition for Jerusalem before its conquest by David; we usually find the term Jebusites, hence this term. We find it as the name of the place only here and in I Chron. 11.4f. On the basis of the biblical information it is often regarded as the name of the city down to its conquest by David, or at least in the period which immediately preceded it. However, the name Jerusalem (Accadian URU–*sālim* or *urusālim*) is already attested in the el-'Amarna archive (fourteenth century) and in the Egyptian execration texts (nineteenth to eighteenth century bc), while Jebus never appears, cf. Jüngling, 210: 'As far as we know, Jerusalem probably never bore the name Jebus.' According to a recent study,[4] Jebus is distinct from Jerusalem, of which it is simply a northern suburb; it is probably present-day *ša'fat* (coord. 172–145). However, Jebusites could live in Jerusalem, which may have caused confusion; and it is not in fact said that this text seeks to identify the two places. [12] 'Gibeah' and 'Ramah' of the following verse : these are places in the southern part of the central highlands; the first, cf. Josh. 18.28, is perhaps present-day *tell el-fūl*, about 6 km. north of Jerusalem and a few yards east of the main road (coord. 172–136); the identification was considered certain until a few years ago, but in 1970 even W. F.

[4]J.M. Miller, 'Jebus and Jerusalem: a Case of Mistaken Identity', *ZDPV* 90, 1974, 115–27.

Albright, Prolegomenon to C. F. Burney*, 1919, 25*, declared that
'there is no completely satisfying proof that Gibeah of Benjamin . . .
was really located at Tell el-Ful. . . '; and justified doubts have been
expressed elsewhere. This is Saul's future homeland. The second place
is present-day *er-rām*. another three kilometres further north, on the
same route (coord. 172–140). Note the duplication of the two phrases
in vv. 12 and 13. However, perhaps 12b is simply an anticipation of
what will happen, a historical figure frequent in Hebrew. [**15**] 'Turned
aside': the place is not directly on the road, as still today. 'The square':
the only spacious place, in front of the city gate; cf. above on 5.11b.
[**16**] As in Gen. 19, a text on which this passage shows marked signs
of dependence, as we have seen above. The hospitality offered by the
stranger contrasts here with the impiety of the local population. [**18**]
Note the recapitulatory character of the levite's reply. 'Home': MT
has 'to the house of Yahweh', which does not make any sense given
that we do not know whether the levite performed any cultic functions,
and if so where; with LXX (εἰς τὸν οἰκόν μου) I read *'el bētī*: the
prenominal suffix in the first person has evidently been confused with
the abbreviation for Yahweh, Moore*, 1897. [**19**] 'Your servant': MT
has the plural, but with Vg, Tg and Syr I have restored the obvious
singular. [**21**] 'Fodder', root *bālal*, 'mix'. Note the difference between
K and Q, which is irrelevant at a semantic level.

(c) The outrage of the inhabitants of Gibeah (19.22–28)

19 22While they were refreshing themselves, a group of people from
the city, toughs, surrounded the house and began to batter on the
door, shouting out to the old man, the master of the house, 'Bring out
the man who has come to your house: we want to have sex with him.'
23But the master of the house went out and said to them, 'I beg you,
brothers, do not commit such an abominable action. Now that this
man has entered my house, do not commit such impiety. 24Look, I
have a daughter who is still a virgin: I will bring her out to you.
Ravish just her, do what you like to her, but do not such a vile thing
to this man.' 25However, the men would not listen to him. Then the
levite took his concubine and led her outside and they ravished her,
violating her all night until the dawn. And when dawn broke they let
her go. 26And as morning appeared, the woman came and fell at the
gate of the house of the man where her husband was staying, and
there she remained until it was light. 27In the morning her husband
got up and opened the door and went out to go on his way; but he
found the concubine fallen there in front of the door, with her hands
on the threshold. 28He said to her, 'Get up, let us be going', but there
was no reply. Then he put her on the ass and returned to his own
country.

[22] 'Toughs': literally, 'men of the city, sons of *b'līya'al'* (Boling*, 1975, 'the local hell raisers'). The term, which appears about twenty-seven times in the Old Testament, almost always in combinations with a construct (Jüngling, 266), is of doubtful etymology and meaning. Rabbinic exegesis, followed by St Jerome, thought of *b'lī- 'ōl*, 'without yoke' (of the *tōrāh*, or of heaven), hence lawless; others of *b'lī-ya'al*, 'without rising (from hell)', an allusion to Sheol, cf. Ps. 18.5 (EVV 18.4)//II Sam. 22.6; but which here, as in I Sam. 1.16; 2.12; 10.27, etc., denotes human beings who act in disregard of all laws, whether human or divine. During the intertestamental period it became the name of a demonic power, which as Beliar appears in Qumran, the Sibylline Oracles, the Testaments of the Twelve Patriarchs, the Ascension of Isaiah and also in the New Testament, II Cor. 6.15. The phrase seems to have been conflated and is perhaps the product of the combination of *'anšē hā'īr* and *'anšē b'nē b'līya'al*. In any case, the formula indicates, irrevocably, that we can expect no good from this intervention. 'Batter' and 'have sex': cf. Gen. 19.5,9. The first is a matter of 'putting shoulders to the door' with the aim of breaking it down, Driver**, 1964; in the second instance we have one of the common meanings of the root *yāda'*: it is in fact obvious that it is not just a matter of making their acquaintance: they had all the time in the world while the group had been sitting in the square. On the other hand, as I have noted, while in Gen. 19 the homosexual violence is a fundamental element, given that the three 'angels' are seen as men, here the theme quickly disappears, as the toughs are happy with the concubine, cf. 20.5. As we have seen, this is manifest proof that this narrative is secondary in comparison with Gen. 19, which, moreover, is a much earlier story. [23] 'Impiety': *n'bālāh* is normally used to express 'foolishness'; however, it also appears generically for a violation of normal relationships (Jüngling, 279), or as a euphemism for sexual matters, cf. Gen. 34.7; Deut. 22.21; II Sam. 13.12; it does not, however, appear in Gen. 19.7–8a, which has only the first part of the speech. 'In my house': read *'el* for the Hebrew *'al*, which does not make sense. [24] 'Virgin': MT adds: 'and that of his concubine' (using an anomalous form which is not repeated, cf. *GesK* § 91d), but the phrase should be deleted, cf. v. 25: the personal pronouns here and in the following verses should therefore always be read in the singular: *'ōtāh*. 'Ravish': literally 'humiliate her', a euphemism. 'Do not': note in Hebrew the use of *lō'* instead of *'al*; the first appears only for absolute prohibitions, the second for contingent prohibitions. [28] 'There was no. . ': the impersonal with G. R. Driver**, 1964; the woman was dead, as LXX and Vg are concerned to add, leaving nothing to the imagination of the reader or the audience.

(*d*) The publicity given to the outrage (19.29f.)

19 ²⁹As soon as he arrived home, he took a knife, laid hold of his concubine and dismembered her into twelve pieces, which he sent throughout the territory of Israel. ³⁰And he gave this order to the men whom he sent: 'Say to the men of Israel, "Has such a thing ever happened since the Israelites came out of Egypt until this day? Consider it, take counsel and think!" ' And when they came, they exclaimed, 'Such a thing has never happened or been seen from the time when the Israelites came out of Egypt, until this day.'

[29] For parallels to this action in the history of religions and in folk-lore cf. T. H. Gaster**, 1969, 443ff.; they are relatively few. A specific case is attested for Mari (*ARM* II, 48) by Wallis, 1952, and by R. G. Boling*, 1975; however, this is a remote parallel: in the Mari text no body is dismembered; what is sent round is simply the head of an executed criminal, to convince the reluctant Haneans that they must assemble their troops for the war. The text might in some way be parallel to I Sam. 11, but certainly not to our one. Furthermore, in I Sam. 11.5ff., Saul dismembers his oxen under the power of the spirit of God, whereas here the only motive force seems to be the desire to inform the others and to arouse a healthy horror for the crime that has been committed. Despite the formal similarity, the substance of the message here is different both from I Sam. 11 and from the Mari text cited. 'Dismembered': literally, 'cut her according to her bones'.
[30] 'Say. . .consider it!': the verse has been reconstructed following LXXᴬ (there is a criticism of this procedure in Jüngling, 312); however, with K. Budde*, 1897, and W. Rudolph**, 1947, I have left what the text already contained, which is presupposed by the following verse, 20.1ff. The phrase which has fallen out is reproduced in Hebrew in *BHK*³ and *BHS*, and so there is no need to cite it here. 'Consider it. . .': Hebrew *śīmū lākem*, implying *lēb*. 'Take counsel': with LXX: θέσθε. . .βουλήν, for *'uṣṣū*, root *yā'aṣ*. LXX does not propose a different reading (against G. F. Moore**, 1895) but only a vague translation. 'Think': literally 'speak'; however, the order of the phrase, 'Consider it, take counsel and speak', shows that this is a deliberation. T. Veijola, 1977, 21f., notes that the reaction of the people anticipates what in fact happens in 20.4,7, and thinks that this is an addition of a Dtr type; however, as we have seen often before, Hebrew style anticipates features which it considers to be important.

(*e*) The assembly of the tribes of Israel (20.1–11)

20¹ Then 'all Israel', as one man, from Dan to Beer-sheba, came out to gather before the face of Yahweh in an assembly at Mizpah, ²ᵇand four hundred thousand men on foot drew the sword. ³ᵃWhen the

Benjaminites learned that the Israelites had gone up to Mizpah, they
refused to go to join them. ²ᵃAnd the chiefs of all the people took up
their positions in the assembly of the people of God, ³ᵇ and said to the
Israelites, 'Explain how such an infamous act was perpetrated.' ⁴The
levite, the husband of the dead woman, replied: 'We had arrived at
Gibeah of Benjamin, I and my concubine, to spend the night. ⁵The
notables of Gibeah rose against me and surrounded the house; they
wanted to kill me, and they ravished my concubine so that she died.
⁶Then I took my concubine, dismembered her, and sent the pieces into
all the regions assigned to Israel: they have committed an abominable
act, impious in Israel. ⁷And now that you are all here, Israelites,
discuss the question and make a resolution here and now.' ⁸Then all
the people rose to their feet as one man and said, 'None of us will
return to his camp and none will return to his home. ⁹This is what we
will do to Gibeah: we will mount a campaign against it according to
lot. ¹⁰We will take ten men of every hundred for every tribe of Israel,
one hundred for every thousand and one thousand for every ten thousand to provide for the victualling of the troops; and in this way we
can requite Gibeah of Benjamin for the impiety which they have
committed in Israel.

11 Thus all the men of Israel gathered against the city, allied and
united as one man.

---

[1] 'Assembly': *qāhāl* is a term used in the late, post-exilic period,
especially in P. 'Mizpah': this time of Benjamin, the place mentioned
with more frequency, later to be the scene of various episodes of the
life of Saul. It is usually identified with present-day *tell en–nāṣbeh*
(coord. 170–143) or, according to others, with *nebī samwīl*, the height
now crowned with a Moslem sanctuary visible from all over Jerusalem,
situated a few kilometres to the north (coord. 167–137). It is mentioned
in Josh. 18.13–26 as a frontier point between Ephraim and Benjamin.
'Dan . . .Beer-sheba' are the extreme northern and southern points of
ancient Israelite Palestine from the time of David onwards. [2f.] The
chronological sequence of events seems to be disturbed in MT; with
some commentators I read them in the following order: vv. 2b, 3a, 2a,
3b, and with W. Rudolph**, 1947, add 'they refused to join them'.
'The chiefs': Hebrew *pinnōt*, literally 'corner stones'; in all, the expression appears four times in the Old Testament, but J. Gray*, 1967,
points out that a similar title was sometimes borne by the sultans of
Turkey. 'Four hundred thousand': the figures are evidently much
exaggerated; however, it does not seem possible here to render 'thousand' as a synonym for a political or military unit, cf. above on 4.6;
6.15; rather, the text is concerned to show how numerous Israel is.
The absence of Benjamin from the debate presages no good. [5]
'Notables': for the expression *ba'alē-X* (name of the place) cf. on 9.1;

however, the note contrasts with 19.22, cf. 20.13, which speaks of 'toughs', unless it is the thesis of the account that the place is so corrupt that the two categories are identical. **[6]** 'Abominable act' is missing in LXX^A. **[9]** 'We will mount. . . ': insert *na⁽ᵃ⁾leh* with LXX. **[10]** 'We can requite. .': in Hebrew with *lābō'*, 'for their going', or 'so that they go', which we correct with LXX^ᵃ into *habbā'īm*, with Moore, Vincent, and Penna; Burney proposes that it should rather be deleted. 'Gibeah': corrected from Geba, a different place, even if it is phonetically similar (present-day *ğeba'*, coord. 175–140), which is not involved here. The confusion can be explained from the phonetic similarity. **[11]** 'Against the city' makes good sense here; LXX^A has ἐκ τῶν πόλεων, as in v. 14; is this confusion, or an *'el* understood as if it were *min*, as in Ugaritic?

(*f*) The demands made on the Benjaminites (20.12–17)

20 ¹²Then the tribes of Israel sent men throughout the tribe of Benjamin with the following message: 'What wicked act is this that has been committed among you? ¹³Now give up those toughs who are at Gibeah, so that we may put them to death and thus purify Israel from the evil.' But the Benjaminites refused to accede to the request of their brothers, the Israelites. ¹⁴And the Benjaminites, too, assembled at Gibeah from their cities, ready to go out to war against the Israelites. ¹⁵In those days the Benjaminites who came out from their cities were estimated to be about twenty-six thousand men bearing arms, without including the inhabitants of Gibeah, and they amounted to seven hundred picked fighters. ¹⁶Of all this company, seven hundred were picked fighters, ambidextrous; everyone could sling a stone at a hair and not miss. ¹⁷The Israelites, excluding Benjamin, were estimated to be four hundred thousand men bearing arms, all instructed in war.

---

[12] 'The tribe': in the plural in Hebrew, either through confusion with the preceding 'tribes of Israel', or as a synonym for clan, which is how traditional Hebrew exegesis understands it. I have corrected the text with LXX and Vg. **[13]** 'Toughs': cf. on 19.22 and 20.5. 'The Benjaminites': Q, followed by LXX and Targ, has *b'nē binyāmīn*, K only *binyāmīn*; both readings make good sense. **[14]** 'Their': with LXX αὐτῶν, necessary in a Western translation, but not in Hebrew. **[15]** 'Amounted to. . .picked fighters' is probably an addition which anticipates the following verse and which some commentators prefer to delete. Here, too, and in the following verses the figures seem exaggerated, but it is not possible to read 'unit' of some kind, cf. on vv. 2f. The figures vary from version to version and in Josephus. **[16]** 'Ambidextrous': for a discussion of the term see on 3.15; however, in the Ehud episode it probably means, 'with an impediment in his right hand', even if the LXX renders it 'ambidextrous', as we have seen. In this text the adjective seems to have been taken from the story of Ehud, but with the different (late?) meaning attested in LXX, cf. Moore*, 1897: 'ambidextrous' or 'left-handed'. Both characteristics offer certain advantages in hand-to-hand fighting, as anyone who has practised fencing or boxing well knows. In I Chron. 12.2 this is the prerogative of an auxiliary corps of David's, also composed of Benjaminites; among other things, they too are skilled with the sling.

(g) The first two battles and defeats (20.18–28)

20 [18]They arose and went up to Bethel, where they enquired of God by means of the oracle. The Israelites asked, 'Which of us shall go up first to fight against the Benjaminites?' Yahweh replied, 'The first will be Judah.' [19]At dawn the Israelites arose and encamped near Gibeah. [20]Then they went out to battle against Benjamin and took up position to attack Gibeah. [21]However, the Benjaminites made a sortie from Gibeah and routed on that day twenty-two thousand men. [23]Then the Israelites went up to weep before Yahweh until the evening, and then they again asked Yahweh by means of the oracle, 'Shall I again do battle against the Benjaminites who are my brothers?' The Lord replied, 'Yes, march against him.' [22]Then the army, the men of Israel, took heart; they returned to draw up in battle in the same place where they had drawn up on the first day.

24 So the Israelites advanced against the Benjaminites that second day. [25]However, on the second day also Benjamin made a sortie from Gibeah and clashed with them; and routed another eighteen thousand men of Israel, all bearing arms. [26]Then all the Israelites and all the people went up to Bethel and resorted to the sanctuary, where they wept, remaining before the face of the Lord and spending the whole day there. There they offered holocausts and peace offerings before the face of Yahweh.

27 Again the Israelites enquired of Yahweh by means of the oracle (for the ark of the covenant of God was there in those days), [28]and Phinehas the son of Eleazar, son of Aaron ministered before it in those days. They asked: 'Shall I again go up to do battle against the Benjaminites who are my brothers, or will it be better to stop?' Yahweh replied: 'Go up against them: tomorrow I will give them into your hands!'

---

[18] 'Bethel': today usually identified with *beitīn* (coord. 172–148), for details see on 1.22. However, apart from being the proper name of a place, the term can have the generic meaning of 'temple ('house') of (a?) god', cf. Vg: ' . . . *venerunt in domum Dei, hoc est, in Silo* . . .' This rendering is based on the mention of the ark in vv. 27b–28 (cf. there),

an object which was located at Shiloh from time immemorial, according to some from the time of the conquest; it was put out of action when it was captured by the Philistines (I Sam. 4.11). This theory has been taken up again now by R. G. Boling*, 1975, who translates *bēt-'el* 'the sanctuary' and understands the place to be Mizpah; J. Gray*, 1967, seems doubtful, cf. also on vv. 27f. However, v. 31 makes it likely that *bēt-'el* here refers to the place of that name, and is not the designation of a sanctuary.[5] 'Enquired . . . oracle': *šā'al b'-X* (name of the deity) is, as we have seen on many occasions (cf. on 18.1), interrogation of the divine oracle. Note the use of *'ᵉlōhīm*, perhaps a reminiscence of the fact that the inquiry was made generically of 'the deity' (but cf. vv. 23, 27). The pattern seems identical with that of 1.1f., this last passage already relatively late in comparison with the traditions which it reports; the present passage will therefore be even later.   **[21]** 'Routed': root *šāḥat*, not to be confused with *šāḥaṭ*, 'slaughter (ritually)'. The 'routed' units remained *hors de combat* for a more or less long period, so that they will not have been reformed, even if only a very small proportion of them had been killed or seriously wounded.   **[22f.]** The commentaries are agreed in inverting the order of the two verses, as I have done here.   **[23]** 'Weep': a cultic lament of a funeral kind.   **[27]** While MT and LXX^A here mention the ark and its priesthood merely in passing, LXX^B has . . .ὅτι ἐκεῖ, thus explaining the cultic act in terms of the presence of the ark; for the reading of Vg see on v. 18. For the ark, cf. on Josh. 3.1ff.[6] In this text, the Hebrew and the versions have slightly different designations: 'the Lord Yahweh', LXX^B; 'the Lord', LXX^A, Tg and Syr; Vg is the same as MT.   **[28]** 'Ministered': *'āmad 'al X* (name of the person) generally indicates service, at table or in the cult; for this second meaning, which is of interest here, cf. Deut. 10.8; 18.17; Ezek. 44.15 and other passages.

This note puts the ark and the person of Phinehas (an Egyptian name, cf. *pȝ,-nḥsy*, 'negro') at Bethel (to which it had perhaps been transported from Shiloh because of the war, cf. a similar case in I Sam. 4); or (cf. the variant of Vg on v. 18) at Shiloh, if *bēt-'el* is understood as 'temple of God'. In fact this is a passing comment of a priestly kind (P) such as we find in Josh. 14.1f.; 18.1–10; 19.51a; 21.1f.; 22.13; these are passages which were independent in the tradition from the context in which they appear.

(*h*) The third battle and the Israelite victory (20.29–48)

The chief difficulty in this narrative is presented by the now generally accepted fact that here we have two accounts of the

---

[5]For the whole problem cf. H.-J. Zobel, ' 'Ārôn', *TWAT* I, 1973, cols. 391–404, who considers the insertion to be historically valid.

[6]Cf. *Joshua*, ad loc., and A. Cody, *A History of Old Testament Priesthood*, AnBibl 35, Rome 1969, index. s.v.

same event, somewhat crudely combined into an apparently
unitary narrative. However, there are clear duplicates and parallels, which provide proof. They are: vv. 19::20: the departure
of Israel and the taking up of positions against Gibeah;
vv. 31::39a: the Israelite retreat; vv. 32a::39b: the Benjaminites
rout Israel and think that they have won a victory as in the
preceding battles; vv. 36a::41a: the Benjaminites see that they
are in trouble; vv. 35::46: the fall of Benjamin; vv. 45::47: the
Benjaminite survivors take refuge in the 'Rock of Rimmon'. By
contrast, vv. 42a, 45 are not a duplicate, but continue the same
account.

It also seems sufficiently clear that the main break between
the two accounts comes between vv. 35 and 36.

It is by no means easy to reconstruct the two narratives. Some
commentators, e.g. A. Penna*, 1963, J. Gray*, 1967, and H.
Rösel**, 1976, 31ff., propose what is apparently the simplest
solution: I: vv. 29–35 (or 36a); II: vv. 36 (or 36b)-48, but the
simplicity of this proposal itself seems suspect in what is clearly
not a simple text. In 1895 G. F. Moore* proposed: I: vv. 29,
36b, 37a, 38, 39, 40–42a, 44, 47; II: vv. 30–36a, 37b, 42b-46,
but there is a difficulty here, since one of the parallels, vv. 35::46,
is included in section II. In 1919, C. F. Burney* proposed a
different division: I: vv. 29, 33a, 34b, 36b, 37–44, 47b, 48; and
II: 30–32, 33b, 34a, 35, 36a, 45a, 47a. Being well aware of the
complexity of the problem and the difficulty of arriving at a
definitive solution (the two texts have been partly disfigured,
partly mutilated by the redactors), I would propose the following division, which is close enough to that proposed by Moore:
I: vv. 29, 36b, 37a, 38–42a, 45, 46; II:vv. 30–36a, 37b, 42b, 47.
For topographical problems the reader must consult the study
by Rösel**, 1976.

I

20[29] Then Israel set ambushes around Gibeah, [36b]and then gave
ground in front of the Benjaminites, trusting in the ambush which
they had set at Gibeah. [37a]And the men in ambush made haste to rush
in the direction of Gibeah. [38]There had been an arrangement between
the Israelites and those set in the main ambush: these last were to
send up a smoke signal from the city, [39]and then the Israelites would
turn in battle. Benjamin began to kill some of the Israelites in retreat,
striking about thirty men, and they said among themselves, 'Look,
they are routed before us, as in the earlier battles.' [40]But the signal, a

column of smoke, began to rise from the city. Benjamin turned and saw the city in smoke like a burnt-offering! [41]Then the men of Israel turned about, and the men of Benjamin were confounded, seeing that disaster was imminent. [42a]So they turned before the men of Israel in the direction of the desert, but the battle overtook them. [43]The Israelites cut Benjamin in pieces and pursued the survivors without respite, reassembling in front of Gibeah, on the side where the sun rises. [44]Eighteen thousand men of Benjamin fell, all picked warriors. [45]The survivors turned their backs and fled towards the desert, towards the 'Rock of Rimmon'. Israel cut down five thousand of them along the route and continued to pursue the others as far as Gidom, killing two thousand of them. [46]All those of Benjamin who fell on that day were twenty-five thousand, men experienced in war, all chosen warriors.

---

[29] A tactic similar to Josh. 8.4ff. and Judg. 9.25ff. Cf. there. [38] 'Main ambush': the expression is followed by the term *hereb*, which most commentators consider impossible; it is an obscure form of the root *rābāh*, 'increase' or 'magnify'; LXX[A] and Hebrew MSS, however, read *hereb*, 'sword', another obscure form here; LXX[B], Vg and Syr omit the term, which many people would prefer to delete. By contrast, G. R. Driver**, 1964, has suggested vocalizing it as *hārāb* and putting the *atnah* here: in that case we would have 'the great ambush', i.e. the 'principal' one. I have adopted this suggestion as being the least strange. [43] 'Cut in pieces': read *kaťtū* or *kāŕtū* with LXX, cf. Vg, for MT, which has 'surround'; Driver would prefer to keep this last term, cf. there for details. 'Without respite' is the most probable solution of the crux *m*c*nūhāh*, which LXX[B] understood as the name of a place, 'from Nohah . . .', thus G. R. Driver. 'Reassembling': the general solution to another crux, *hidrīkūhū*, is 'crushing them'; with Driver I prefer the rendering given here. (45) The place has not been identified with any certainty. For the 'Rock', Vincent*, 1958, proposes *er-rammūn*, about three kilometres south of *tayībeh* (which I take to be Ophrah, cf. on 6.11), coord. 192–223.

II

20 [30]Then the Israelites marched against the Benjaminites on the third day. They drew up against Gibeah as on the other occasions. [31]The Benjaminites made a sortie from the city to confront the army, and were drawn away from the city. As on previous occasions they began to smite and to kill people from the army along the roads, one of which goes up to Bethel and the other to Gibeon: about thirty of the Israelites in the open country. [32]The Benjaminites said, 'They are routed by us as on the other occasions.' But the Israelites said, 'Let us flee and draw them away from the city, towards the road.' [33]Then all the Israelites arose from their position and drew up at Baal-tamar, while the men in ambush broke out from their positions in the vicinity of Geba. [34]And there came against Gibeah eight thousand chosen men from all Israel, and the battle became more violent. The Benjaminites did not know that disaster was imminent. [35]And Yahweh smote Benjamin before Israel: the Israelites routed in that day twenty five thousand and one hundred men, all skilled in the use of arms. [36a]And the Benjaminites saw that they were defeated. [37b]Then those who had been in ambush took up position and smote the city, putting it to the sword. [42b]Those who came out of the city they routed, catching them between two fires. [47]They turned their backs and fled towards the desert, to the 'Rock of Rimmon': six hundred men, and they stayed at the 'Rock of Rimmon' for four months.

48 Then the Israelites again turned against the Benjaminites and put the population to the edge of the sword, men and animals, as many as they found. And they set fire to all the towns on their route.

---

[31] 'Drawn away': the hophal of *nātaq* is a *hapax legomenon*, and many would prefer to read the niphal: *wayyinnatᵉqū*, cf. the commentaries. However, the alternative reading is unnecessary, cf. *KB³*. 'The roads': *mᵉsillāh* is not a footpath made by regular walking, but the road proper, constructed by engineering work (root *sālal*, 'fill', 'fill in'). 'Gibeon': corrected by all the commentaries from the 'Gibeah' of MT (Gibeah, Geba and Gibeon are easily confused, given the phonetic similarity). The place proposed is almost certainly the present-day village of *eǧ-ǧib* (coord. 167–139). At Gibeah the roads for Bethel and Gibeon parted. [33] 'Baal-tamar': an unidentified place; according to Vincent*, 1958, it is perhaps *rās et-tawīl*, a little north of *tell el-fūl* (coord. 173–138). 'Broke out': *gyḥ* is a verb used only for water, cf. the name of the river Gihon, Gen. 2.13; I Kings 1.33–45//II Chron. 32.30; 33.14. 'In the vicinity': not to be corrected to *mimmaᵃrāb*, 'from the west', with Vg; despite what is said in the commentaries, the Hebrew *mimmᵃrēh* fits well. 'Geba': coord. 175–140, present-day *ǧebaʿ*, a few kilometres north of Gibeah. [37b] 'Took up position': for this sense of *māšak* cf. above on 4.6. [42b] 'Out of the city': read the singular with Vg, Tg and LXX^MSS. The final *mem* seems to be the product of dittography with the beginning of the following word. 'Between two fires': literally, 'in the midst', but read either *battāwek* or *bᵉtōkām*.
[48] 'Men': read with Vg *mᵉtīm* for the incomprehensible *mᵉtōm*, 'from the complete to . . .'; for the expression *ʿīr mᵉtīm* cf. Deut. 2.34; 3.6; and Job 24.12.

(i) Women of Jabesh for Benjamin (21.1–14)

21 ¹The men of Israel had sworn the following oath at Mizpah: 'No one of us shall give his daughter in marriage to a Benjaminite.' ²The people went to Bethel and remained before the face of God until evening; and there they lamented in a loud voice. ³They said, 'Why, O Yahweh, God of Israel, has such a thing happened in Israel? Why today has a tribe been removed from Israel?' ⁴And on the next day the people rose at dawn, built an altar there and offered burnt offerings and peace offerings.

5 Then the Israelites asked, 'Is there anyone from all the tribes of Israel who did not come up to Yahweh, in the assembly at Mizpah?' They had pronounced a grave oath against those who had not come up to Yahweh at Mizpah, 'He deserves death!'

6 The people of Israel had compassion on Benjamin, their brother, and said: 'Today a tribe has been cut off from Israel. ⁷What shall we do for wives for those who are left?' ⁸Then they asked, 'Is there a tribe of Israel which has not come up to Yahweh at Mizpah?' And behold, no one had come up to the camp from Jabesh in Gilead, to the assembly. ⁹The people passed in review and in fact there were none of the inhabitants of Jabesh in Gilead. ¹⁰Then the assembly sent there ten thousand men who were especially valiant, and gave them this command: 'Go and smite the inhabitants of Jabesh in Gilead, put them to the edge of the sword, including the women and the children. ¹¹But this is what you shall do: every male and every woman who has cohabited with a man, you shall utterly destroy; but the virgins you are to leave alive.' And that is what they did. ¹²Among the inhabitants of Jabesh there were four hundred young virgins who had not lived with any man. They took them to the camp in Shiloh, in the land of Canaan. ¹³Then all the assembly sent messengers to the Benjaminites who were at the 'Rock of Rimmon' to offer them peace. ¹⁴And the Benjaminites returned at that time, and Israel gave them the women of Jabesh-gilead who had been left alive; but there were not enough of them.

---

[1] I have translated with the pluperfect. I do not see the need to render it as having happened in the immediate past, as do all the commentaries, thus presupposing the existence of an oath before the battle. [5] 'Deserves death': for this rendering of *mōt yūmāt (tāmūt)* cf. my 1963 study:[7] the expression indicates not so much the execution of the condemned man as the penalty to be inflicted for a particular crime. [8] 'Jabesh': a place in Transjordan but of uncertain location;

[7]Cf. my 'Osservazioni filologico-linguistiche al secondo capitolo della Genesi', *Bibl* 44, 1963, 521–30 (English in *OTOS*, 169–78), esp. §3.

Y. Aharoni**, 1967, 223ff., 254ff.[8] thinks of *tell el-maqlūb*, coord. 214–201; its name is perpetuated by the *wādī yabīś*, which runs into the Jordan about the level of Beth-shean. The city was to play an important role in the assumption of the crown by Saul, I Sam. 11.1ff.; in this last passage the city seems to be normally populated and to have good relations with the rest of Israel, features which make the notes in the present passage problematical. **[10]** 'The assembly': Hebrew *ʿēdāh*, a late term (P), cf. vv. 13, 16. **[11]** 'But the virgins . . .' An addition with LXX[B] and Vg; it is indispensable for producing a comprehensible text. **[12]** 'Shiloh': we do not know the reason for this new move, but the terminology is again the same as that of the P passages, Josh. 21.2; 22.23. The alternation of Mizpah, Bethel and Shiloh is understood by older authors (Moore and Burney) as a feature supporting the existence of sources; however, without denying the existence of tensions, this hypothesis is not necessary. **[13]** The offer of peace here also means restoring the covenant relation between the rebellious Benjaminites and the other tribes. 'There were not enough of them', literally, 'they did not find enough': this refers to the fact that there were six hundred survivors from Benjamin, but only four hundred women. The formula introduces the transition to the next section.

(*j*) The rape of the women of Shiloh (21.15–25)

21 [15]And the people had compassion on Benjamin, because Yahweh had produced a catastrophe among the tribes of Israel. [16]And the elders of the assembly said, 'What shall we do for wives for those who are left?' The women had in fact been exterminated in Benjamin. [17]And they said again, 'How will there be some sort of survivors from Benjamin, so that one tribe is not blotted out from Israel? [18]We cannot give them our daughters in marriage, because the Israelites swore by means of an oath: "Cursed by anyone who gives a wife to Benjamin." [19]So they suggested, 'Look, there is an annual feast at Shiloh in honour of Yahweh' (the place is to the north of Bethel, to the east of the road which runs from Bethel to Shechem, to the south of Lebonah). [20]And they commanded the Benjaminites, 'Go and hide in the vineyards. [21]When you see the daughters of Shiloh come out to dance in a circle, come out of the vineyards and seize each man one for himself and then go to the land of Benjamin. [22]And if their fathers and their brothers should protest to us, we shall say to them, "Have compassion on them; they did not obtain a wife for each of them in war. If you had given them to them, then you would have been guilty." '

23 That is what the Benjaminites did: they took wives according to

[8]On the basis of M. Noth, 'Jabes-Gilead', *ZDPV* 69, 1953, 28–41 = *ABLAK* I, 476–88.

their number from the dancers whom they had captured, and then returned to their territory, where they built cities and lived in them.

24 And the Israelites also departed from there, each one to his own tribe and his own clan, and they returned to their own territory.

25 In those days, when there was no king in Israel, each one did what seemed to him to be right.

---

[15] This story is certainly parallel to the previous one, to which it is now connected in a somewhat precarious way. 'Catastrophe': for this rendering of *pereṣ*, instead of 'breach', 'void', cf. II Sam. 6.8 and Moore*, 1895. • [17] 'How will there be. . .?' LXX^mss have πῶς ἔσται κλῆρος διασωζόμενος τῷ Β. . ., cf. Syr, i.e. *ʾēn tiššāʾrāh* (or *tiššāʾēr*, or *tiwwāšeᵃʾ*) *bᵉbinyāmīn*, a reading which I adopt: MT has the impossible 'an inheritance for the survivors for Benjamin'; G. R. Driver**, 1964, wants to understand it in the sense of 'heirs', but his proposal is not convincing. Vg, too, did not understand and paraphrases: *Et magna nobis cura ingentique studio providendum est, ne una tribus. . .* [19] 'Feast': Hebrew *ḥag*, a periodic festival connected with a pilgrimage (not mentioned here, but cf. I Sam. 1.2), cf. Arabic *ḥaǧǧ*. For 'Shiloh', cf. above on 21.12; it is usually identified nowadays with *ḥirbet seilūn* (coord. 177–162). The topographical description of the location of Shiloh can hardly be put on the lips of 'the elders of the assembly': it would be too artificial. So I accept the existence of a note of a topographical kind, precariously added to the context, which is why I have put it in parentheses. The reference to the 'road' (for the term cf. on 20.31) recalls Alt's theory of the pilgrimage from Shechem to Bethel;[9] in this case we would not have an ordinary line of communication but the route of an ancient periodical pilgrimage, on which Shiloh was probably an important stage. For Bethel cf. 1.22ff. and 20.18; for Shechem cf. on 9.1ff. 'Lebonah' is probably present-day *lubbān* (coord. 173–164). [20] 'Commanded' : K singular, Q plural. [21] 'Dance' : cf. on 11.34. [22] 'Fathers. . .brothers': with the masculine suffix, as often happens in Hebrew. For brothers as protectors of sisters cf. Gen. 34.1ff. and elsewhere. 'Protest': K *lārōb*, Q *lārīb*; for the first term cf. on 6.32. The verb is used as a technical term to indicate a lawsuit in a judicial setting. 'To us': LXX and Vg have 'to you'; it is difficult to say which is the correct reading, here and immediately afterwards. 'To us' presupposes a protest to the tribes who, having punished the misdeed of Benjamin, had allowed, if not instigated, another misdeed by them, namely the rape; 'to you' presupposes a direct objection over the rape to those who had carried the women off. The problem appears almost the other way round in the

---

[9] A. Alt, 'Die Wallfahrt von Sichem nach Bethel' (Riga 1938), *KlSchr* I, Munich 1953, 79–88.

sequel. 'Have compassion' (the tribes are speaking) appears in LXX^A and Vg; instead, MT, with LXX^B and Tg, has 'Leave them. . . ' However, the first reading continues the previous reading of MT and the second that of LXX and Vg. 'Then. . .':˙read *kī ʻattāh* for *kāʻēt*, an erroneous vocalization of the same consonants (as the text now stands it means 'in time', 'at the right time'). **[25]** The phrase which, as we have seen, goes against the existence of a tribal organization and is clearly in favour of the monarchy, might originally have concluded the narrative of ch. 19 (Jüngling, 335ff.)

1. In the introduction to the present section I pointed out a series of inconsistencies and difficulties which are to be found in chs. 19–21; they arise from the fact that we have to do with a series of units which a redactor has collected together into a single narrative. A first unit is that of the levite and his wife, who are subjected to the agression at Gibeah (19.1–28), with an appendix and an epilogue in 19.29f. and a conclusion in 21.25; a second is made up of the session of the assembly and the decision taken at the end (20.1–11), followed by the ultimatum to Benjamin (20.12–17); then we have the account of the war: the first two campaigns, ending in a defeat for Israel (20.18–28), and the final battle, ending in the Israelite victory (20.29–48). Finally, in ch. 21, we have two more epilogues, the capture of the women of Jabesh (21.1–14) and the rape of the women of Shiloh (21.14–24). As we have seen, the last two texts were originally independent and parallel; the theme of both of them is the reconstitution of the tribe of Benjamin by bringing women from other groups; however, as things now stand, in the passage from one episode to another, which are now thought to have taken place successively, the first episode ends with a reference to the inadequacy of the attempt (21.14); thus the second is needed because the first has not been enough. I also showed how the episode of the levite is meant to support the usefulness of the institution of the monarchy, whereas that of the session and the decision of the assembly is meant, rather, to show how useless it was, compared with the existence of a representative organ of all the tribes, fully capable of maintaining law and order in Israel, by force if necessary. Thus it is evident that these two descriptions of the institutions existing or not existing in the prehistory of Israel are contradictory; the existence of the two descriptions side by side can probably be explained by attributing the pro-monarchical text to the earliest phase of Dtr,

DtrH, and that of the other text to the later anti-monarchical phase, DtrN.

2. However, if this composite character of the narrative only appears as a result of a thorough study, we cannot deny that the story is presented as a unity, not only at first sight (as I indicated to the introduction), but certainly also in the intentions of the final redactors. A. Penna*, 1963, 251, therefore does well to say, 'The account is much more of a unity than it seems to be according to certain analyses with a predilection for continuous fragmentation.' Quite apart from the useless polemical thrust, the difficulty in the text arises on the one hand from its composite character (it is the product of a number of originally independent narratives) and on the other from its unitary impression (the narratives in question have been skilfully combined into one thematic narrative which gives the impression of being a unity). The criterion which governed this unification by the redactors seems to be the declaration which we find repeated, 'Has such a thing ever happened from the time when the Israelites came out of Egypt to the present day. . .?' (19.30; 20.6b-7). This seems to be the theme of the redactors: certain things should not happen in Israel because they are incompatible with the concept of the people of God which the redactors proclaim. The redactors therefore propose to their hearers and readers a very high ethical standard: certain things may happen among other peoples, but they must not come about in Israel; where they do come about all the same, the event suspends every criterion of tribal solidarity: the guilty ones must be handed over to the institutions responsible for the punishment which they deserve. And it is precisely this consideration which is the connecting link between the narrative of the levite and that of the war against Benjamin.

We should not therefore be surprised that this section in particular has the pan-Israelite interpretation which in the course of our study we have seen always to be relatively late: especially here it seems to presuppose the whole doctrine of the election of Israel which appears in the writings of Dtn and Dtr, cf. Deut. 4.9,32–40; 5.32f.; 7.1–6; 9.1–6; 11.2ff.; 28.15–26, 58–68; 29.21–28; Josh. 1.18; 23.11–13; II Kings 17.7ff. and so many others: here the election of Israel is described not just as a privilege but as a vocation, a mission and a responsibility, and an unfaithful people will lose its own land. Benjamin here appears to be to some extent the example of what had happened to Israel at the end of the eighth century and Judah at the beginning of the seventh: some exterminated, the rest exiled, with only a few survivors who had escaped the national catastrophe almost by a miracle.

In the section in question we find a quite detailed description of how the redactors saw the functioning of an institution like the tribal assembly (*qāhāl* and *'ēdāh*). The place where it gathered seems to have been Mizpah, 20.1;21.1, which also seems to be the case in the latest of the three traditions of the coronation of Saul (I Sam. 10.17ff.), traditions which Veijola, 1977, 39ff. and 119, assigns to DtrN. Both the texts have the theme of the sovereign assembly which, when functioning at its best, shows the superfluous, if not downright impious character of the institution of the monarchy. The power of the assembly to implement its decisions is vividly indicated by the note that four hundred thousand armed foot soldiers were ready to intervene to see that they were carried out. The assembly seems to be composed of 'chiefs' (*pinnōt*, a term which the Old Testament uses only rarely with this meaning and which is of uncertain date). Thus they are the ones who form 'the people' (20.8). The assembly is first of all concerned with basic decisions, here the case of the levite and the outrage; however, it does not disdain to be interested in technical questions of detail (20.9ff.). It might seem strange to the modern reader (and yet another feature suggesting the artificial character of the construction) that at a first stage Benjamin is offered no alternative. The war seems to be resolved upon from the point when (20.3) Benjamin decides not to join in the assembly; when the assembly then resolves to require Benjamin to hand over the culprits (20.11ff.), it does so with arms already in its hands, i.e. in such a way as almost to invite the tribe in question, well known for its pride and arrogance, *not* to hand them over. In other words, the redactors begin from the fact of the war with Benjamin and avoid any feature which could avert it: given the tone of the request, just as it was, Benjamin virtually had to refuse.

This narrative seems to be remarkably unified, except probably for the incidental Priestly note in 20.27b-28: there is not in fact a conflict between Mizpah and Bethel, given that the first place is the seat of the assembly and the second the place where the oracle was consulted. The functions of the two sanctuaries are thus essentially different and there is no need to suppose that they are parallels.

3. The situation over the account of the outrage is a different matter. As we have seen, the people involved are not clearly described: they are all anonymous, and it is not clear why the protagonist is a levite (the theory according to which the harshness of the reaction from the tribes is to be attributed to his status, cf. Jüngling, 315ff., is obviously untenable, cf. there). Too many features are taken from Gen. 19 (J) and I Sam. II; thus this is a tradition which is hardly earlier than that of chs. 17–18 (cf. there); moreover, both seek to indicate the advantages of the monarchy by describing the chaotic and arbitrary situation which existed before it was instituted. However, as we have seen, both make use of a phrase which appears in Deut. 12.8–12 (cf. above on 17.6, p. 265). It is a text which describes the religious situation of the people before the entry into Canaan as that in which 'each one did what seemed to him to be right' over cultic matters; however, this commandment is that the situation is to be changed when the people have entered the country, by means of the centralization of the cult. The reference to the monarchy in 17.6; 21.25, cf. 18.1; 19.1, can therefore easily be connected with the phrase in Deut. 12, in the sense that the monarchy was the institution which had brought private judgment to an end in both the religious and the political spheres (thus Veijola, loc. cit., but cf. Jüngling, 140f.).

The episode ends in 19.30, and 21.25 is probably the final conclusion, now put by the redactors at the end of the whole episode; it is also a particularly good conclusion from a pro-monarchical point of view if we accept that in the original narrative no steps are taken, and that the horror of those who see the severed remains of the woman is limited to a purely verbal level. In this way Judg. 17–18 and 19; 21.25 in fact form an excellent text for the transition to a narrative which describes the institution of the monarchy in a favourable way (I Sam. 9.1–10.16).

4. As we have seen, the tradition of the tribal war against Benjamin may be early, even if it has now been completely revised so as to fit the present account. In origin (Eissfeldt), it probably spoke only of Benjamin and its northern neighbour Ephraim, and perhaps Manasseh, hence Joseph; then this tradition, too, has been amplified in a pan-Israelite direction with the inclusion even of Judah (20.18), albeit merely in terms which are too reminiscent of 1.1f. to be original. The state of the narrative is now such that it is difficult to reconstruct the events

which underlie it. It is enough to remember that Benjamin found itself hard-pressed between its large and powerful neighbours to the north and south, and that the war can be connected with an attempt to make a minimum of living space. Of course a fact of this kind is to be put in the pre-monarchical period: during the united monarchy Benjamin in fact belonged to the north, and whether in the time of Saul or in that of David, there are no signs that it had once been exterminated; when the kingdoms divided it passed over to the south, to Judah (I Kings 12.21//II Chron. 11.1), and it does not seem probable that anything of the kind happened in this period either. However, in the period before the monarchy we have another certain case of civil war between two tribes (Judges 12.4–6, cf. there). Now of course the ancient tradition, completely revised and distorted, serves only to show how certain things were intolerable in Israel and automatically led to catastrophe; the solidarity demonstrated towards the criminals of Gibeah disqualified all the tribe and delivered it over the just judgment of its brethren (20.10b).

5. The conclusion of the narrative presents two episodes the theme of which is, as we have seen, the provision of wives for the survivors of the tribe; the members of the other tribes had in fact made a vow not to give their daughters to the wicked Benjaminites. The second story re-echoes well-known themes, cf. T.H. Gaster**, 1969, 445: from Rome we have the rape of the Sabine women, and in Greece the Messenians snatch virgins during a feast of Artemis. This last episode, perhaps the least known, is certainly the most interesting parallel because it has its special setting in the cult. In Israel, too, we cannot exclude the possibility of the survival of Canaanite cults on the occasion of harvest in general and the gathering of the grapes in particular, cf. 9.27, where. the episode narrated partly takes place in the temple of Shechem (cf. there). Here the scene takes place among the vines, where the young men apparently associated with girls in a ceremony of an orgiastic type which, as Gray*, 1967, rightly points out, recalls what happens at Baal-peor in Num. 25.1–3. It is possible that here we have an ancient recollection of the celebration of the feast of booths, in its original agricultural setting. Such a celebration appears in the Mishnah, *Taan.* 4. 8, for the Day of Atonement and other festivals. There is an obvious inconsistency between such a celebration during the autumn festival and absolute mourning, but this could be a sign of great antiquity. However, these are only indications;

there is no specific element. Here, too, our text is concerned to narrate other things, so that any interference must remain highly speculative. We are also completely in the dark about the expedition against Jabesh; it is enough to note (cf. above on 21.8, pp. 297f.) that the place was inhabited in the time of Saul and closely connected with Benjamin and especially with Gibeah. It may therefore be that in origin the account seeks to explain the reason for such a close union between two rather distant places, situated in such different regions. Here, too, however we cannot say more.

6. If, as is generally accepted (but cf. the recent doubts on pp. 286f. above), Gibeah is present-day *tell el-fûl*, it should be pointed out that the excavations conducted there at the beginning of the 1930s show a destruction of the place at the beginning of the twelfth century, a destruction which the majority of scholars[10] tend to connect with the war against Benjamin. Abandoned or barely occupied for about a century and a half, it was then reconstructed at the end of the eleventh century, a fact which scholars connect with the reign of Saul. Here once again, archaeologists can report discoveries, leaving to biblical scholarship the task of connecting them with features known through the tradition. If this confirms the possibility of civil war, it does not tell us who took part in it, much less what the causes of it were. And this is the obvious limitation of any archaeological excavation when confronted with the texts.

Thus the book of Judges ends, as it were, in suspense. It is clear that according to its present, final structure, it has to be continued elsewhere, because its narrative now forms part of a wider context, that of the Dtr history.

---

[10]L. A. Sinclair, 'An Archaeological Study of Gibeah (tell el-Fûl)', *AASOR* 34/35, 1954-56 [1960], 1–52, cf. the review by M. Noth, *ZDPV* 78, 1962, 91–3, and P.W. Lapp, 'Tell el-Fûl', *BA* 28, 1965, 2–10. There is a bibliography of earlier work in the study by Sinclair.

ADDITIONAL BIBLIOGRAPHIES

On p. xx:
Monographs and articles
H. M. Niemann, *Die Daniten*, FRLANT 135, Göttingen 1985

On the 'Judges' and on the title
B. Lindars, 'The Israelite Tribes in Judges', *VTS* 30, 1979, 95–112;
H. N. Rösel, 'Die "Richter Israels", Rückblick und neuer Ansatz', *BZ* 25, 1981, 180–203

On p.6:
Chronology:
B. Lindars, 'The Israelite Tribes in Judges', *VTS* 30, 1979, 95–112;
G. W. Ramsey, *The Quest for the Historical Israel*, Atlanta and London 1981, 75–77.

On p. 12:
Text and translations

W. R. Bodine, *The Greek Text of Judges*, Harvard Semitic Monographs, Cambridge, Mass. 1980.

On p. 18
H. N. Rösel, 'Die Überleitungen vom Josua ins Richterbuch', *VT* 30, 1980, 342–50 (on the parallels between Josh. 24 and Judg. 1–2); A. Marx, 'Forme et fonction de Juges 2, 1–5', *RHPR* 59, 1979, 341–50; J. van Seters, *In Search of History*, New Haven and London 1983, 242ff.; R. Smend, 'Das uneroberte Land', in G. Strecker (ed.), *Das Land Israel in biblischer Zeit*, Göttingen 1981, 91–102.

On p. 27
Add to first paragraph:

According to Van Seters 1983 the whole section is late and must be attributed to P; according to Smend 1981 the section vv. 27–35 is certainly late.

On p. 37
A. Marx, 'Forme et fonction de Juges 2,1–5', *RHPR* 59, 1979, 341–50; H. N. Rösel, 'Die Überleitungen vom Josua ins Richterbuch', *VT* 30, 1980, 342–50; J. Van Seters, *In Search of History*, New Haven and London 1983, 337–42.

On p. 48

L. Alonso Schökel, 'Erzählkunst im Buche der Richter', *Bibl* 42, 1961, 143–72; J. Trebolle Barrera, 'El simbolo de los dones (2 Re 8,7–15; Jue 3,15–28)', in *El misterio de la Palabra, homenajes a L. Alonso Schökel*, Madrid 1983, 161–76: 172ff.

On p. 61

L. Alonso Schökel, 'Erzählkunst im Buche der Richter', *Bibl* 42, 1961, 143–72. For v. 18: E. Wilkinson, 'The *hapax legomenon* of Judges IV 18', *VT* 33, 1983, 512f.; D. F. Murray, 'Narrative Structure and Technique in the Deborah-Barak Story (Judges IV 4–22)', *VTS* 30, 1979, 155–89 (which I have been unable to use). For a history of the region, cf. recently A. F. Rainey, 'The Military Camp Ground at Taanach by the Waters of Megiddo', *ErIsr* 15, 1981, 61–6. For v. 21: M. Heltzer, *The Suteans*, Naples 1981, 101–4; Y. Zakovich, 'Sisseras Tod', ZAW 93, 1981, 364–74.

On pp. 89–90

L. Alonso Schökel, 'Erzählkunst im Buche der Richter', *Bibl* 42, 1961, 143–72; G. Grottanelli, 'L'inno a Hermes e il canto di Deborah: due facce di un tema mitico', *RSO* 56, 1982 [1985], 27–37; A. J. Hauser, 'Judges 5: Parataxis in Hebrew Poetry', *JBL* 99, 1980, 23–41; B. Lindars, 'Deborah's Song: Women in the Old Testament', *BJRL* 65, 1982–83, 158–75; B. Mazar, 'Yahweh Came Out from Sinai', in A. Biran (ed.), *Temples and High Places in Biblical Times*, Jerusalem 1981, 5–9; J. F. A. Sawyer, ' "From Heaven Fought the Stars" ', Judges V 20', *VT* 31, 1981, 87–9; J. A. Soggin, 'Bemerkungen zum Deboralied, Richter Kap. 5', *TLZ* 106, 1981, 625–39; 'Amaleq und Ephraim, Richter 5, 14', *ZDPV* 98, 1982, 58–62; J. G. Taylor, 'The Song of Deborah and Two Canaanite Goddesses', *JSOT* 23, 1982, 99–108; M. Weinfeld, 'Divine Intervention in War in Ancient Israel and in the Ancient Near East', in H. Tadmor and M. Weinfeld (eds.), *History, Historiography and Interpretation . . .*, Jerusalem 1983, 121–47:125–31. For a history of the region, cf. A. F. Rainey, 'The Military Camp Ground at Taanach by the Waters of Megiddo', *ErIsr* 15, 1981, 61–6.

On p. 102

J. A. Emerton, 'The "Second Bull" in Judges 6,26–28', *ErIsr* 14, 1978, 52*–55*.

On p. 103

C. Schäfer-Lichtenberger, *Stadt und Eidgenossenschaft*, Heidelberg theological dissertation 1979, 25–32, and *Stadt und Eidgenossenschaft im Alten Testament*, BZAW 156, Berlin 1983, 229ff. (on 6.11–24); H. Spieckermann, *Juda unter Assur in der Sargonidenzeit*, FRLANT 129, Göttingen 1983, 204–7 (on 6.25–32); K. Galling, *BRL*, ²1978, 289–92; B. Margalith, 'The Episode of the Fleece (Judges 6, 36–40) in the Light of Ugaritic', *Shnaton* 5–6, LV–LXII (in Hebrew with an English summary).

On p. 163

M. Haran, *Temples and Temple Service in Ancient Israel*, Oxford 1978, 299f. (for v. 27); V. Fritz, 'Abimelek und Sichem, in Jdc IX', *VT* 32, 1982, 129–44; H. N. Rösel, 'Überlegungen zu "Abimelek und Sichem" in Jdc IX', *VT* 33, 1983, 500–3; C. Schäfer-Lichtenberger, *Stadt und Eidgenossenschaft im Alten Testament*, BZAW 156, Berlin 1983, 213–20; E. F. Campbell, 'Judges 9 and Biblical Archaeology', in *The Word of the Lord shall Go Forth – Essays . . . D. N. Freedman*, Philadelphia 1983, 263–71; M. D. Fowler, 'A Closer Look at the "Temple of El Berith" at Shechem', *PEQ* 115, 1983, 49–53; R. Bartelmus, 'Die sogenannte Jothamfabel – eine politisch-religiöse Parabeldichtung', *TZ* 41, 1985, 97–120; T. A. Bogaart, 'Stone for Stone: Retribution in the Story of Abimelek and Shechem', *JSOT* 32, 1985, 45–56; I have not been able to use the last two articles.

On p. 183

S. Springer, *Neuinterpretationen im Alten Testament*, Stuttgart 1979, 16ff.

On p. 195

A. L. Hansen, 'The "Minor Judges" – A Revaluation', *JBL* 94, 1975, 190–200; J. A. Soggin, 'Das Amt der "Kleinen" Richter in Israel', *VT* 30, 1980, 245–8; E. T. Mullen, 'The "Minor Judges": Some Literary and Historical Considerations', *CBQ* 44, 1982, 185–201; M. Tsevat, 'Two Old Testament Stories and their Hittite Analogue', *JAOS* 103, 1983, 321–62; C. Schäfer-Lichtenberger, *Stadt und Eidgenossenschaft*, Heidelberg theological dissertation 1979, 205–12, 237–42, and *Stadt und Eidgenossenschaft im Alten Testament*, BZAW 156, Berlin 1983, 256, 347–52.

On p. 200

K. H. Keukens, 'Richter 11, 37f.: Rite de passage und Übertsetzungprobleme', *BN* 19, 1982, 41f.; P. Kaswalder, 'Giudici 11, 20a: problemi testuali e grammaticali', *BeO* 26, 1984, 129–42; id., 'Aroer e Iazer nella disputa diplomatica da Giudici 11, 12–28', *Studii Biblici Franciscani Liber Annuus* 34, 1984, 25–42.

On p. 219
A. F. L. Beeston, 'Hebrew *Šibbolet* and *Šobel*', *JSS* 24, 1979, 175–7; P. Swiggers, 'The Word *šibbōlet* in Jud. XII 6', *JSS* 26, 1981, 205–7.

On p. 225
J. C. Exum, 'Promise and Fulfillment; Narrative Art in Judges 13', *JBL* 99, 1980, 43–59; ead., 'Aspects of Symmetry and Balance in the Samson Saga', *JSOT* 19, 1981, 3–29; D. Grimm, 'Der Name des Gottesboten in Richter 13', *Bibl* 62, 1981, 92–8; O. Margalith, 'Samson's Foxes', *VT* 35, 1985, 224–9. I was unable to make use of J. Kegler, 'Simson – Widerstandskämpfer und Volksheld', in *Theologische Brosamen für Lothar Steiger*, Beihefte zu den Dielheimer Blätter zum Alten Testament 5, Heidelberg 1985, 233–55; P. Nel, 'The Riddle of Samson', *Bibl* 66, 1985, 534–45.

On p. 264
W. J. Dumbrell, ' "In those days there was no King in Israel – Everyman did what was right in his own eyes" ', *JSOT* 25, 1983, 23–33; A. A. Macintosh, 'The Meaning of *mklym* in Judges XVIII 7', *VT* 35, 1985, 68–97. I have not been able to use H. M. Niemann, *Die Daniten*, FRLANT 135, Göttingen 1985.

On p. 279
M. Haran, *Temples and Temple Service in Ancient Israel*, Oxford 1979, 299f. (for 21.19). S. Niditch, 'The "Sodomite" Theme in Judges 19–20: Family, Community and Social Disintegration', *CBQ* 44, 1982, 365–78; C. Schäfer-Lichtenberger, *Stadt und Eidgenossenschaft*, Heidelberg theological dissertation 1979, 214–22, and *Stadt und Eidgenossenschaft im Alten Testament*, BZAW 156, Berlin 1983, 268ff.; S. Lasine, 'Guest and Host in Judges 19: Lot's Hospitality in an Inverted World', *JSOT* 29, 1984, 37–59; E. J. Revell, 'The Battle with Benjamin (Judges XX 29–48) and Hebrew Narrative Technique', *VT* 35, 1985, 417–33.